This is a 3D computer graphics image of the Black Order created by
Shotaro, a friend of one of my assistants. It's so realistic! But it looks
more like the headquarters of some evil organization.

—**Katsura Hoshino**

Shiga Prefecture native Katsura Hoshino's hit manga series
D.Gray-man has been serialized in *Weekly Shonen Jump* since 2004.
Katsura's debut manga, "Continue," appeared for the first time in
Weekly Shonen Jump in 2003.

Katsura adores cats.

GRAPH
HOSHI
NO.
V. 6

D.GRAY-MAN
VOL. 6
SHONEN JUMP ADVANCED
Manga Edition

STORY AND ART BY
KATSURA HOSHINO

English Adaptation/Lance Caselman
Translation/Toshifumi Yoshida
Touch-up Art & Lettering/Kelle Han
Design/Yukiko Whitley
Editor/Gary Leach

VP, Production/Alvin Lu
VP, Sales & Product Marketing/Gonzalo Ferreyra
VP, Creative/Linda Espinosa
Publisher/Hyoe Narita

D.GRAY-MAN © 2004 by Katsura Hoshino. All rights reserved.
First published in Japan in 2004 by SHUEISHA Inc., Tokyo.
English translation rights arranged by SHUEISHA Inc.

Printed in the U.S.A.

Published by VIZ Media, LLC
P.O. Box 77010
San Francisco, CA 94107

10 9 8 7 6
First printing, August 2007
Sixth printing, April 2010

www.viz.com

SHONEN JUMP ADVANCED MANGA EDITION

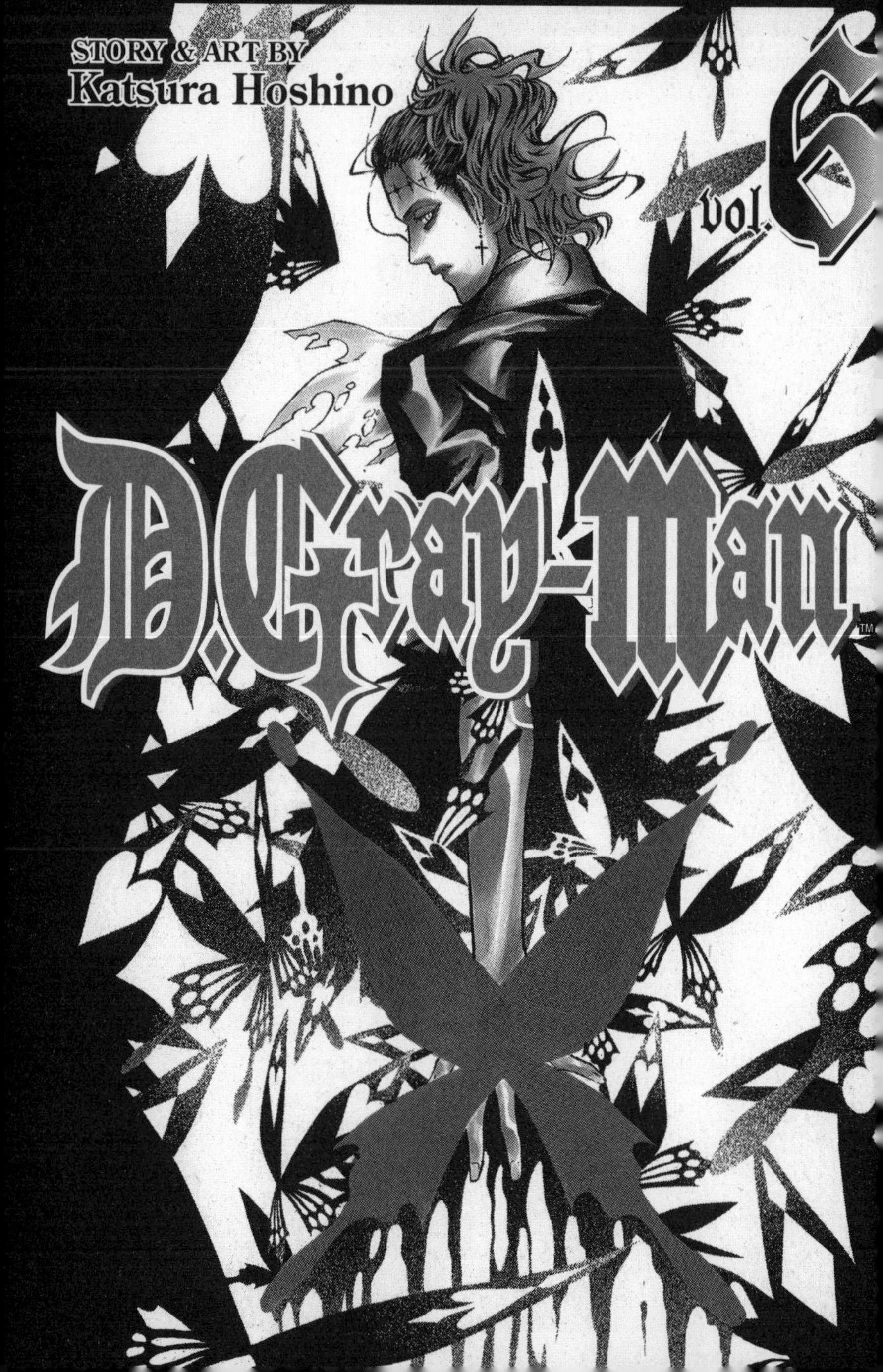
STORY & ART BY
Katsura Hoshino
vol. 6
D.Gray-man™

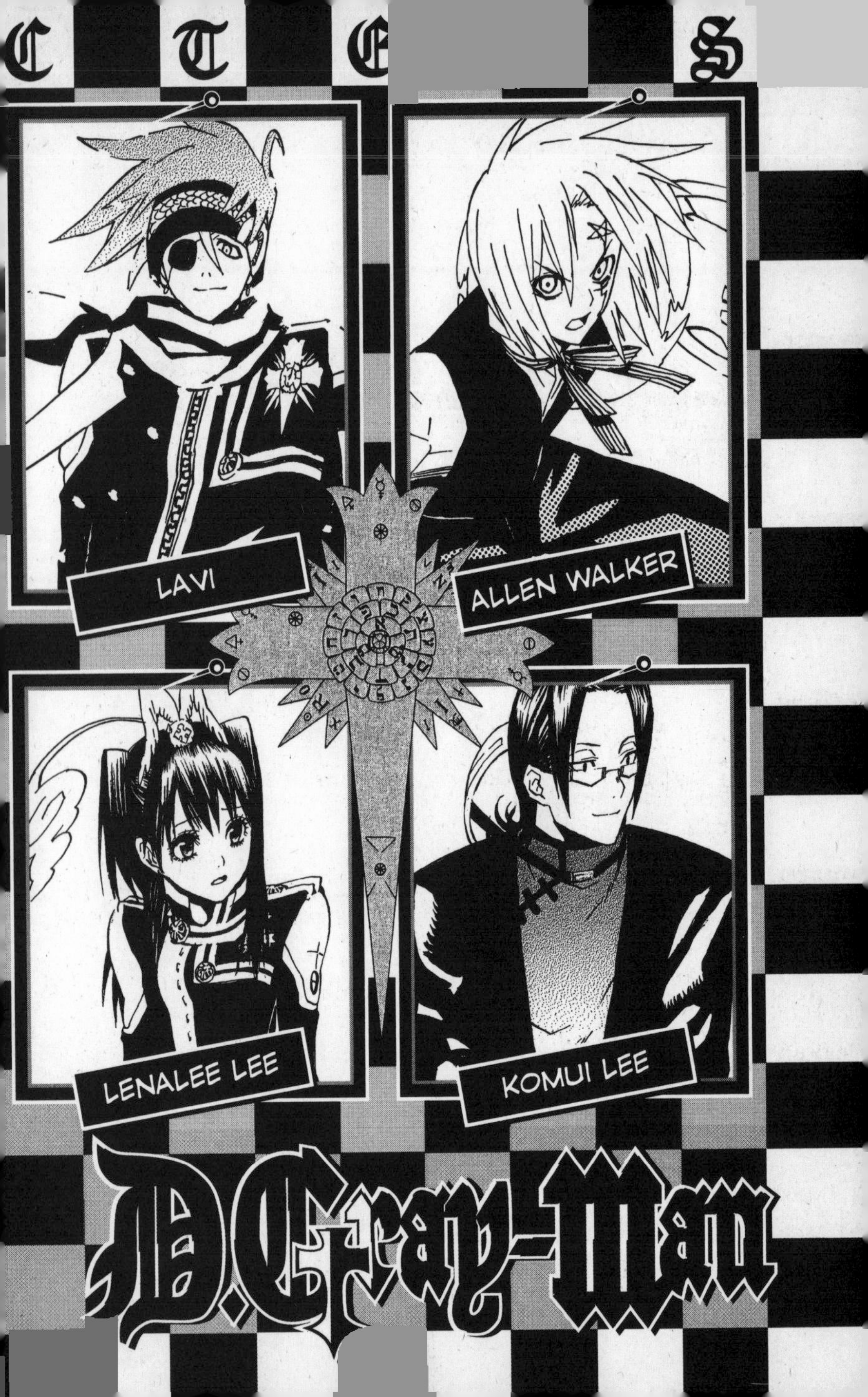
C T E S
ALLEN WALKER
LAVI
KOMUI LEE
LENALEE LEE
D.Gray-man

CHARA

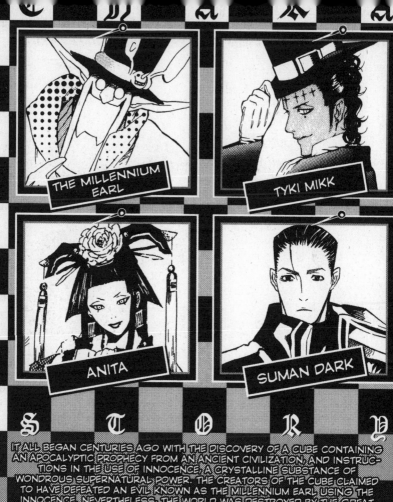

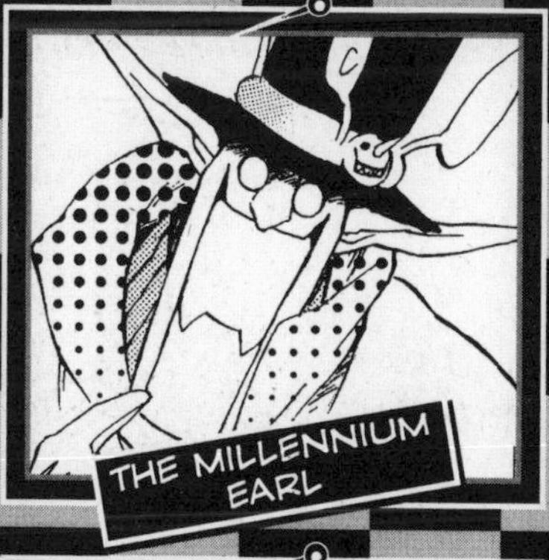
THE MILLENNIUM EARL

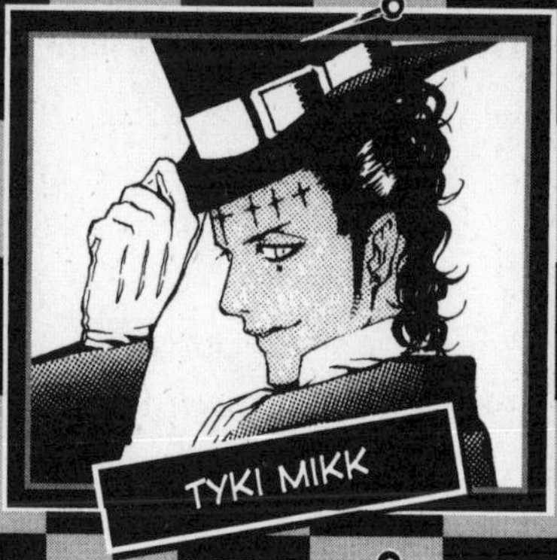
TYKI MIKK

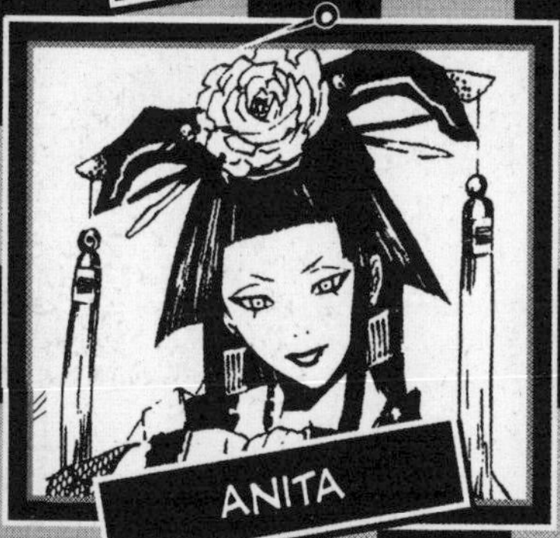
ANITA

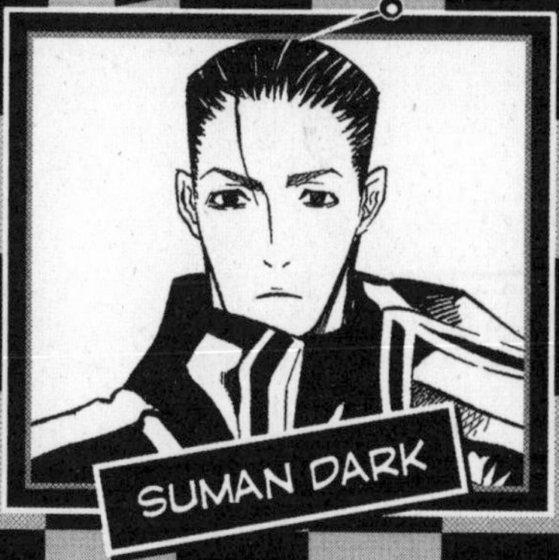
SUMAN DARK

STORY

IT ALL BEGAN CENTURIES AGO WITH THE DISCOVERY OF A CUBE CONTAINING AN APOCALYPTIC PROPHECY FROM AN ANCIENT CIVILIZATION, AND INSTRUCTIONS IN THE USE OF INNOCENCE, A CRYSTALLINE SUBSTANCE OF WONDROUS SUPERNATURAL POWER. THE CREATORS OF THE CUBE CLAIMED TO HAVE DEFEATED AN EVIL KNOWN AS THE MILLENNIUM EARL USING THE INNOCENCE. NEVERTHELESS, THE WORLD WAS DESTROYED BY THE GREAT FLOOD OF THE OLD TESTAMENT. NOW TO AVERT A SECOND END OF THE WORLD, A GROUP OF EXORCISTS WIELDING WEAPONS MADE OF INNOCENCE MUST BATTLE THE MILLENNIUM EARL AND HIS TERRIBLE MINIONS, THE AKUMA.

FORCES OF THE MILLENNIUM EARL LAUNCH A MASSIVE ATTACK AGAINST THE BLACK ORDER IN AN ATTEMPT TO OBTAIN THE HEART, AN INNOCENCE OF FANTASTIC POWER. MORE THAN A HUNDRED EXORCISTS PERISH IN THE ONSLAUGHT. BUT THERE IS LITTLE TIME TO MOURN AS ALLEN AND HIS COMPANIONS PREPARE TO SAIL FOR JAPAN IN PURSUIT OF GENERAL CROSS. BUT EVEN AS THEY SET OUT, A VAST SWARM OF AKUMA DARKENS THE SKIES...

D.GRAY-MAN
Vol. 6

CONTENTS

THE 47TH NIGHT: POINT OF THE ATTACK

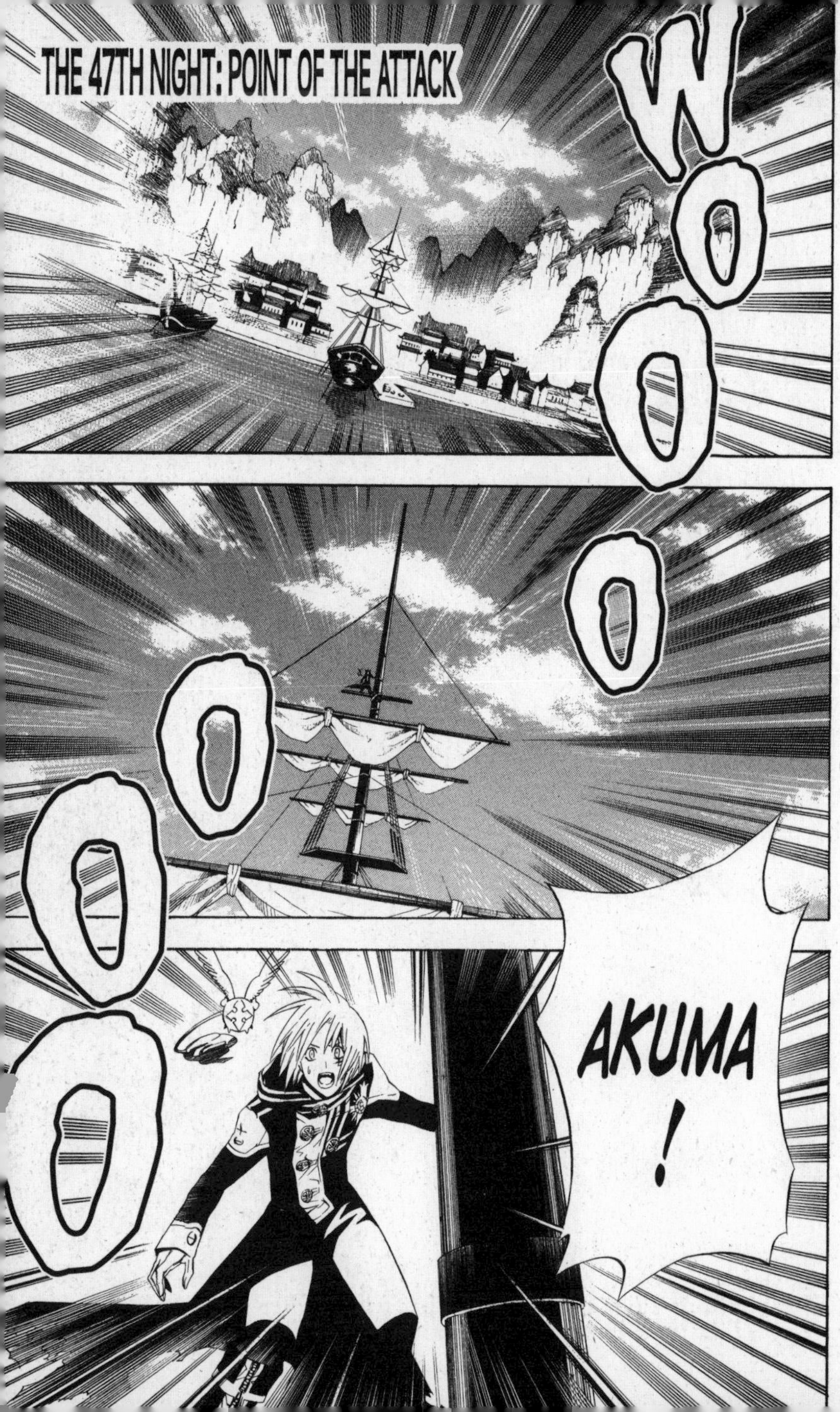
WOOOOOO
AKUMA!

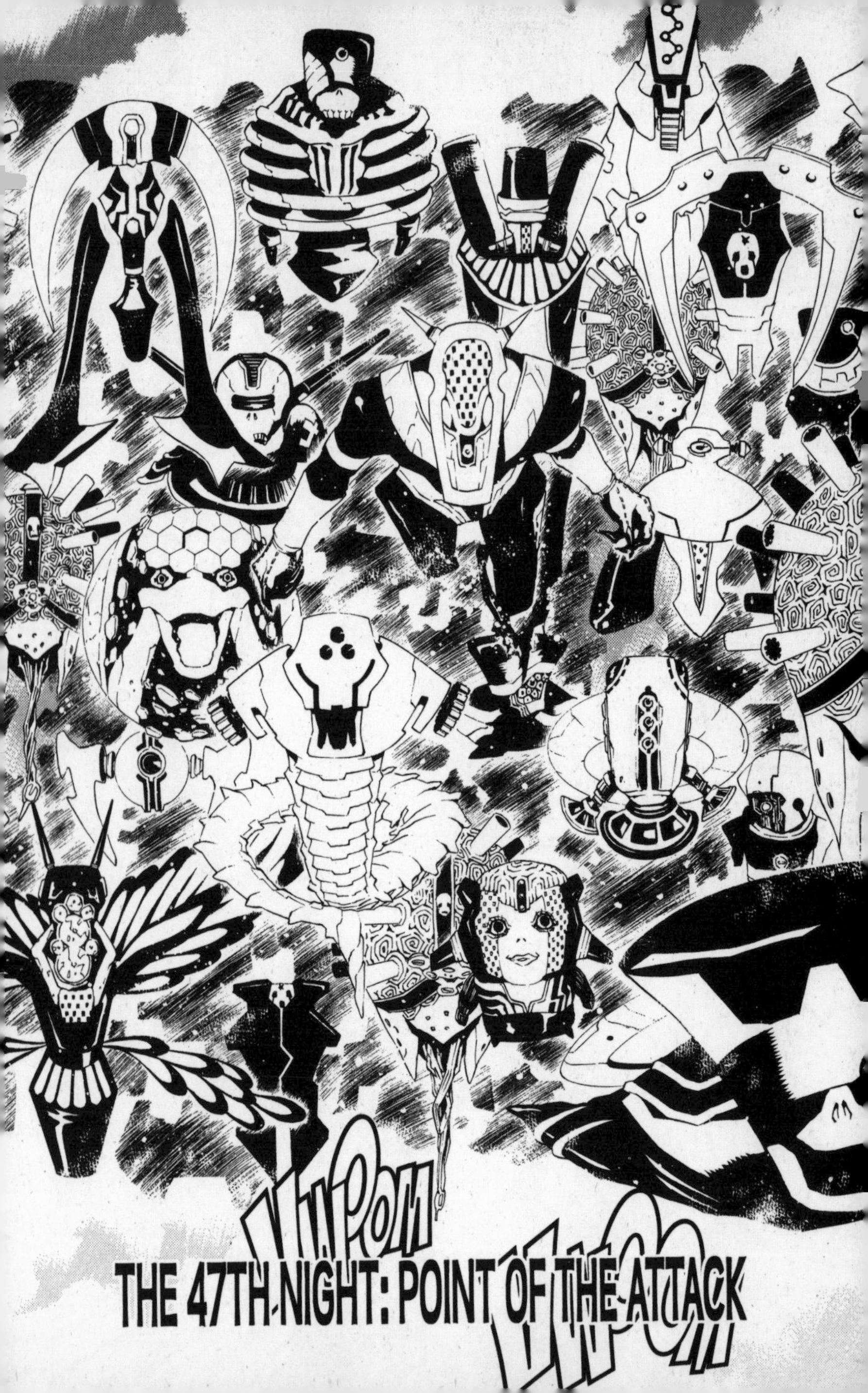
THE 47TH NIGHT: POINT OF THE ATTACK

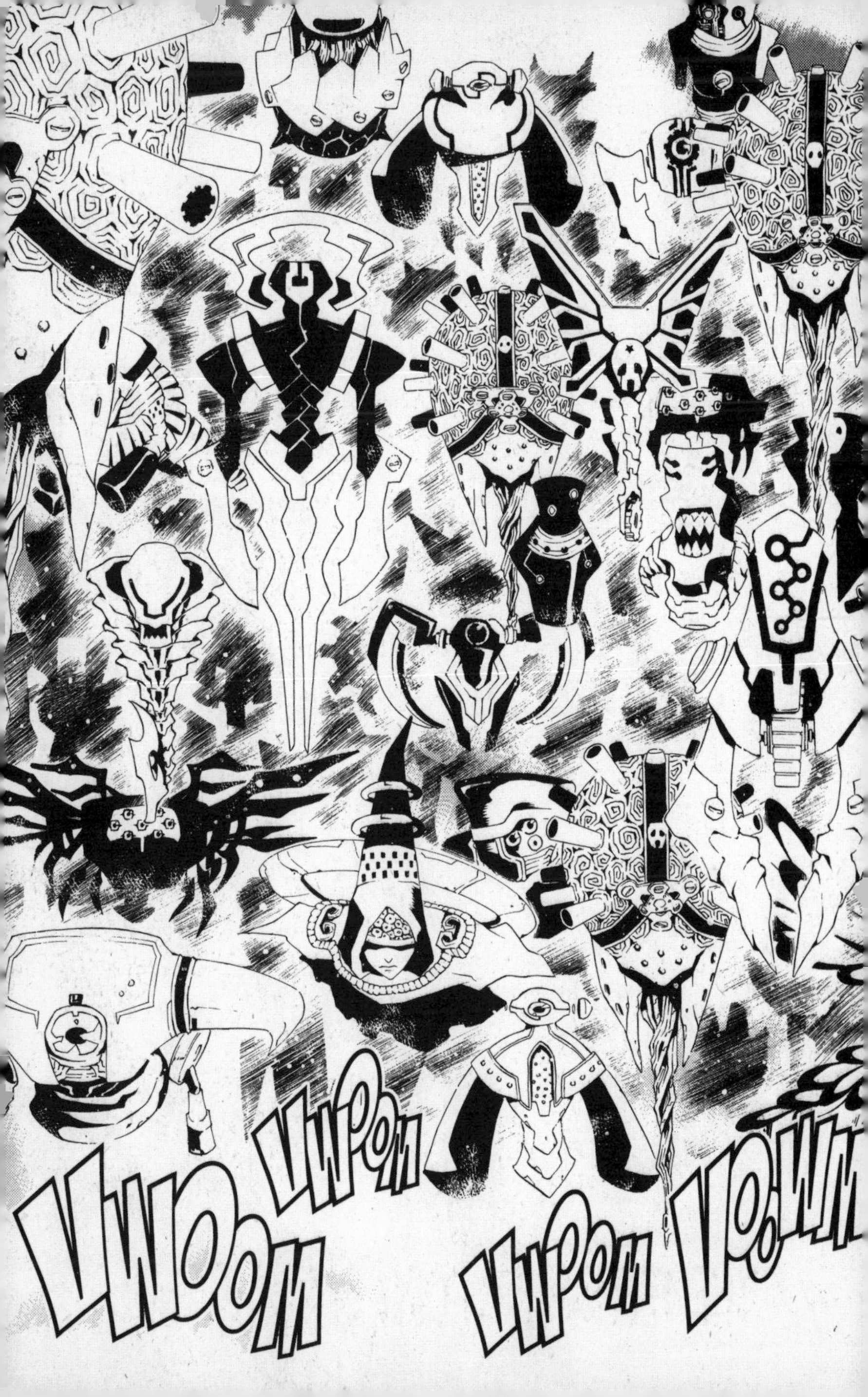
VOOWM
VWOOM
VWOOM
VWOOM

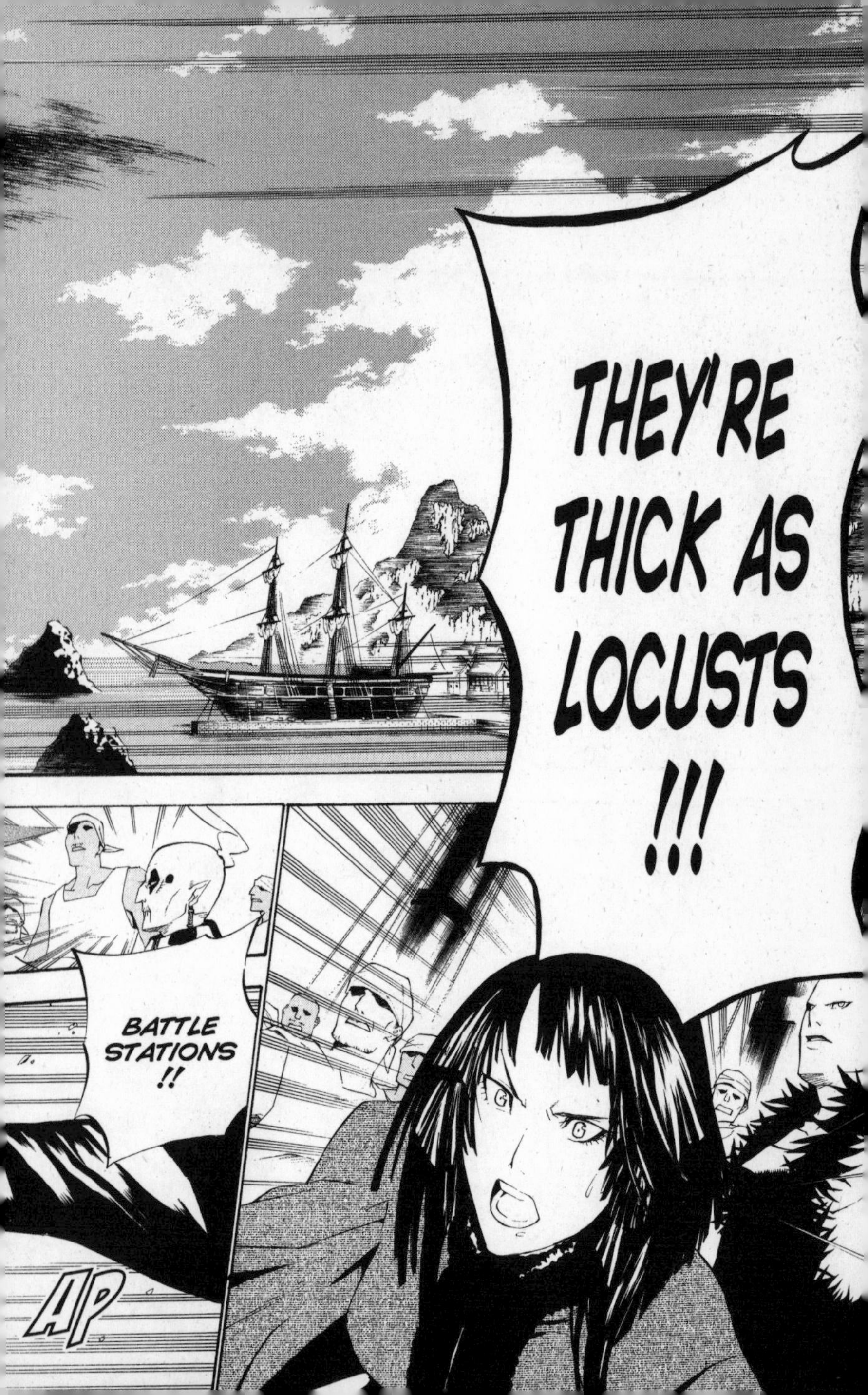
THEY'RE THICK AS LOCUSTS !!!
BATTLE STATIONS !!
AP

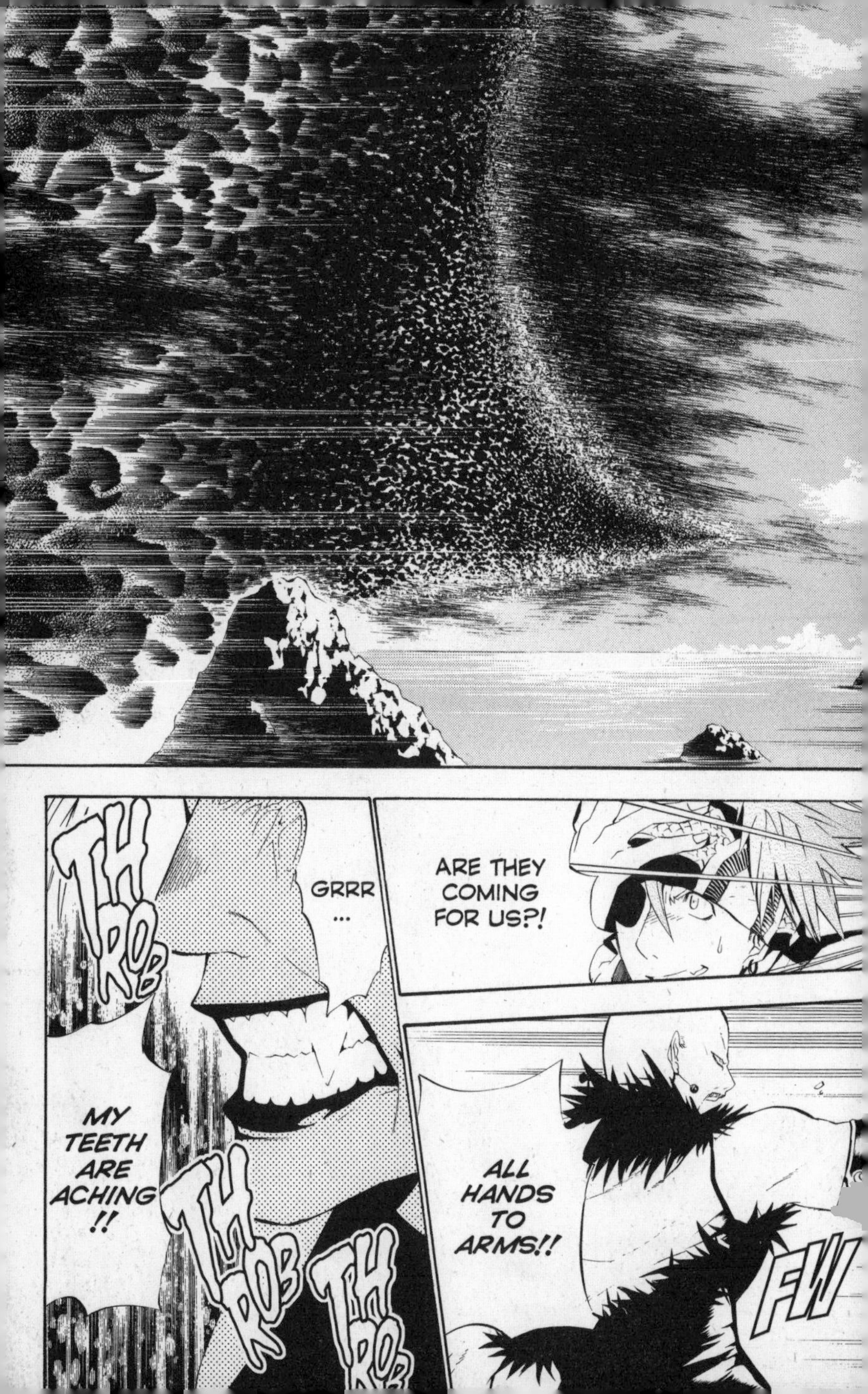
ARE THEY COMING FOR US?!
ALL HANDS TO ARMS!!
FW
THROB
GRRR ...
MY TEETH ARE ACHING!!
THROB
THROB

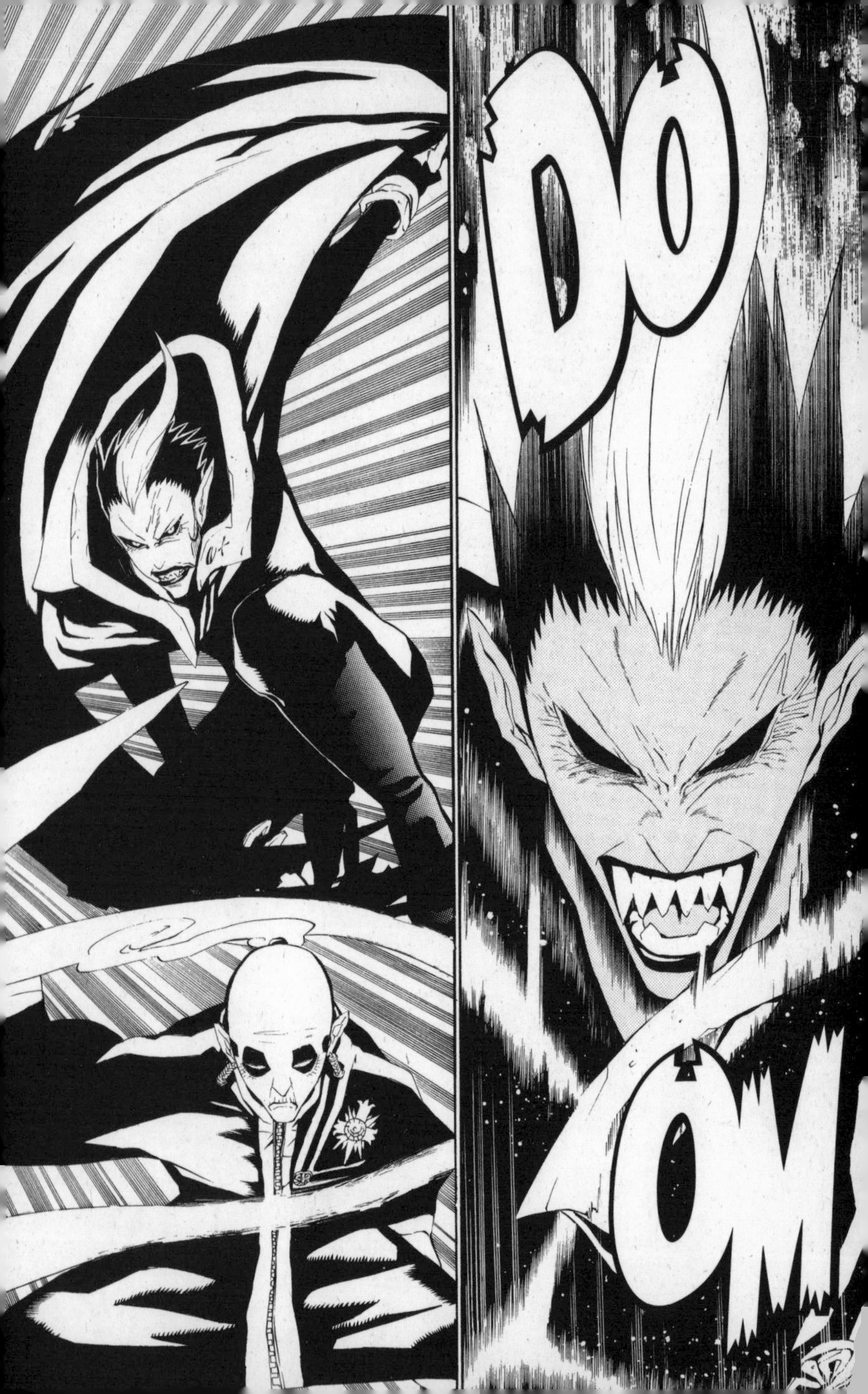
DOOM!

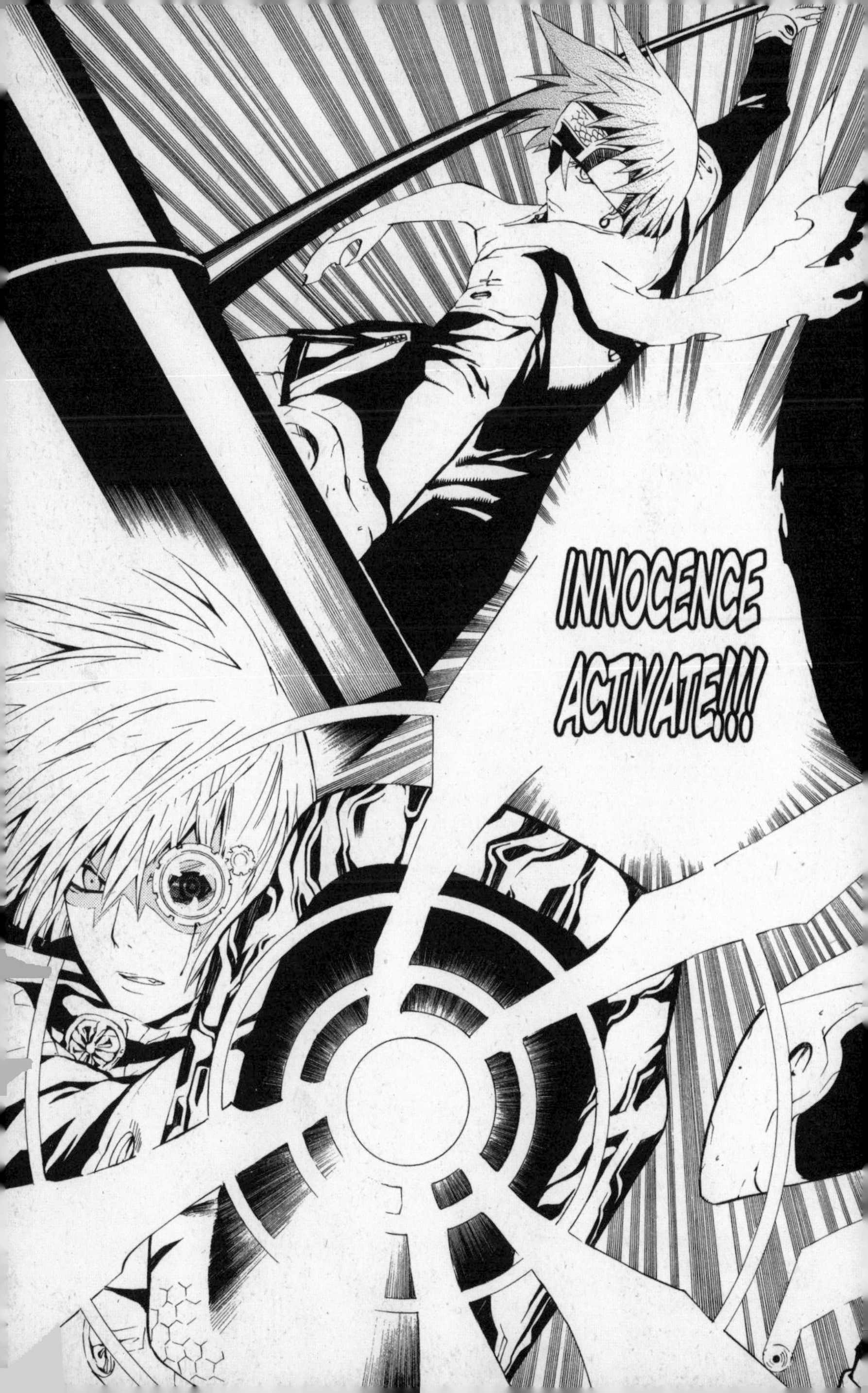
INNOCENCE
ACTIVATE!!!

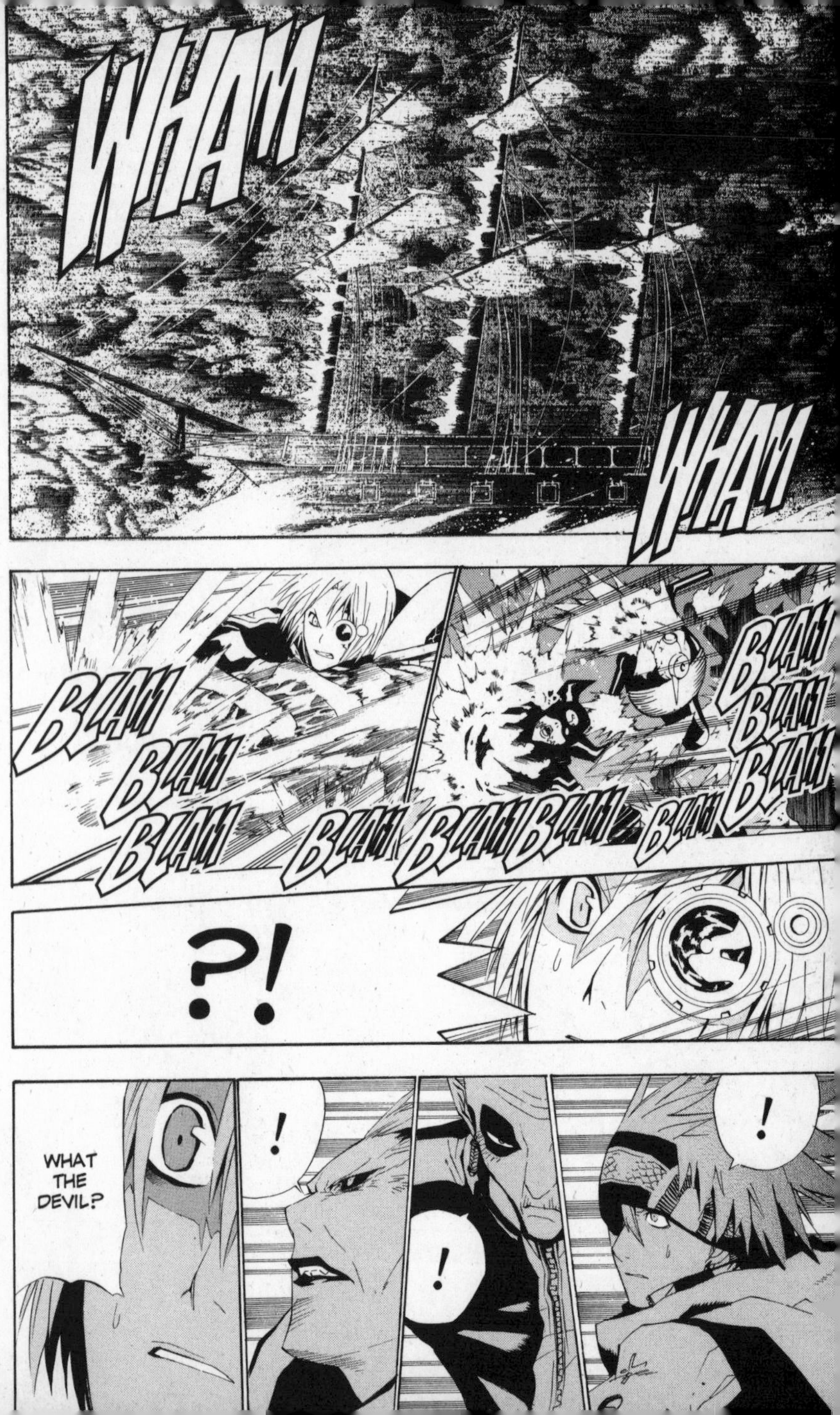
WHAM
WHAM
BLAM
BLAM
BLAM
BLAM
BLAM
BLAM
BLAM
BLAM
BLAM
BLAM
BLAM
?!
!
!
!
WHAT THE DEVIL?

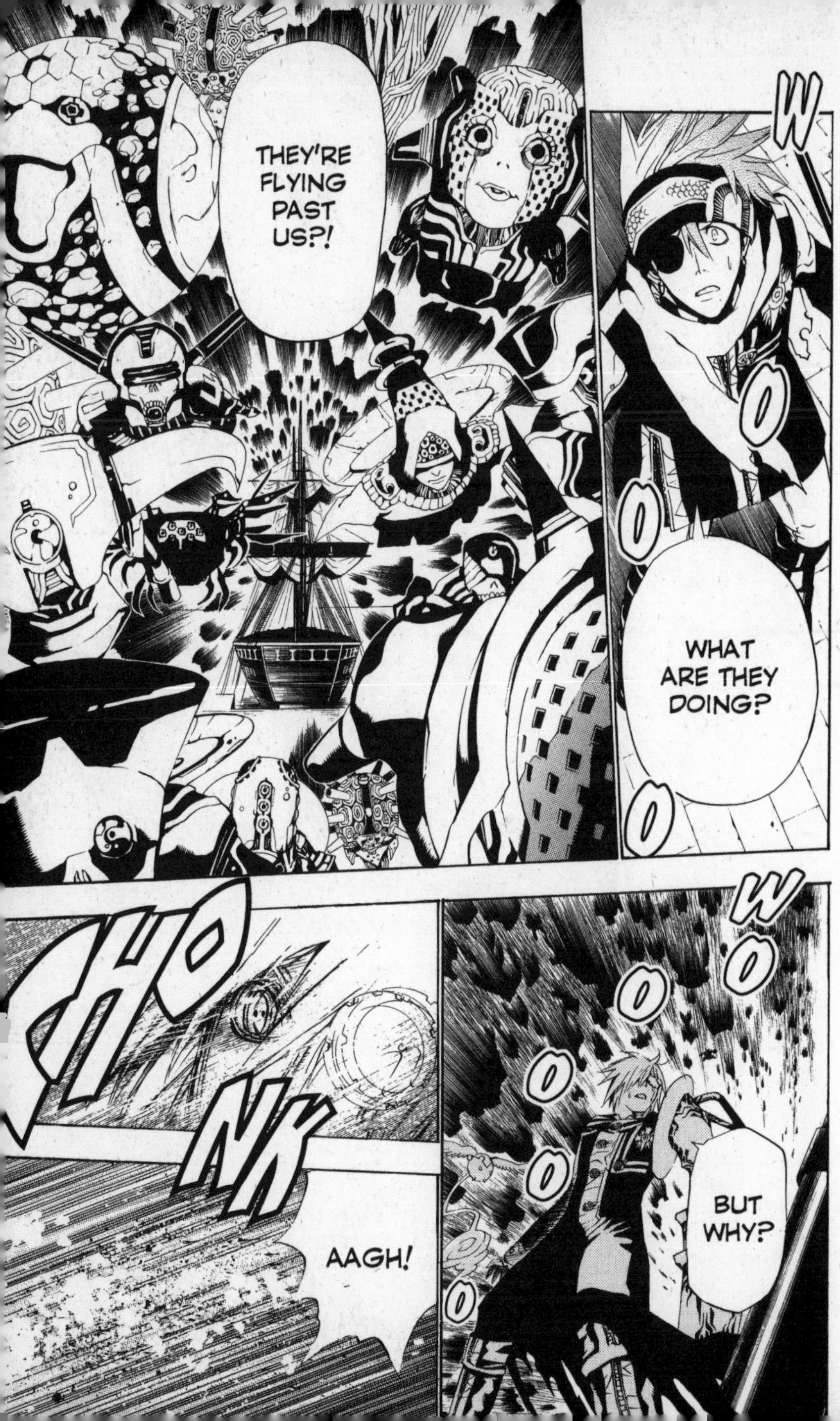
WOOOO
WHAT ARE THEY DOING?
THEY'RE FLYING PAST US?!
WOOOOOOO
BUT WHY?
CHONK
AAGH!

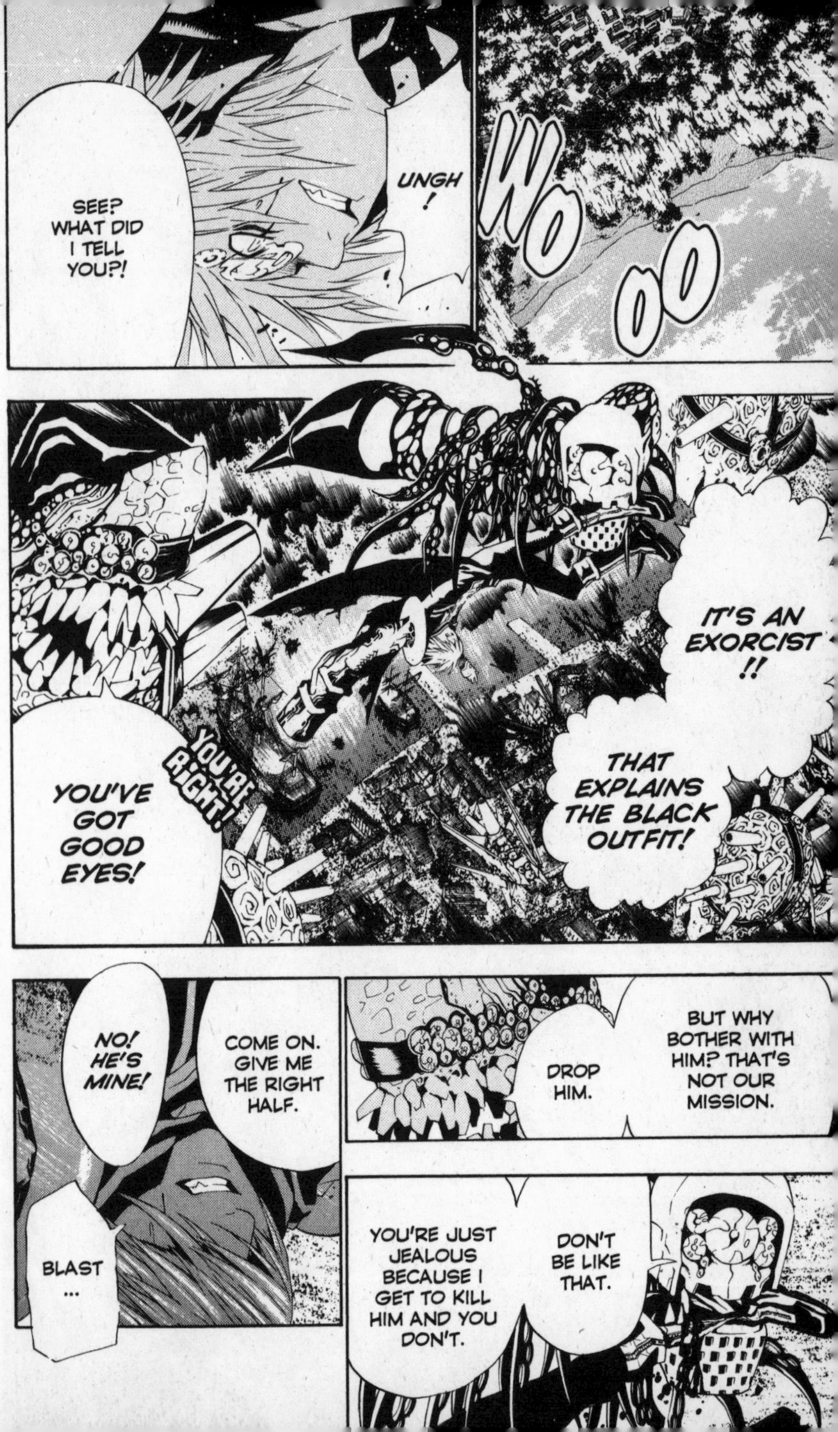
WOOOO
UNGH!
SEE? WHAT DID I TELL YOU?!
IT'S AN EXORCIST!!
THAT EXPLAINS THE BLACK OUTFIT!
YOU'RE RIGHT!
YOU'VE GOT GOOD EYES!
BUT WHY BOTHER WITH HIM? THAT'S NOT OUR MISSION.
DROP HIM.
DON'T BE LIKE THAT.
YOU'RE JUST JEALOUS BECAUSE I GET TO KILL HIM AND YOU DON'T.
COME ON. GIVE ME THE RIGHT HALF.
NO! HE'S MINE!
BLAST ...

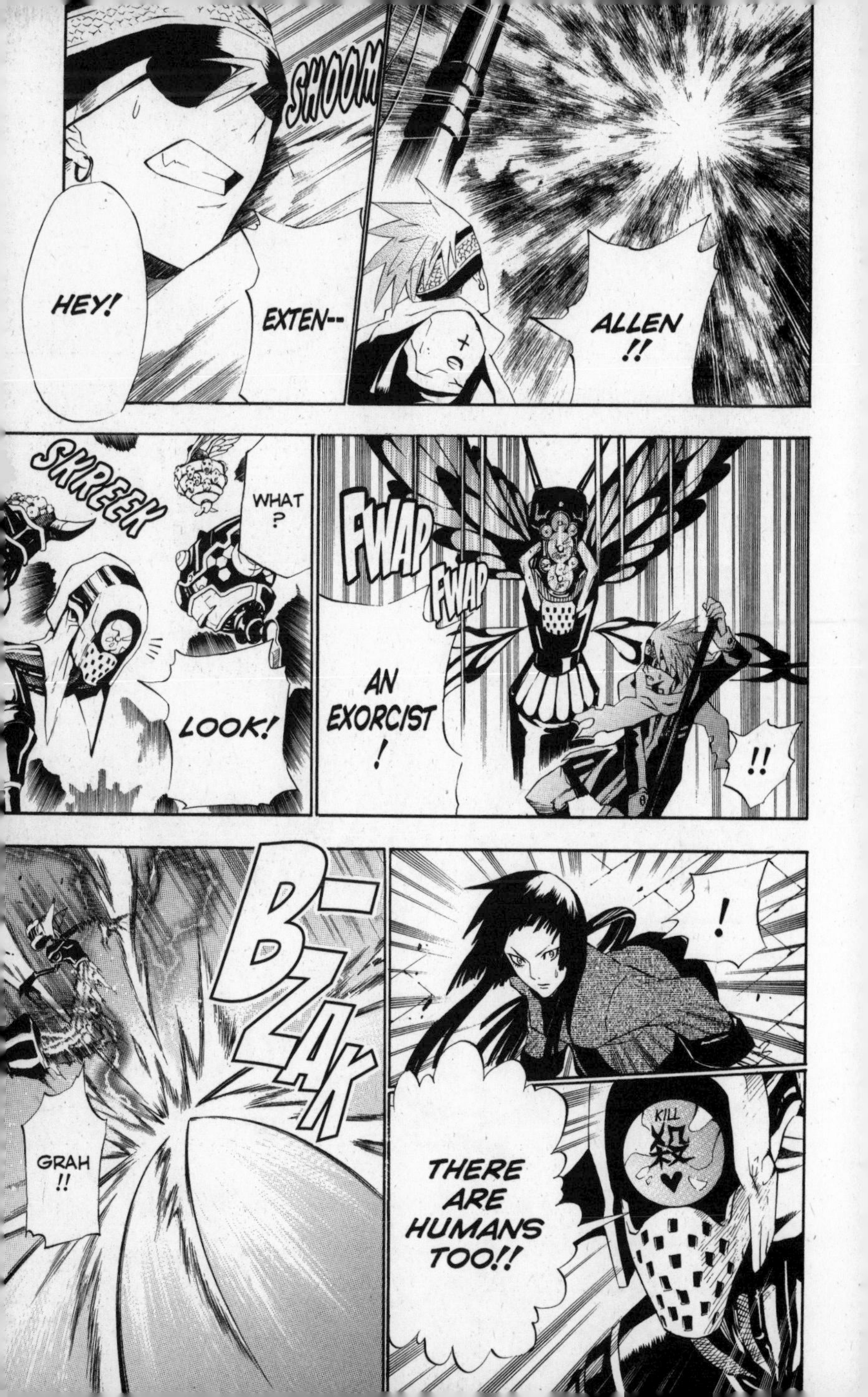
ALLEN !!
SHOOM
EXTEN--
HEY!
FWAP
FWAP
AN EXORCIST !
!!
WHAT ?
SKREEK
LOOK!
!
KILL
殺
THERE ARE HUMANS TOO!!
B-ZAK
GRAH !!

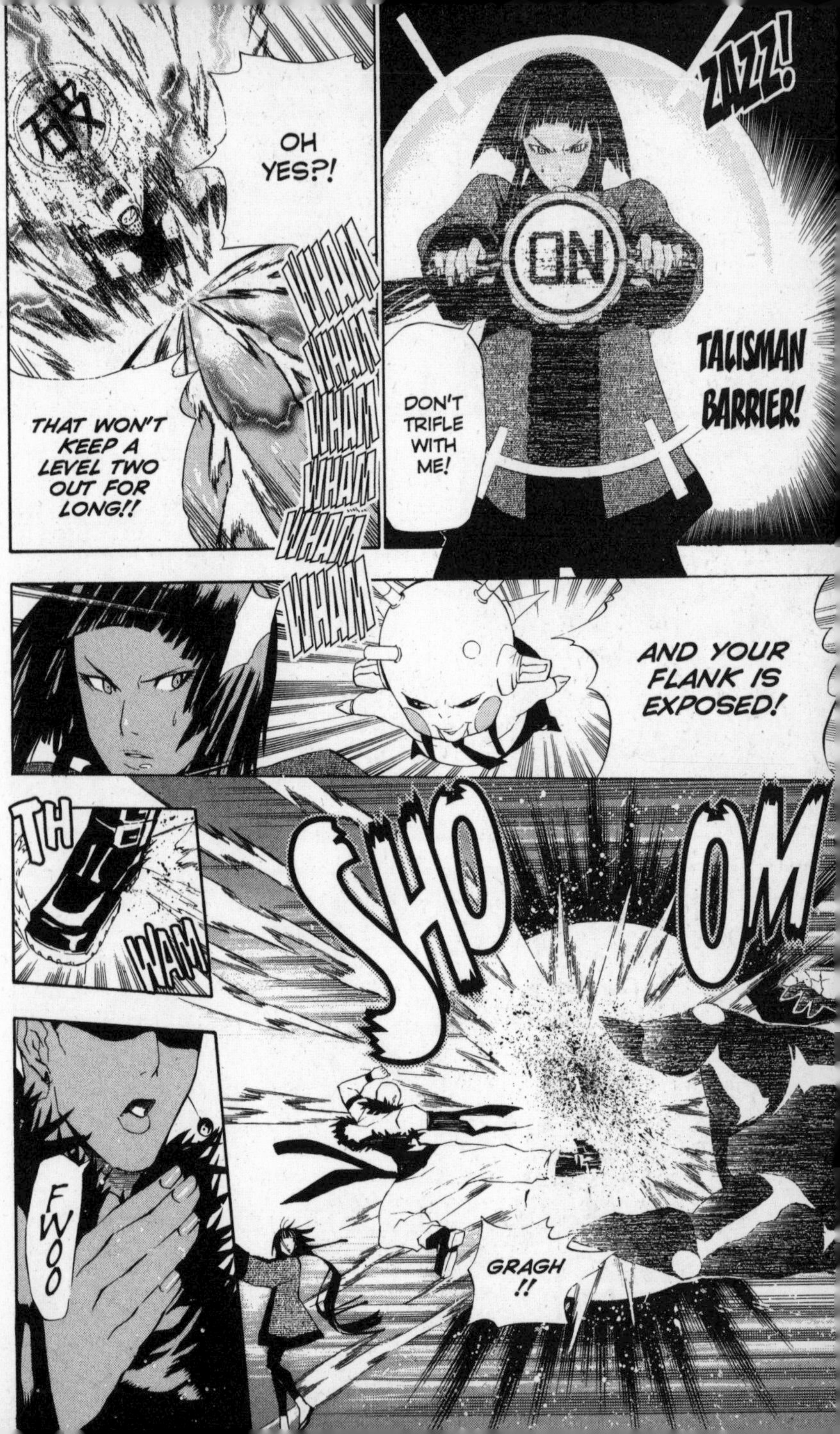
ZAZZ!
TALISMAN BARRIER!
DON'T TRIFLE WITH ME!
OH YES?!
WHAM WHAM WHAM WHAM WHAM WHAM
THAT WON'T KEEP A LEVEL TWO OUT FOR LONG!!
AND YOUR FLANK IS EXPOSED!
SHO OM
TH
WAM
GRAGH!!
FWOO

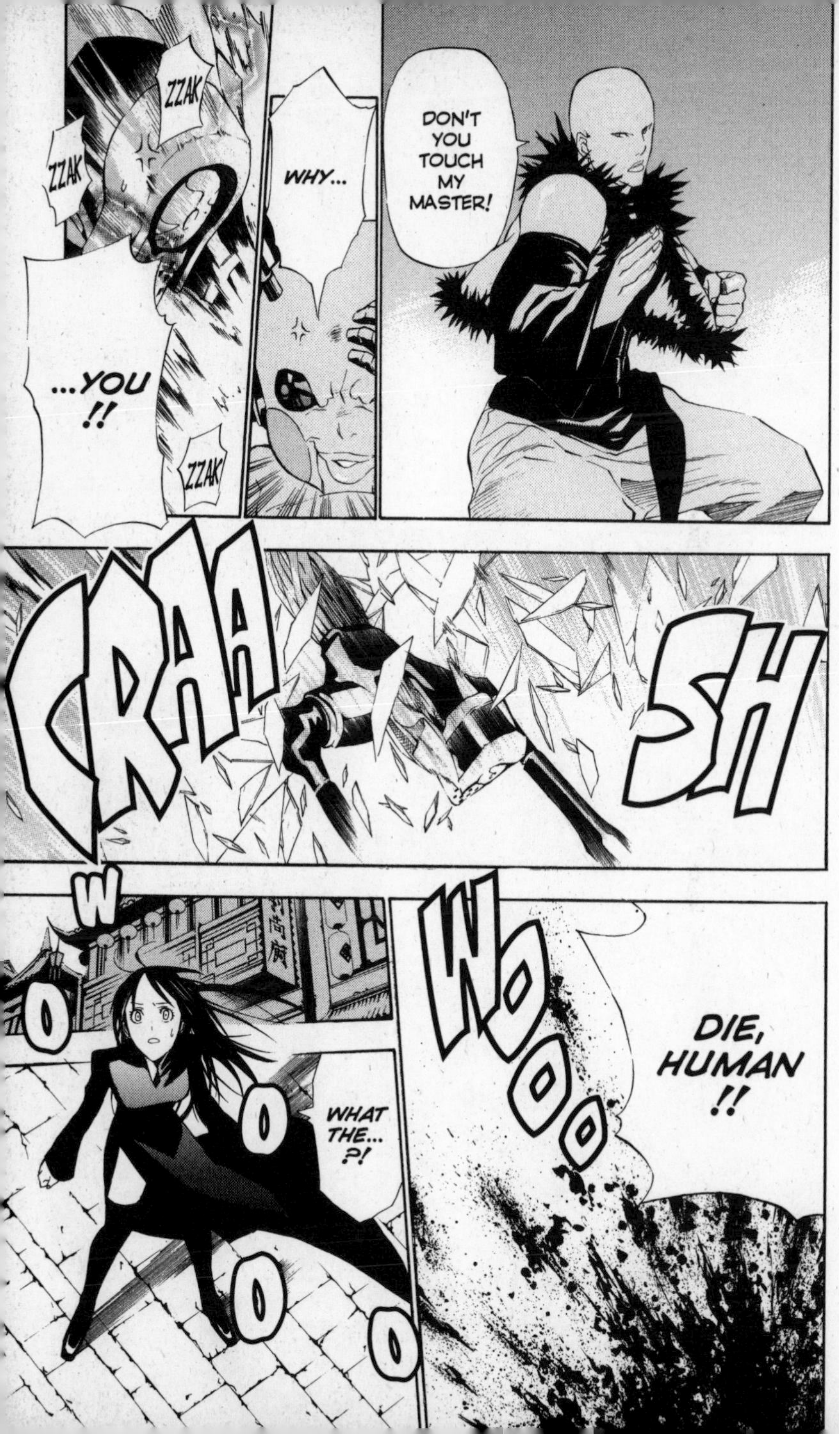
DON'T YOU TOUCH MY MASTER!
WHY...
ZZAK
ZZAK
...YOU!!
ZZAK
CRAASH
WOOOO
DIE, HUMAN!!
WOOOOO
WHAT THE...?!

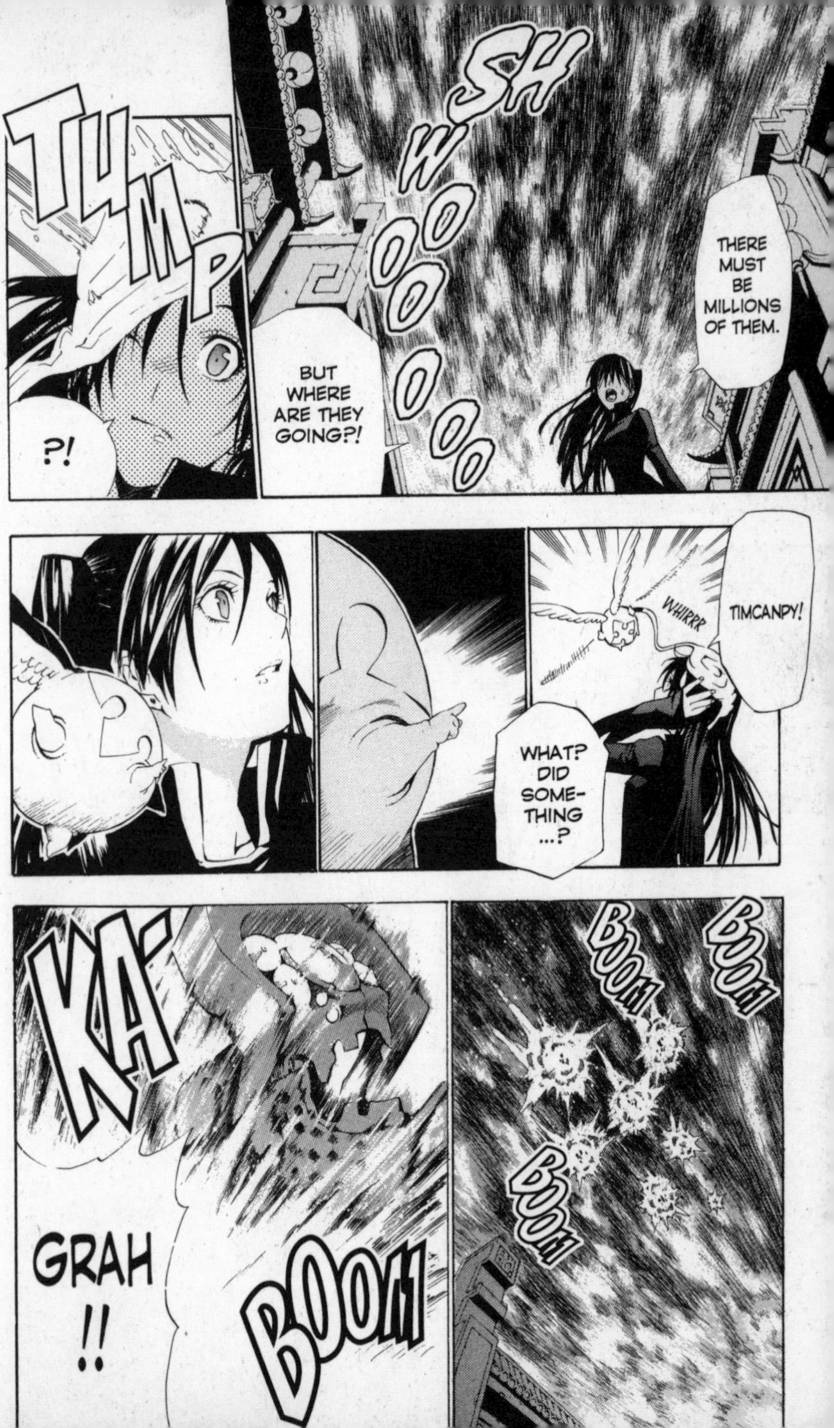
SHWOOOOOOOOO
THERE MUST BE MILLIONS OF THEM.
BUT WHERE ARE THEY GOING?!
THUMP
?!
TIMCANPY!
WHIRRR
WHAT? DID SOME-THING ...?
BOOM
BOOM
BOOM
KA-
BOOM
GRAH !!

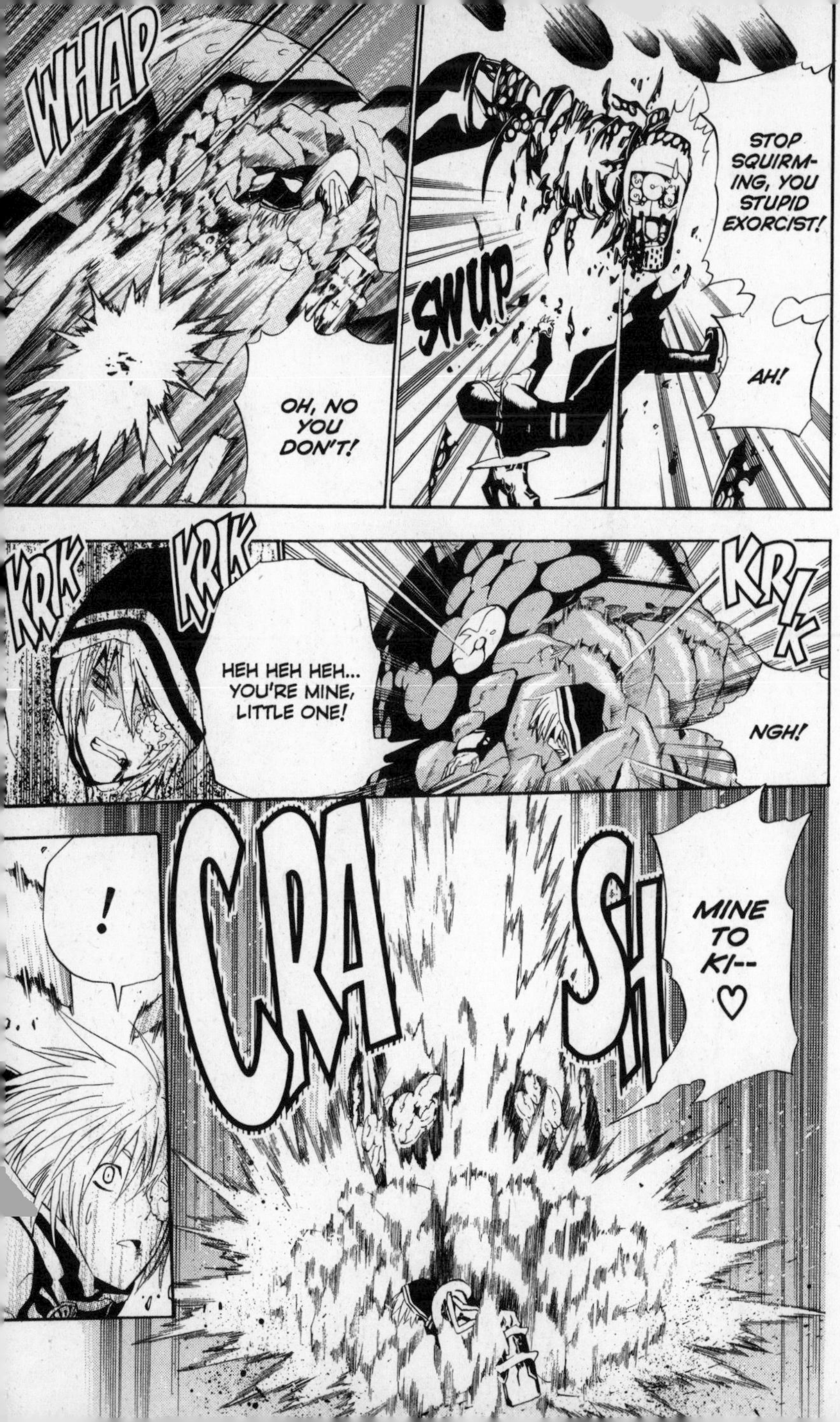
STOP SQUIRMING, YOU STUPID EXORCIST!
AH!
SWUP
WHAP
OH, NO YOU DON'T!
KRIK
NGH!
HEH HEH HEH... YOU'RE MINE, LITTLE ONE!
KRIK
KRIK
MINE TO KI-- ♡
CRASH
!

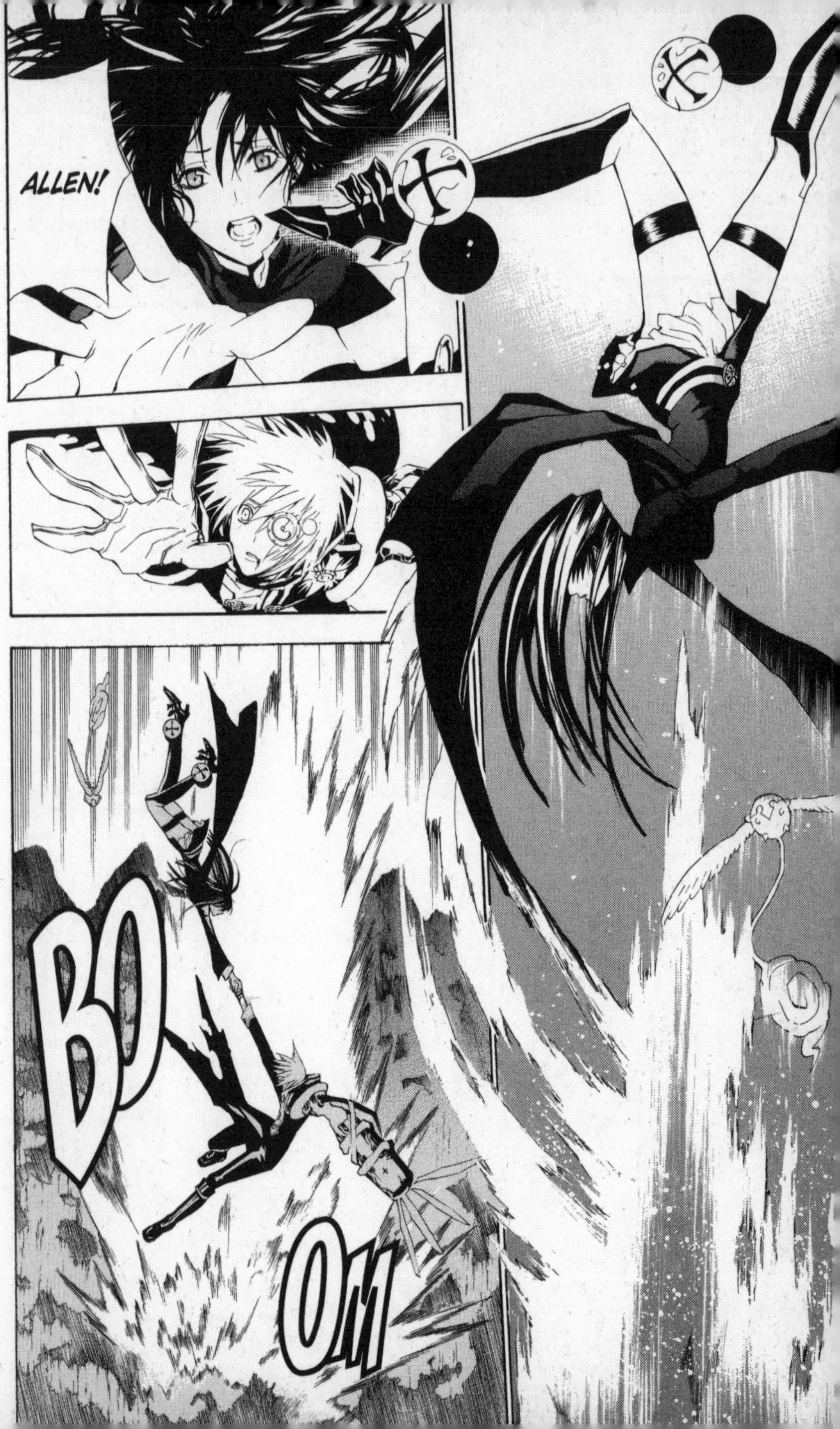
ALLEN!
BO
OM

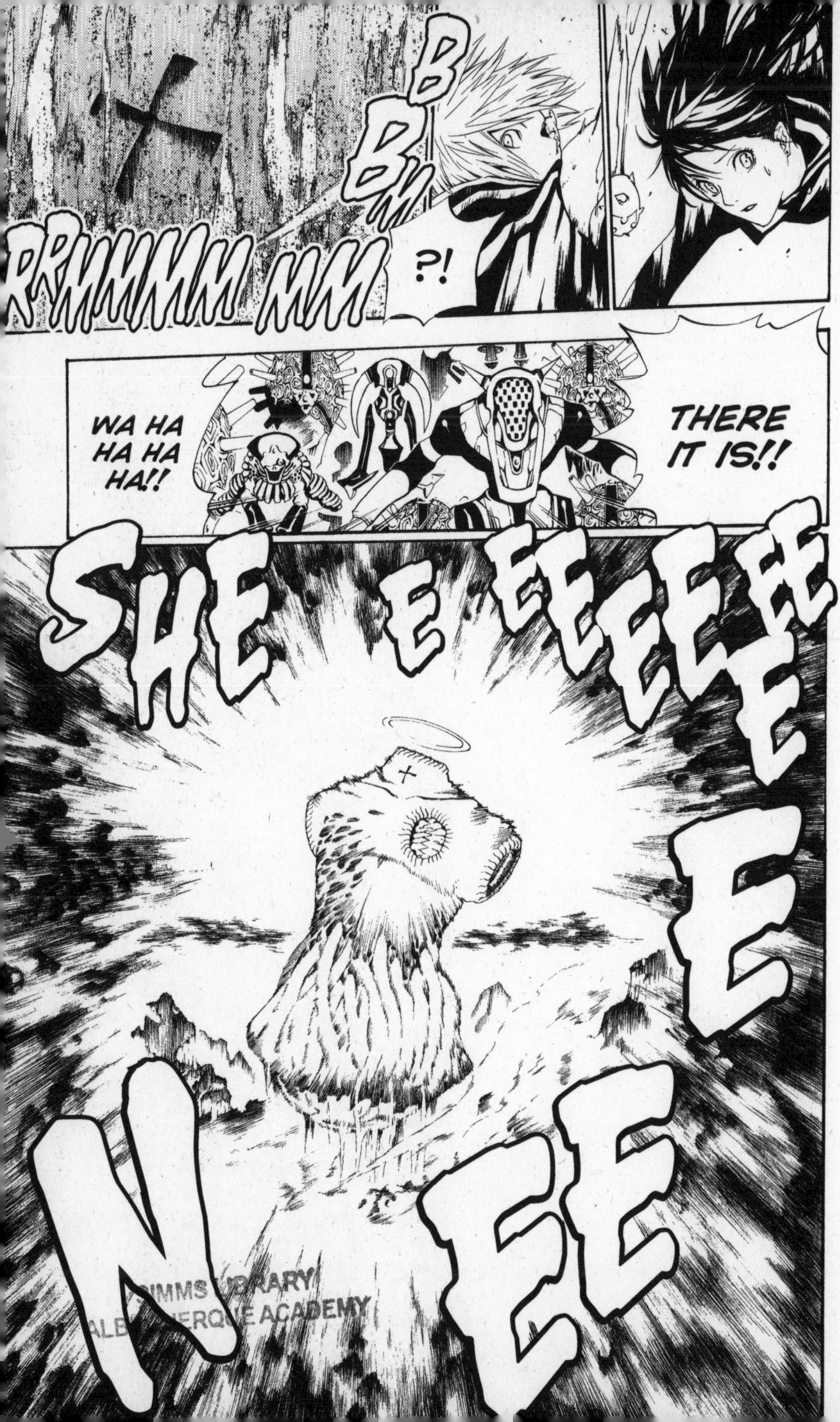
?!
BBM
RRMMMM MM
THERE IT IS!!
WA HA HA HA HA!!
SHEEEEEEEEEE
EEE
NEE

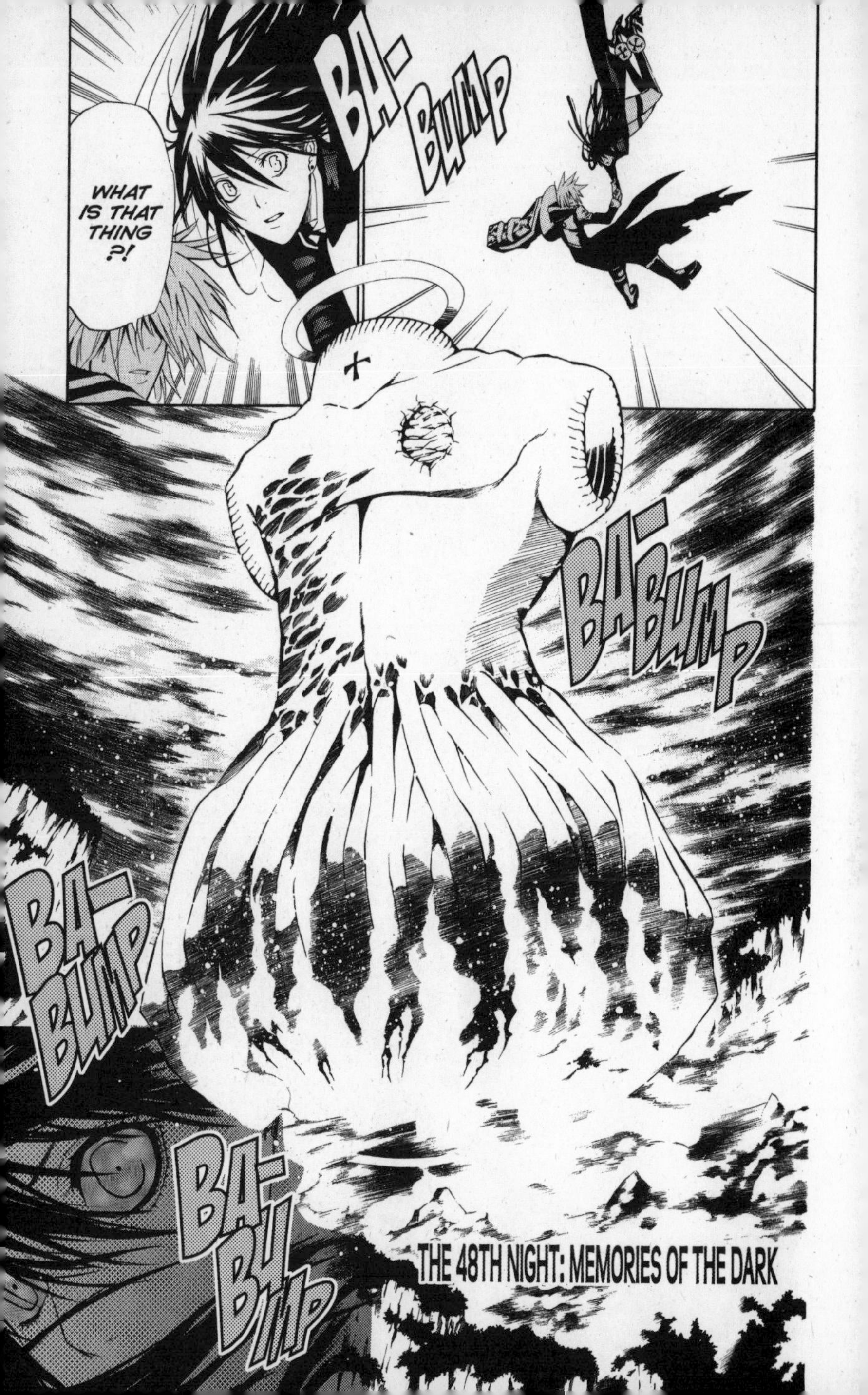
BA-BUMP
WHAT IS THAT THING ?!
BA-BUMP
BA-BUMP
BA-BUMP
BA-BU-BUMP
THE 48TH NIGHT: MEMORIES OF THE DARK

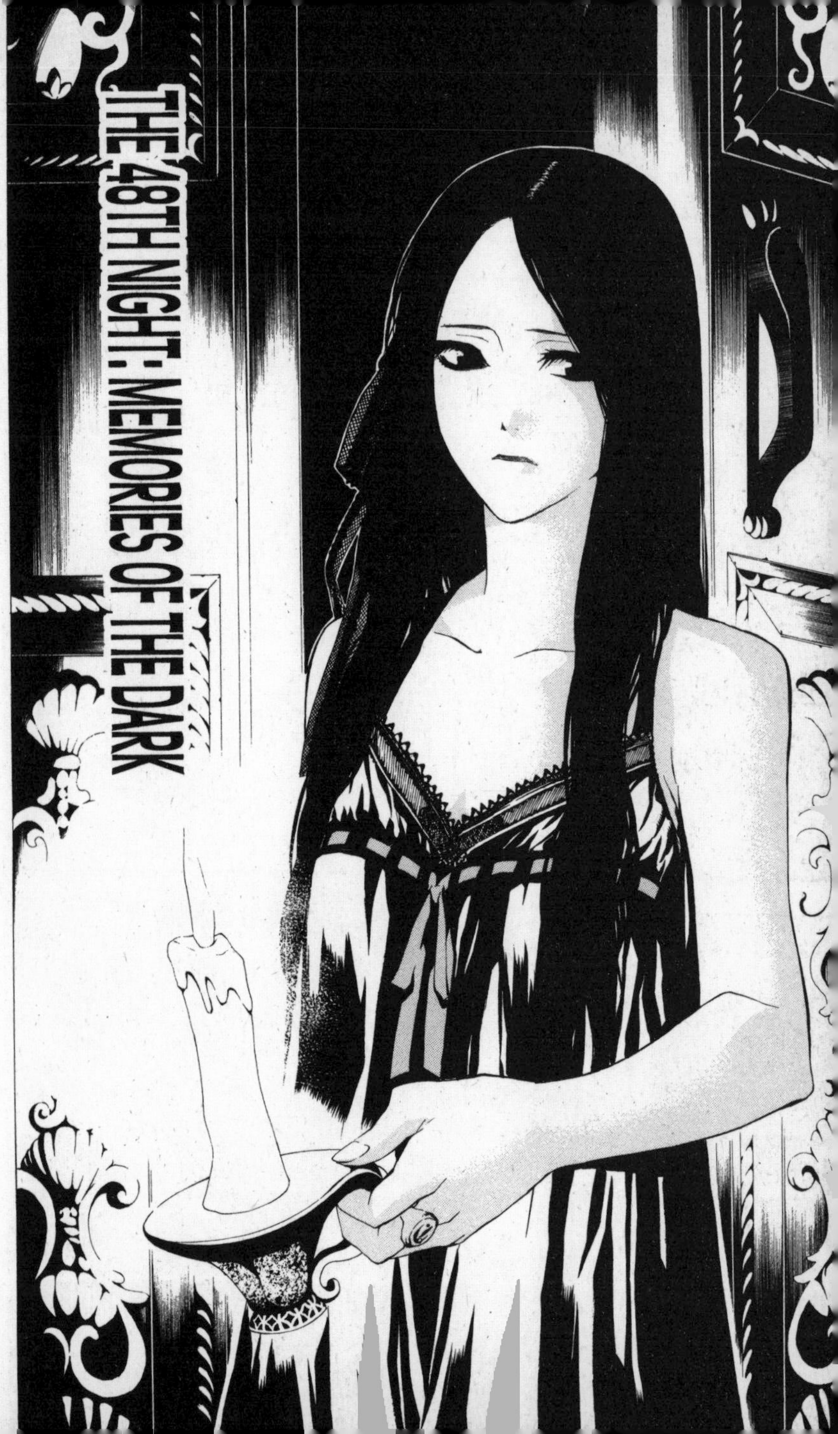
THE 48TH NIGHT: MEMORIES OF THE DARK

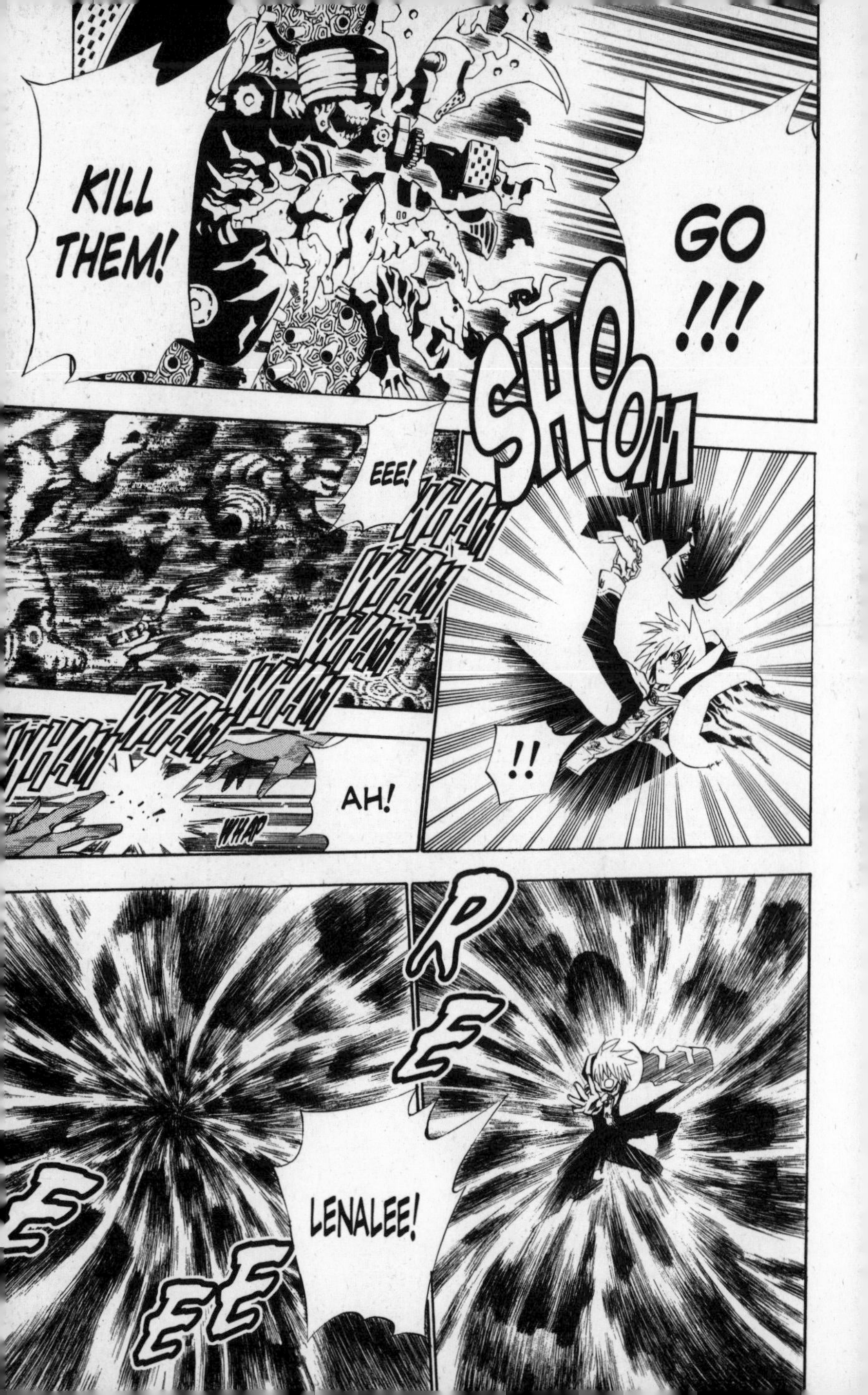
GO!!!
KILL THEM!
SHOOM
!!
EEE!
AH!
WHAP
REEEEE
LENALEE!

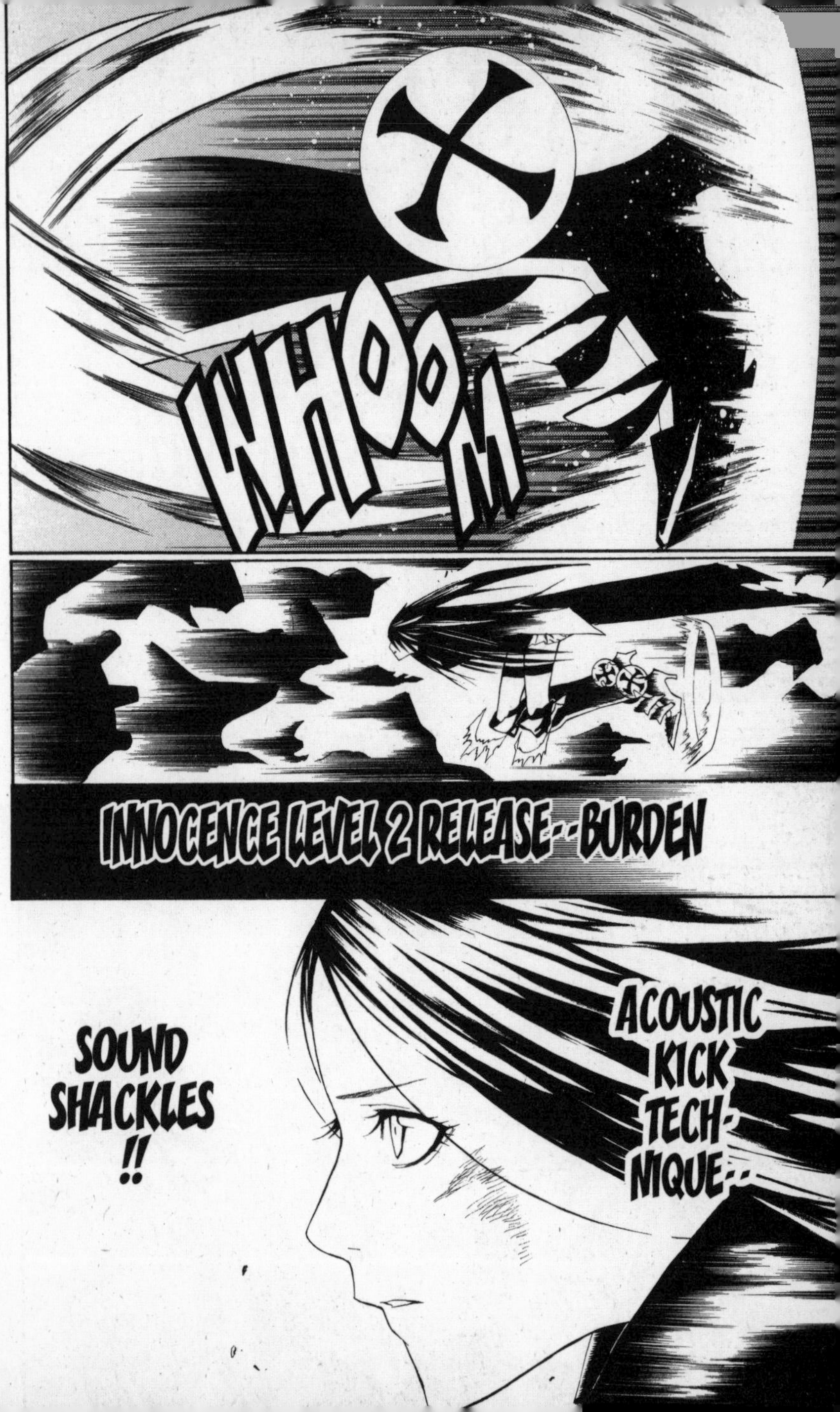
WHOOM
INNOCENCE LEVEL 2 RELEASE--BURDEN
ACOUSTIC KICK TECH-NIQUE--
SOUND SHACKLES!!

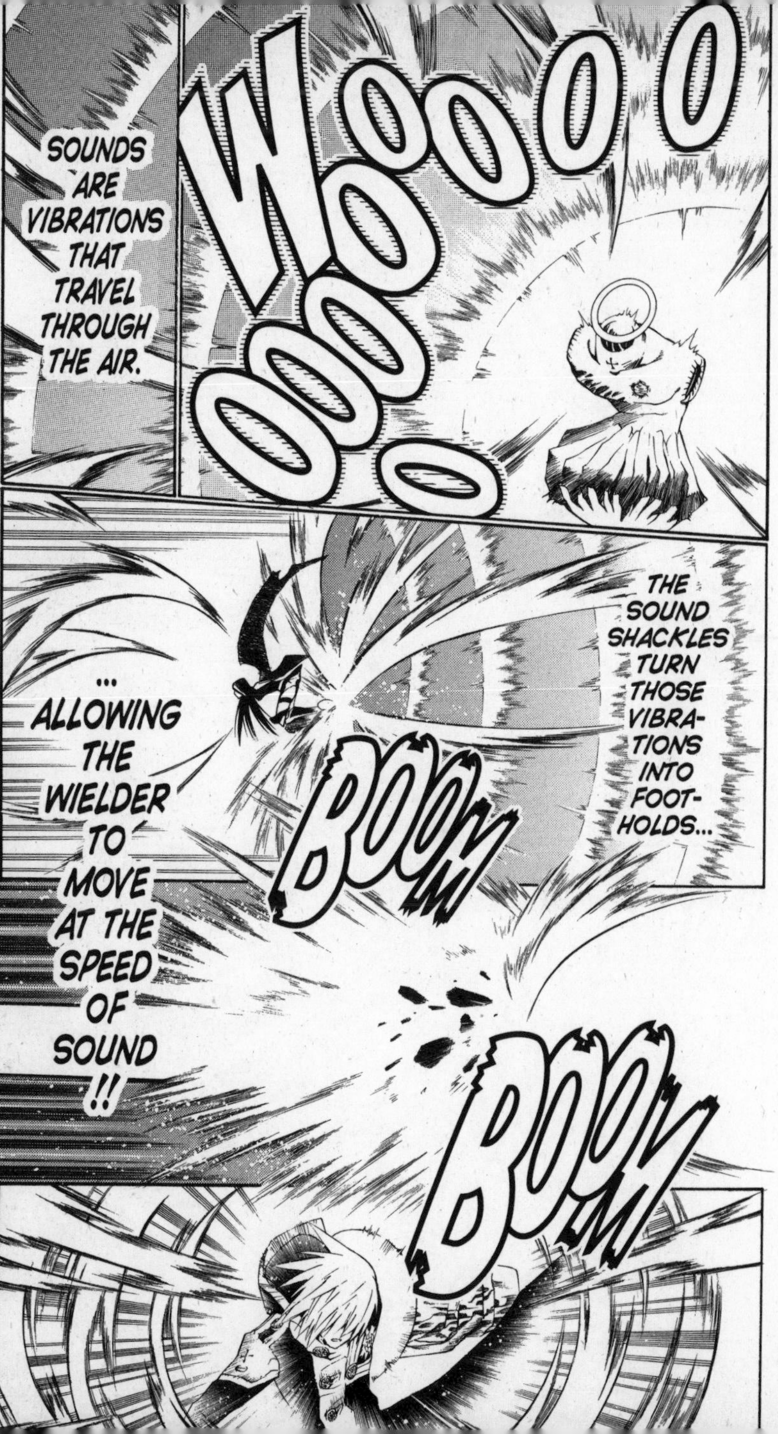
WOOOOOOOOOO
SOUNDS ARE VIBRATIONS THAT TRAVEL THROUGH THE AIR.
THE SOUND SHACKLES TURN THOSE VIBRATIONS INTO FOOTHOLDS...
... ALLOWING THE WIELDER TO MOVE AT THE SPEED OF SOUND !!
BOOM
BOOM

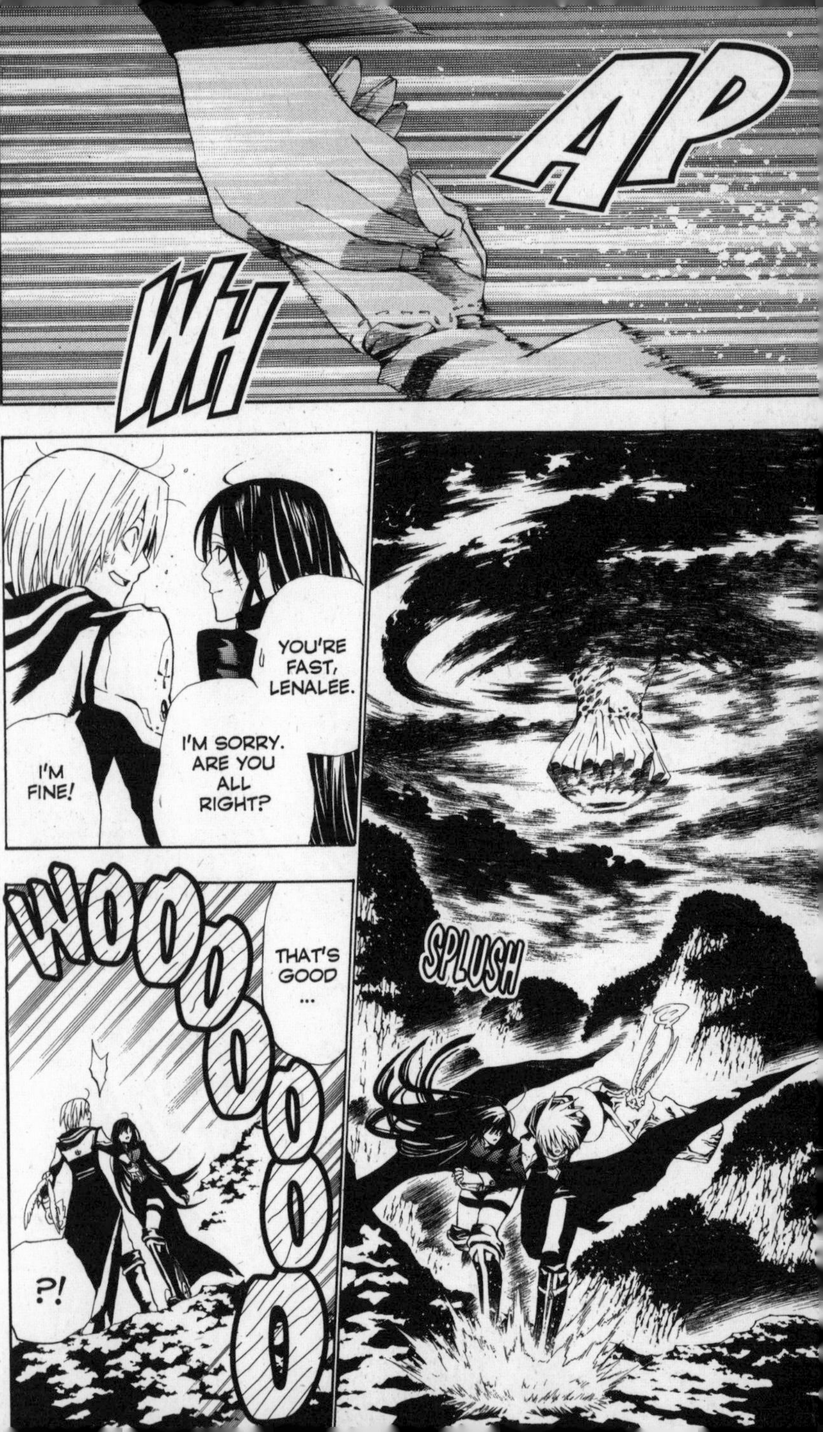

WHAP
SPLUSH
YOU'RE FAST, LENALEE.
I'M SORRY. ARE YOU ALL RIGHT?
I'M FINE!
THAT'S GOOD ...
WOOOOOOOOOO
?!

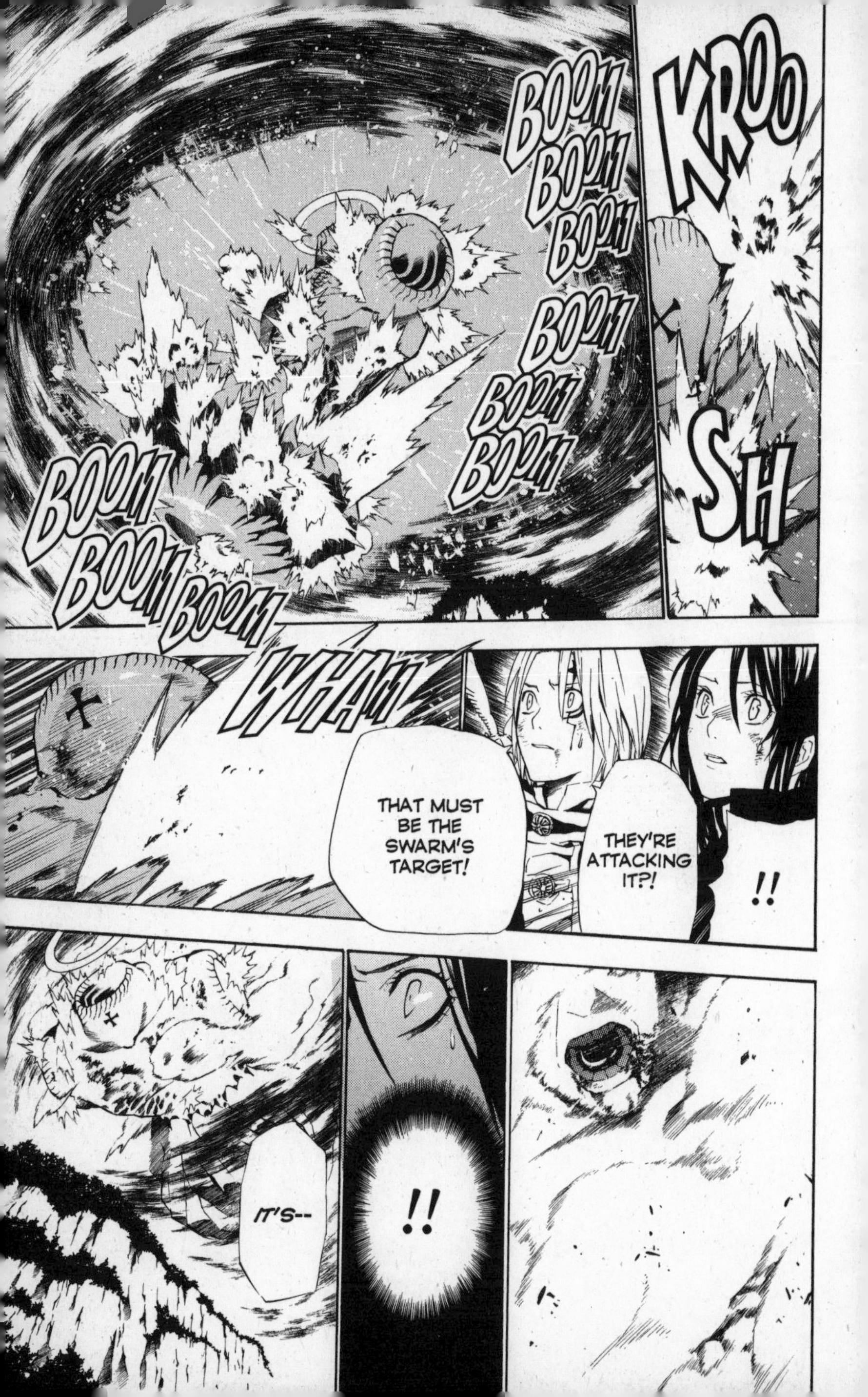
KROO
SH
BOOM BOOM BOOM
BOOM BOOM BOOM
BOOM BOOM BOOM
WHAM
!!
THEY'RE ATTACKING IT?!
THAT MUST BE THE SWARM'S TARGET!
!!
IT'S--

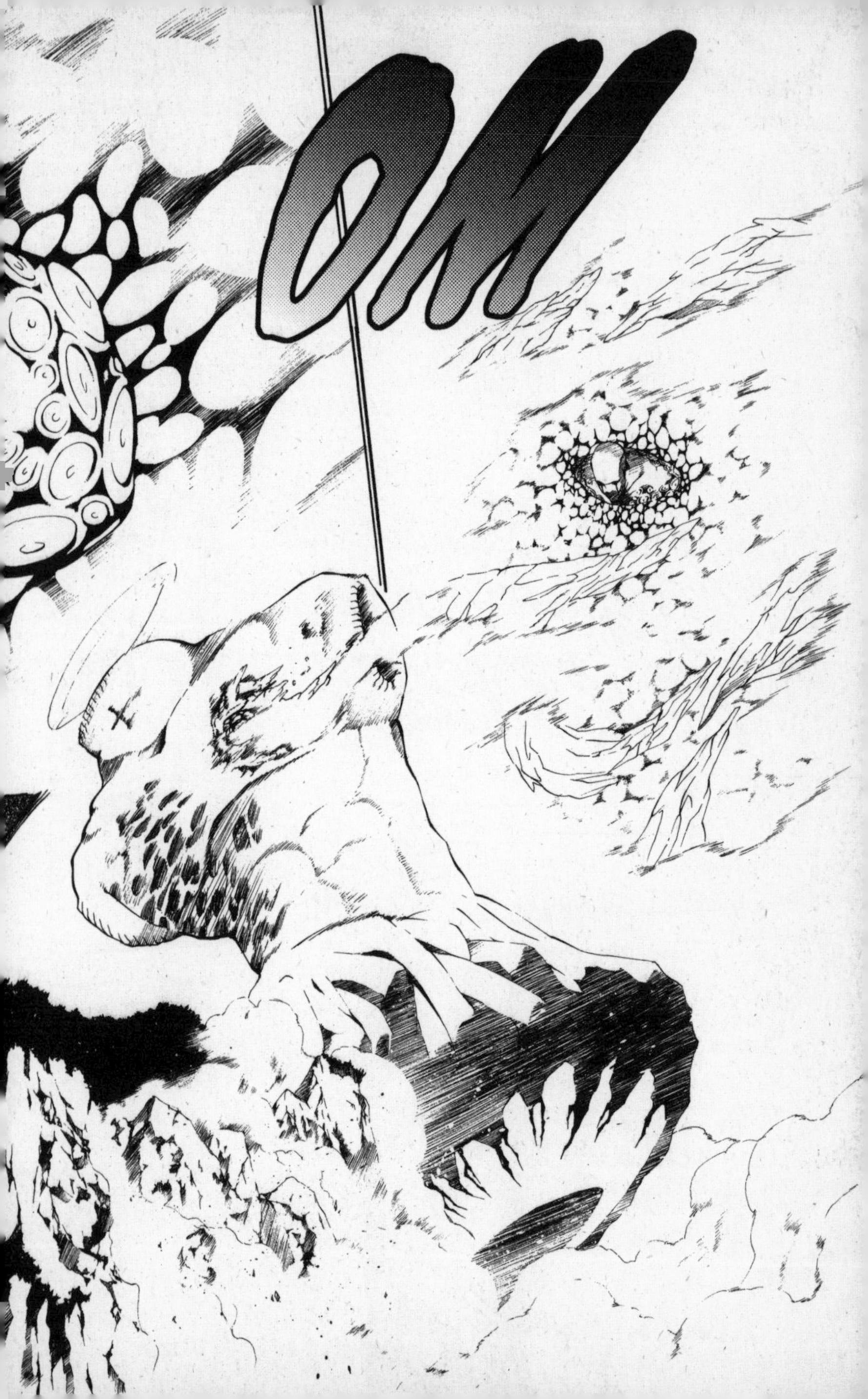
OM

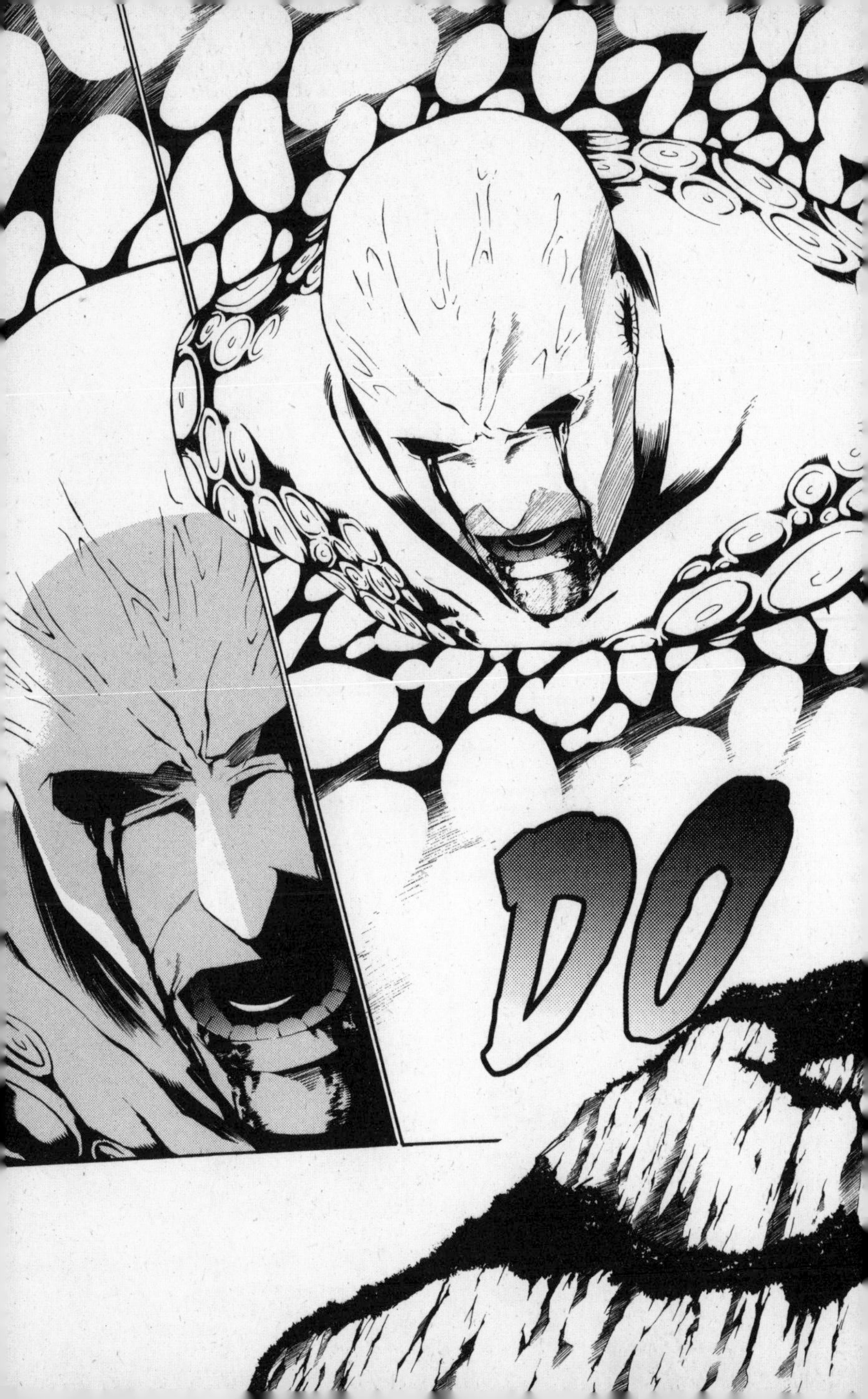
DO

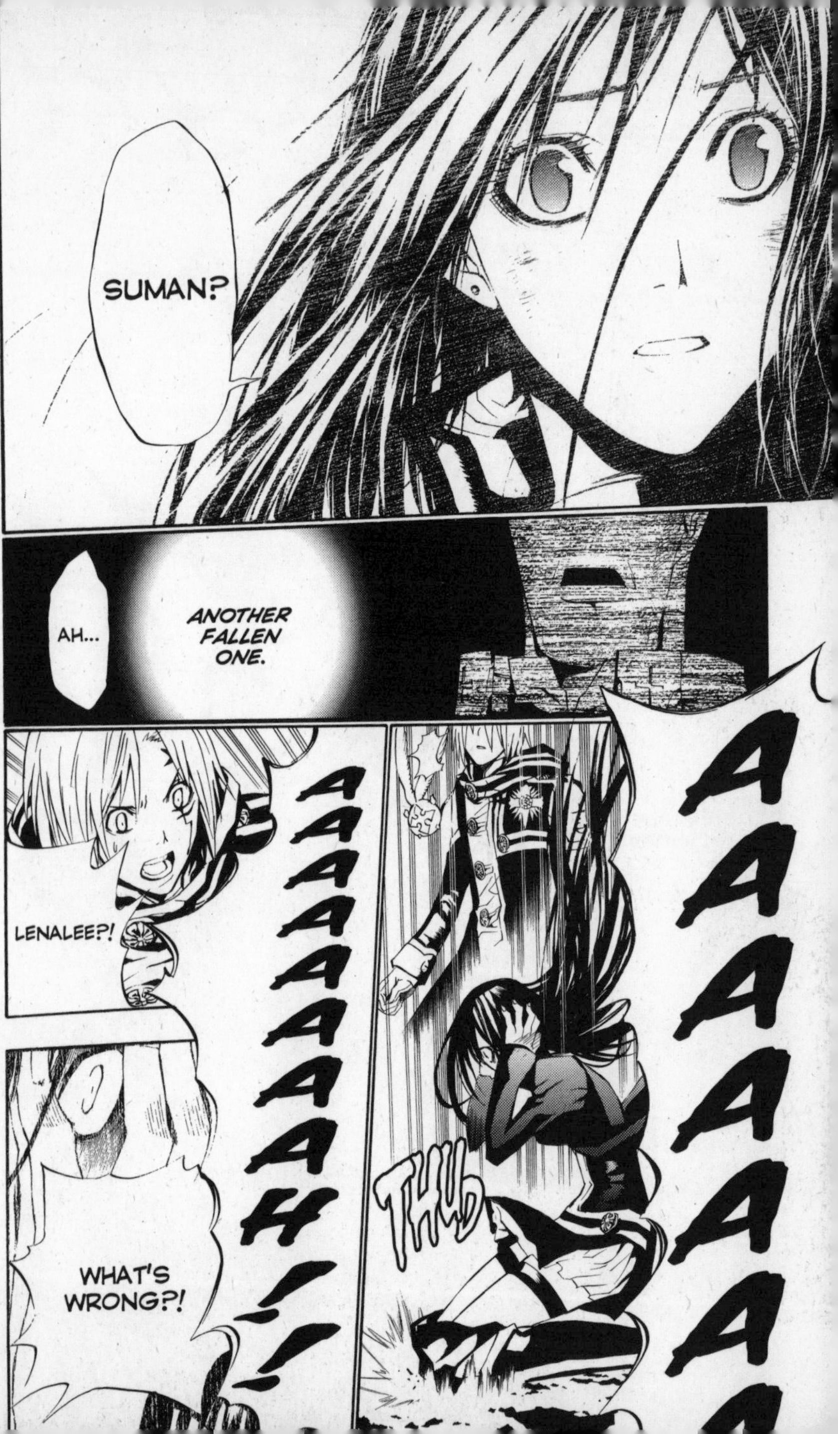
SUMAN?
AH...
ANOTHER FALLEN ONE.
AAAAAAAAA
THUD
AAAAAAAAAAH!!!
LENALEE?!
WHAT'S WRONG?!

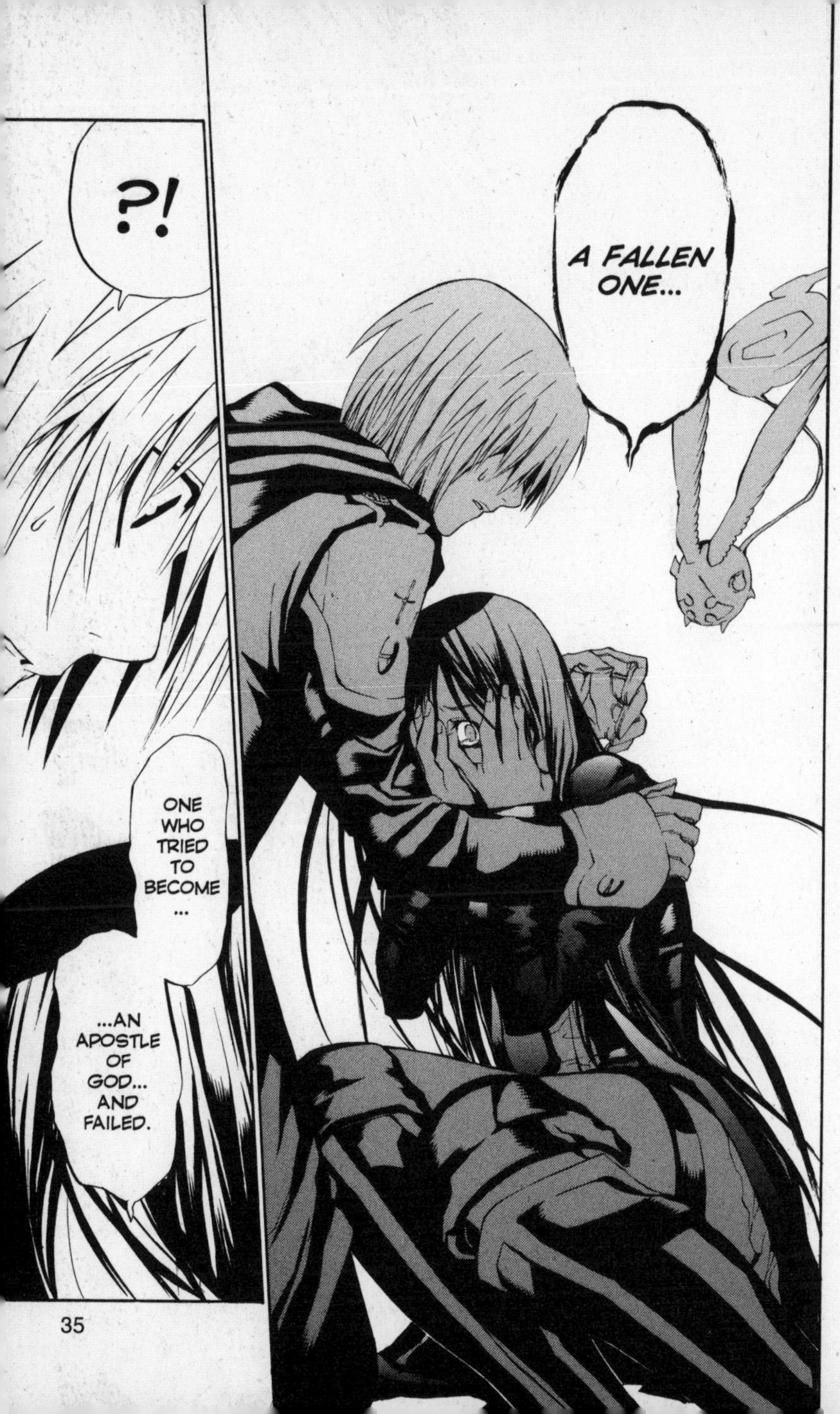
A FALLEN ONE...
?!
ONE WHO TRIED TO BECOME ...
...AN APOSTLE OF GOD... AND FAILED.

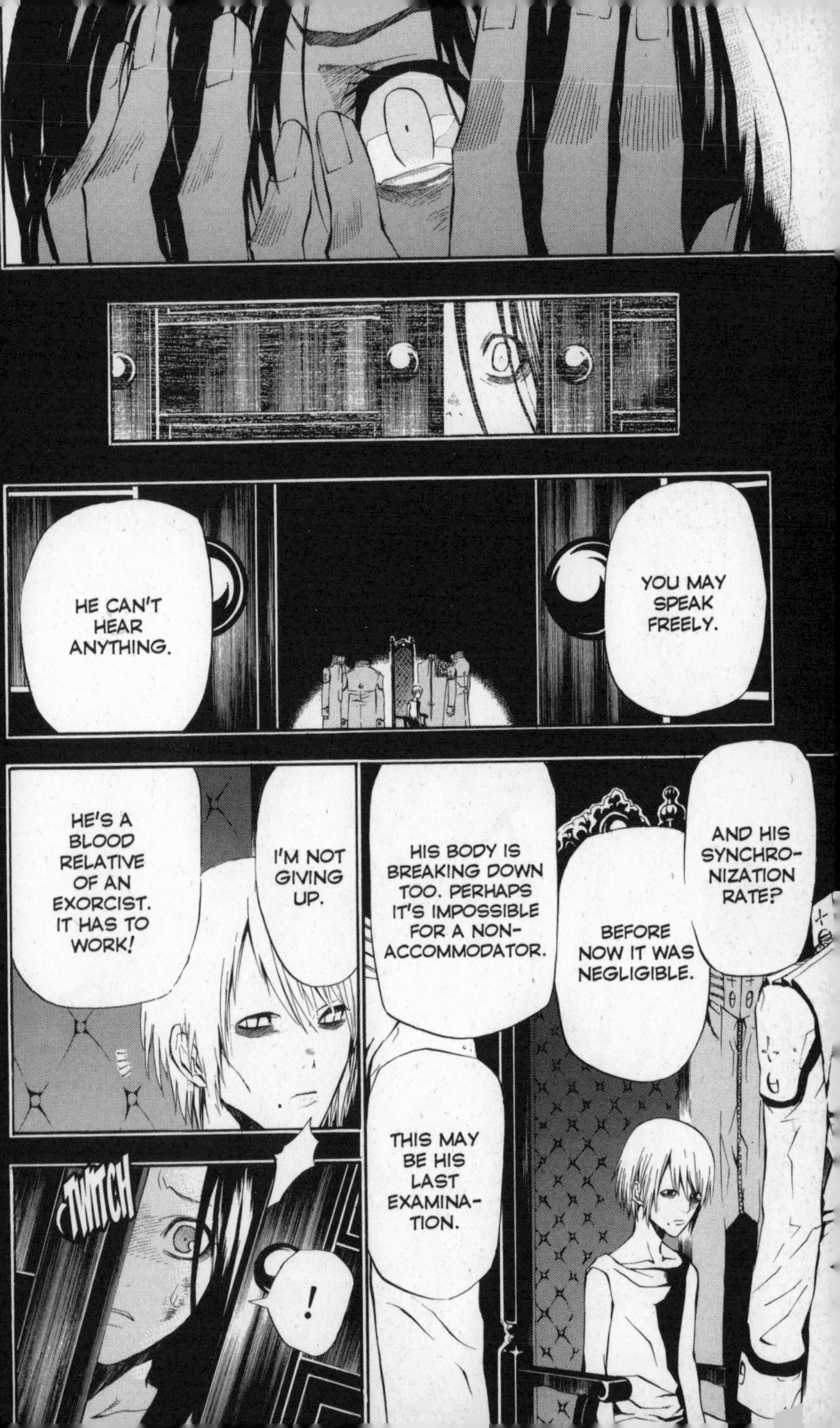
YOU MAY SPEAK FREELY.
HE CAN'T HEAR ANYTHING.
AND HIS SYNCHRONIZATION RATE?
BEFORE NOW IT WAS NEGLIGIBLE.
HIS BODY IS BREAKING DOWN TOO. PERHAPS IT'S IMPOSSIBLE FOR A NON-ACCOMMODATOR.
THIS MAY BE HIS LAST EXAMINATION.
I'M NOT GIVING UP.
HE'S A BLOOD RELATIVE OF AN EXORCIST. IT HAS TO WORK!
TWITCH
!

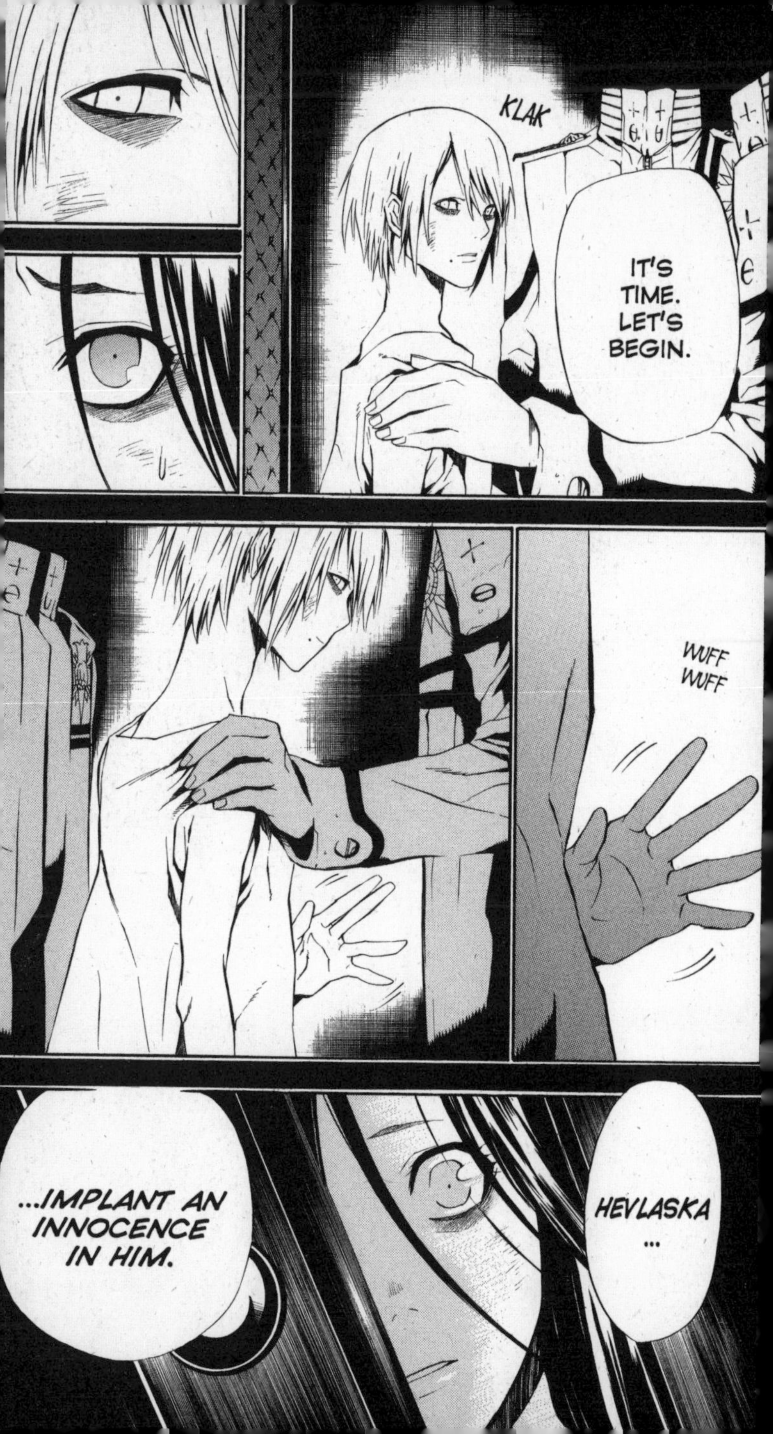
KLAK
IT'S TIME. LET'S BEGIN.
WUFF WUFF
HEVLASKA ...
...IMPLANT AN INNOCENCE IN HIM.

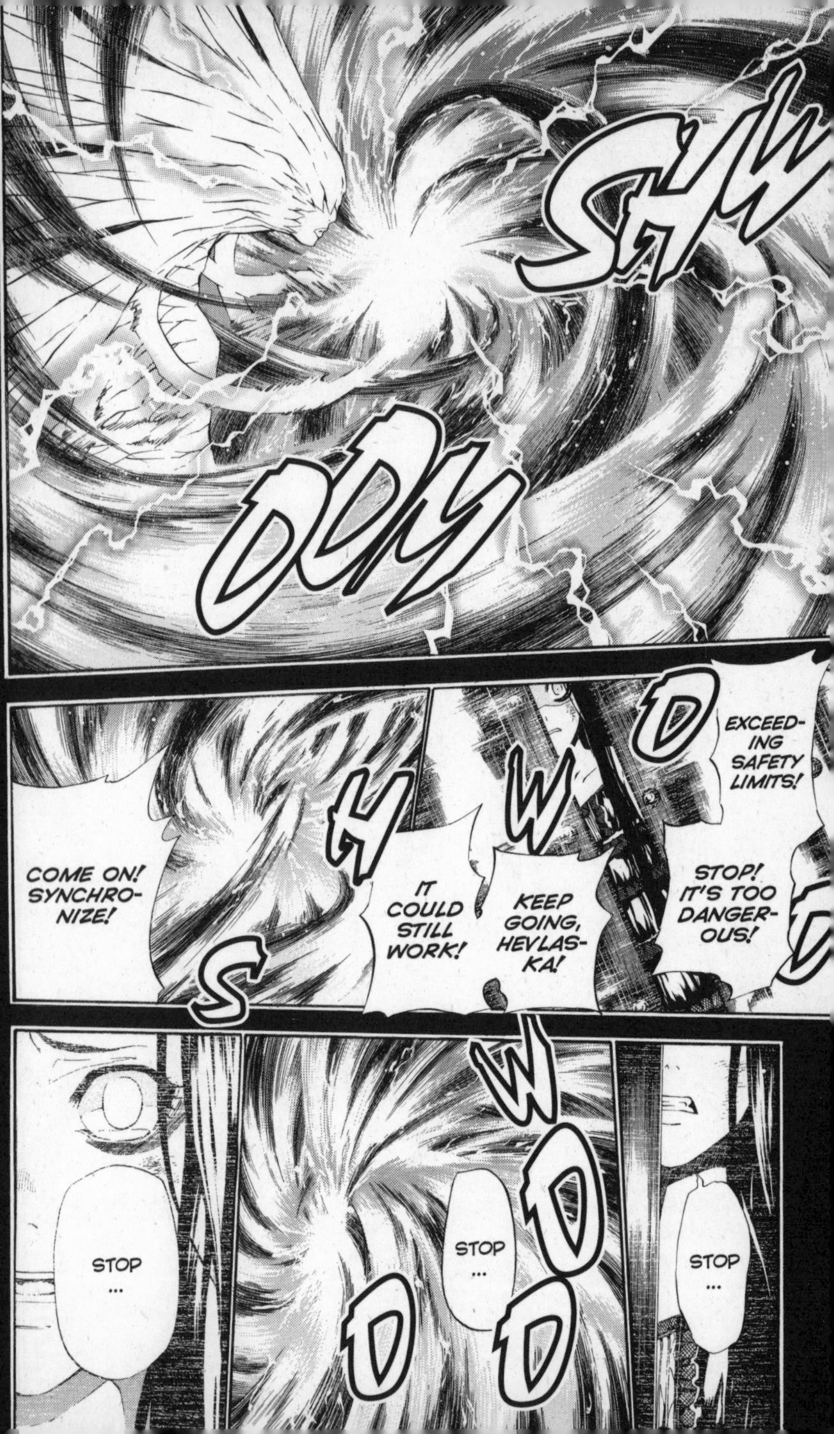
EXCEED-ING SAFETY LIMITS!
STOP! IT'S TOO DANGER-OUS!
KEEP GOING, HEVLAS-KA!
IT COULD STILL WORK!
COME ON! SYNCHRO-NIZE!
STOP ...
STOP ...
STOP ...

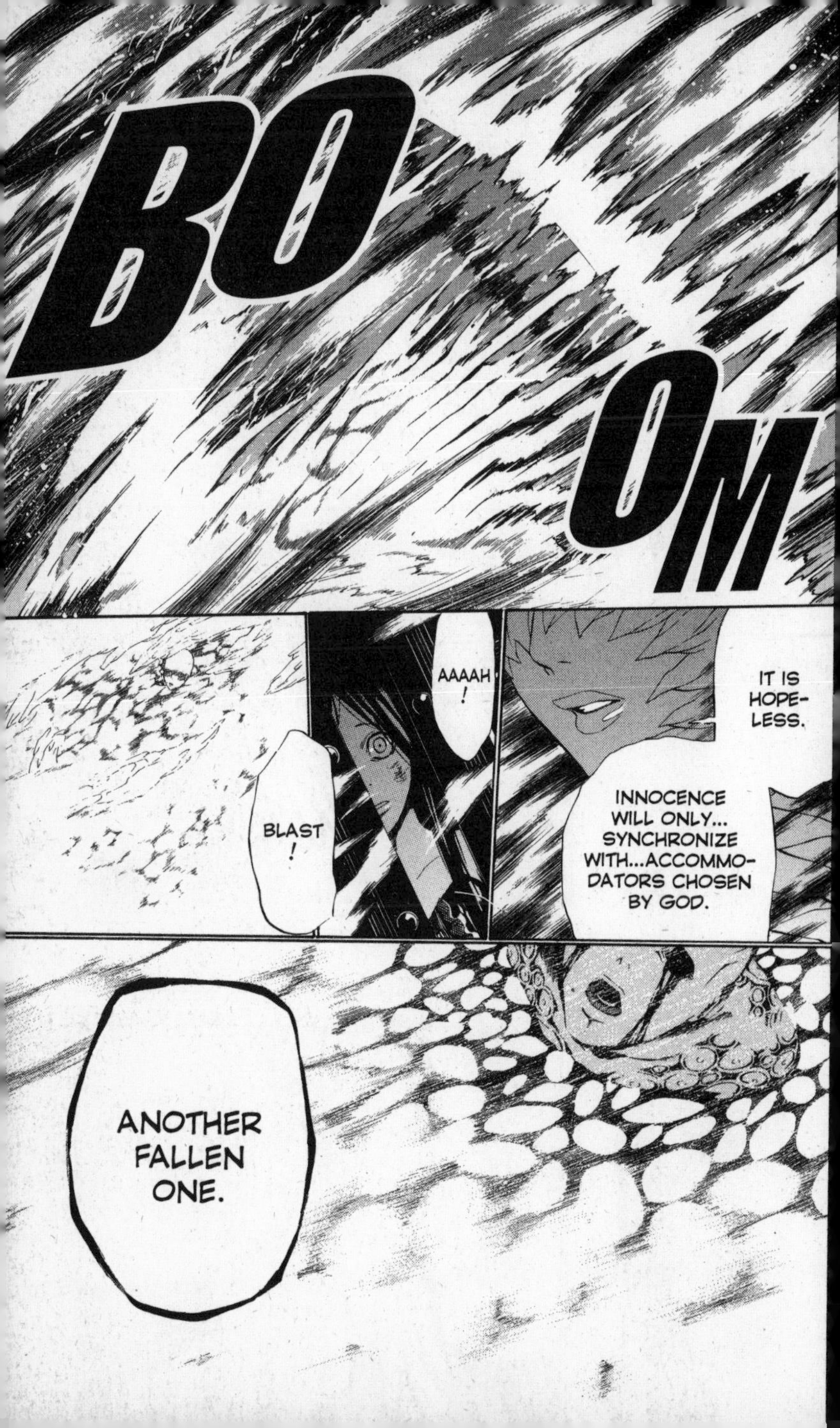
BOOM
IT IS HOPE-LESS.
INNOCENCE WILL ONLY... SYNCHRONIZE WITH...ACCOMMO-DATORS CHOSEN BY GOD.
AAAAH!
BLAST!
ANOTHER FALLEN ONE.

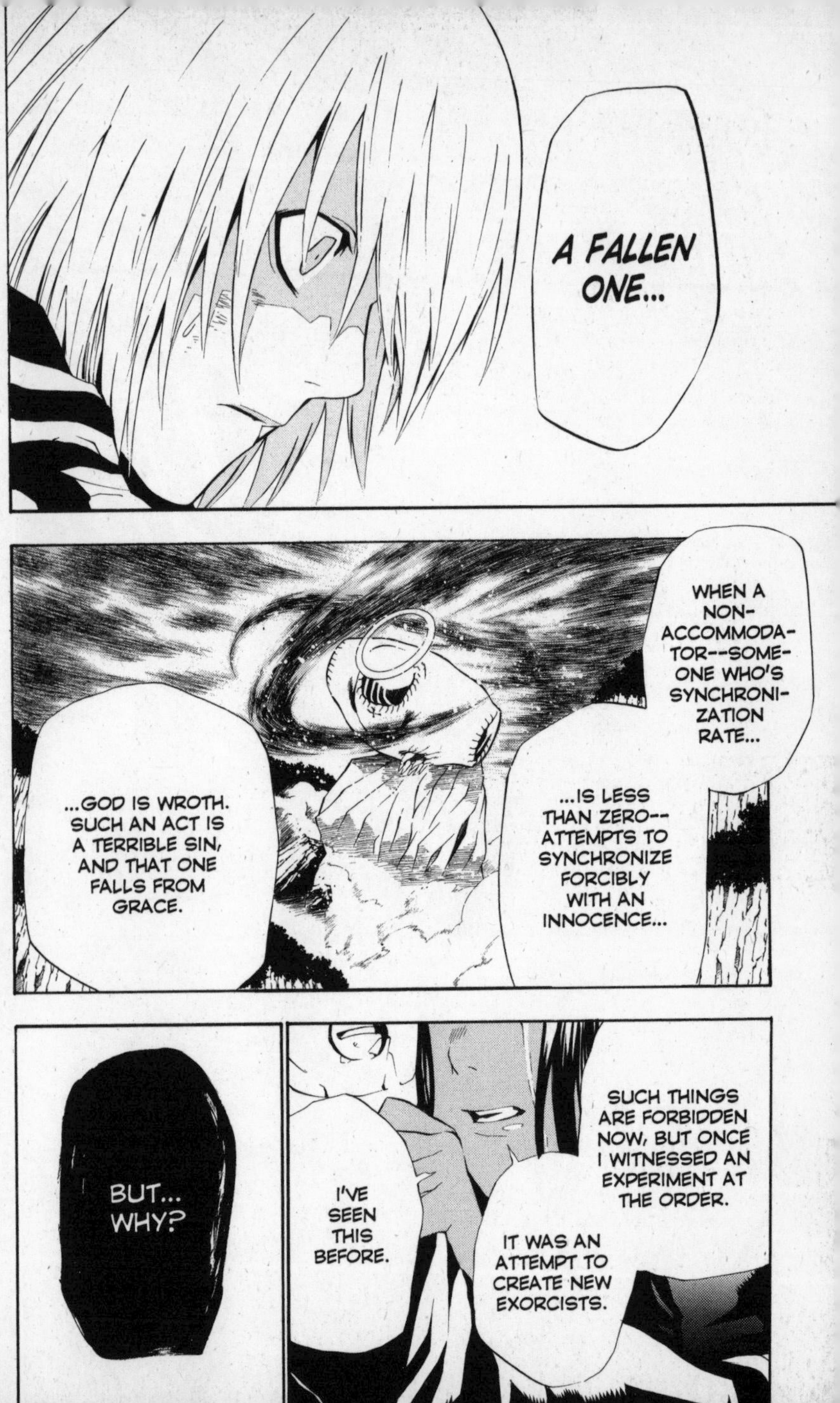
A FALLEN ONE...
WHEN A NON-ACCOMMODATOR--SOMEONE WHO'S SYNCHRONIZATION RATE...
...IS LESS THAN ZERO--ATTEMPTS TO SYNCHRONIZE FORCIBLY WITH AN INNOCENCE...
...GOD IS WROTH. SUCH AN ACT IS A TERRIBLE SIN, AND THAT ONE FALLS FROM GRACE.
SUCH THINGS ARE FORBIDDEN NOW, BUT ONCE I WITNESSED AN EXPERIMENT AT THE ORDER.
I'VE SEEN THIS BEFORE.
IT WAS AN ATTEMPT TO CREATE NEW EXORCISTS.
BUT... WHY?

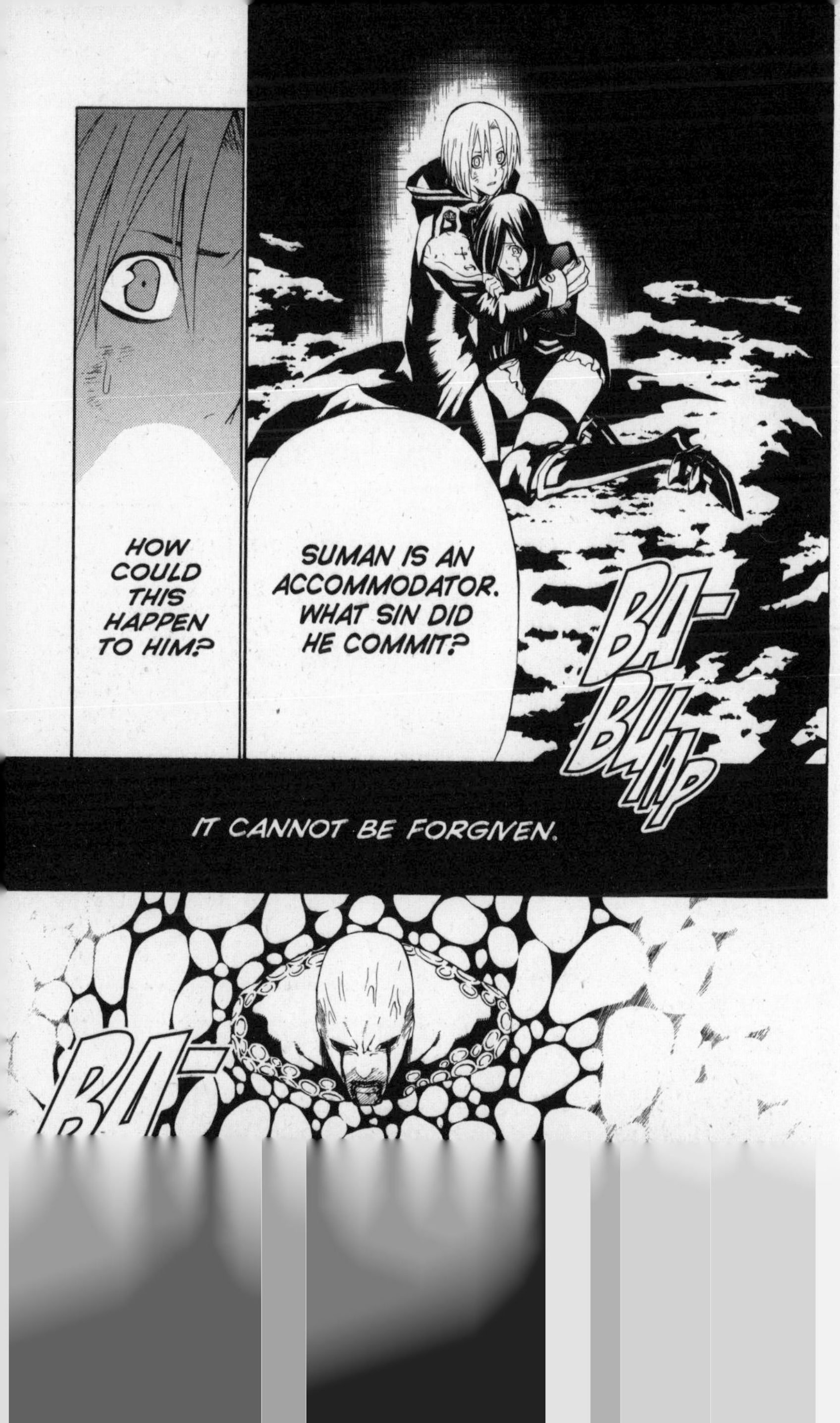
SUMAN IS AN ACCOMMODATOR. WHAT SIN DID HE COMMIT?
HOW COULD THIS HAPPEN TO HIM?
BA-BUMP
IT CANNOT BE FORGIVEN.
BA-

KOMUI'S DISCUSSION ROOM VOL. 1

HEY, WHAT AM I DOING HERE? YOU WANT ME TO
ANSWER QUESTIONS FROM THE READERS? WHY
ME? WHAT HAPPENED TO THAT HOSHINO GUY? A
BELLYACHE? HOW LONG IS HE GOING TO MILK THAT
EXCUSE? HE'S BEEN SAYING THAT SINCE VOL. 4!

HE SHOULD STOP EATING ALL THOSE HAMBURGERS
AND EAT SOBA NOODLES INSTEAD. THEY'RE GOOD
FOR YOU. REALLY. WELL, FINE, IT'S A PAIN, BUT
I'LL DO IT. WHAT DO YOU WANT TO KNOW?

Q. WHAT ARE THE CORRECT SPELLINGS OF THE NAMES OF
THE D.GRAY-MAN CHARACTERS?

A. WHAT AN ANNOYING QUESTION. OKAY, I'M ONLY GOING TO
DO THIS ONCE, SO TAKE NOTE.

YU KANDA
LENALEE LEE
LAVI
ALLEN WALKER
KOMUI LEE
REEVER WENHAM
BOOKMAN
(CONTINUED IN VOL. 2)

THE 49TH NIGHT: SIN

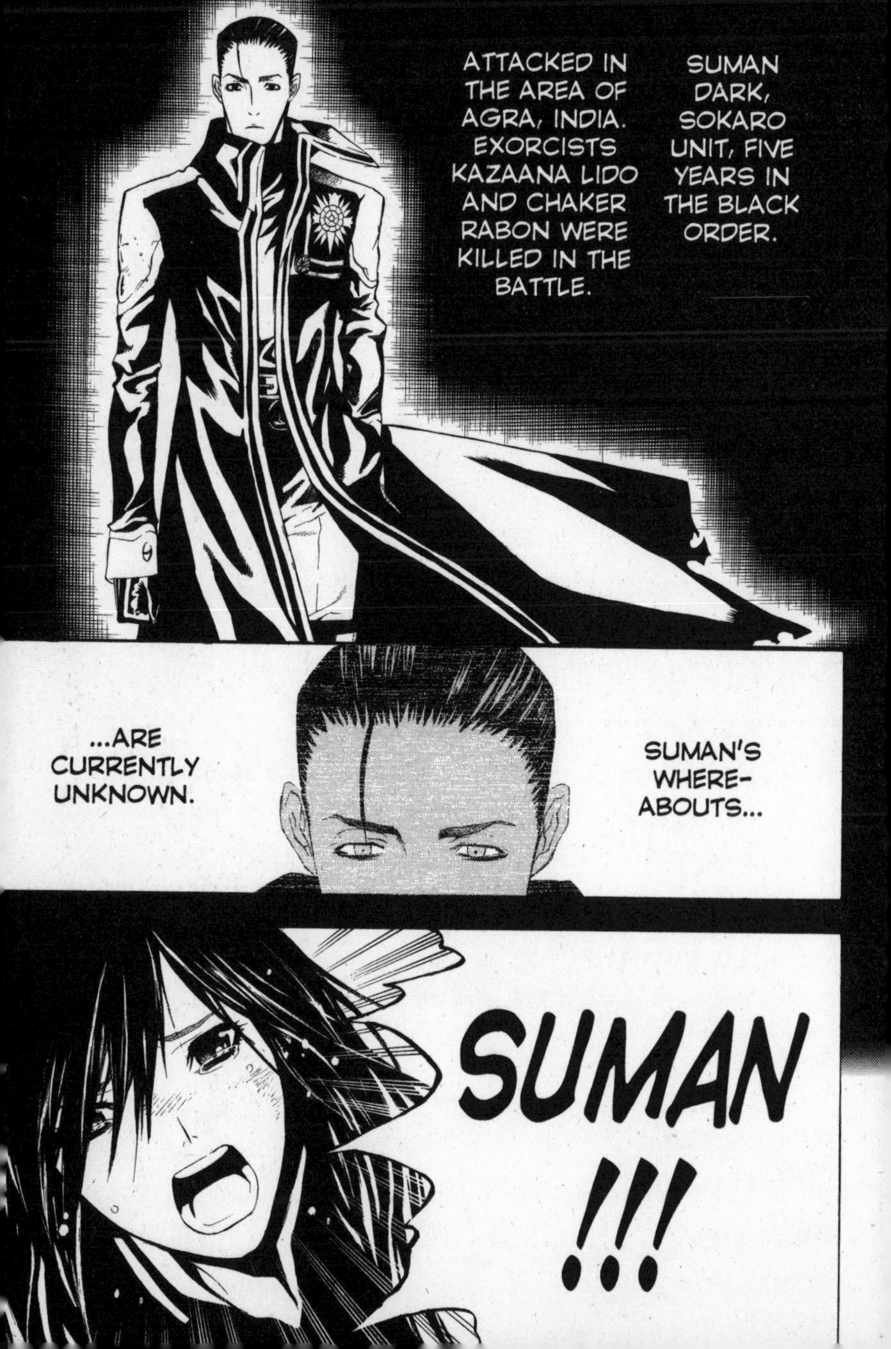
SUMAN DARK, SOKARO UNIT, FIVE YEARS IN THE BLACK ORDER.
ATTACKED IN THE AREA OF AGRA, INDIA. EXORCISTS KAZAANA LIDO AND CHAKER RABON WERE KILLED IN THE BATTLE.
SUMAN'S WHERE-ABOUTS...
...ARE CURRENTLY UNKNOWN.
SUMAN !!!

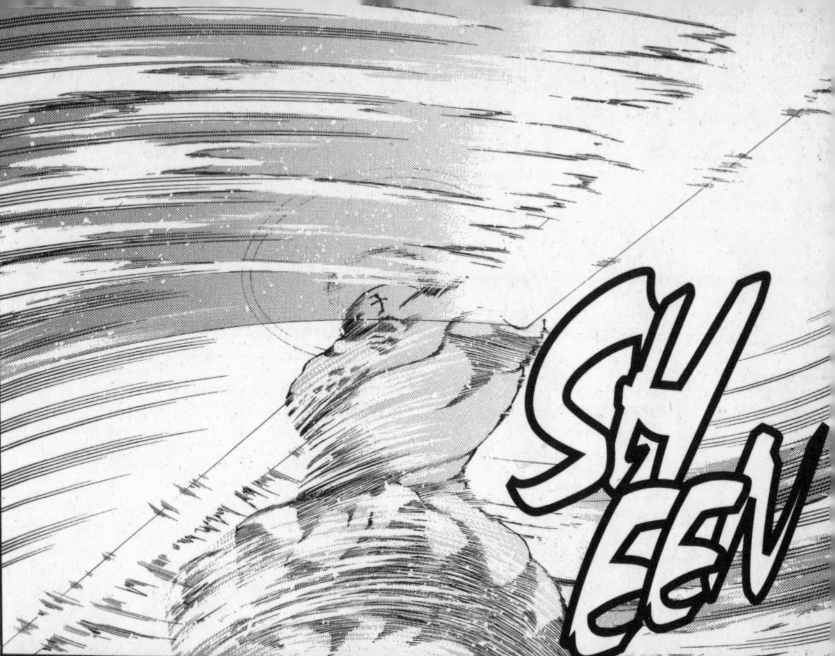
SHEEN

THE 49TH NIGHT: SIN

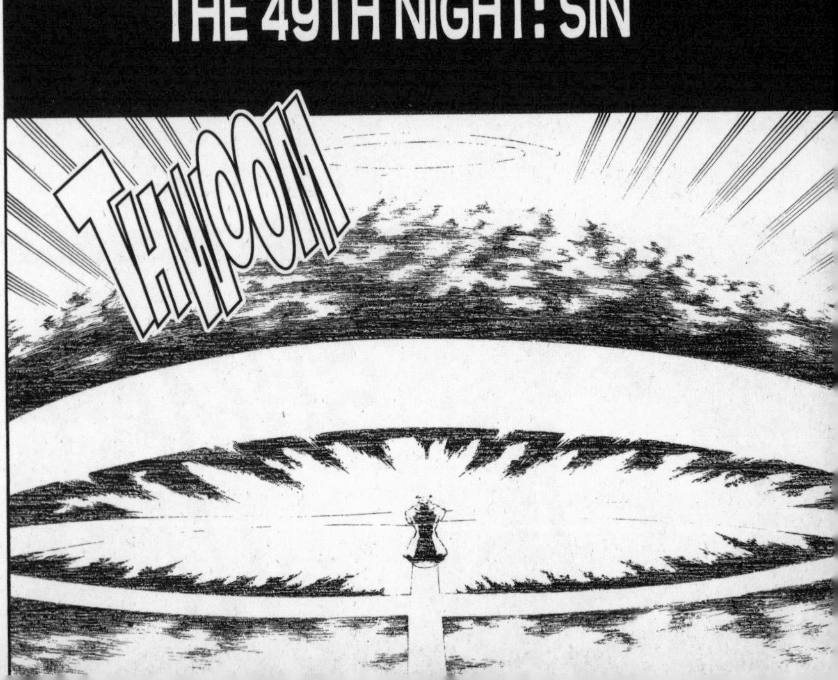
THWOOM

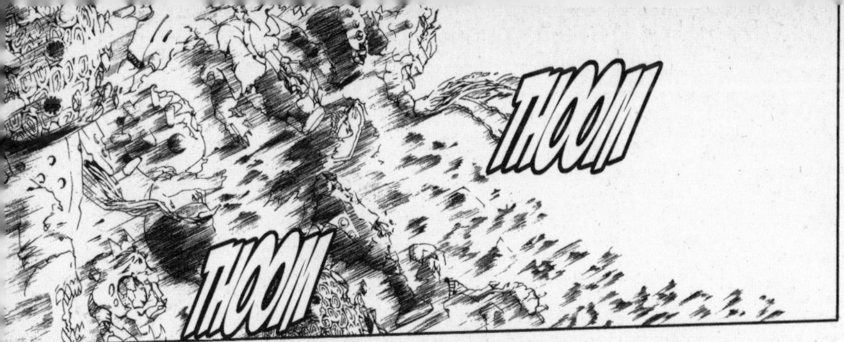
THOOM
THOOM

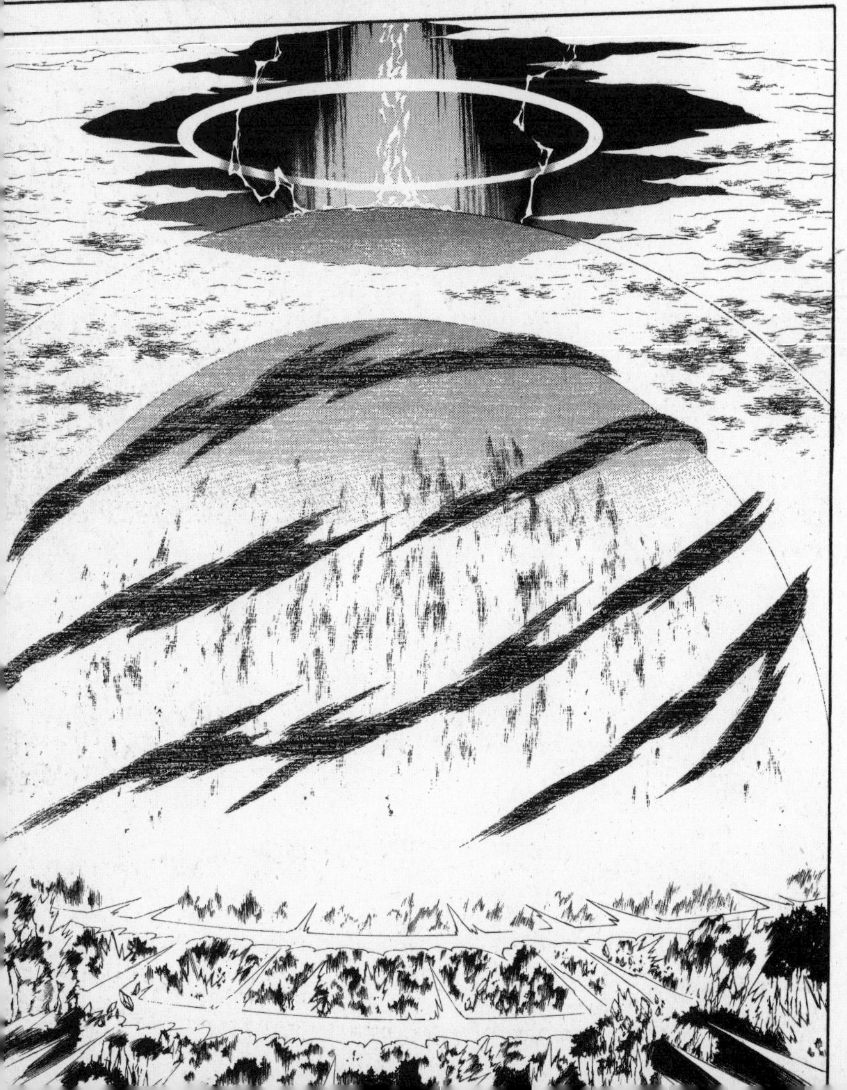

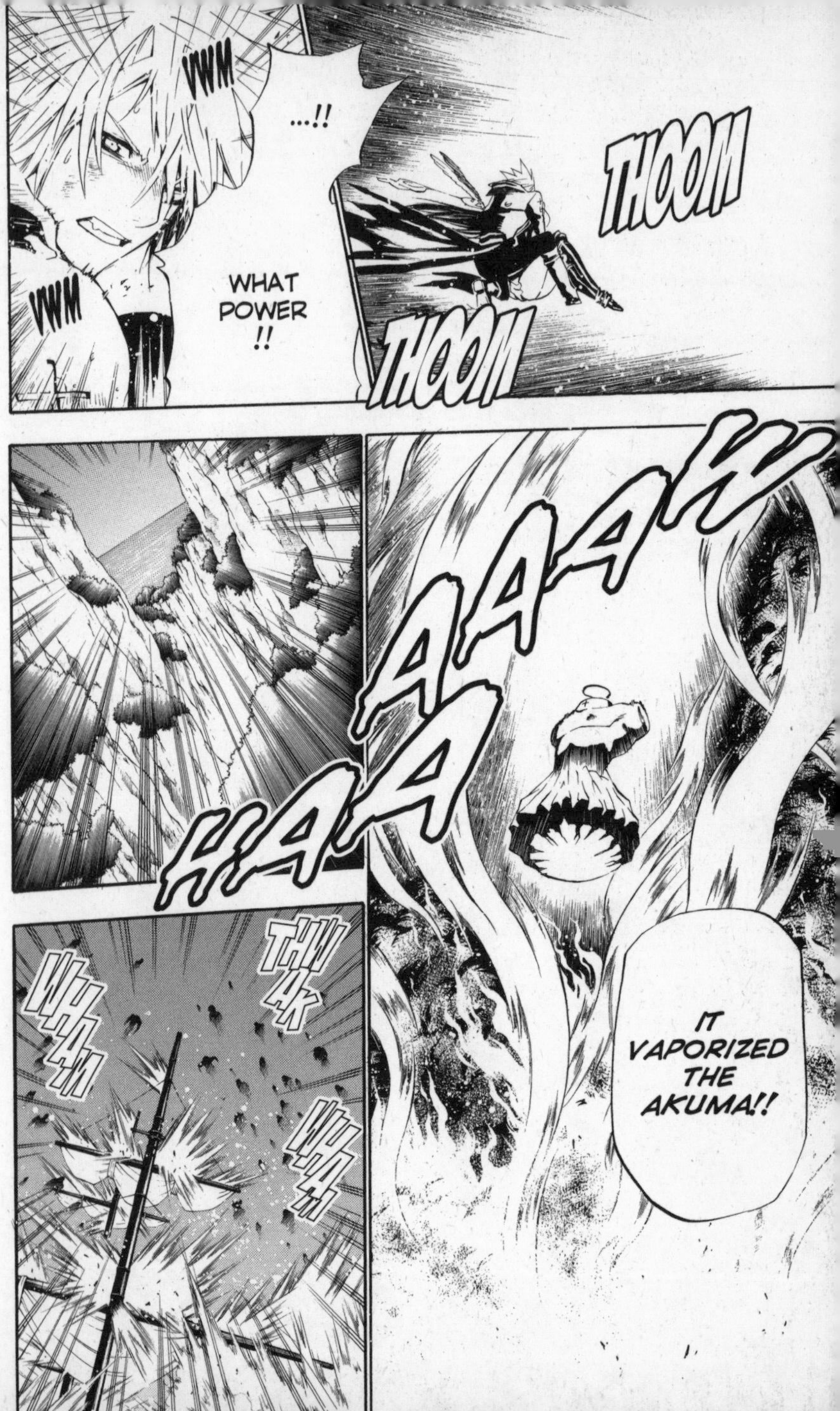
THOOM
THOOM
VWM
...!!
WHAT POWER !!
VWM
HAAAAAA!!
IT VAPORIZED THE AKUMA!!
THWAK
WHAM
WHAM

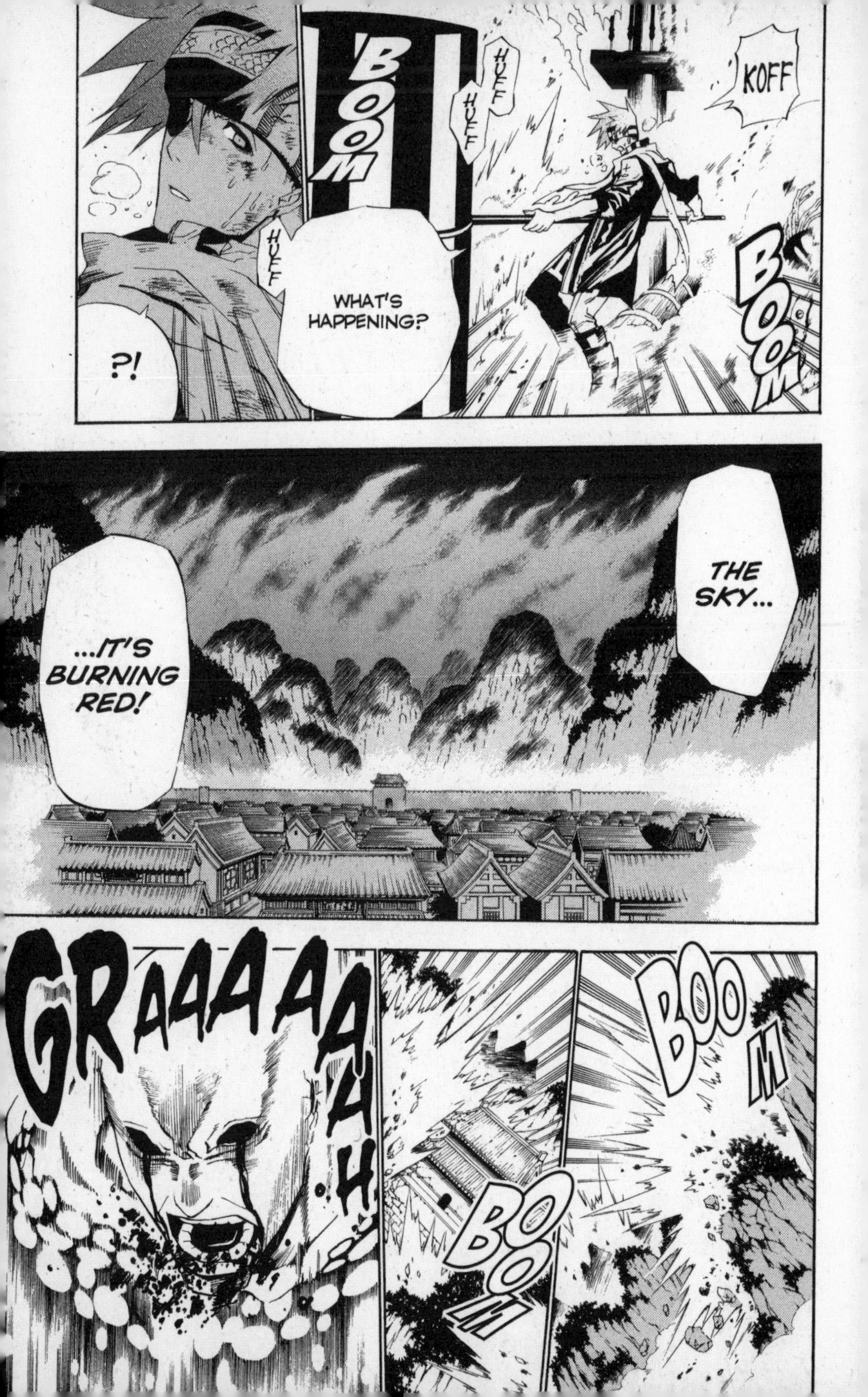
KOFF
HUFF HUFF
BOOM
BOOOM
HUFF
WHAT'S HAPPENING?
?!
THE SKY...
...IT'S BURNING RED!
BOOM
BOOOM
GRAAAAAAH

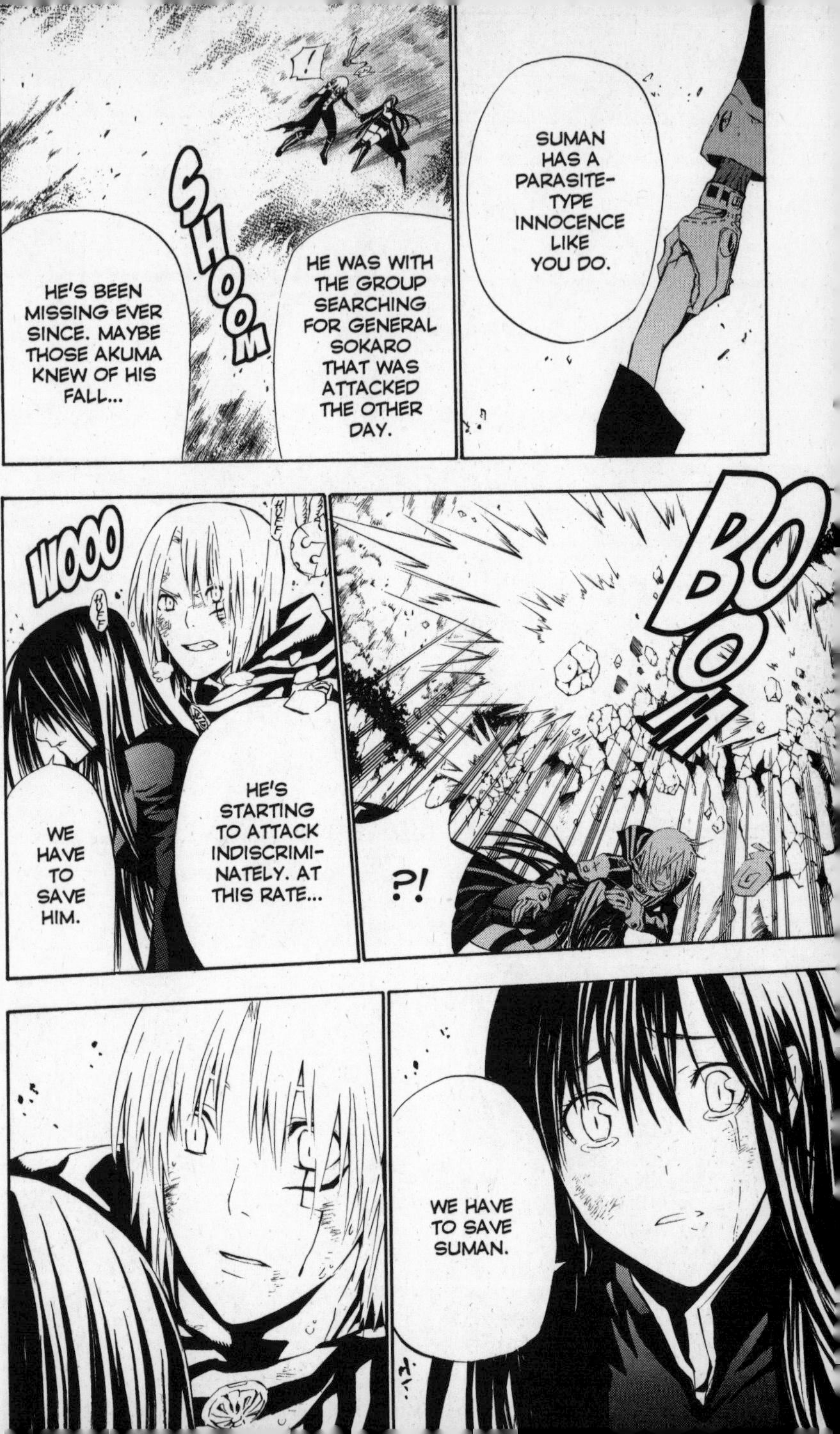
SUMAN HAS A PARASITE-TYPE INNOCENCE LIKE YOU DO.
!
SHOOM
HE WAS WITH THE GROUP SEARCHING FOR GENERAL SOKARO THAT WAS ATTACKED THE OTHER DAY.
HE'S BEEN MISSING EVER SINCE. MAYBE THOSE AKUMA KNEW OF HIS FALL...
BOOM
?!
HUFF
WOOO
HUFF
HE'S STARTING TO ATTACK INDISCRIMI-NATELY. AT THIS RATE...
WE HAVE TO SAVE HIM.
WE HAVE TO SAVE SUMAN.

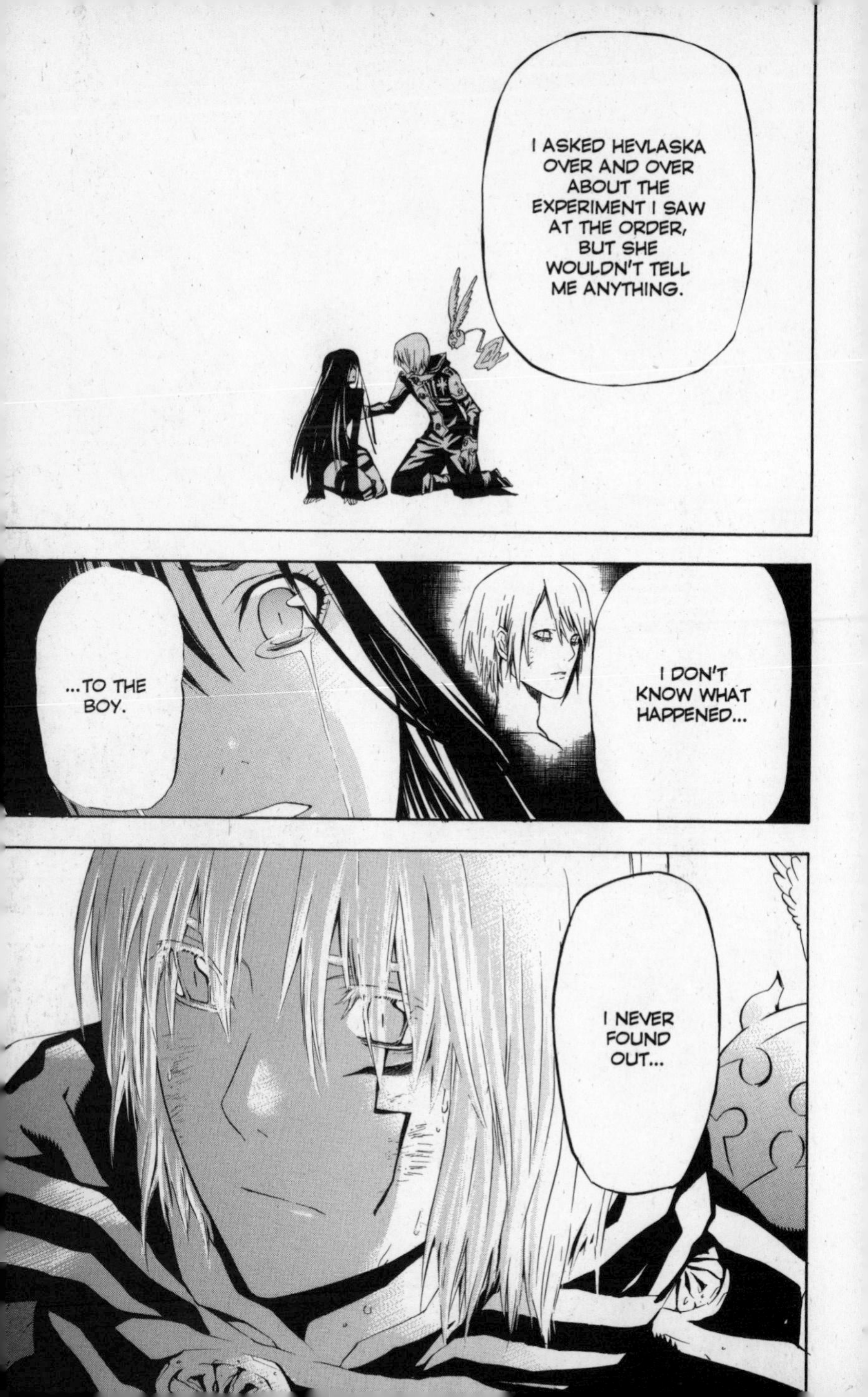
I ASKED HEVLASKA OVER AND OVER ABOUT THE EXPERIMENT I SAW AT THE ORDER, BUT SHE WOULDN'T TELL ME ANYTHING.
I DON'T KNOW WHAT HAPPENED...
...TO THE BOY.
I NEVER FOUND OUT...

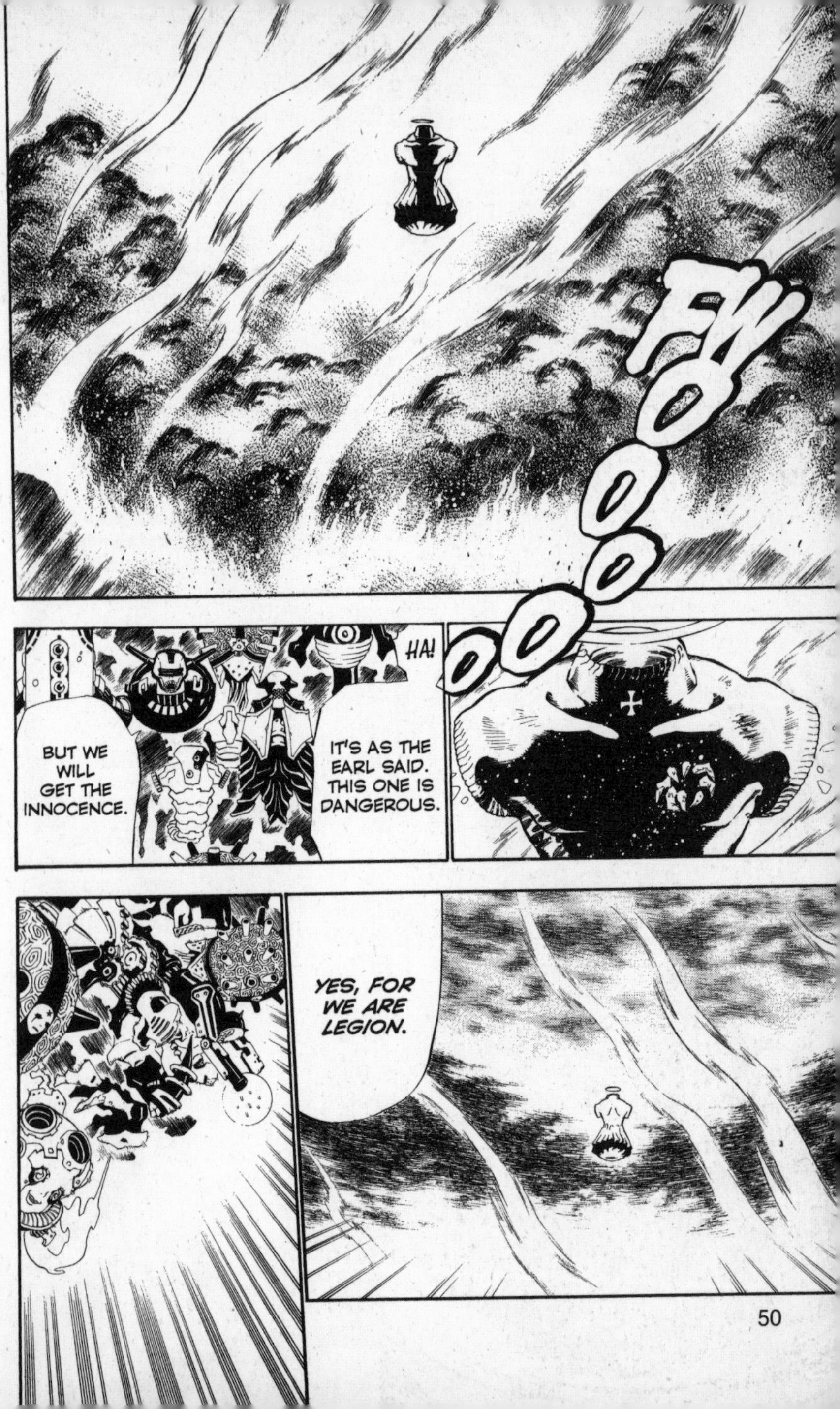
FWOOOOOOO
HA!
IT'S AS THE EARL SAID. THIS ONE IS DANGEROUS.
BUT WE WILL GET THE INNOCENCE.
YES, FOR WE ARE LEGION.

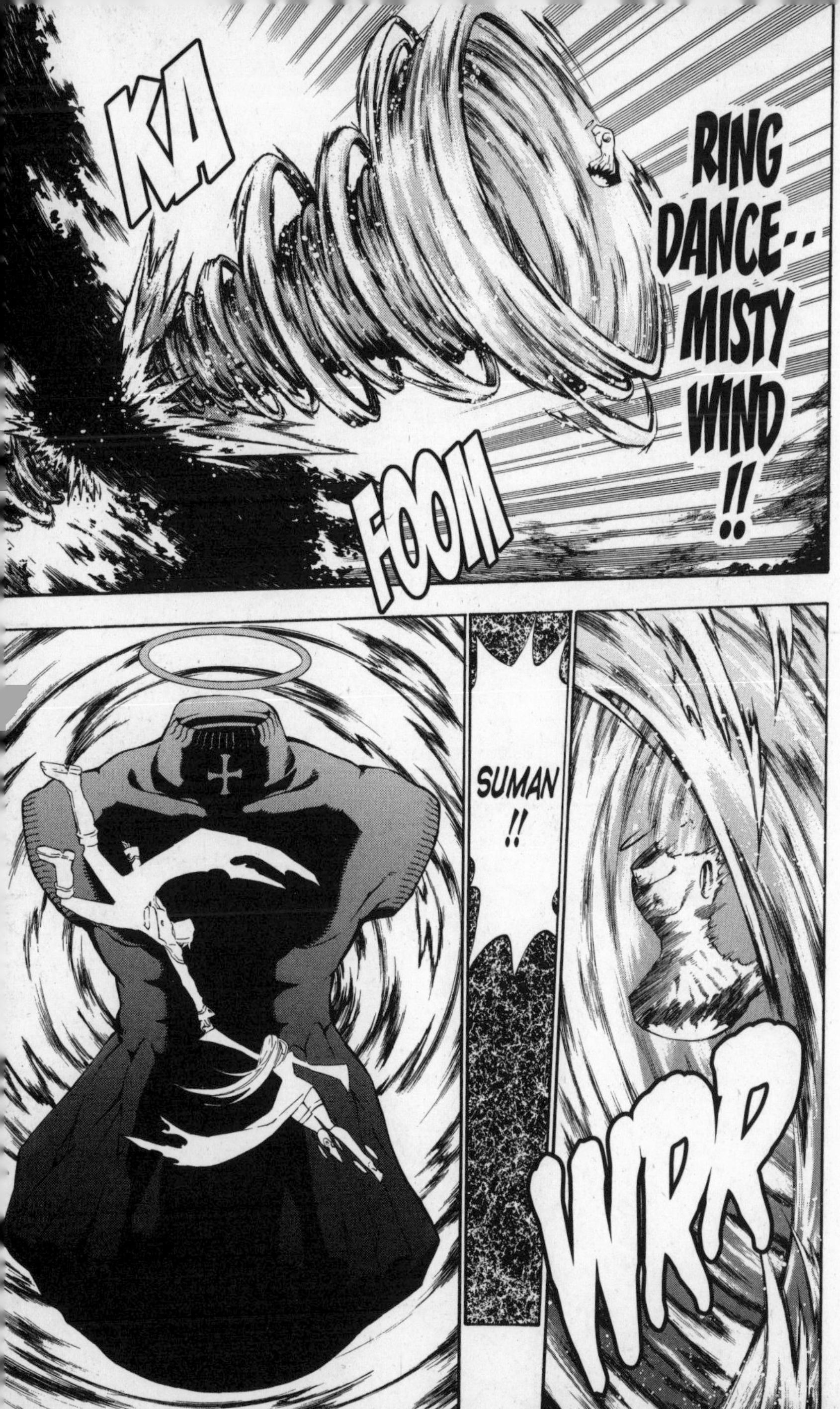
RING DANCE... MISTY WIND!!
KA
FOOM
SUMAN!!
WRR

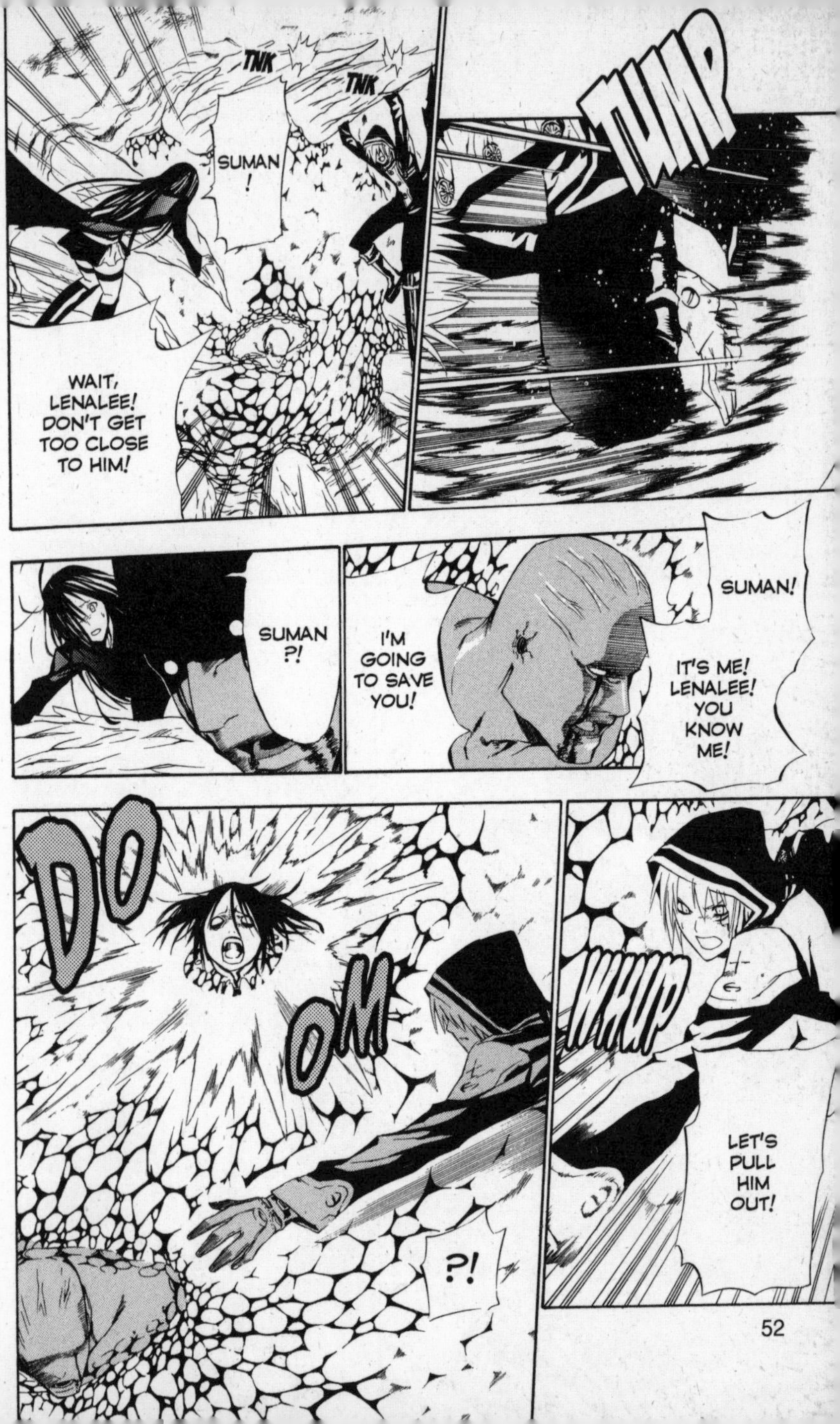
TUMP
TNK
TNK
SUMAN!
WAIT, LENALEE! DON'T GET TOO CLOSE TO HIM!
SUMAN!
IT'S ME! LENALEE! YOU KNOW ME!
I'M GOING TO SAVE YOU!
SUMAN ?!
WHUP
LET'S PULL HIM OUT!
DO
OM
?!

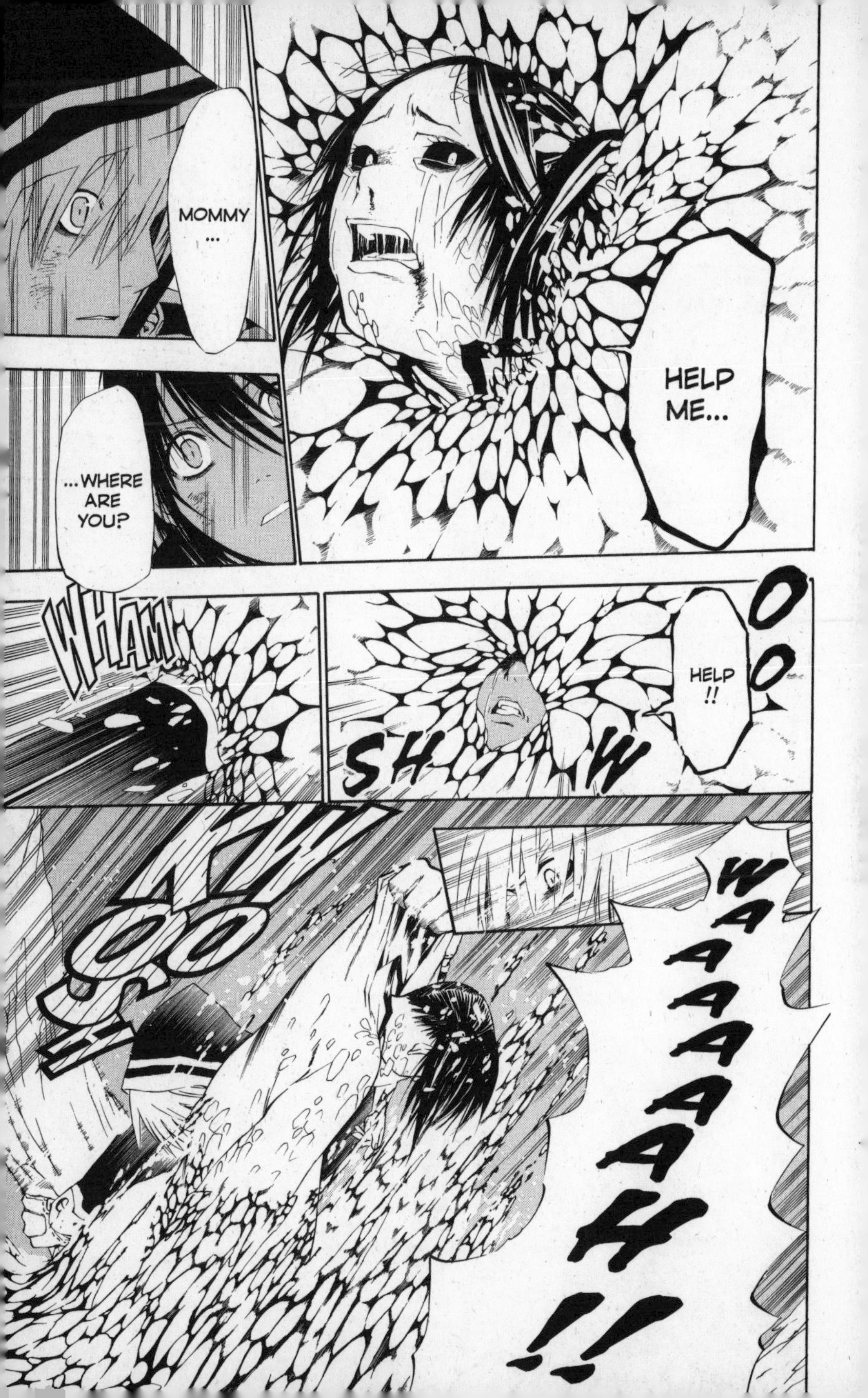

HELP ME...
MOMMY ...
...WHERE ARE YOU?
OOO
HELP!!
SHW
WHAM
WAAAAAAAH!!

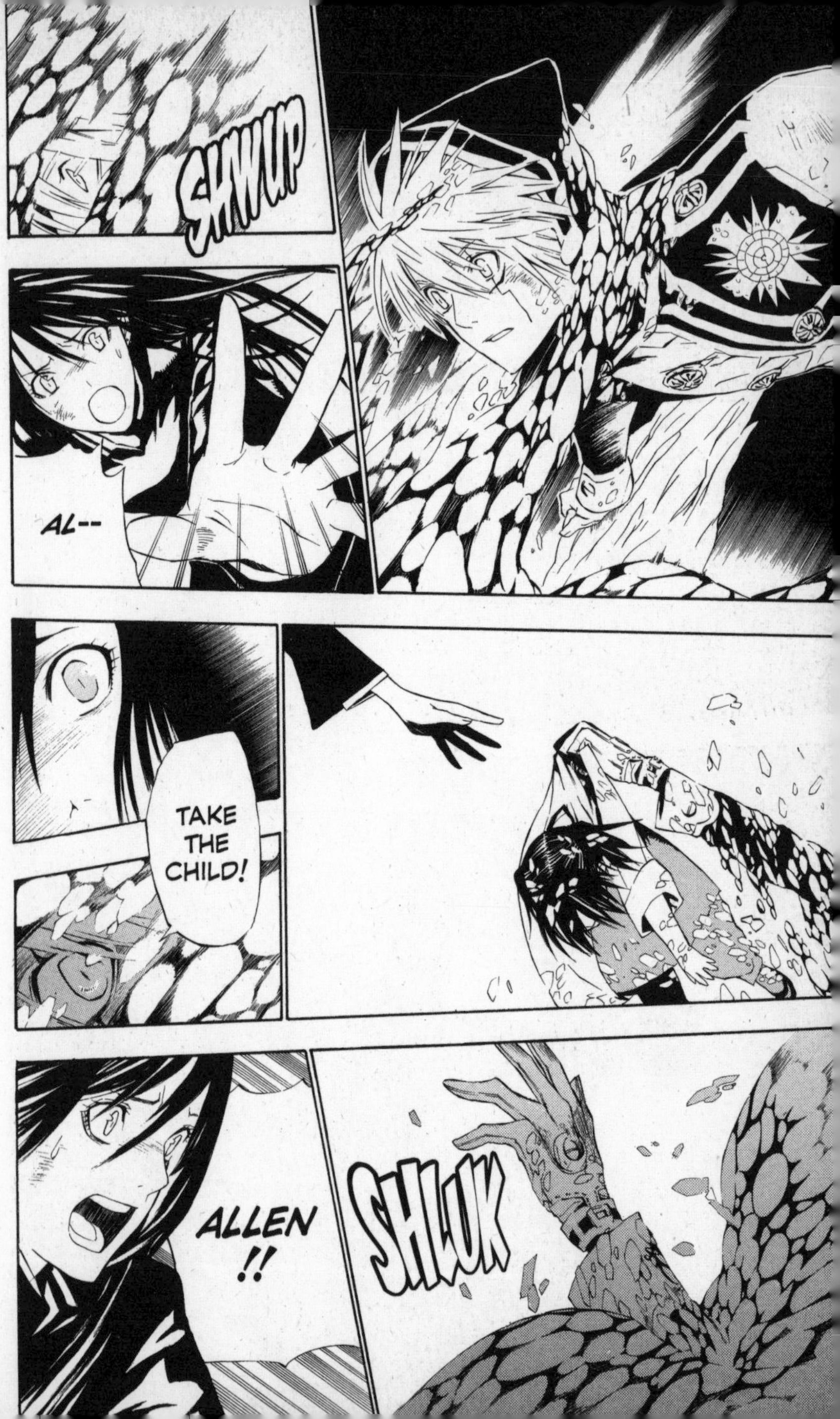
SHWUP
AL--
TAKE THE CHILD!
SHLUK
ALLEN !!

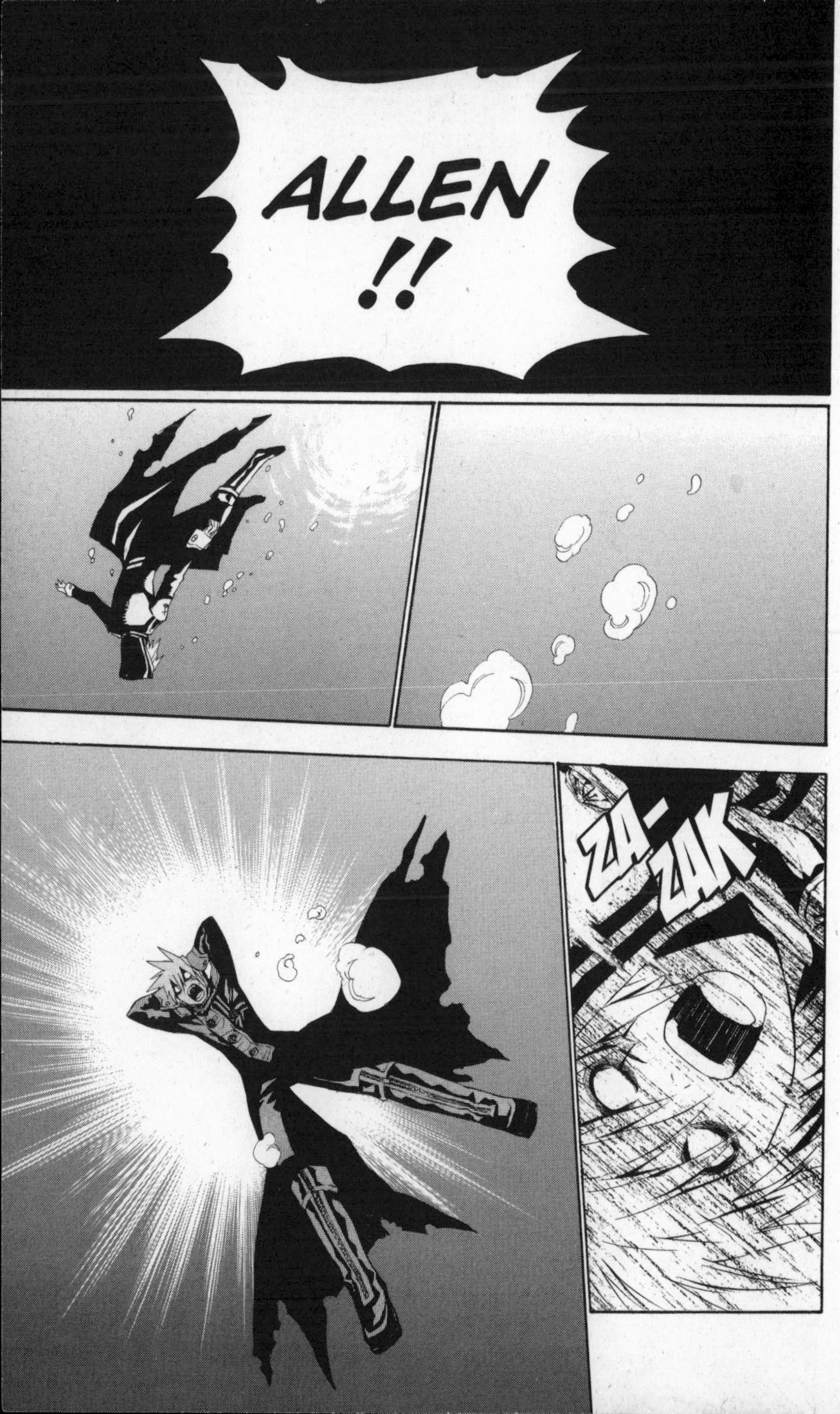
ALLEN!!
ZA-ZAK

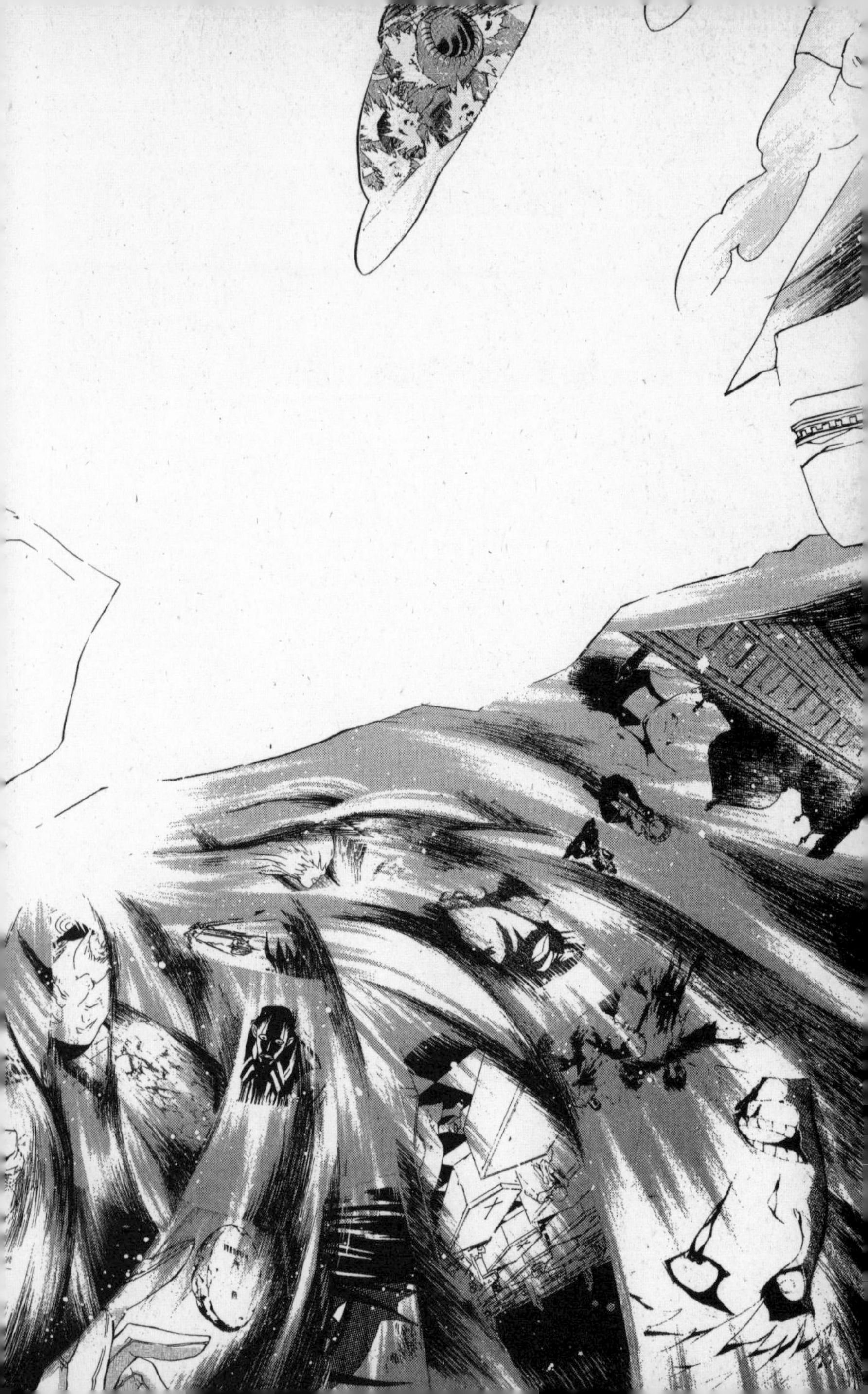

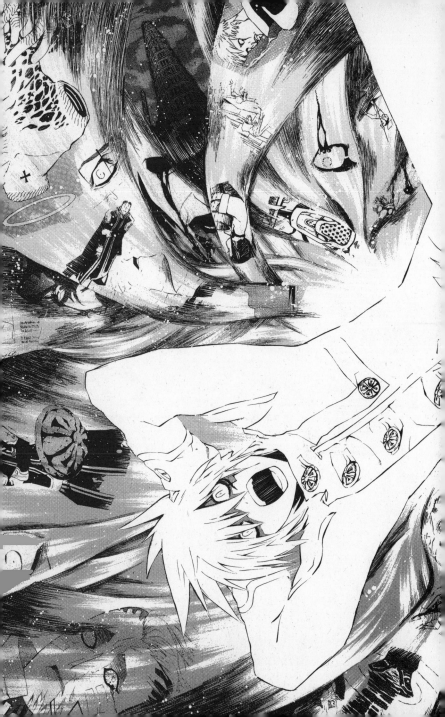

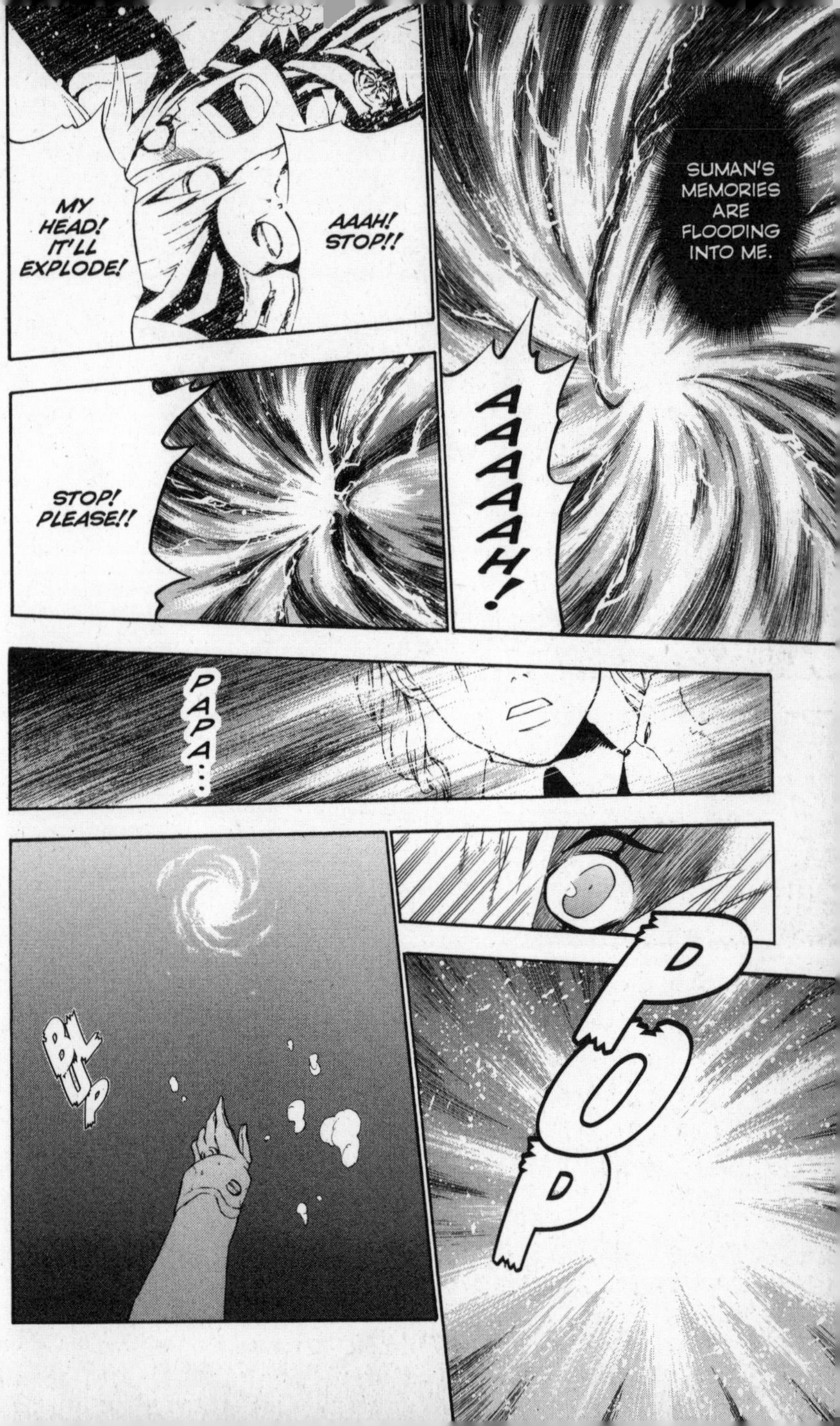
SUMAN'S MEMORIES ARE FLOODING INTO ME.
AAAAAAH!
AAAH! STOP!!
MY HEAD! IT'LL EXPLODE!
STOP! PLEASE!!
PAPA...
POP
BLUP

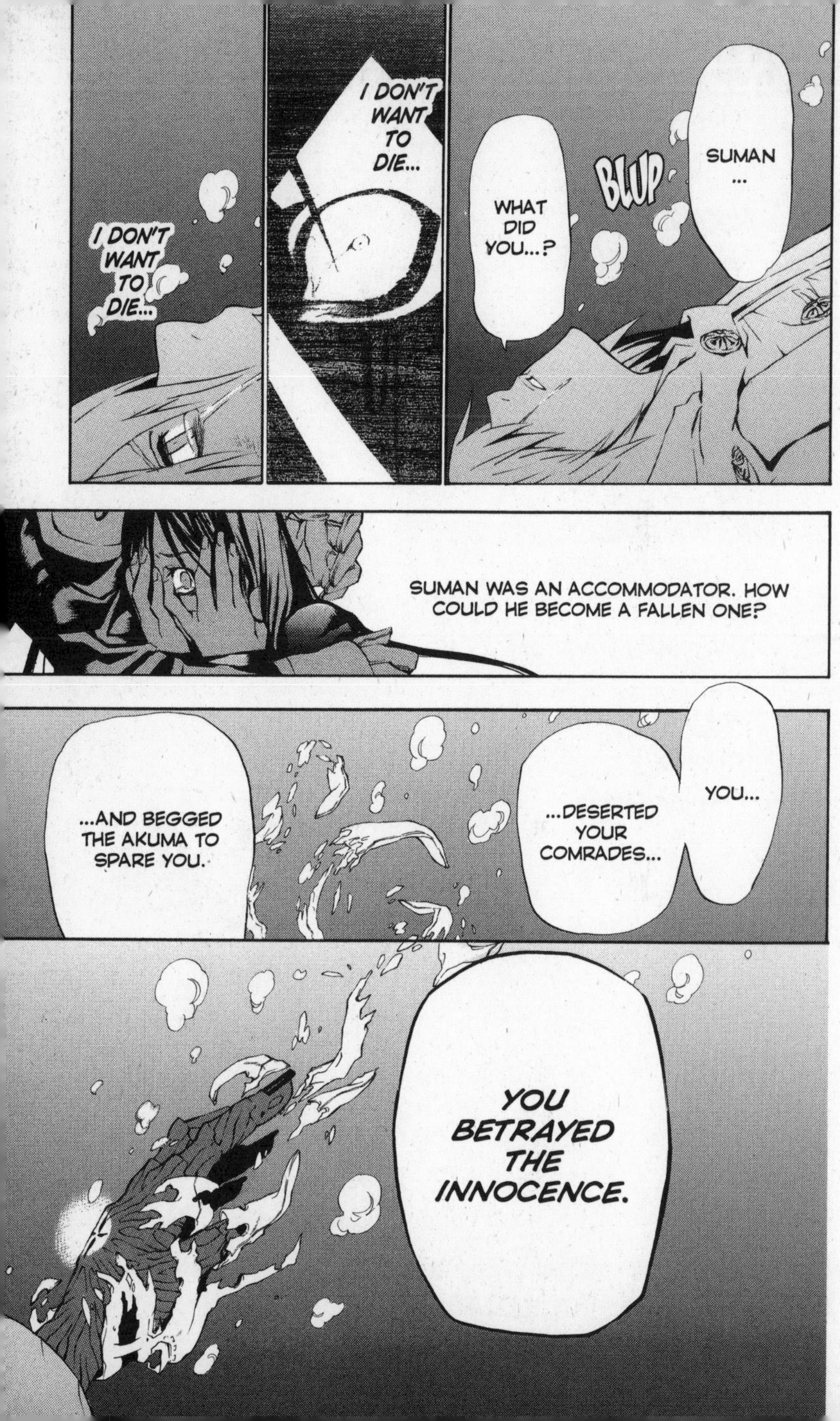
SUMAN ...
BLUP
WHAT DID YOU...?
I DON'T WANT TO DIE...
I DON'T WANT TO DIE...
SUMAN WAS AN ACCOMMODATOR. HOW COULD HE BECOME A FALLEN ONE?
YOU...
...DESERTED YOUR COMRADES...
...AND BEGGED THE AKUMA TO SPARE YOU.
YOU BETRAYED THE INNOCENCE.

KOMUI'S DISCUSSION ROOM VOL. 2

MIRANDA LOTTO
ARYSTAR KRORY
NOISE MARIE
CROSS MARIAN
FROI TIEDOLL
HEVLASKA
SUMAN DARK
DAISYA BARRY
KEVIN BARRY
KEVIN YEEGAR
JERRY
THE MILLENNIUM EARL
LERO
ROAD KAMELOT
TYKI MIKK
TIMCANPY

THAT'S IT! (PHEW)

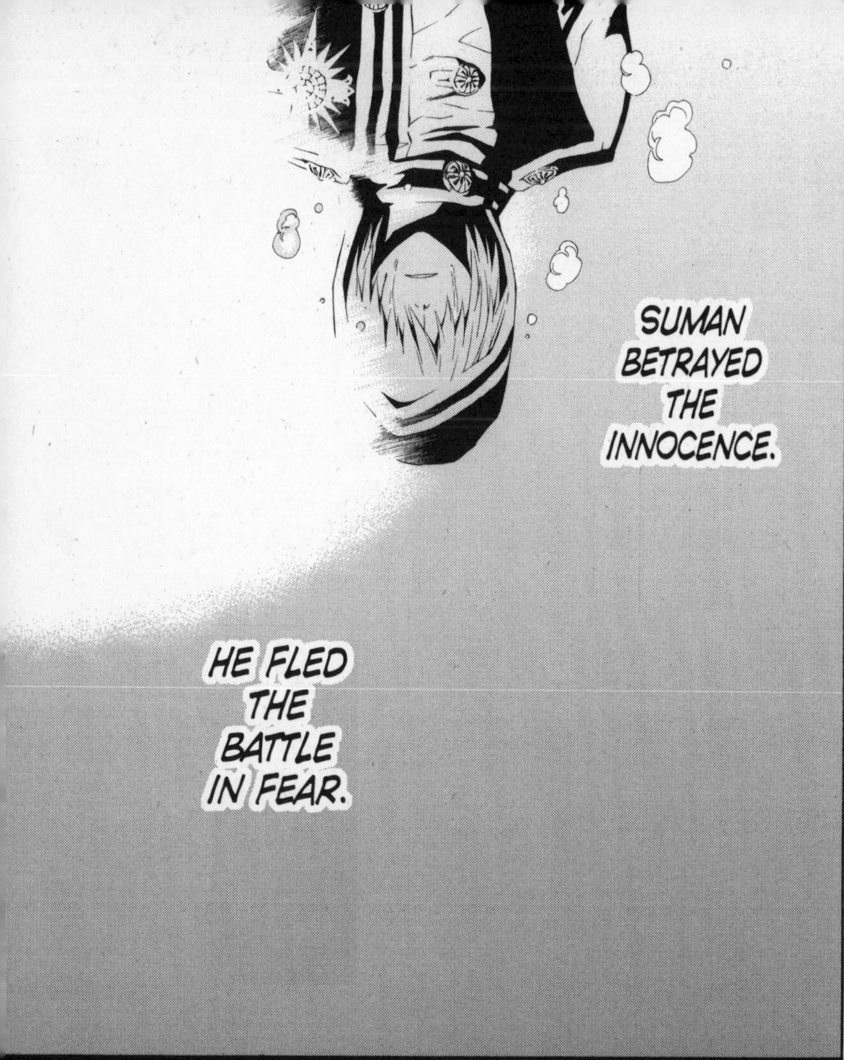
SUMAN BETRAYED THE INNOCENCE.
HE FLED THE BATTLE IN FEAR.

THE 50TH NIGHT: VOICES OF COMRADES

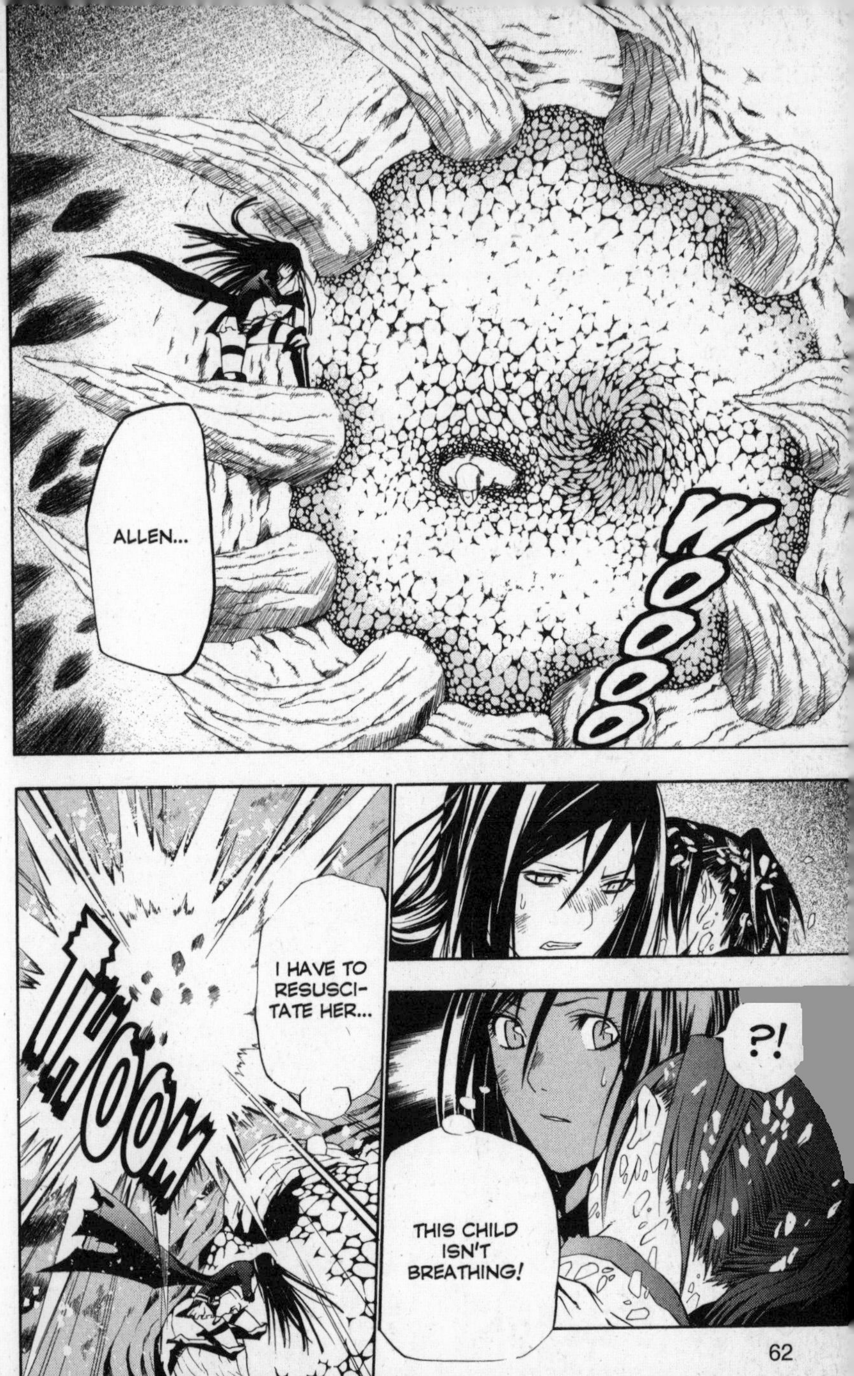
ALLEN...
WOOOOO
?!
THIS CHILD ISN'T BREATHING!
I HAVE TO RESUSCI-TATE HER...
FOOM

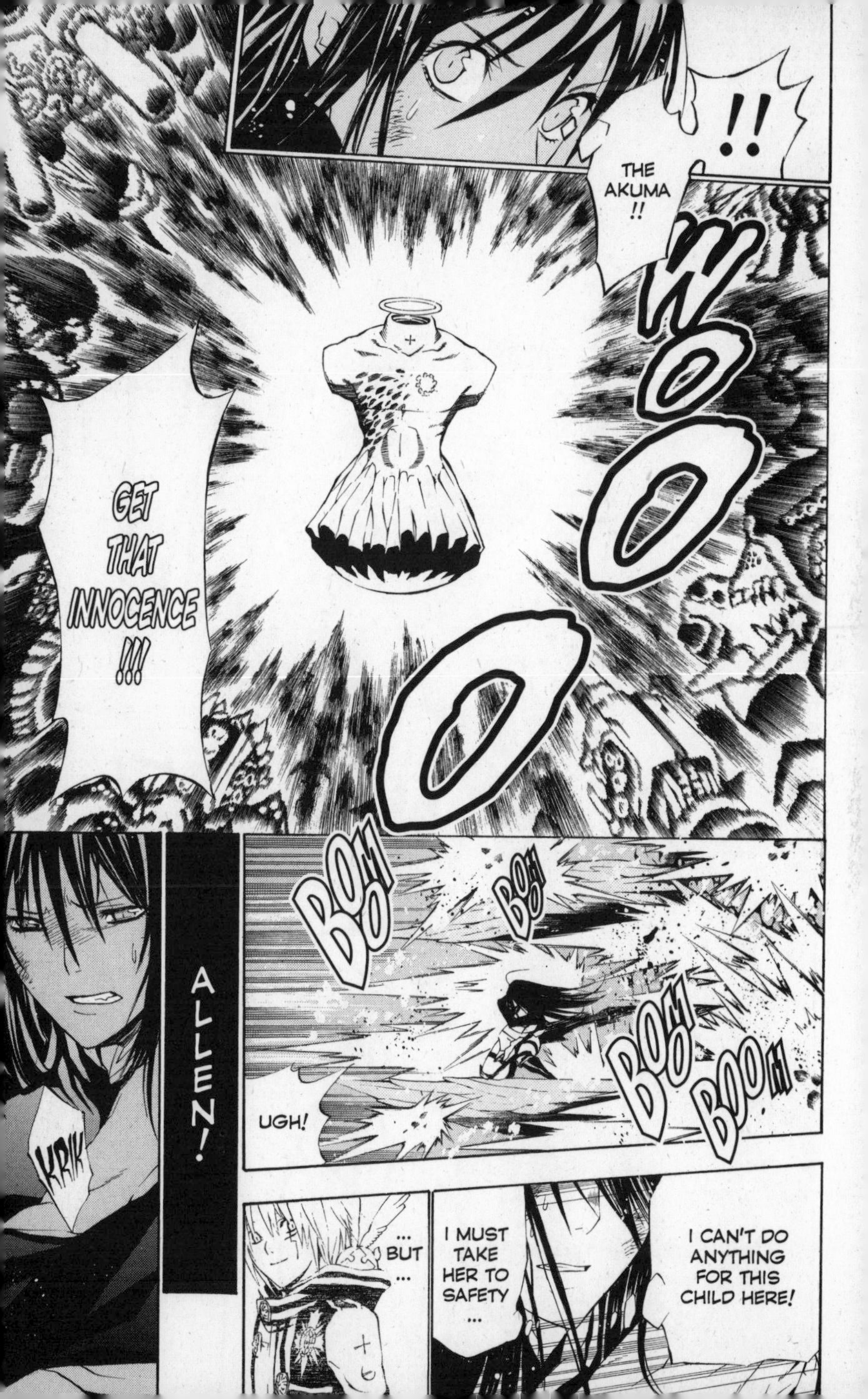
!!
THE AKUMA !!
WOOOO
GET THAT INNOCENCE !!!
BOOM
BOOM
BOOM
BOOM
UGH!
I CAN'T DO ANYTHING FOR THIS CHILD HERE!
I MUST TAKE HER TO SAFETY ...
... BUT ...
ALLEN!
KRIK

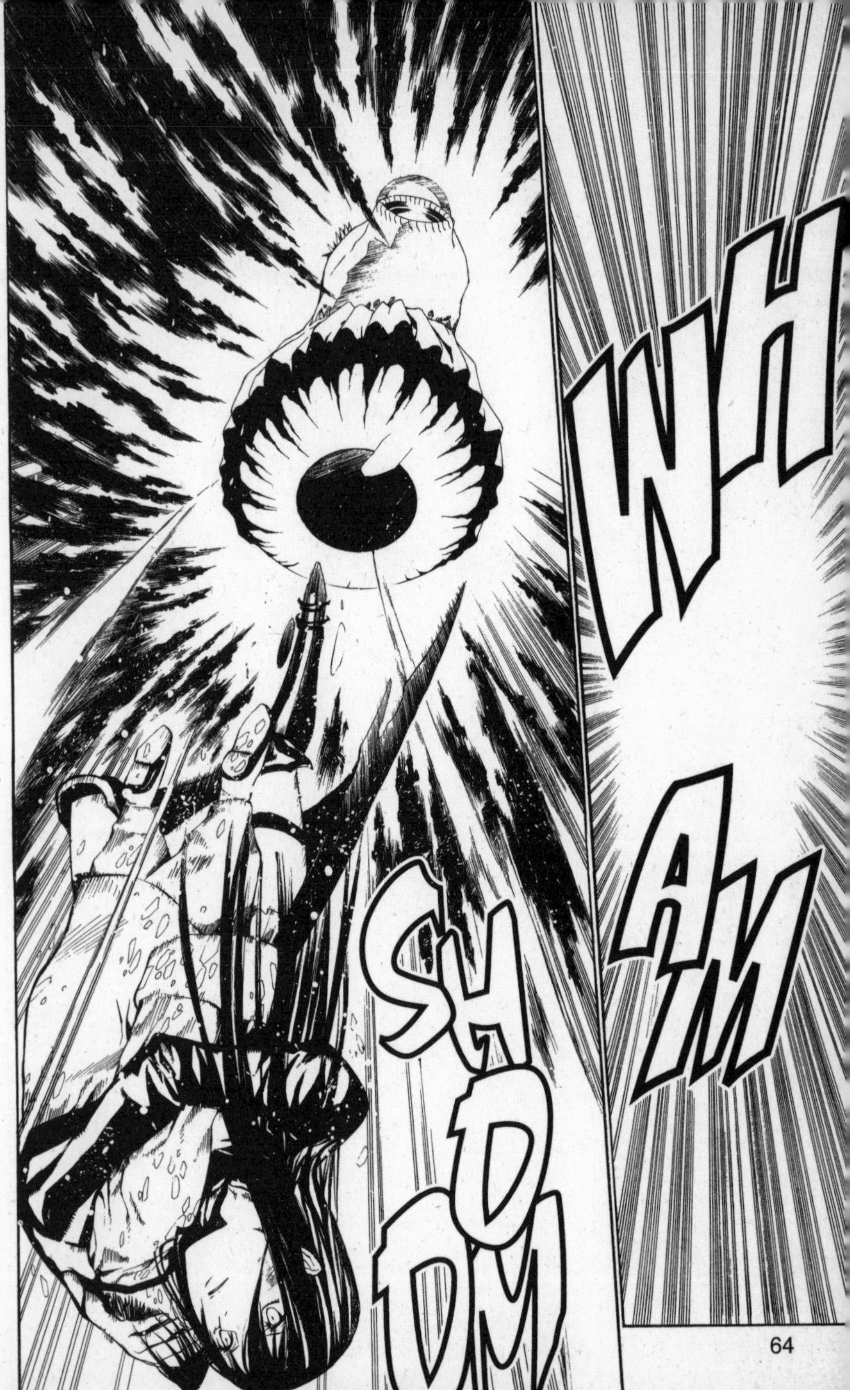
WHAM
SHOOM

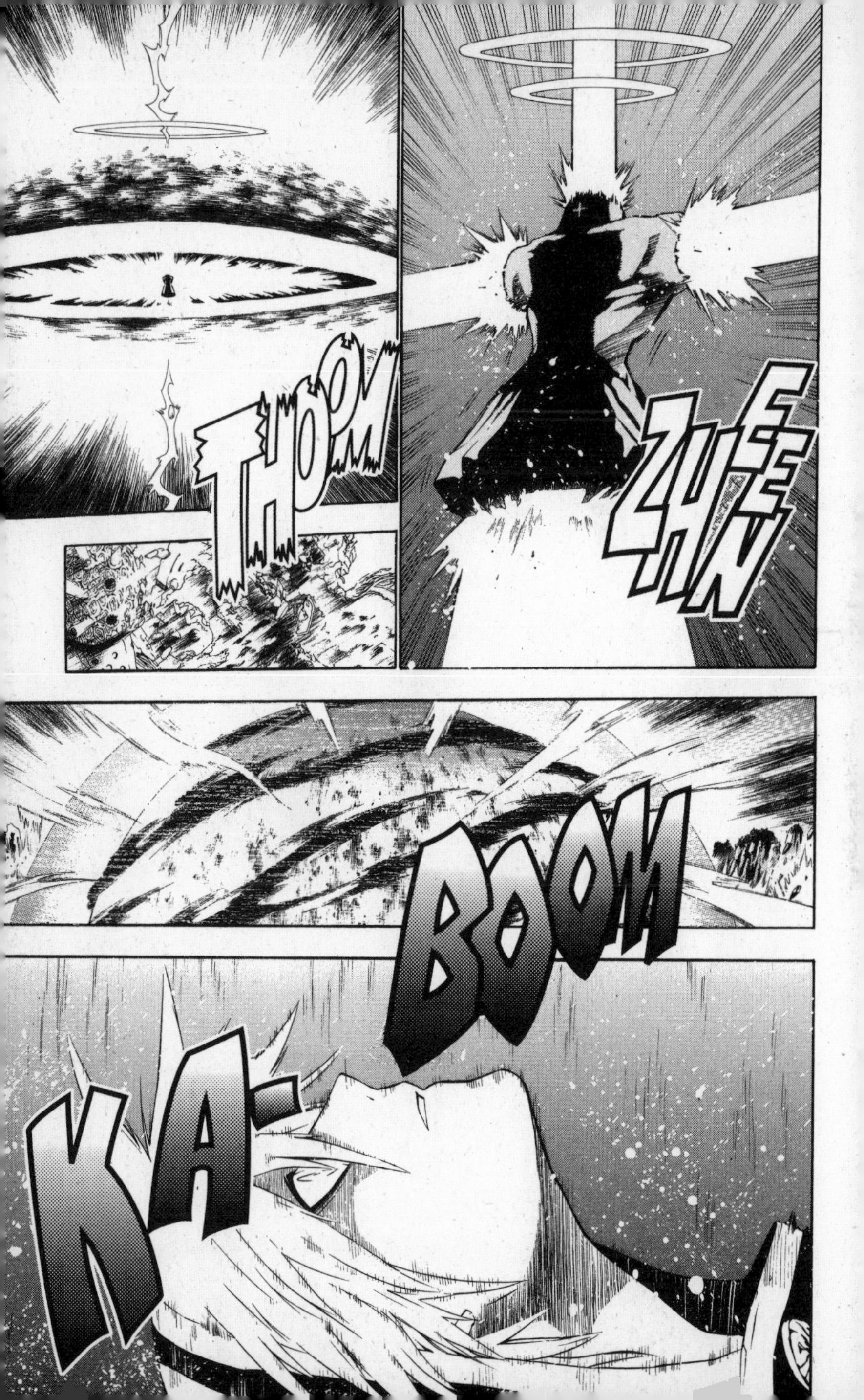
ZUEEEN
THOOM
BOOM
KA-

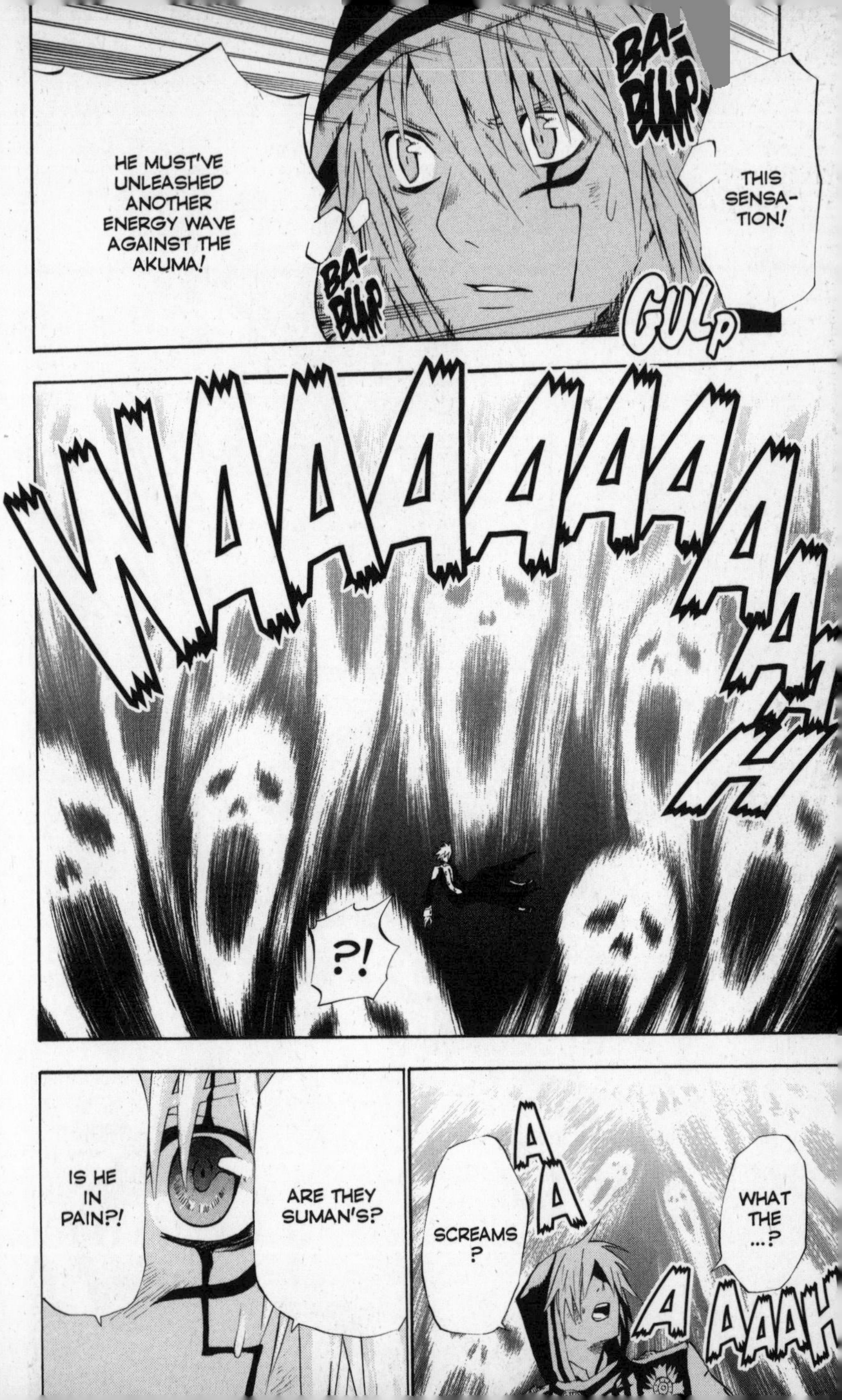

BA-BUMP
THIS SENSATION!
GULP
BA-BUMP
HE MUST'VE UNLEASHED ANOTHER ENERGY WAVE AGAINST THE AKUMA!
WAAAAAAAAAH
?!
WHAT THE ...?
AAA
SCREAMS?
A AAAH
ARE THEY SUMAN'S?
IS HE IN PAIN?!

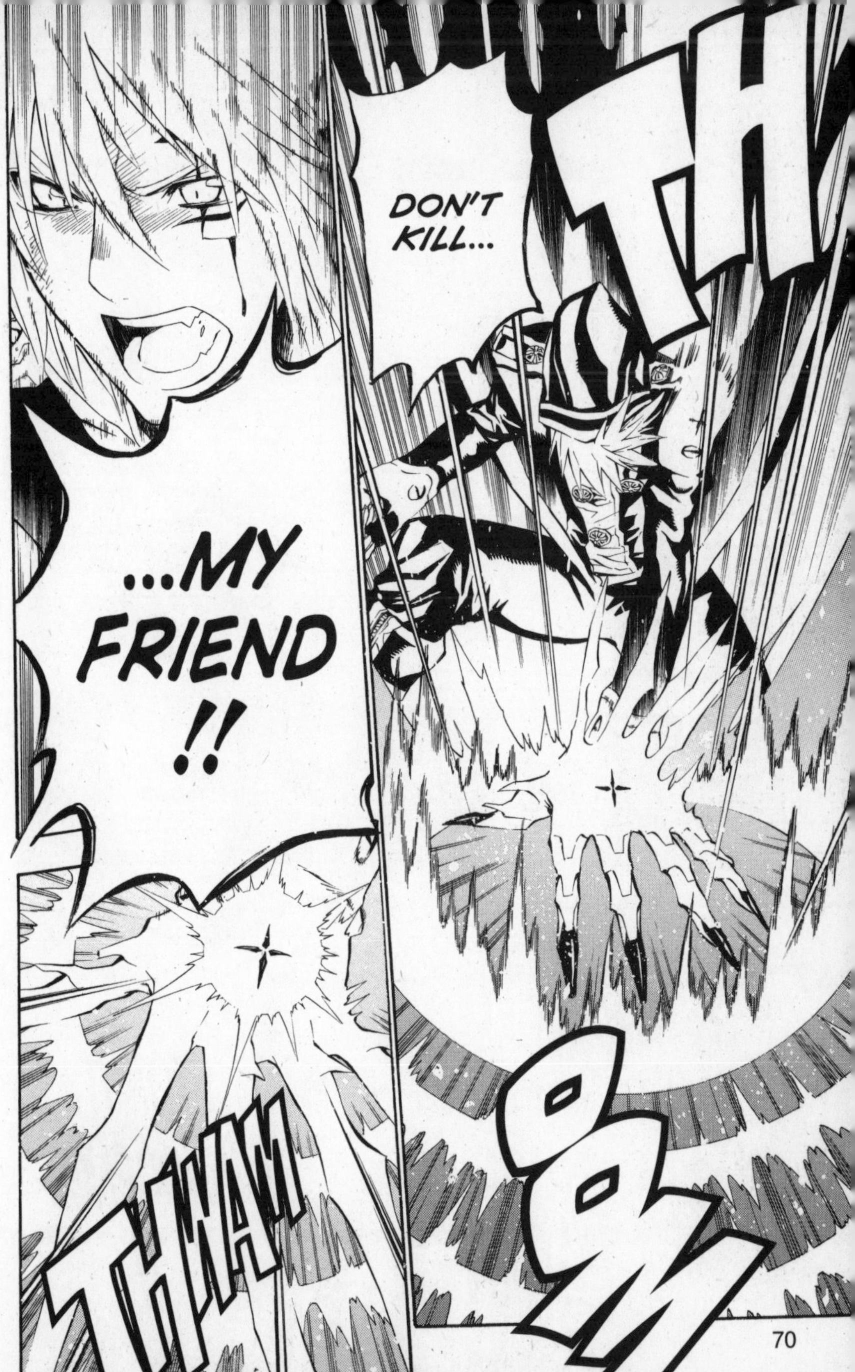
DON'T KILL...
...MY FRIEND !!
THWAM

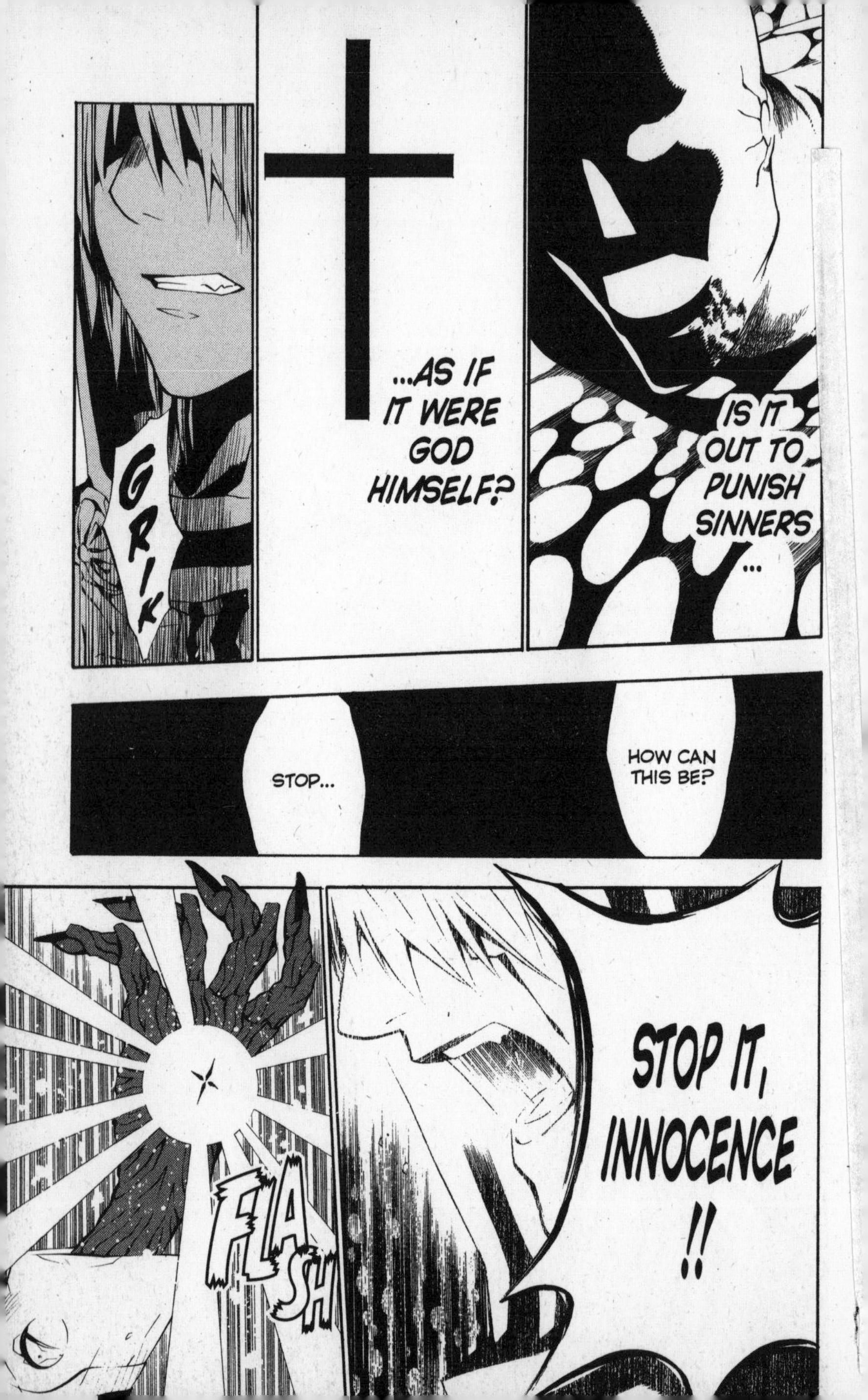
IS IT OUT TO PUNISH SINNERS ...
...AS IF IT WERE GOD HIMSELF?
GRIK
HOW CAN THIS BE?
STOP...
STOP IT, INNOCENCE !!
FLASH

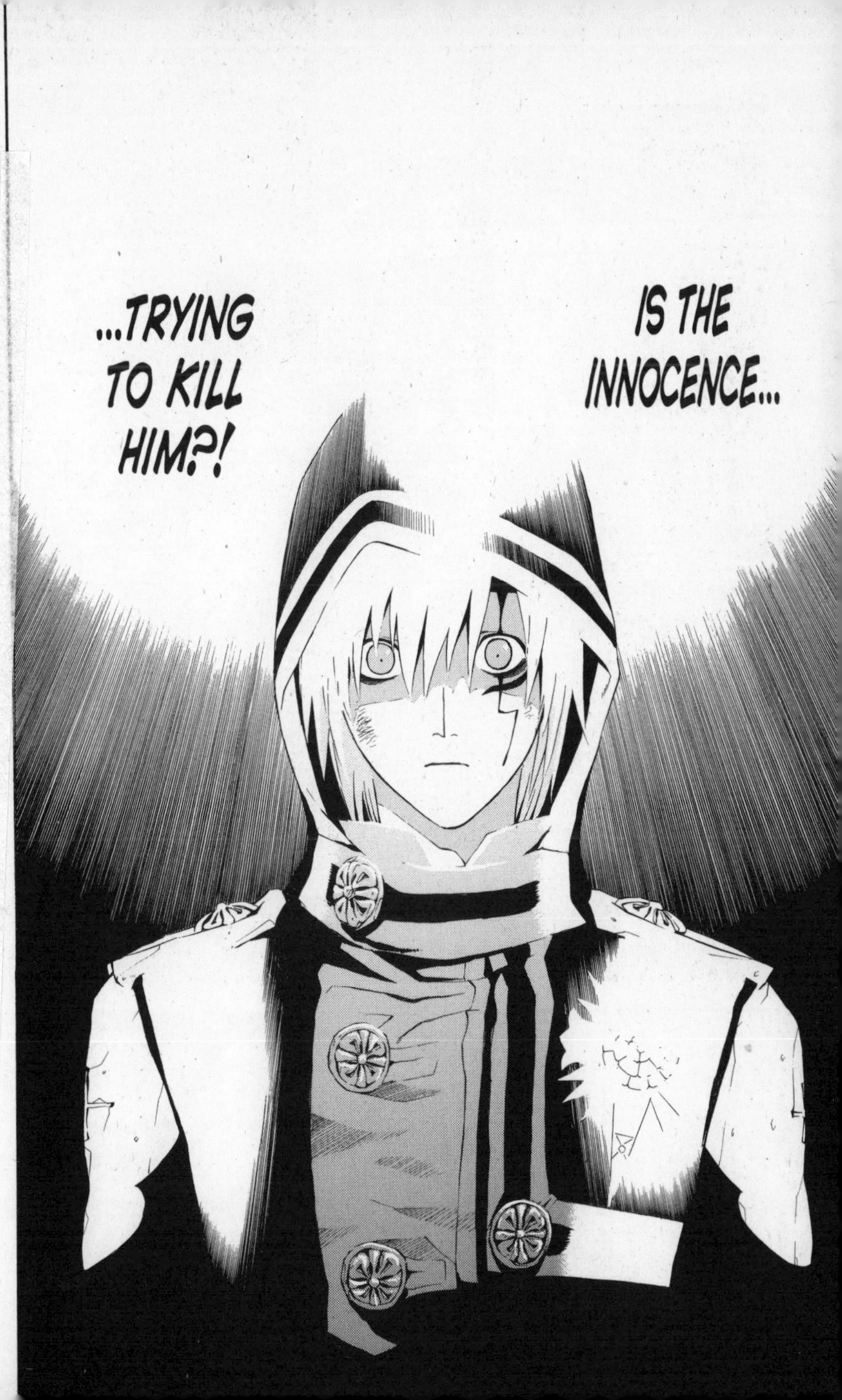
IS THE INNOCENCE...
...TRYING TO KILL HIM?!

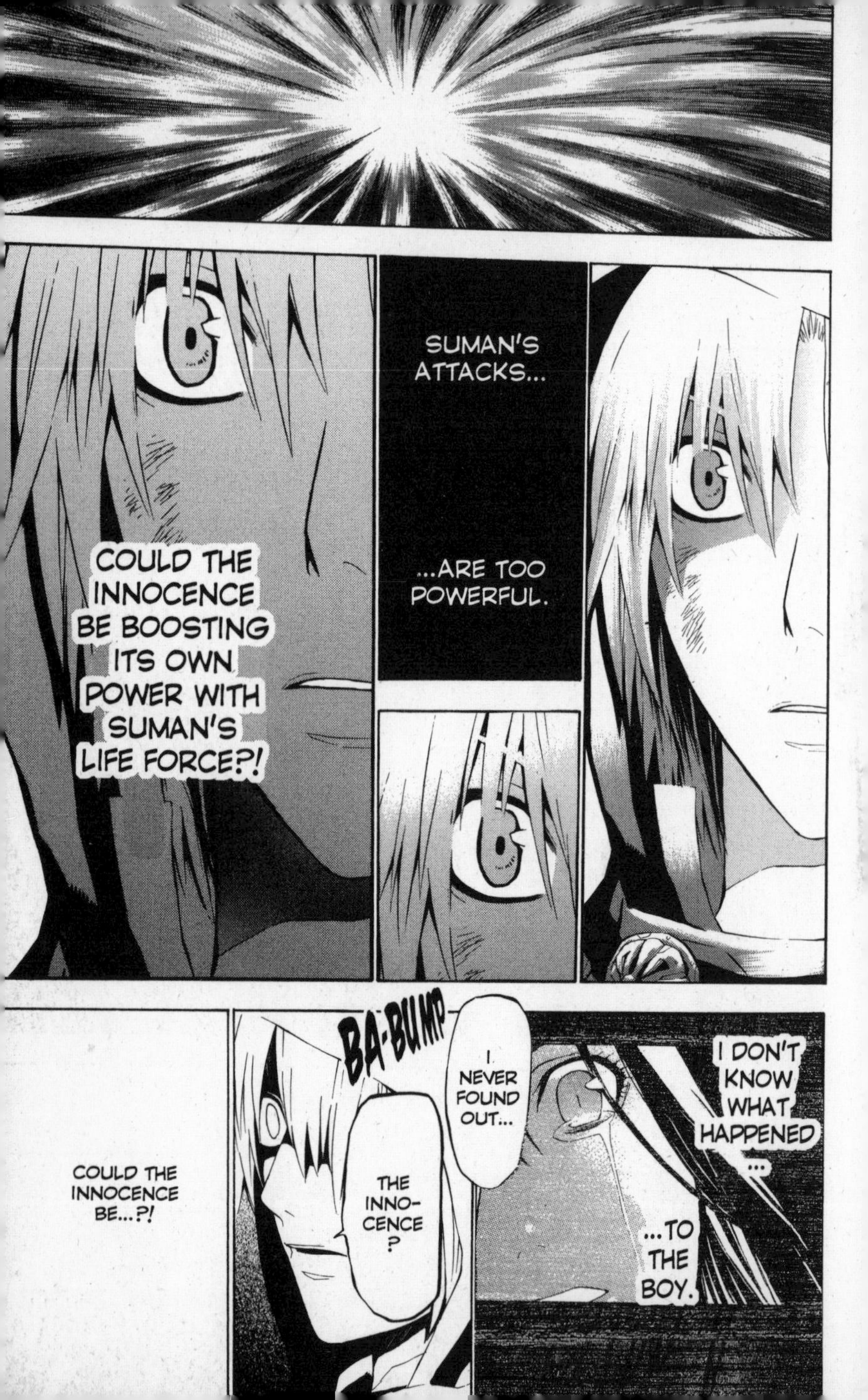
SUMAN'S ATTACKS...
...ARE TOO POWERFUL.
COULD THE INNOCENCE BE BOOSTING ITS OWN POWER WITH SUMAN'S LIFE FORCE?!
I DON'T KNOW WHAT HAPPENED ...
...TO THE BOY.
I NEVER FOUND OUT...
BA-BUMP
THE INNO-CENCE?
COULD THE INNOCENCE BE...?!

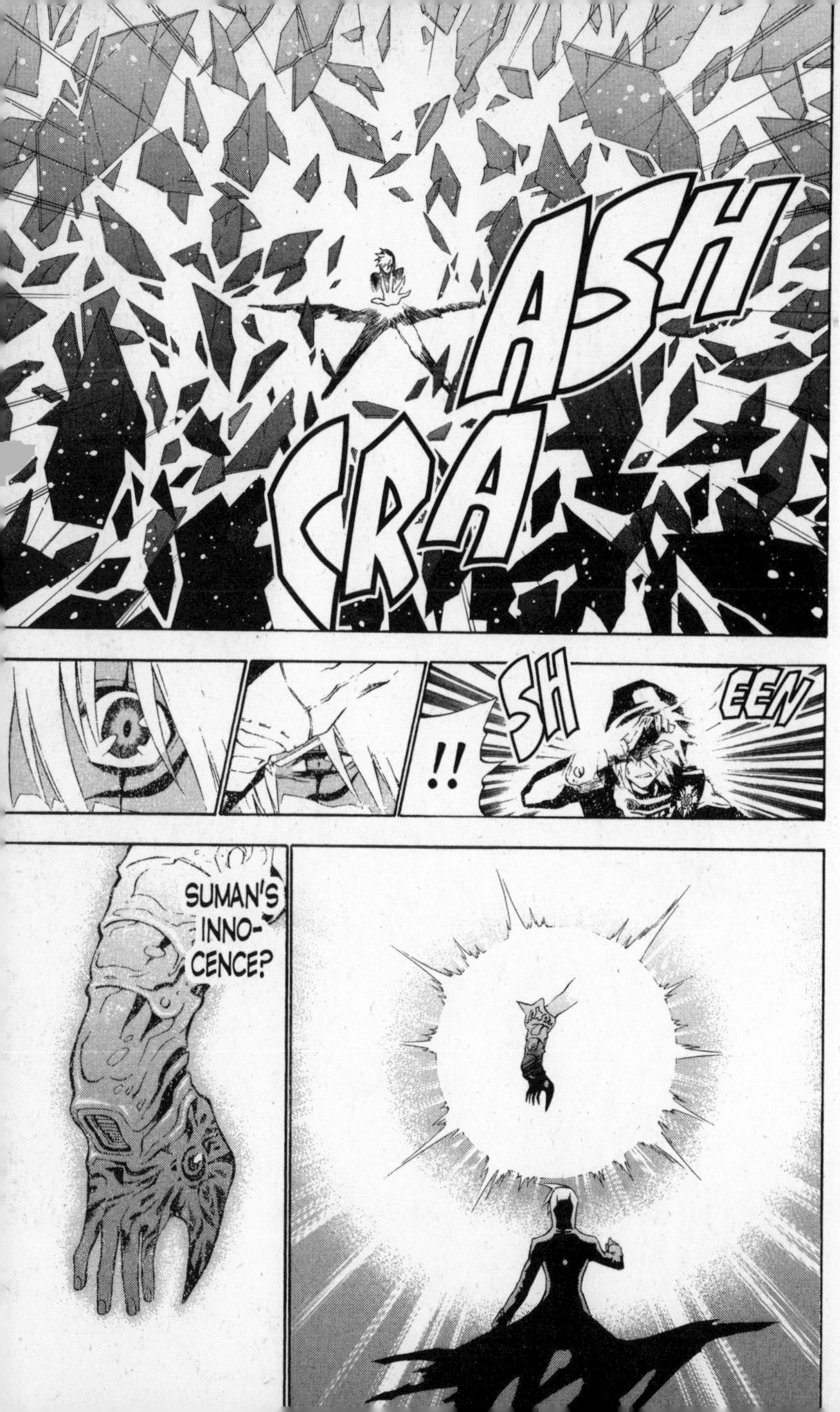
CRA
ASH
SH
EEN
!!
SUMAN'S INNO-CENCE?

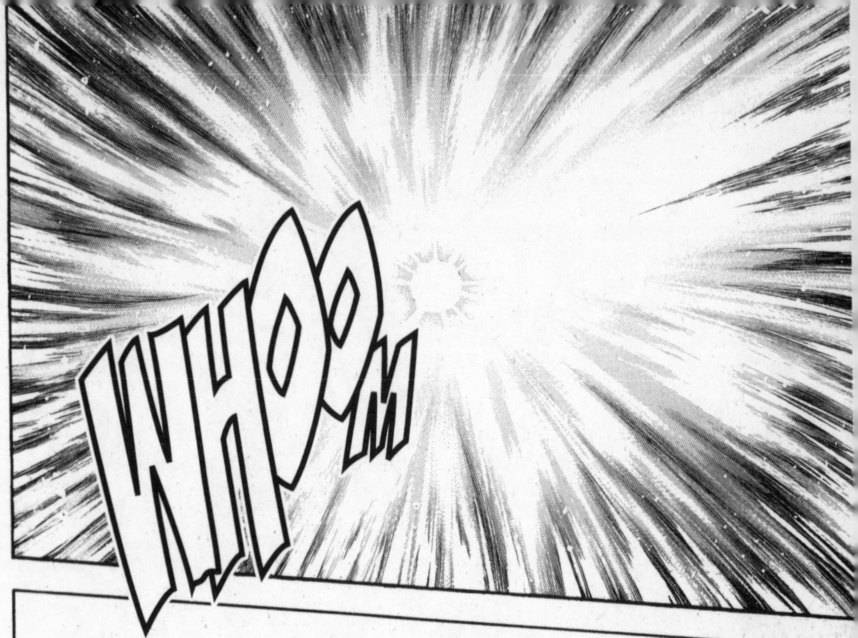
WHOOM
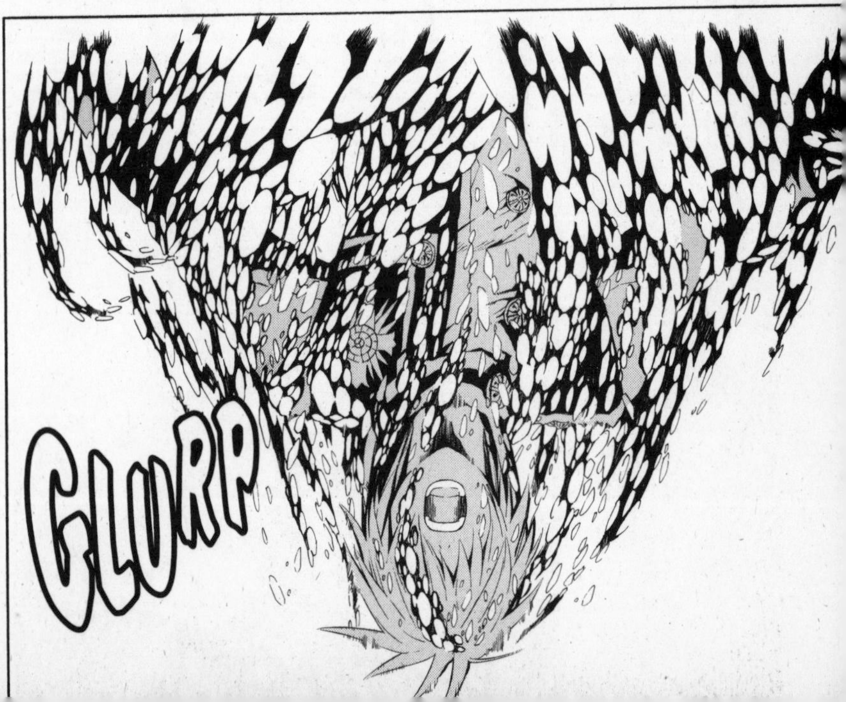
GLURP

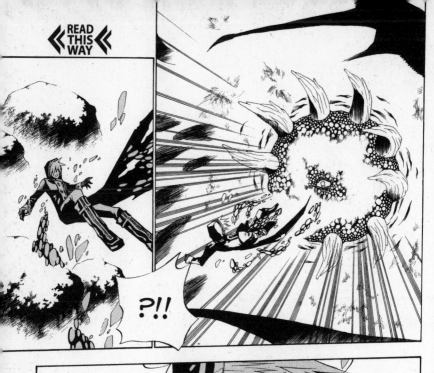

READ
THIS
WAY

?!!

IT SPAT
ME
OUT!!

I'M
OUT-
SIDE?!

UGH
...

SHWIP

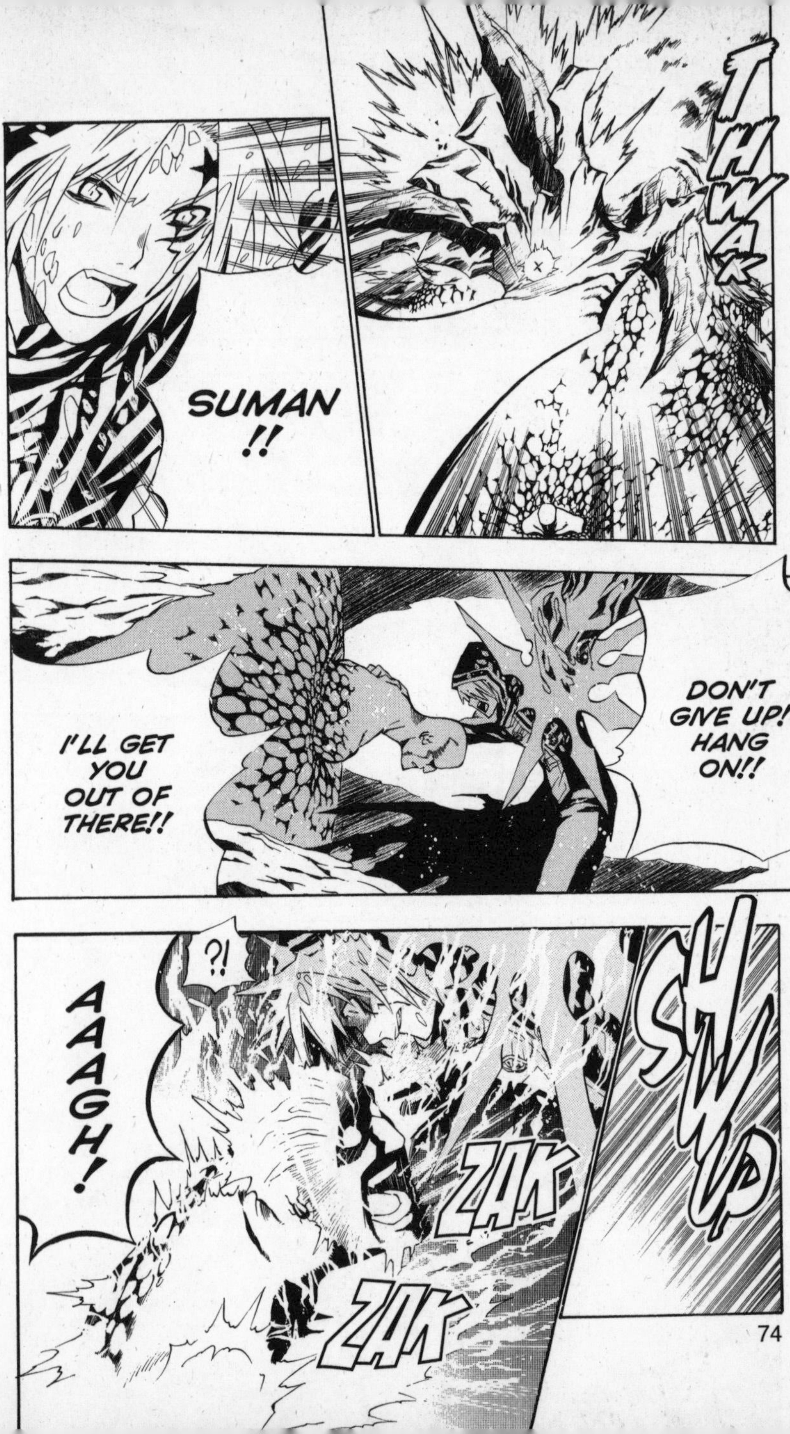
THWAK
SUMAN !!
DON'T GIVE UP! HANG ON!!
I'LL GET YOU OUT OF THERE!!
SHWP
?!
AAAGH!
ZAK
ZAK

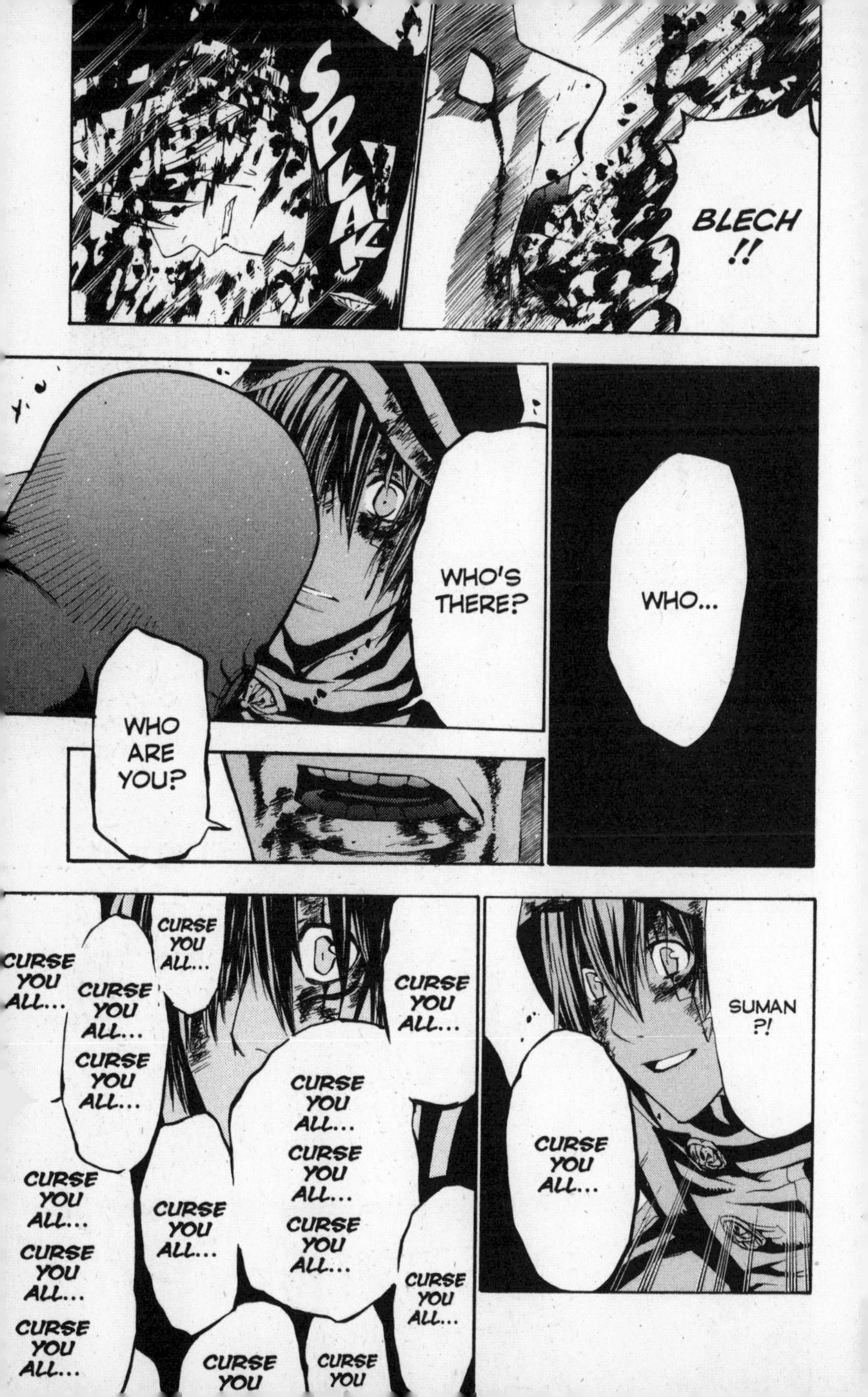

BLECH !!
SPLAK
WHO...
WHO'S THERE?
WHO ARE YOU?
SUMAN ?!
CURSE YOU ALL...
CURSE YOU ALL...
CURSE YOU ALL...
CURSE YOU ALL...
CURSE YOU ALL...
CURSE YOU ALL...
CURSE YOU ALL...
CURSE YOU ALL...
CURSE YOU ALL...
CURSE YOU ALL...
CURSE YOU ALL...
CURSE YOU ALL...
CURSE YOU ALL...
CURSE YOU ALL...
CURSE YOU
CURSE YOU

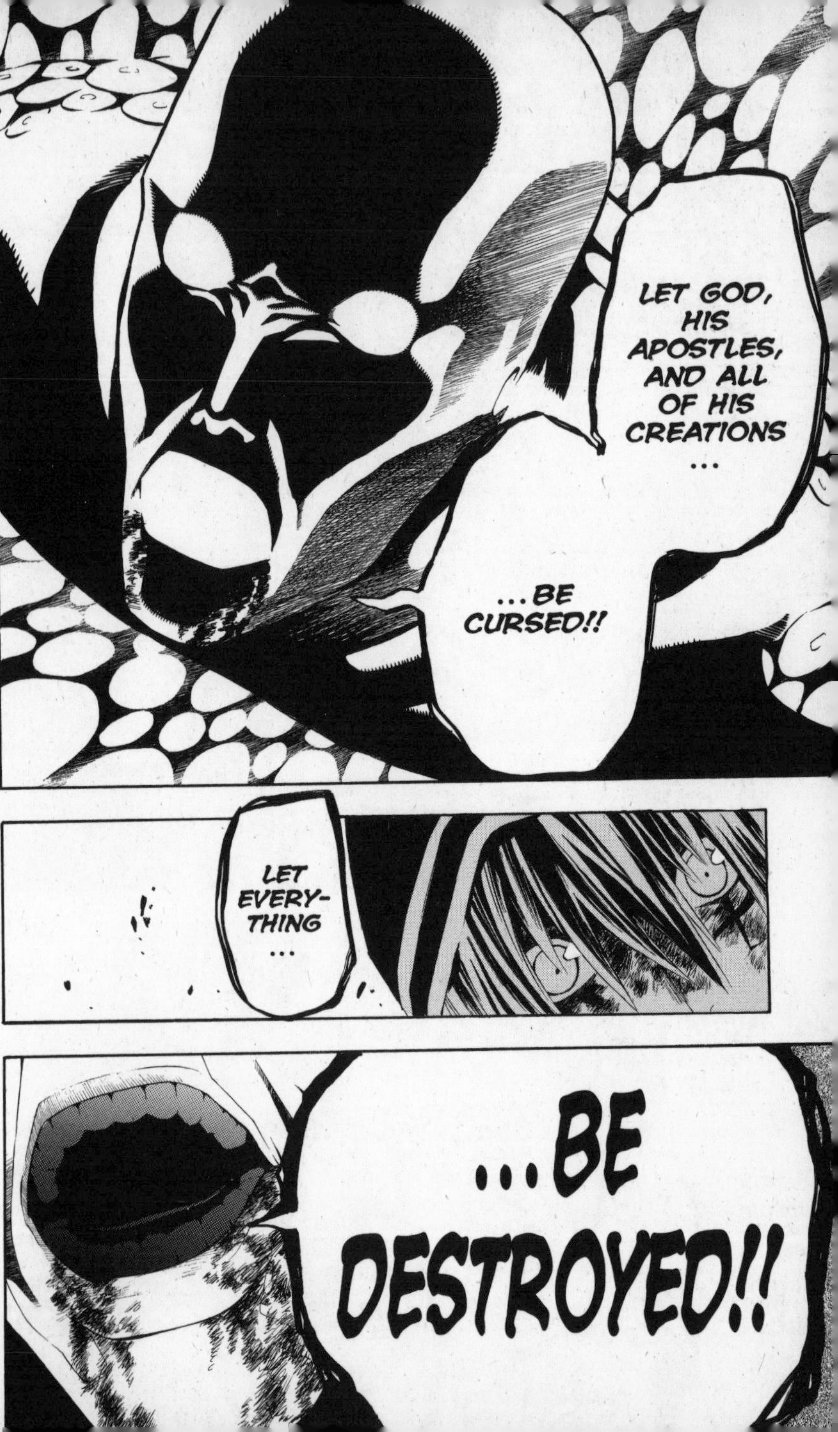
LET GOD, HIS APOSTLES, AND ALL OF HIS CREATIONS ...
...BE CURSED!!
LET EVERY-THING ...
...BE DESTROYED!!

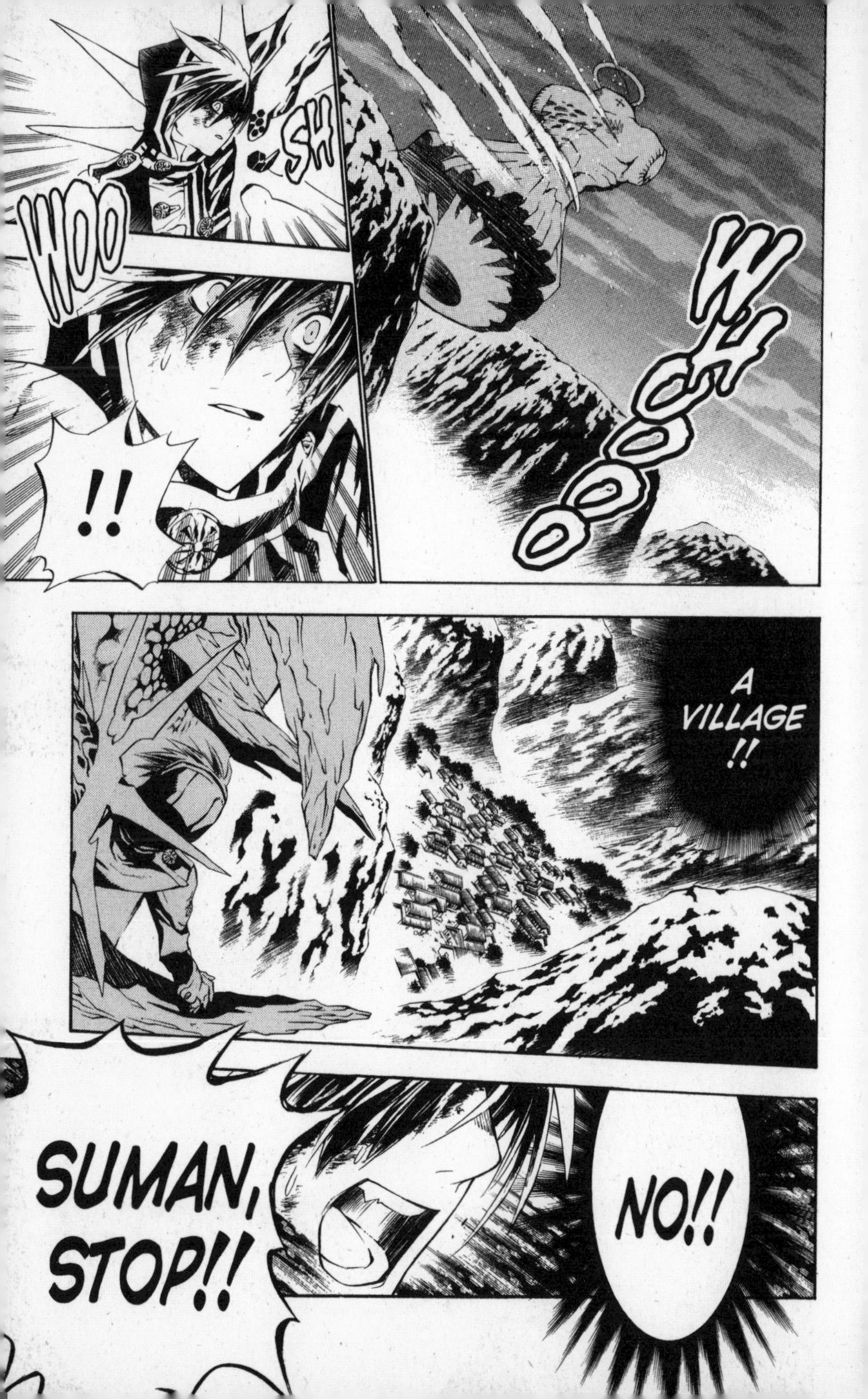
WHOOOOO
WOOSH
!!
A VILLAGE!!
NO!!
SUMAN, STOP!!

KOMUI'S DISCUSSION ROOM VOL. 3

Q. DOES KANDA LIKE ANY NOODLES OTHER THAN SOBA (LIKE UDON AND SUCH)? DOES HE CONSIDER NOODLES THAT AREN'T SOBA AN ABOMINATION?

A. WHAT KIND OF STUPID QUESTION IS THAT?

Q. HOW MUCH SLEEP DOES REEVER WENHAM GET IN A TYPICAL DAY?

A. HOW SHOULD I KNOW?

Q. WHO DOES ALLEN FEAR MORE, GENERAL CROSS OR CHIEF KOMUI?

A. DON'T ASK ME QUESTIONS ABOUT THAT GUY.

Q. IF ALLEN, LENALEE, KANDA, LAVI, KRORY, AND BOOKMAN WERE TO RUN THE 100-METER DASH, WHO WOULD WIN?

A. ...(AFTER A MOMENT OF THOUGHT) PROBABLY LENALEE.

Q. IF ALLEN AND KANDA WERE TO FIGHT EACH OTHER FOR REAL (USING THEIR INNOCENCES), WHO WOULD WIN?

A. I'D CUT HIM IN TWO.

Q. WHAT DOES KANDA'S ROOM LOOK LIKE?

A. NONE OF YOUR BUSINESS.

Q. ISN'T IT DIFFICULT TO DRAW THE ROSE CROSS ALL THE TIME?

A. HOW SHOULD I KNOW?

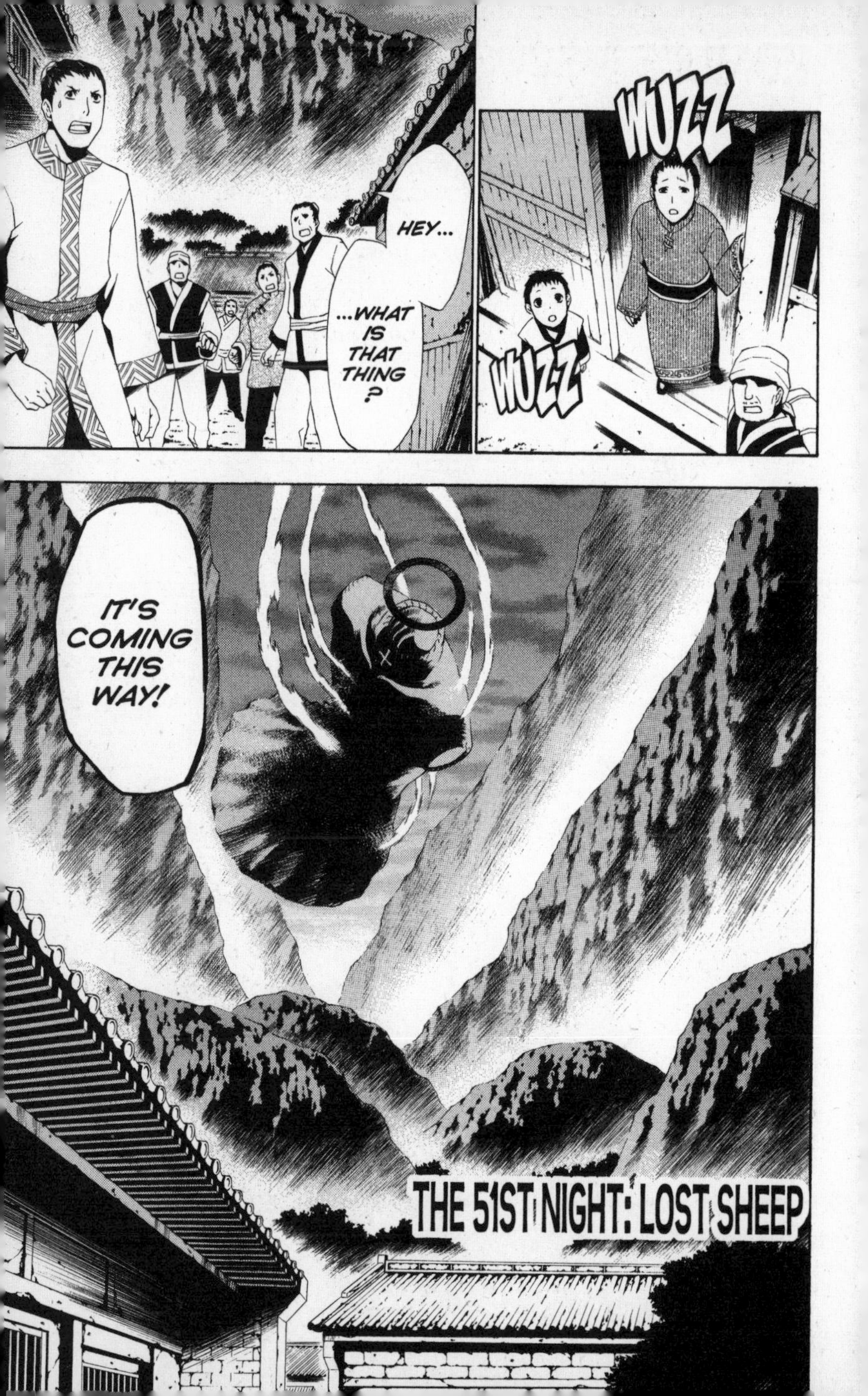
WUZZ
WUZZ
HEY...
...WHAT IS THAT THING?
IT'S COMING THIS WAY!
THE 51ST NIGHT: LOST SHEEP

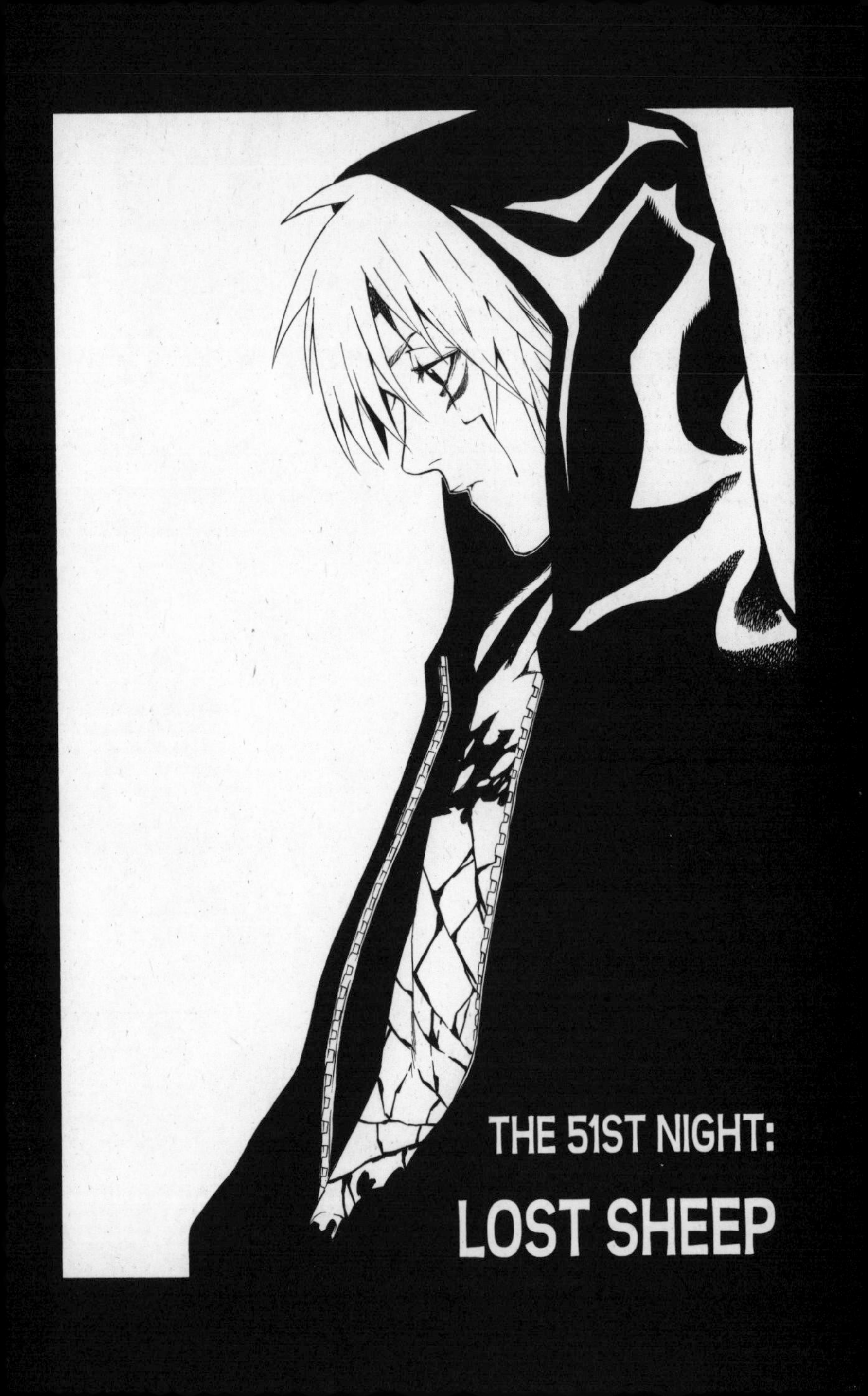
THE 51ST NIGHT:
LOST SHEEP

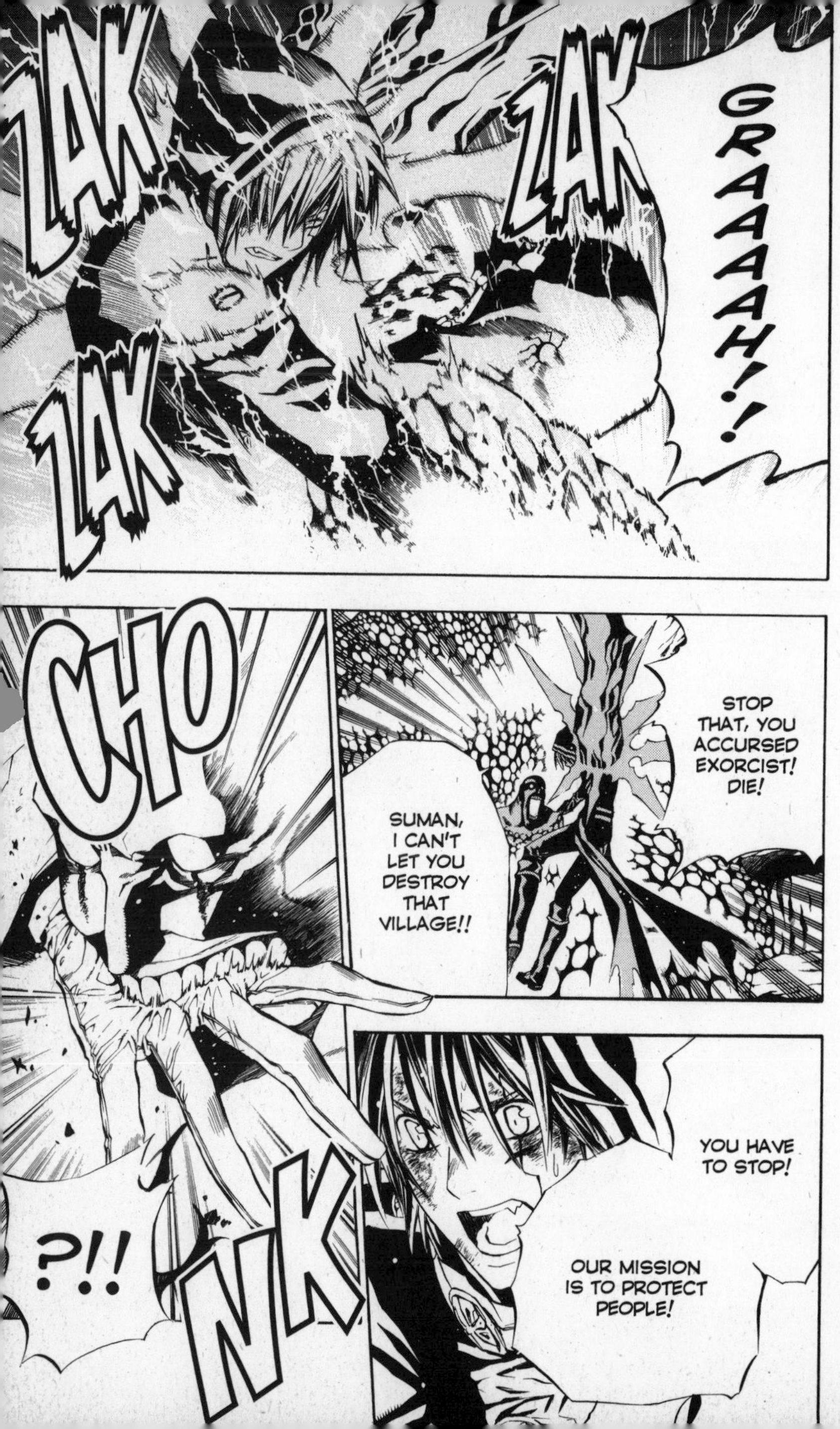
GRAAAAAH!!
ZAK
ZAK
ZAK
STOP THAT, YOU ACCURSED EXORCIST! DIE!
SUMAN, I CAN'T LET YOU DESTROY THAT VILLAGE!!
YOU HAVE TO STOP!
OUR MISSION IS TO PROTECT PEOPLE!
CHONK
?!!

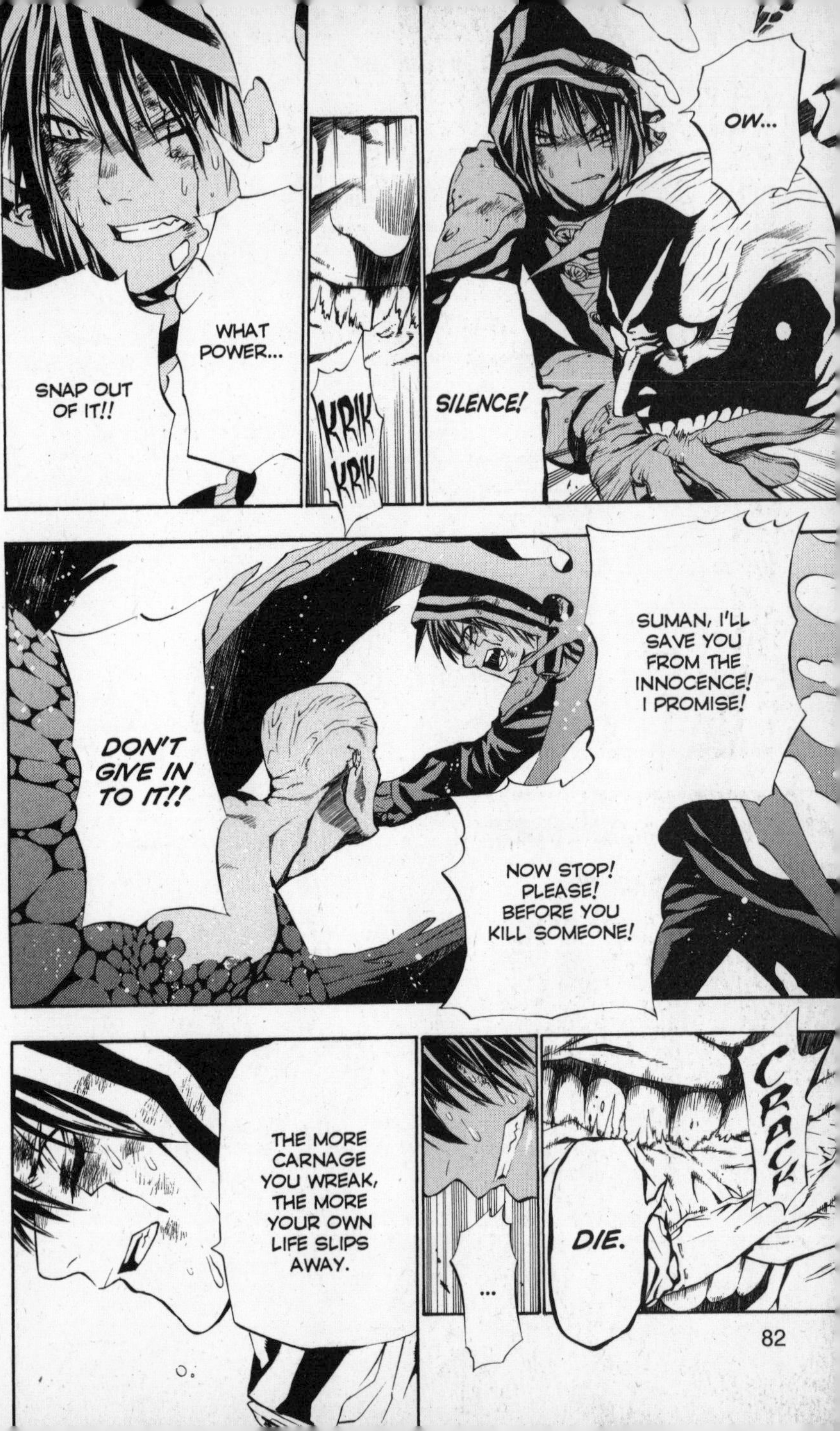
OW...
SILENCE!
KRIK KRIK
WHAT POWER...
SNAP OUT OF IT!!
SUMAN, I'LL SAVE YOU FROM THE INNOCENCE! I PROMISE!
NOW STOP! PLEASE! BEFORE YOU KILL SOMEONE!
DON'T GIVE IN TO IT!!
CRACK
DIE.
...
THE MORE CARNAGE YOU WREAK, THE MORE YOUR OWN LIFE SLIPS AWAY.

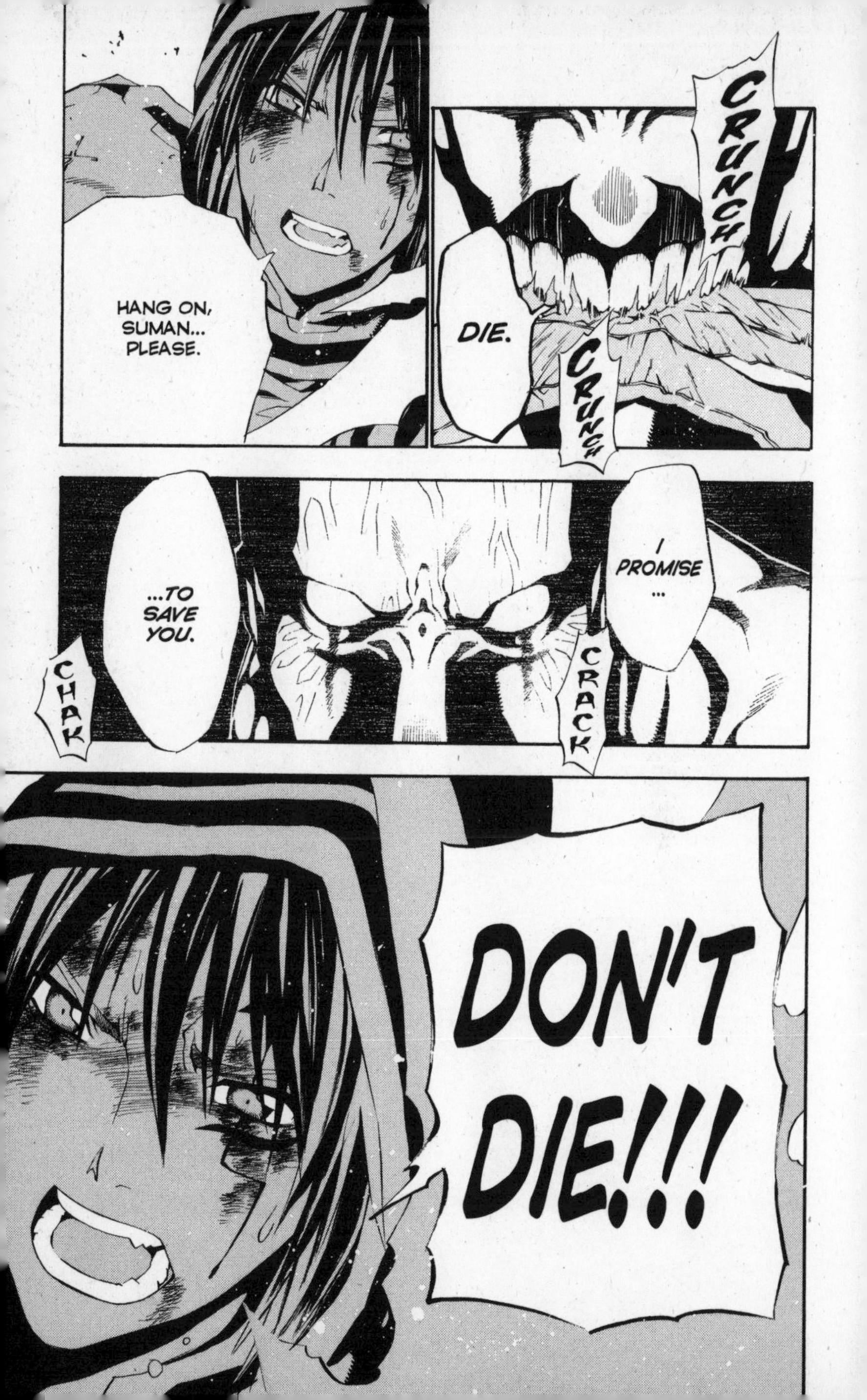
CRUNCH
DIE.
CRUNCH
HANG ON, SUMAN... PLEASE.
I PROMISE ...
CRACK
...TO SAVE YOU.
CHAK
DON'T DIE!!!

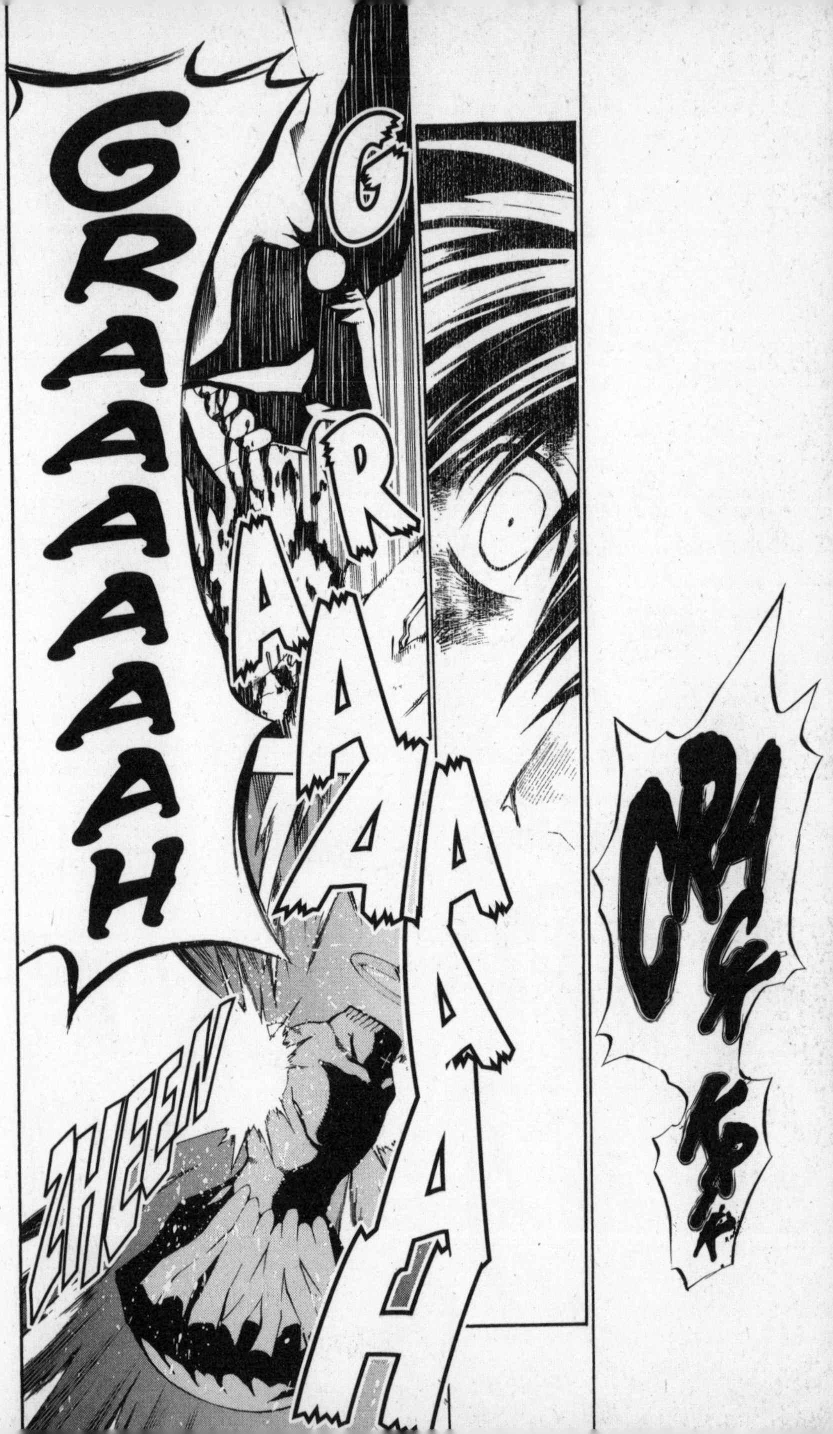
CRACK
KRK
GRAAAAAAH
GRAAAAAAH
ZHEEN

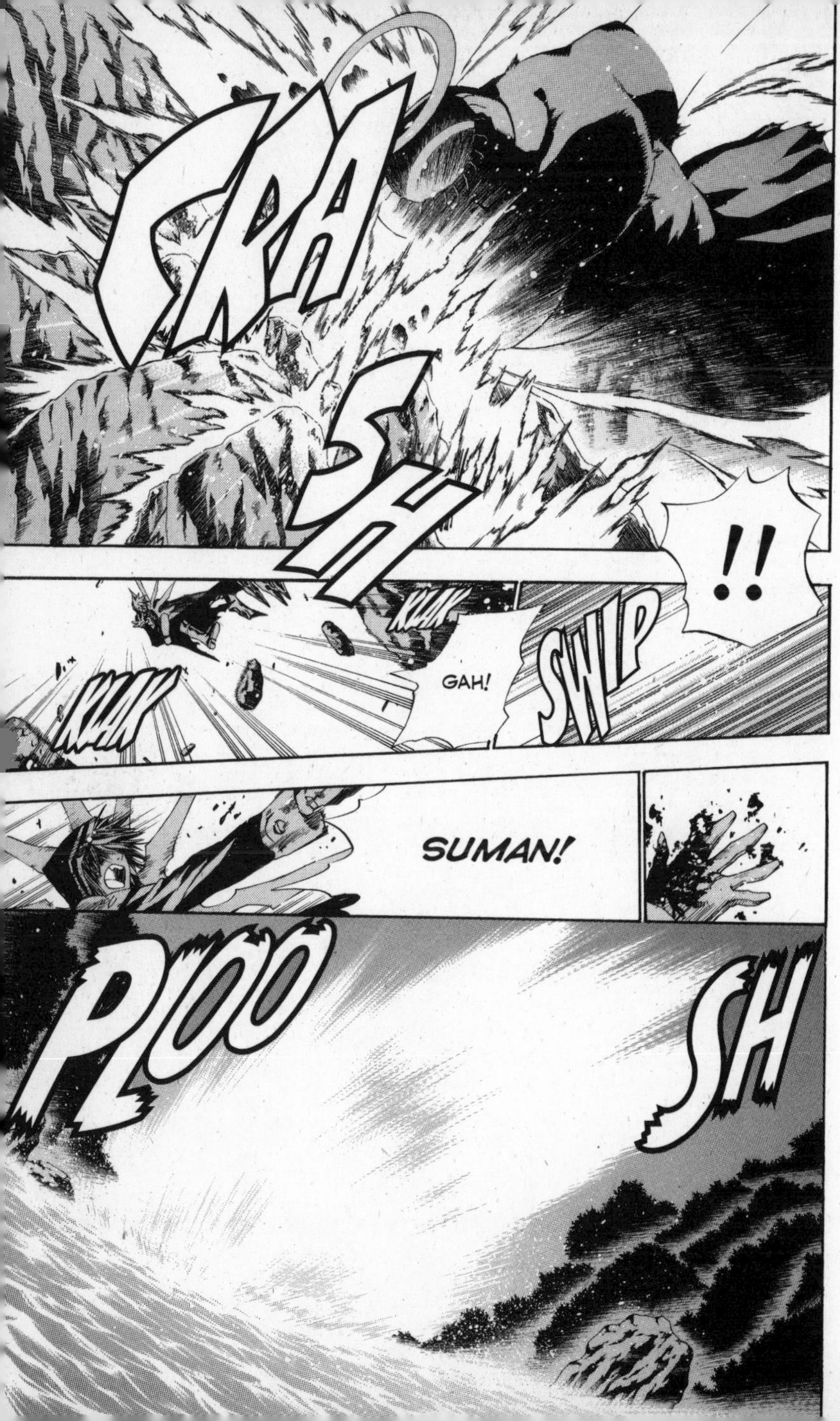
CRASH
!!
SWIP
KLAK
GAH!
KLAK
SUMAN!
PLOOSH

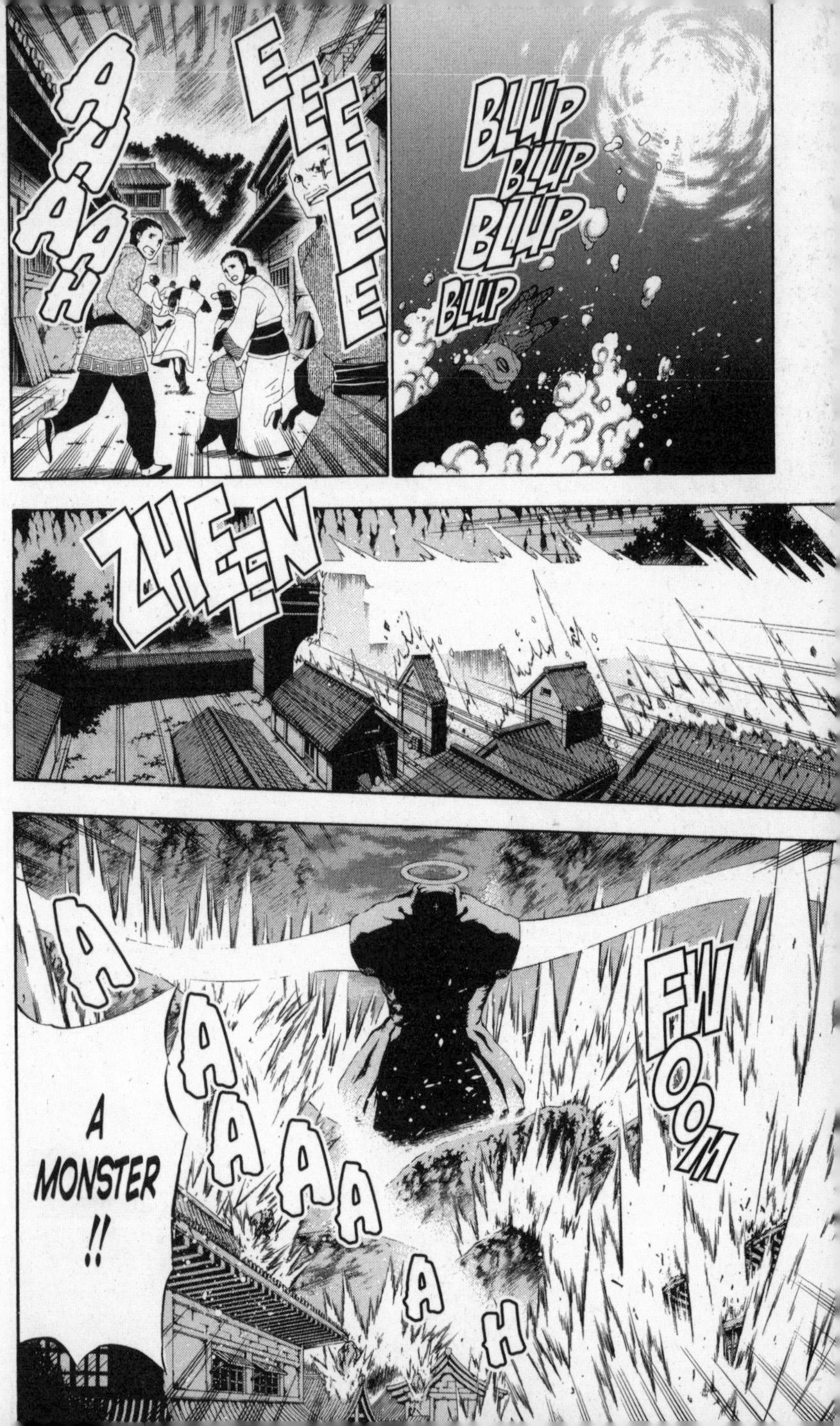

BLUP BLUP BLUP BLUP
AAAAH
EEEEEE
ZHEEEN
FWOOOM
AAAAAAAH
A MONSTER!!

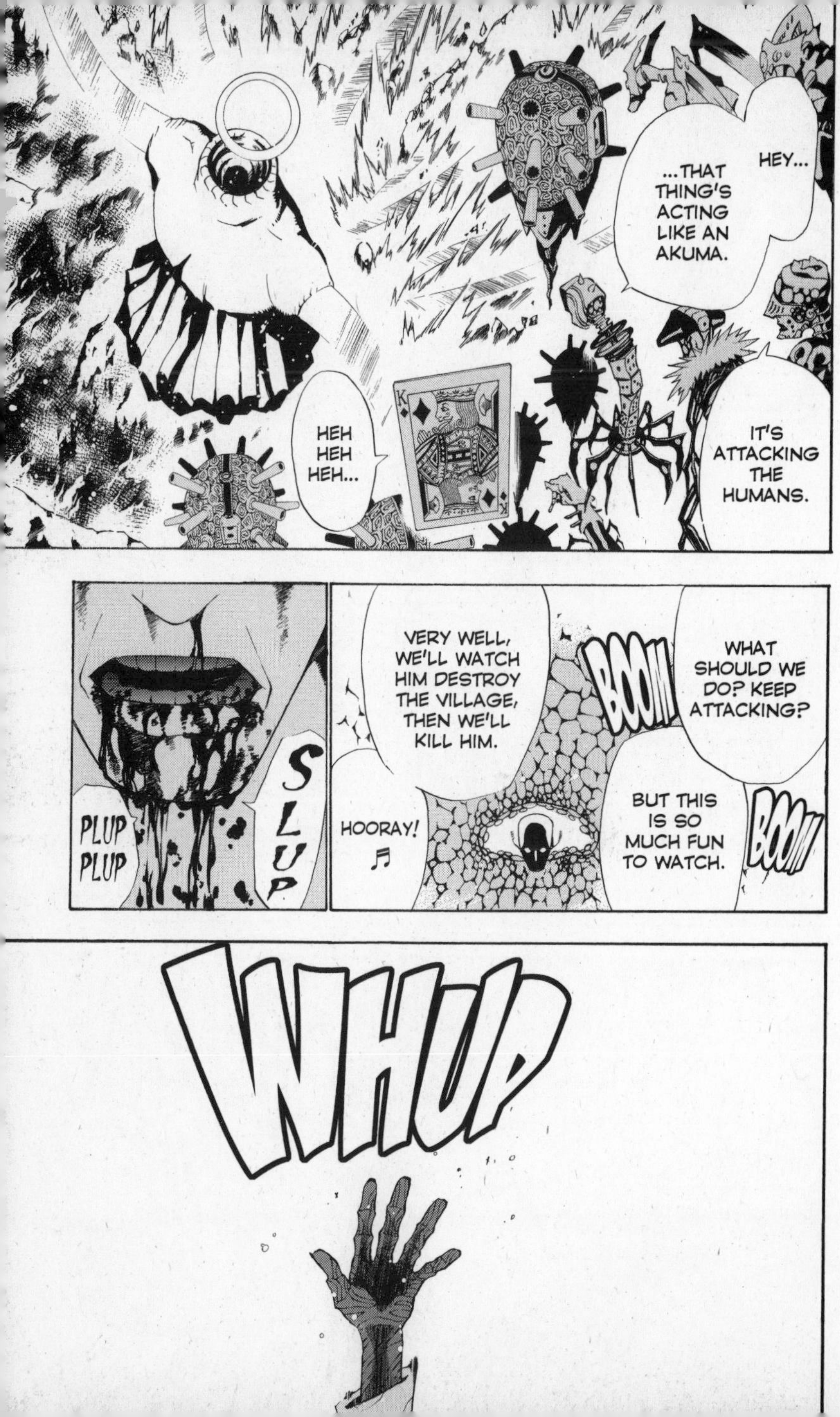
HEY...
...THAT THING'S ACTING LIKE AN AKUMA.
IT'S ATTACKING THE HUMANS.
HEH HEH HEH...
BOOM
WHAT SHOULD WE DO? KEEP ATTACKING?
BOOM
BUT THIS IS SO MUCH FUN TO WATCH.
VERY WELL, WE'LL WATCH HIM DESTROY THE VILLAGE, THEN WE'LL KILL HIM.
HOORAY! ♫
SLUP
PLUP PLUP
WHUD

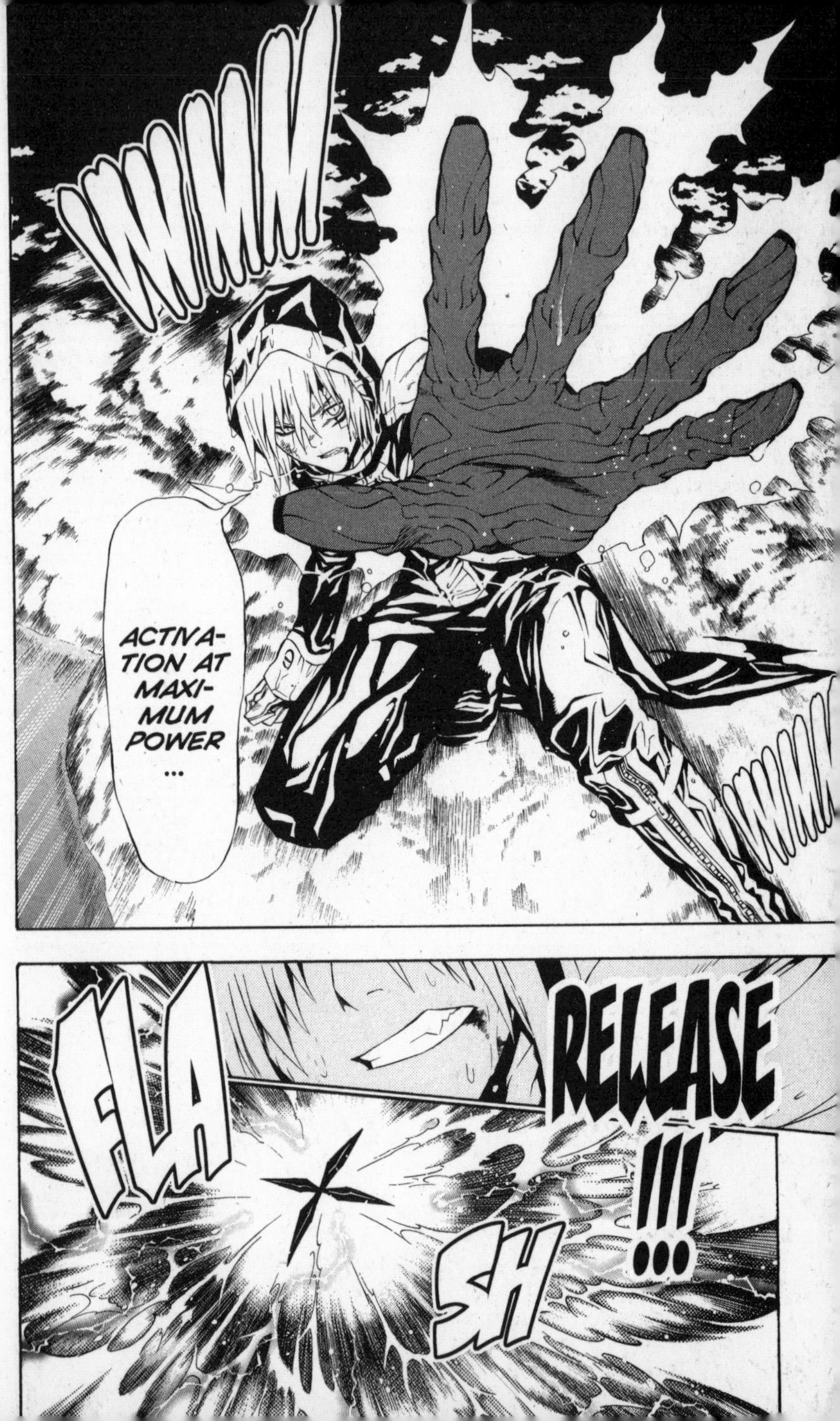
WNNNM
ACTIVATION AT MAXIMUM POWER ...
RELEASE!!!
FLASH

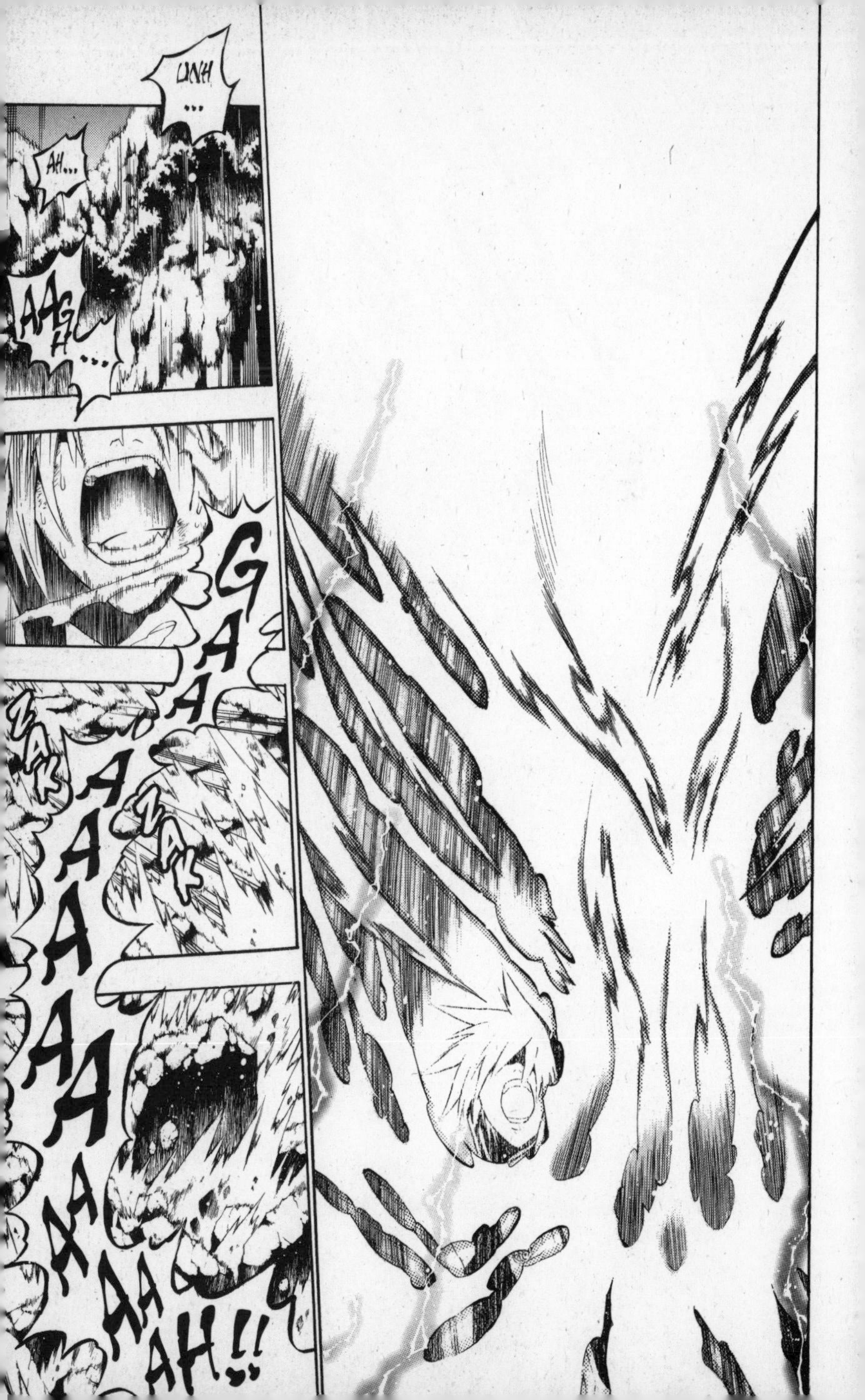
UNH ...
AH...
AAGH...
GAAAAAAAAAAAAAAAH!!
ZAK ZAK

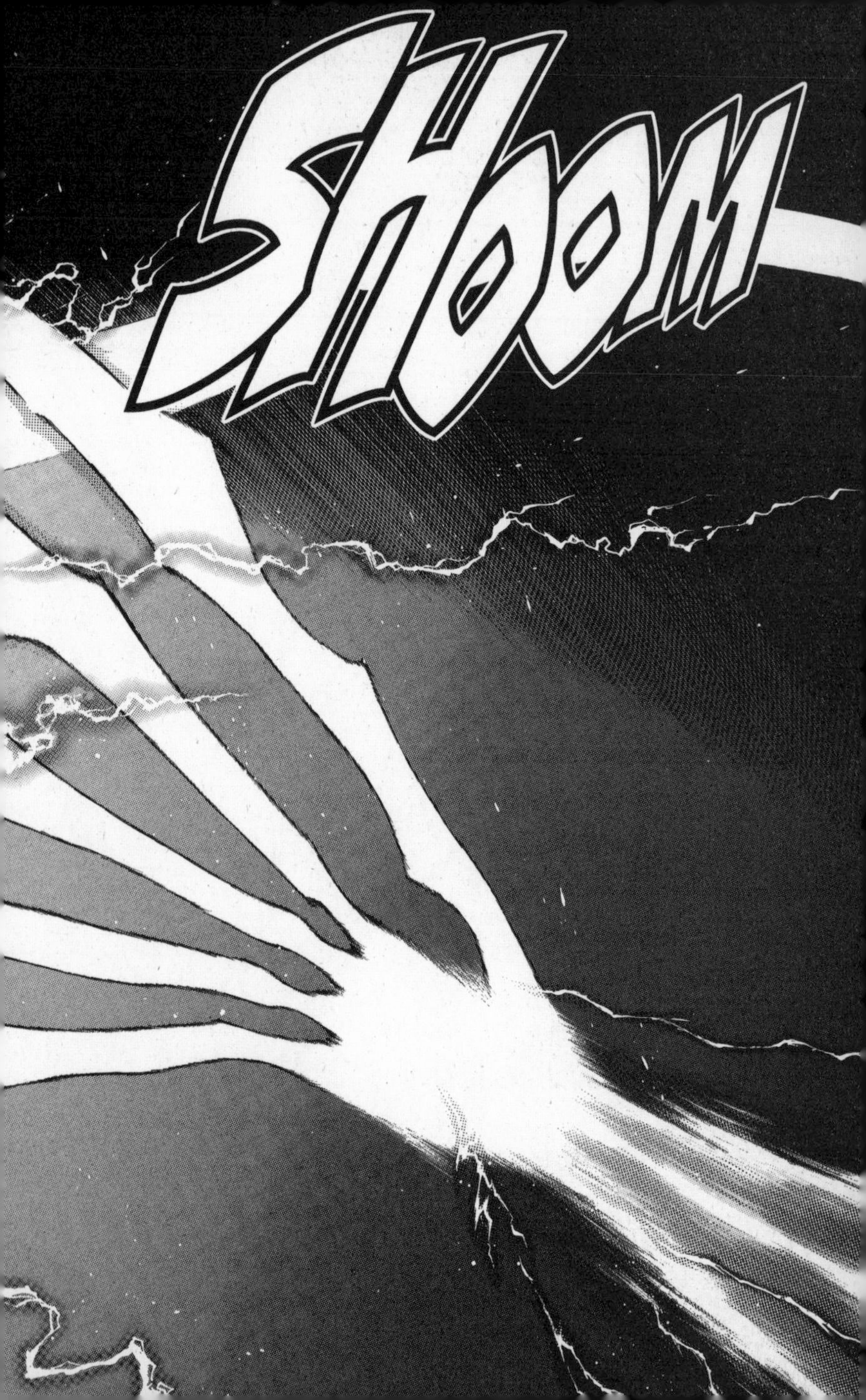
SHOOM

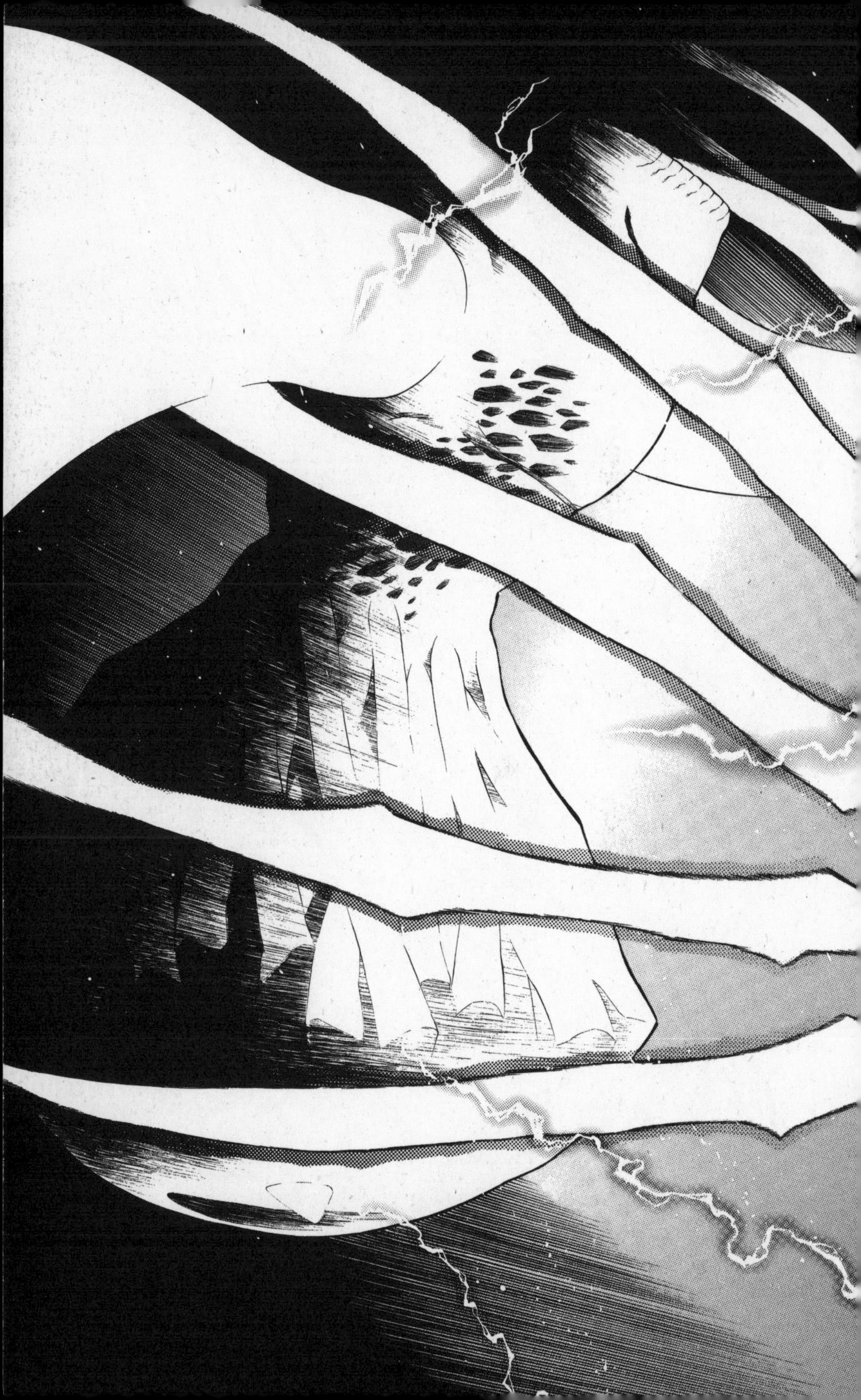

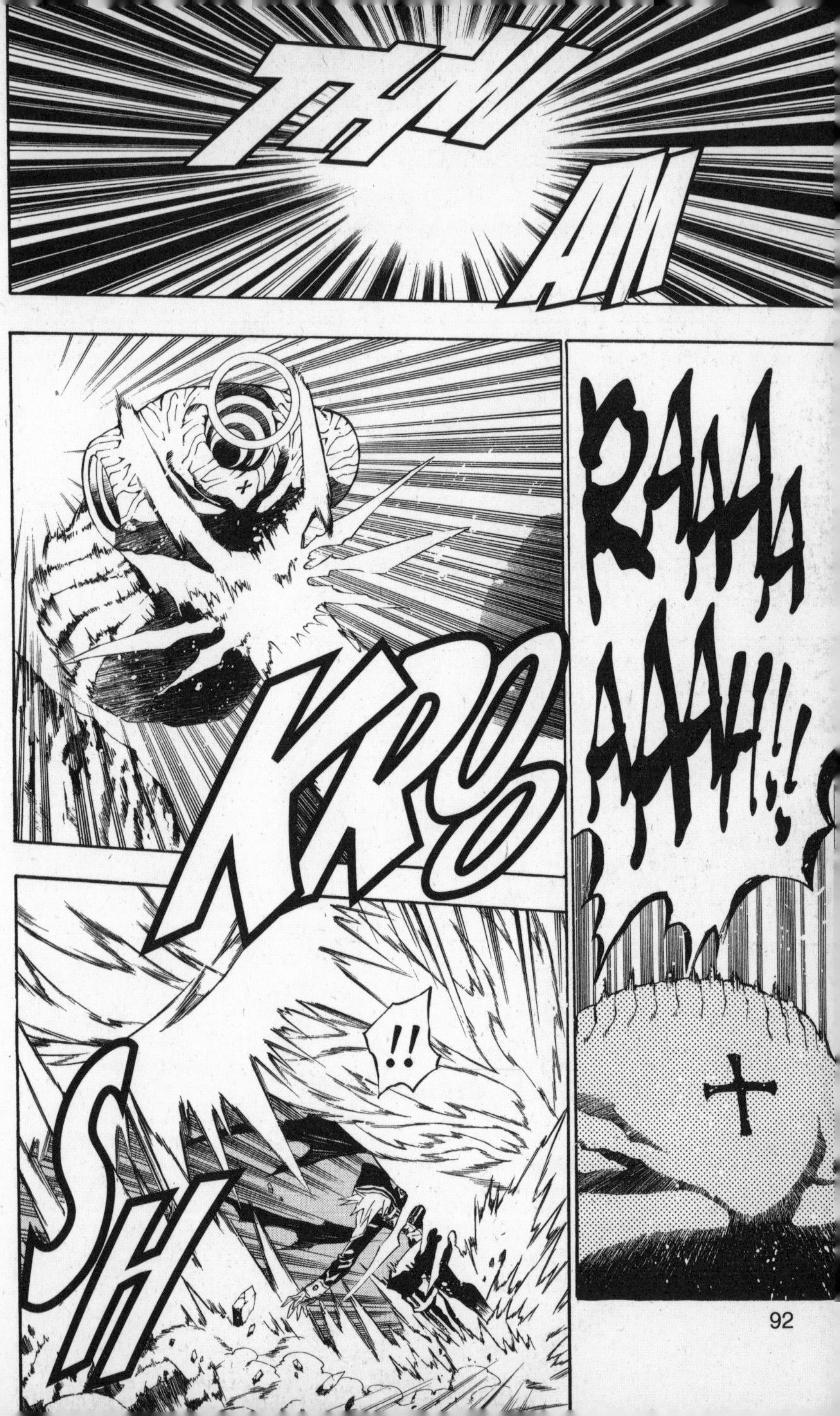
THWAM
RAAAAAAAH!!
KRS
!!
SH

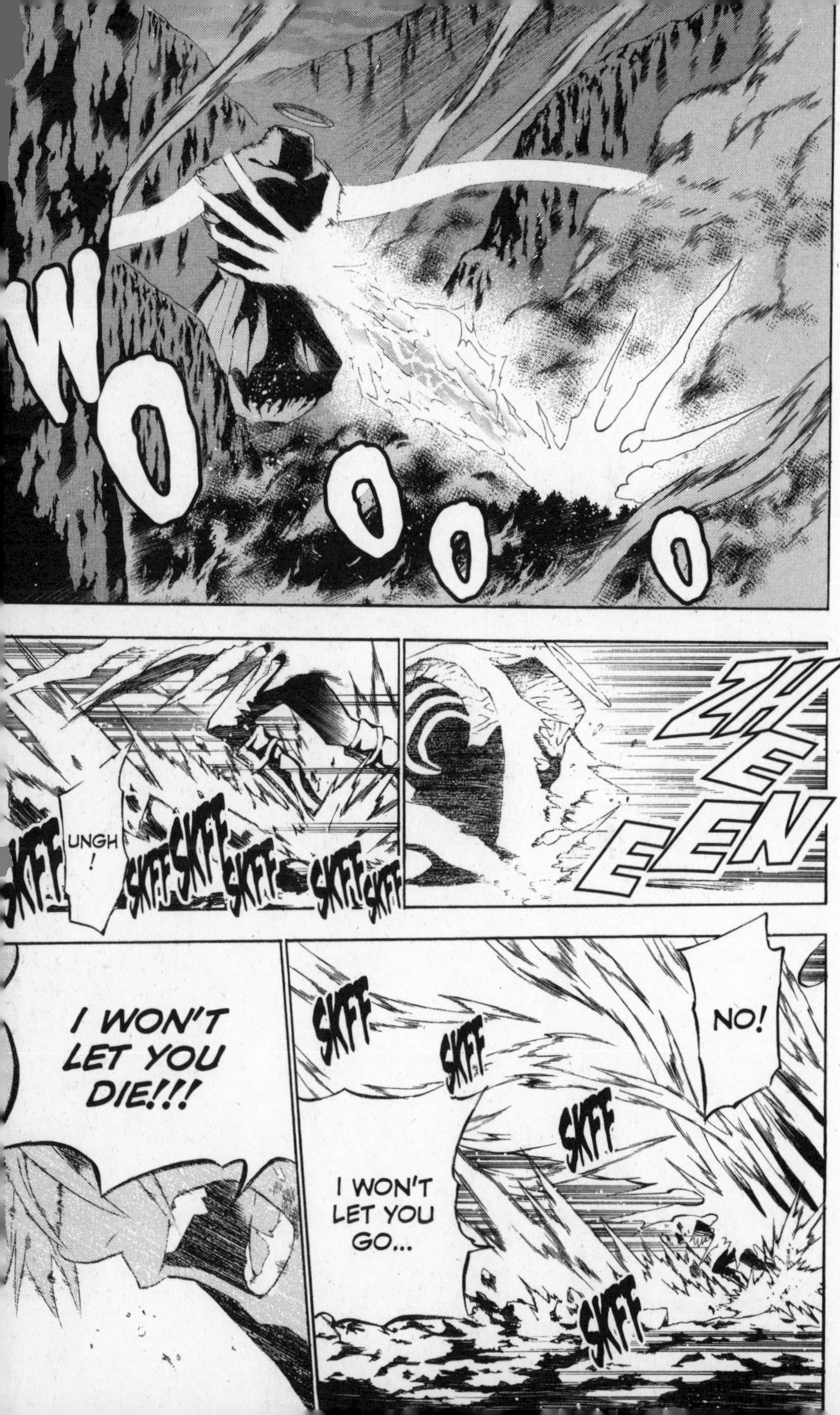
WOOOO
ZHEEEEN
SKFF
UNGH!
SKFF SKFF SKFF
SKFF SKFF
NO!
SKFF
SKFF
SKFF
I WON'T LET YOU GO...
SKFF
I WON'T LET YOU DIE!!!

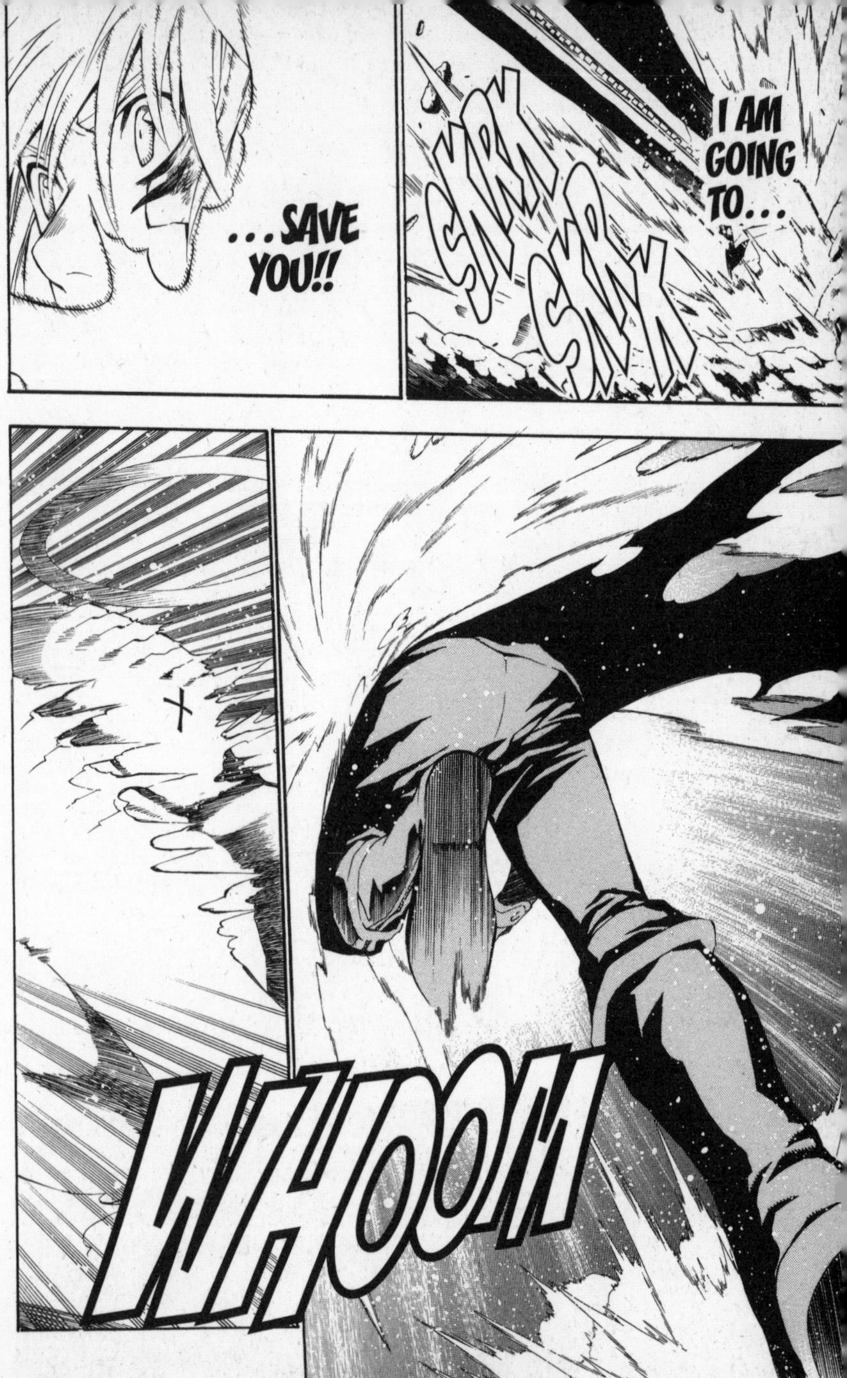
I AM GOING TO...
SKRK SKRK
...SAVE YOU!!
WHOOM

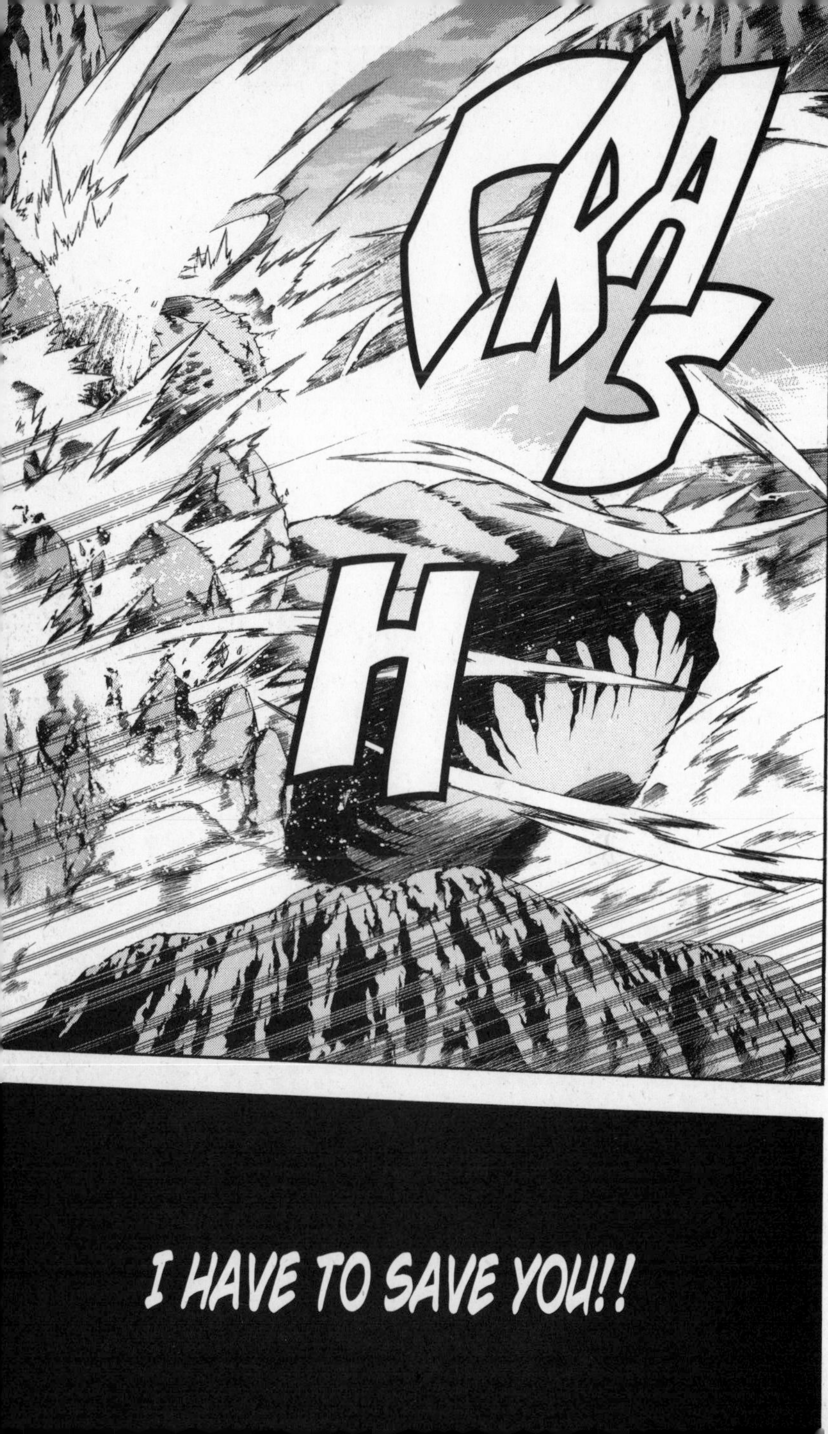
CRASH
I HAVE TO SAVE YOU!!

KOMUI'S DISCUSSION ROOM VOL. 4

Q. REEVER'S CUP HAD THE KANJI FOR BUBBLE/FOAM ON IT. WHAT WAS IN IT?

A. LEMON SODA. I DON'T GET IT, BUT IT'S SUPPOSED TO BE GOOD.

Q. THERE WAS A RUBBER DUCKY FLOATING IN THE BATH IN VOL. 4. DID KANDA PUT IT THERE?

A. GRR...

Q. IN VOLUME 4'S "DISCUSSION ROOM," ALLEN THANKED THE READER FOR THE VALENTINE'S DAY CHOCOLATES, BUT IN VOLUME 5 REEVER SAYS THAT ALLEN DOESN'T LIKE CHOCOLATE. SO WHICH IS IT?

A. I TOLD YOU NOT TO ASK ME QUESTIONS ABOUT THAT GUY!

Q. I'M SERIOUSLY IN LOVE WITH ALLEN!!! I'M EVEN LEARNING TO COOK SO THAT I CAN COOK FOR HIM! I BOUGHT A BOOK ON MAKING MITARASHI DANGO AND I'VE BEEN PRACTICING! IF I LEARN TO MAKE THEM WELL, WILL HE GO OUT WITH ME?

A. TWITCH

Q. ALLEN IS A BOY, RIGHT? BUT HE'S SO PRETTY!! I LOVE ALLEN!

A. DO YOU PEOPLE WANT TO DIE?!!! (GRRR...)

DUE TO KANDA DRAWING HIS SWORD, THIS INSTALLMENT OF THE DISCUSSION ROOM IS NOW OVER. (HOSHINO)

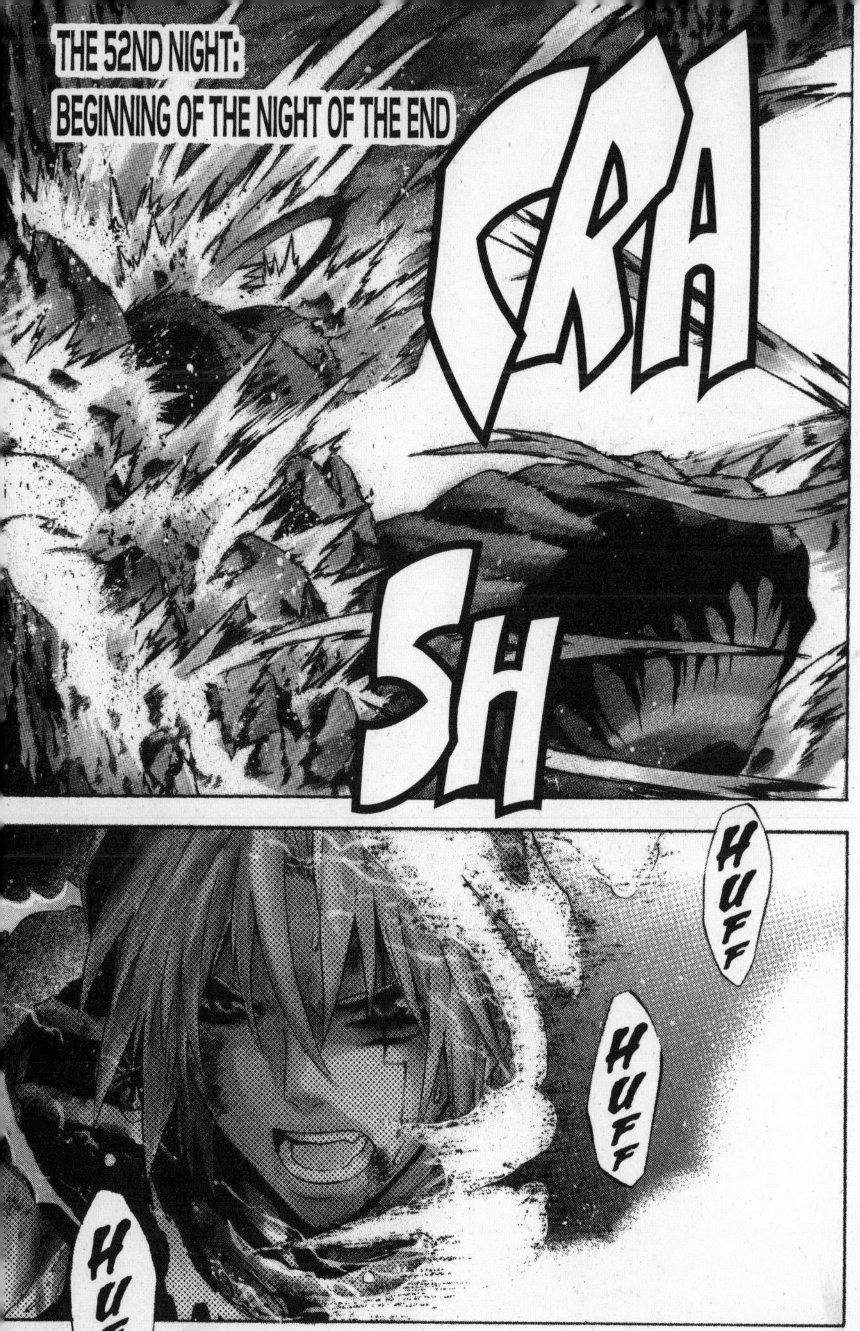
THE 52ND NIGHT:
BEGINNING OF THE NIGHT OF THE END
CRA
SH
HUFF
HUFF
HUFF

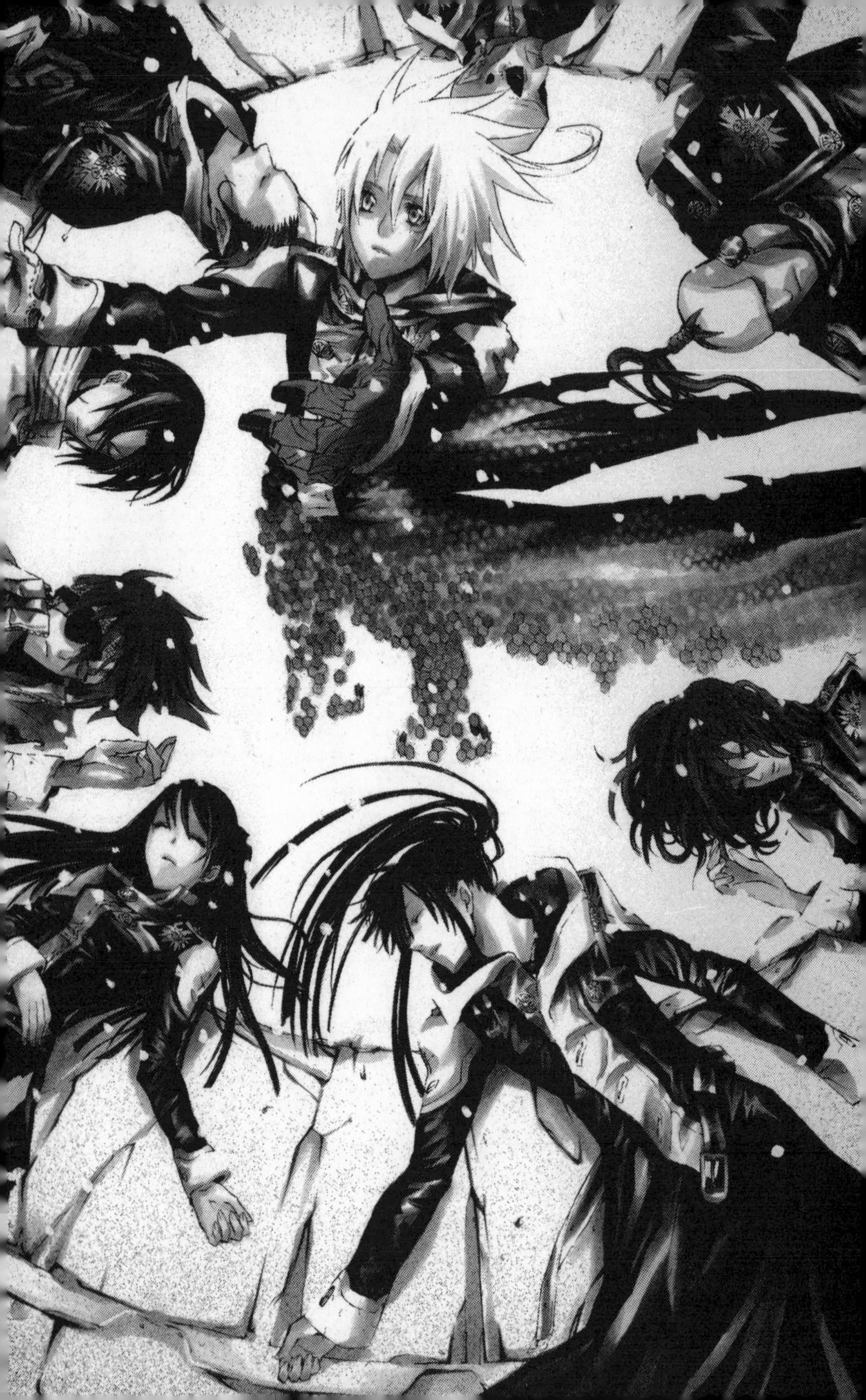

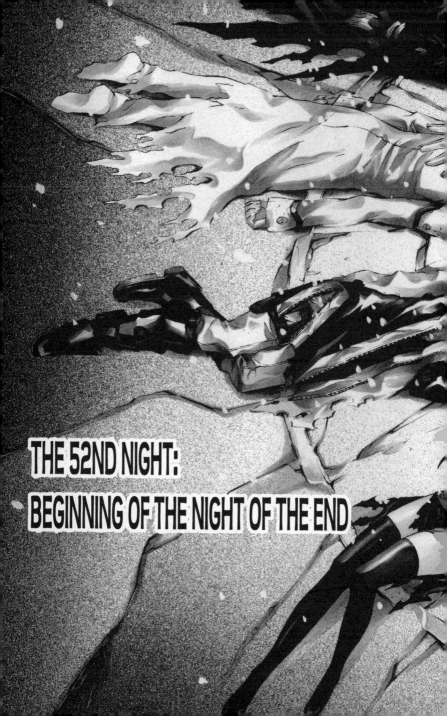

THE 52ND NIGHT:

BEGINNING OF THE NIGHT OF THE END

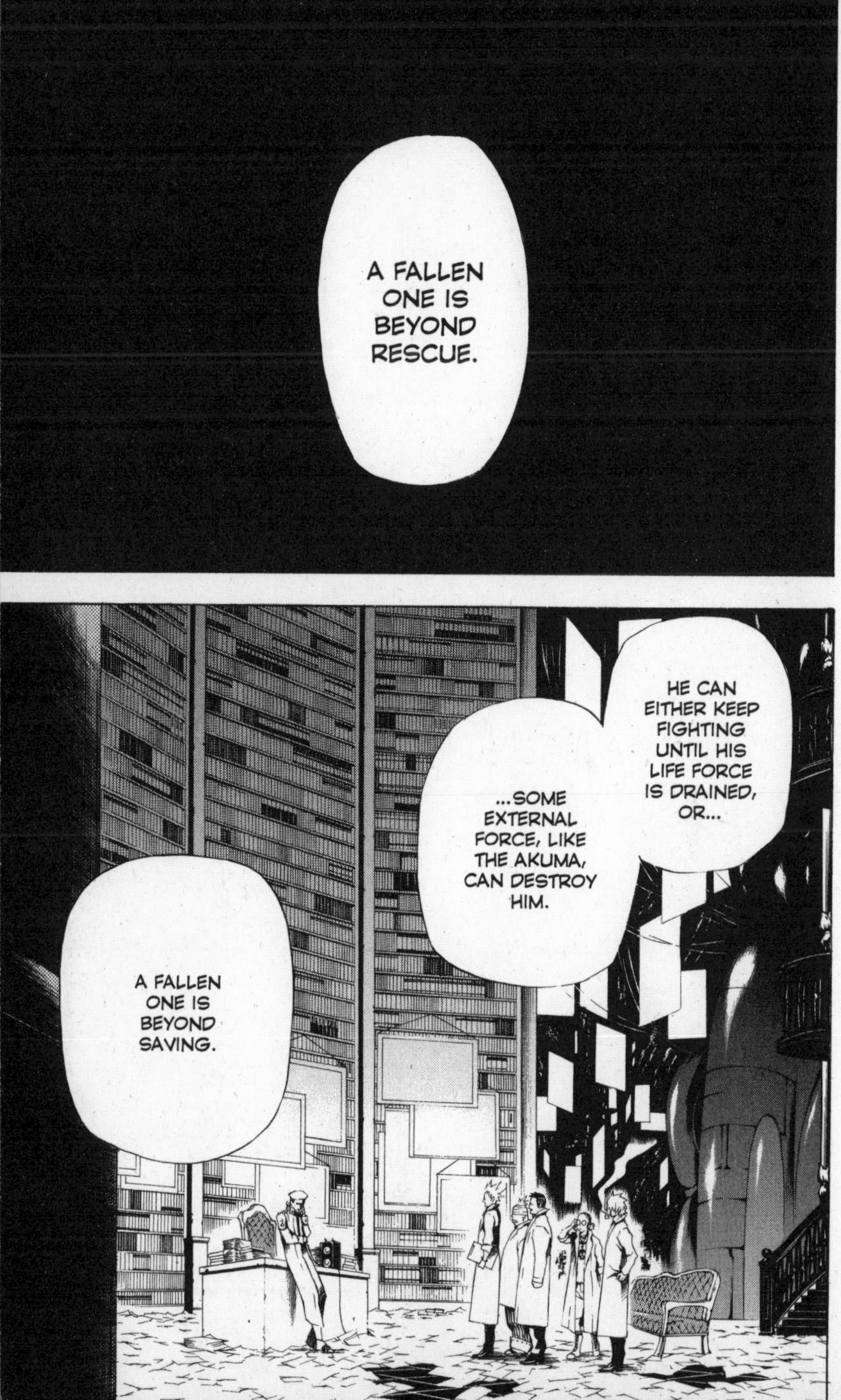
A FALLEN ONE IS BEYOND RESCUE.
HE CAN EITHER KEEP FIGHTING UNTIL HIS LIFE FORCE IS DRAINED, OR...
...SOME EXTERNAL FORCE, LIKE THE AKUMA, CAN DESTROY HIM.
A FALLEN ONE IS BEYOND SAVING.

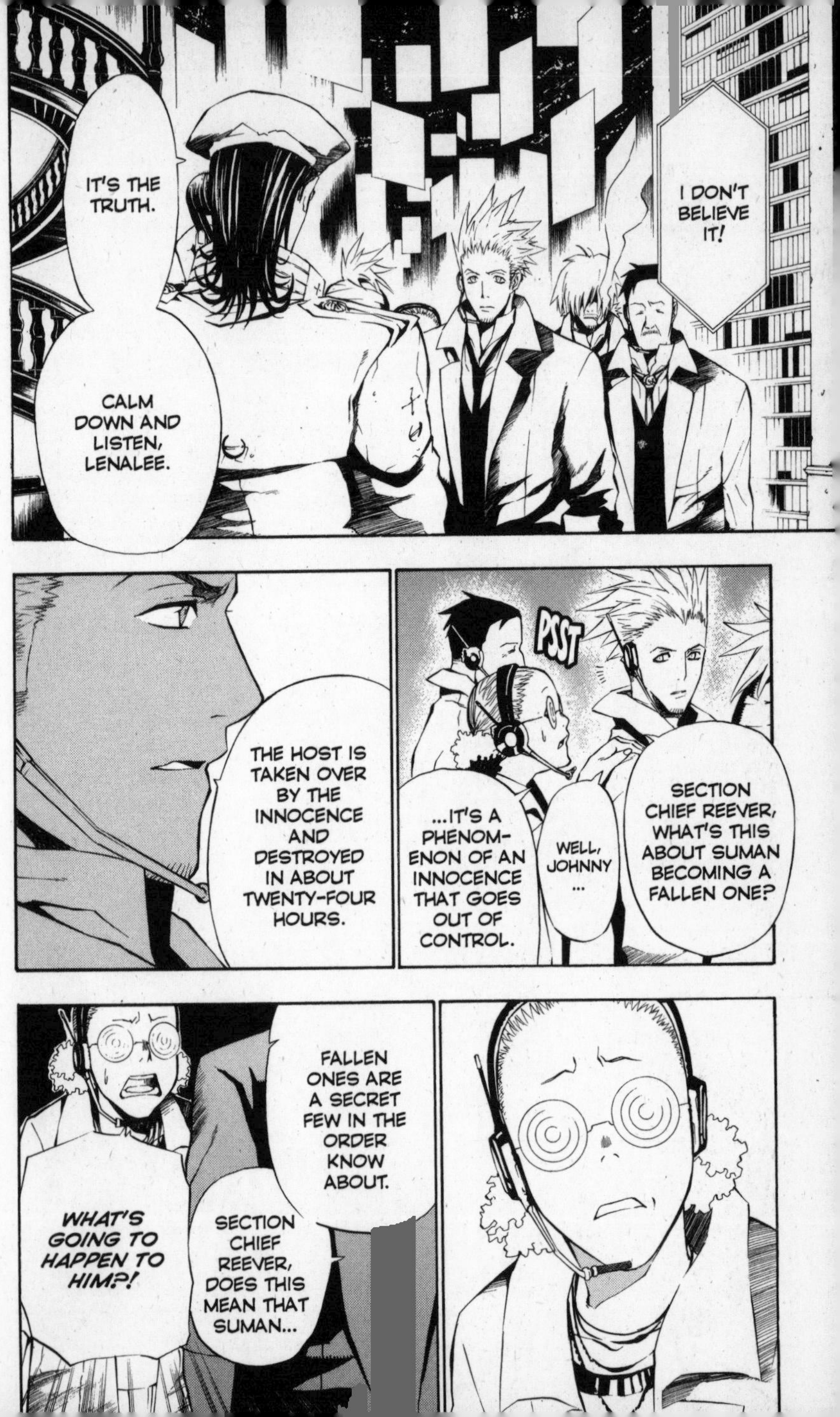
I DON'T BELIEVE IT!
IT'S THE TRUTH.
CALM DOWN AND LISTEN, LENALEE.
PSST
SECTION CHIEF REEVER, WHAT'S THIS ABOUT SUMAN BECOMING A FALLEN ONE?
WELL, JOHNNY...
...IT'S A PHENOM-ENON OF AN INNOCENCE THAT GOES OUT OF CONTROL.
THE HOST IS TAKEN OVER BY THE INNOCENCE AND DESTROYED IN ABOUT TWENTY-FOUR HOURS.
FALLEN ONES ARE A SECRET FEW IN THE ORDER KNOW ABOUT.
SECTION CHIEF REEVER, DOES THIS MEAN THAT SUMAN...
WHAT'S GOING TO HAPPEN TO HIM?!

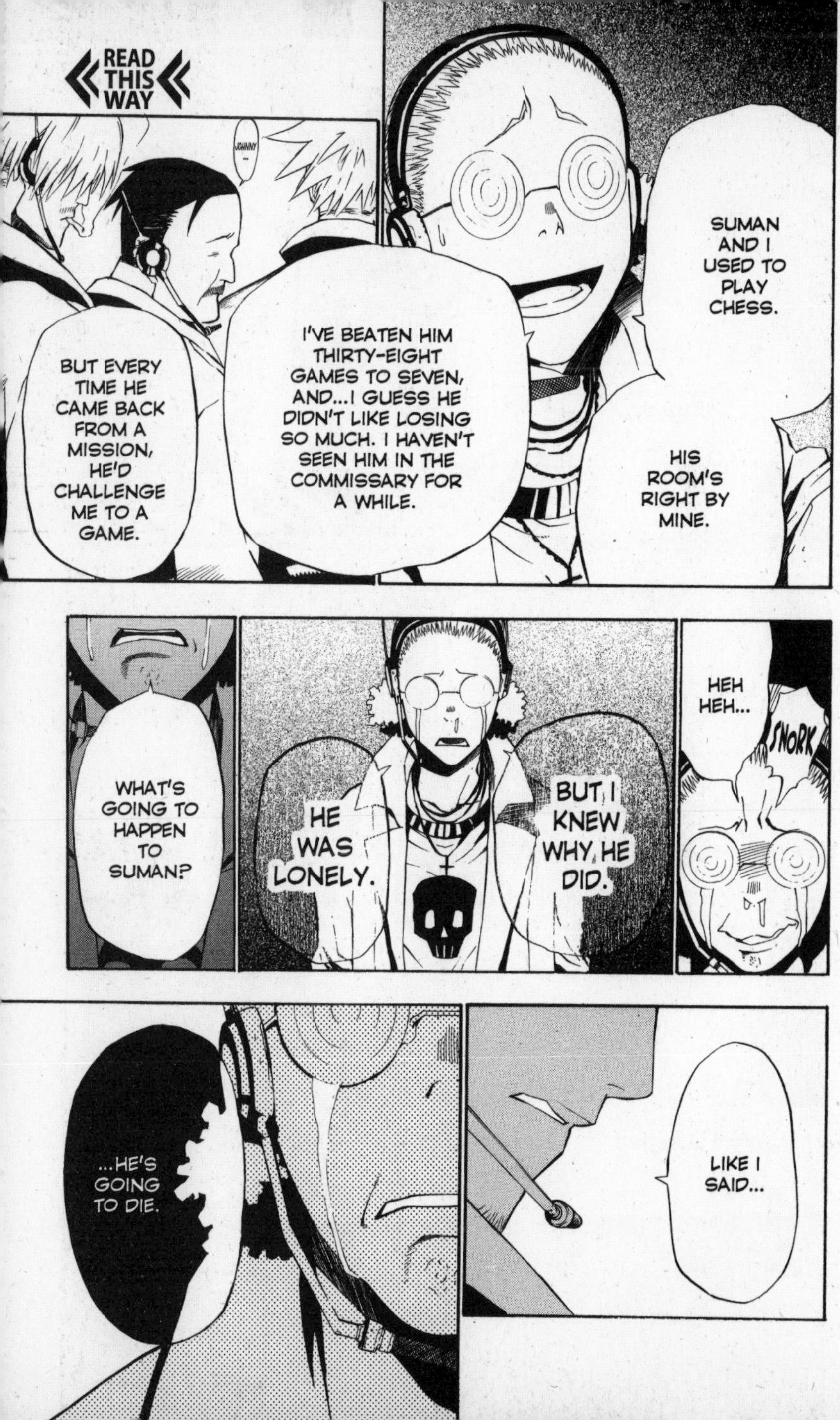
READ THIS WAY
SUMAN AND I USED TO PLAY CHESS.
HIS ROOM'S RIGHT BY MINE.
JOHNNY—
I'VE BEATEN HIM THIRTY-EIGHT GAMES TO SEVEN, AND...I GUESS HE DIDN'T LIKE LOSING SO MUCH. I HAVEN'T SEEN HIM IN THE COMMISSARY FOR A WHILE.
BUT EVERY TIME HE CAME BACK FROM A MISSION, HE'D CHALLENGE ME TO A GAME.
HEH HEH...
SNORK
BUT I KNEW WHY HE DID.
HE WAS LONELY.
WHAT'S GOING TO HAPPEN TO SUMAN?
LIKE I SAID...
...HE'S GOING TO DIE.

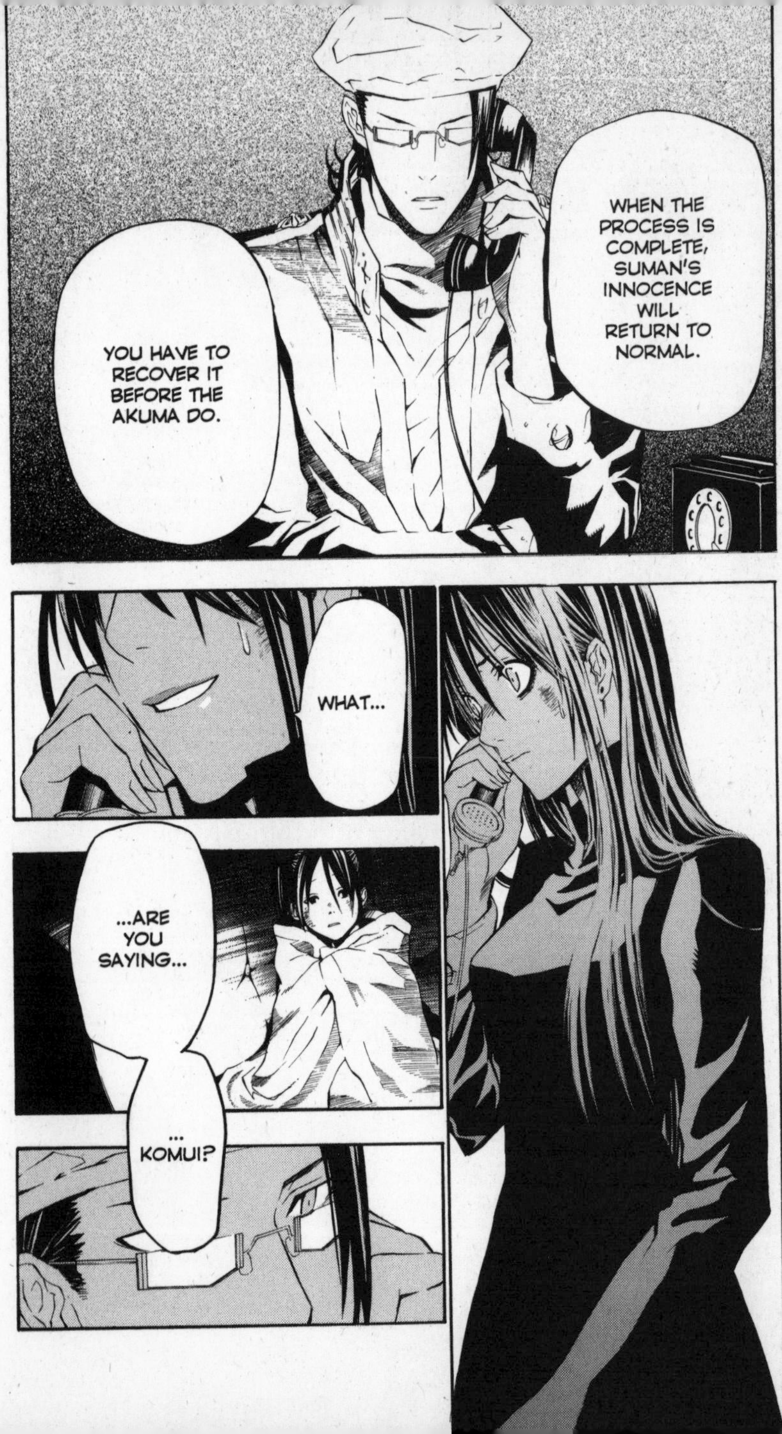
WHEN THE PROCESS IS COMPLETE, SUMAN'S INNOCENCE WILL RETURN TO NORMAL.
YOU HAVE TO RECOVER IT BEFORE THE AKUMA DO.
WHAT...
...ARE YOU SAYING...
...KOMUI?

READ THIS WAY

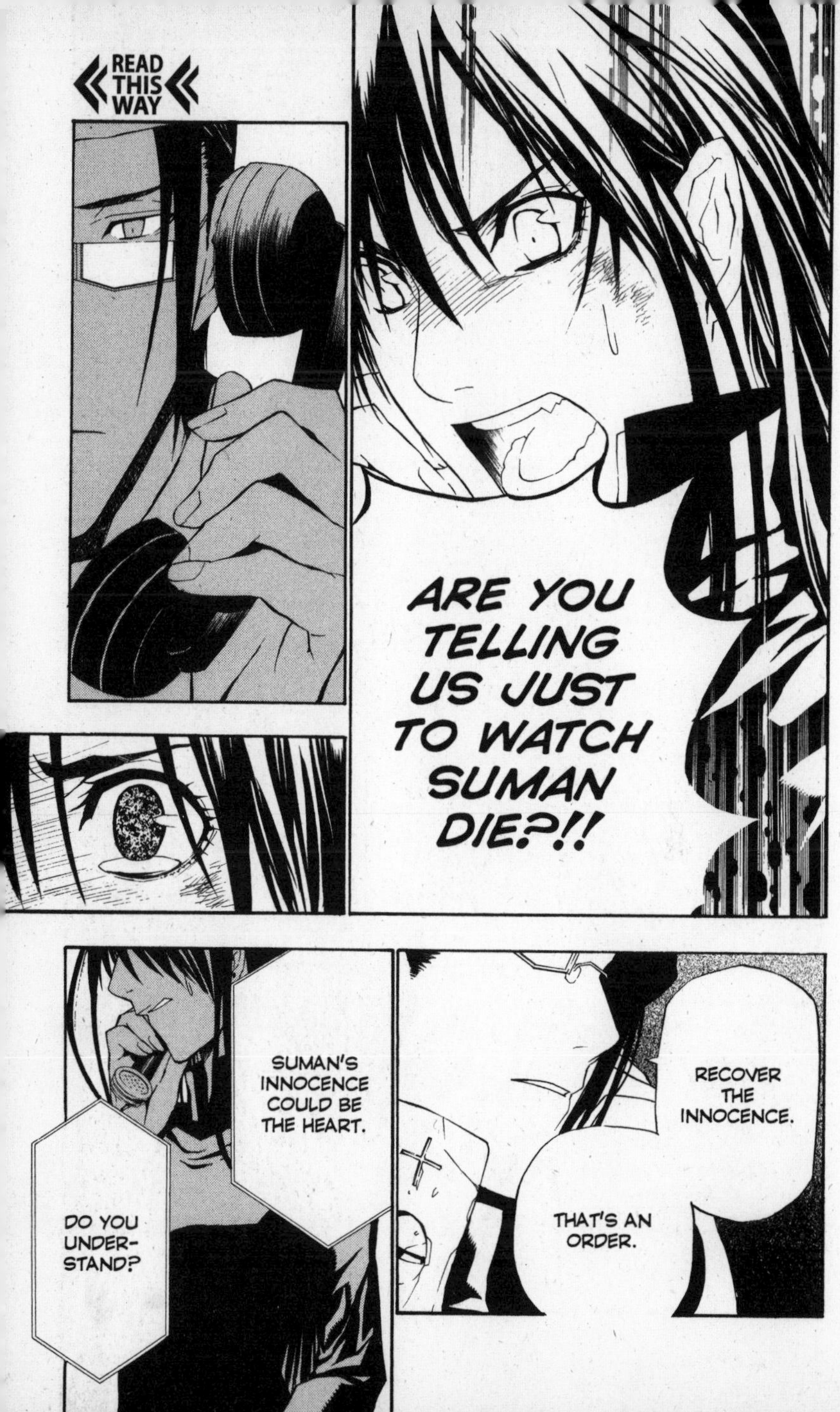
ARE YOU TELLING US JUST TO WATCH SUMAN DIE?!!
RECOVER THE INNOCENCE.
THAT'S AN ORDER.
SUMAN'S INNOCENCE COULD BE THE HEART.
DO YOU UNDER-STAND?

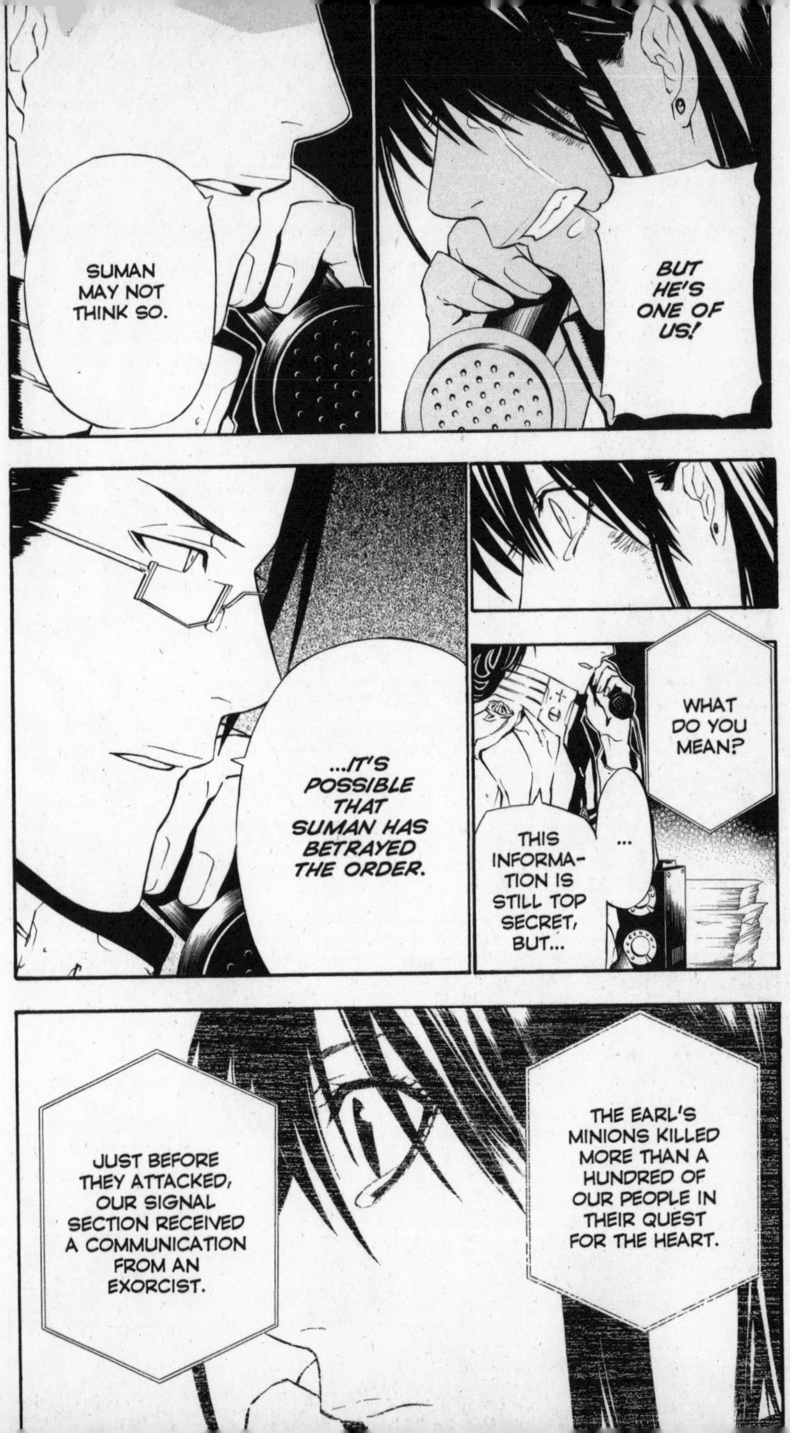
BUT HE'S ONE OF US!
SUMAN MAY NOT THINK SO.
WHAT DO YOU MEAN?
...
THIS INFORMATION IS STILL TOP SECRET, BUT...
...IT'S POSSIBLE THAT SUMAN HAS BETRAYED THE ORDER.
THE EARL'S MINIONS KILLED MORE THAN A HUNDRED OF OUR PEOPLE IN THEIR QUEST FOR THE HEART.
JUST BEFORE THEY ATTACKED, OUR SIGNAL SECTION RECEIVED A COMMUNICATION FROM AN EXORCIST.

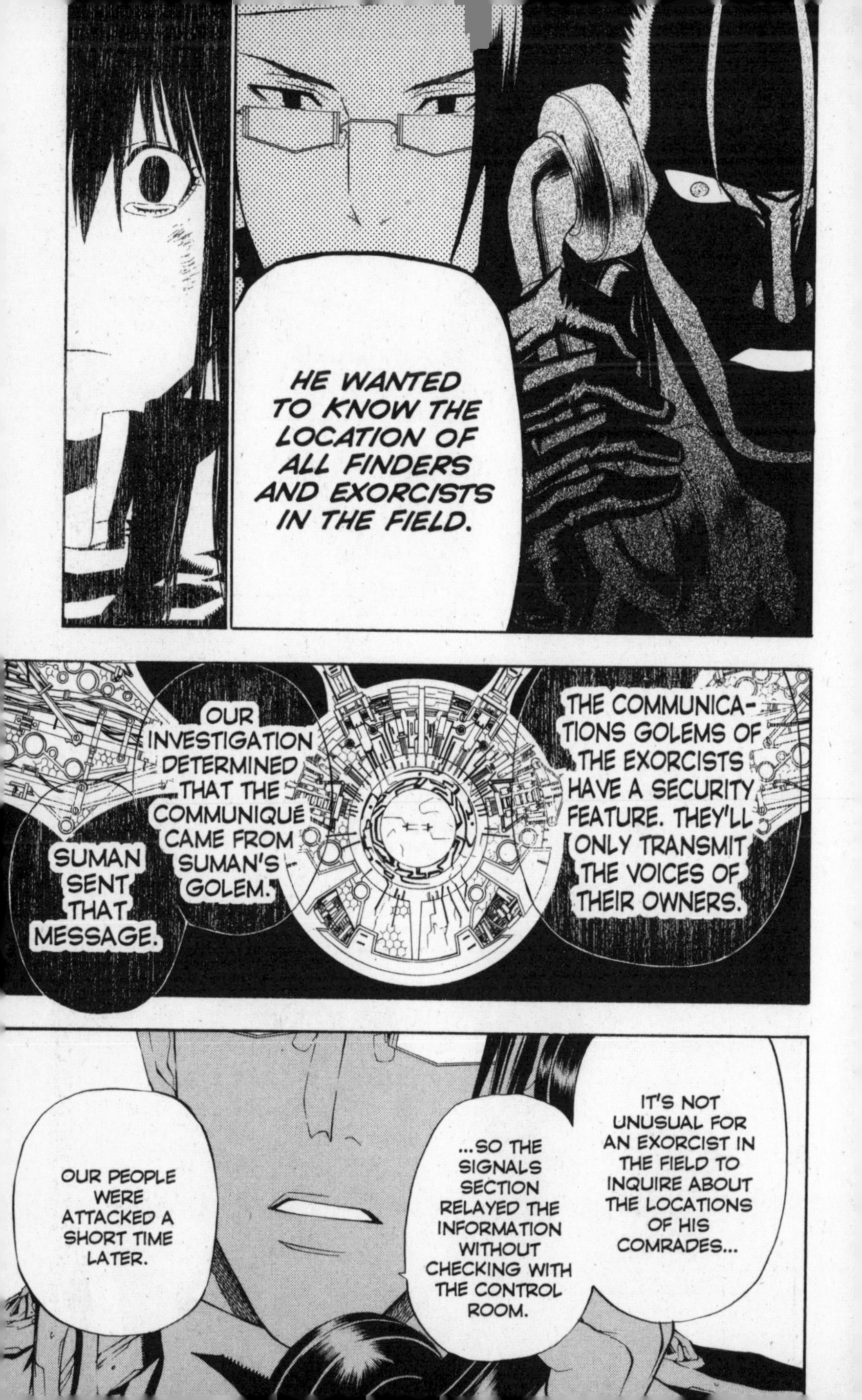
HE WANTED TO KNOW THE LOCATION OF ALL FINDERS AND EXORCISTS IN THE FIELD.
THE COMMUNICATIONS GOLEMS OF THE EXORCISTS HAVE A SECURITY FEATURE. THEY'LL ONLY TRANSMIT THE VOICES OF THEIR OWNERS.
OUR INVESTIGATION DETERMINED THAT THE COMMUNIQUÉ CAME FROM SUMAN'S GOLEM.
SUMAN SENT THAT MESSAGE.
IT'S NOT UNUSUAL FOR AN EXORCIST IN THE FIELD TO INQUIRE ABOUT THE LOCATIONS OF HIS COMRADES...
...SO THE SIGNALS SECTION RELAYED THE INFORMATION WITHOUT CHECKING WITH THE CONTROL ROOM.
OUR PEOPLE WERE ATTACKED A SHORT TIME LATER.

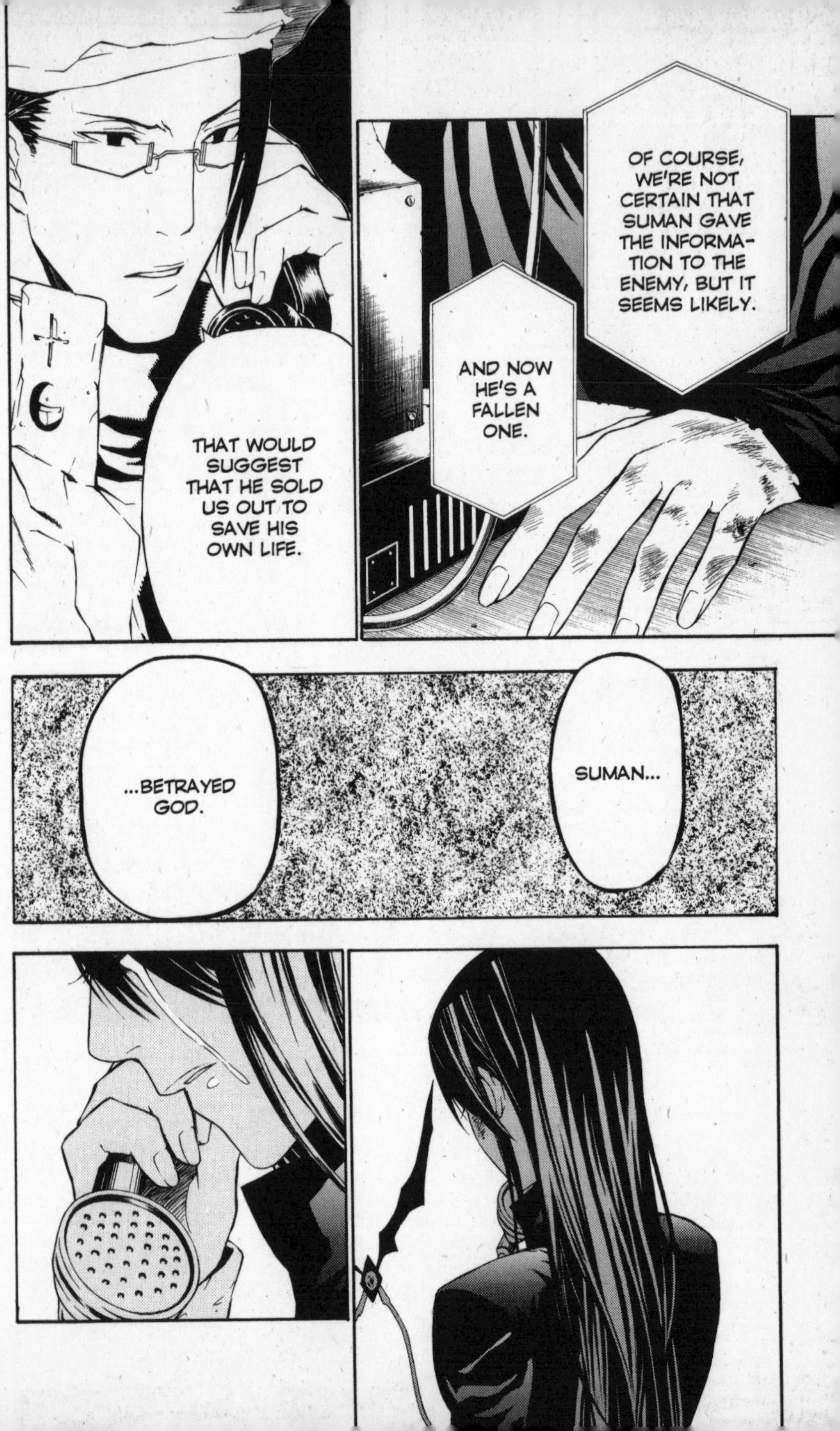
OF COURSE, WE'RE NOT CERTAIN THAT SUMAN GAVE THE INFORMA-TION TO THE ENEMY, BUT IT SEEMS LIKELY.
AND NOW HE'S A FALLEN ONE.
THAT WOULD SUGGEST THAT HE SOLD US OUT TO SAVE HIS OWN LIFE.
SUMAN...
...BETRAYED GOD.

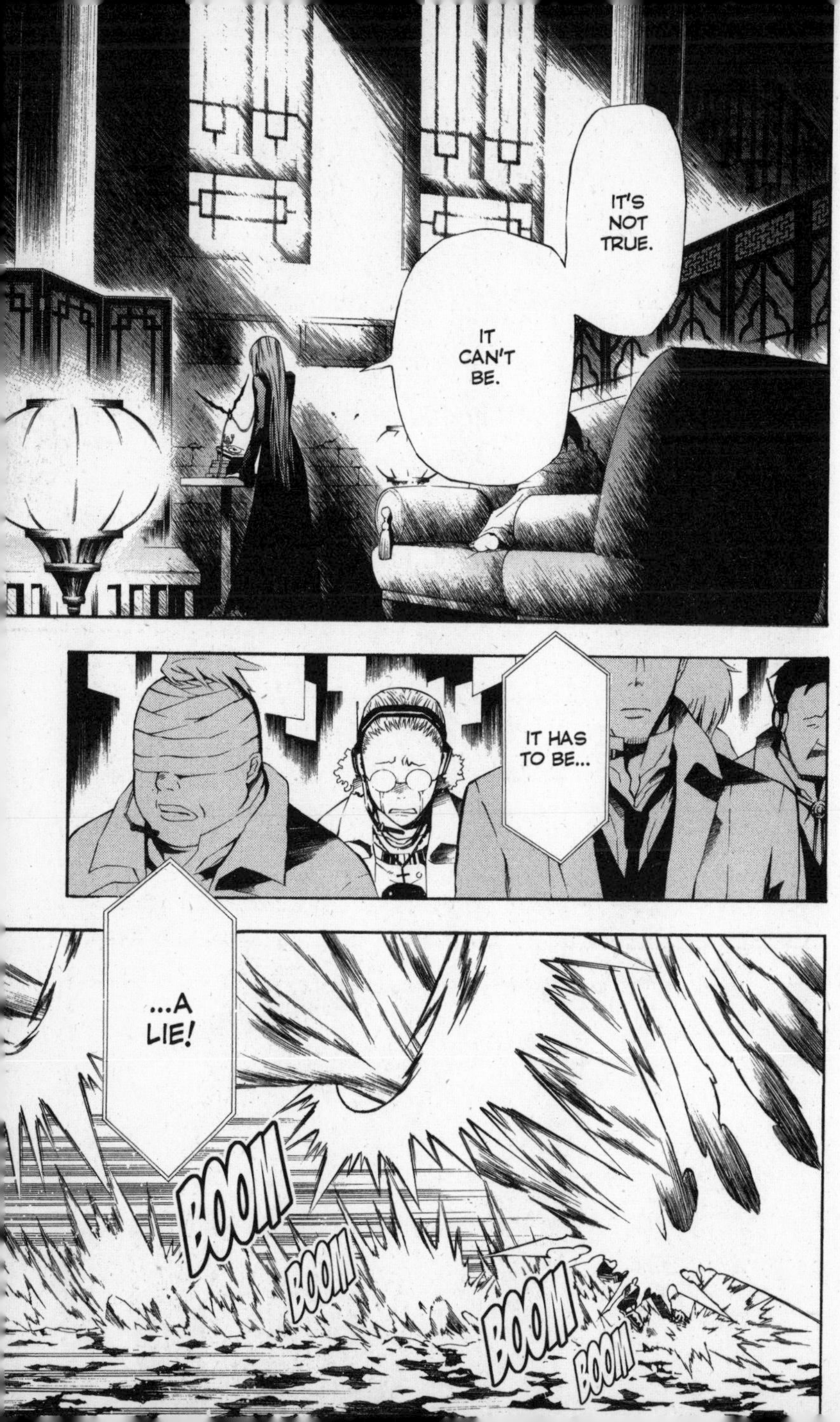
IT'S NOT TRUE.
IT CAN'T BE.
IT HAS TO BE...
...A LIE!
BOOM
BOOM
BOOM
BOOM

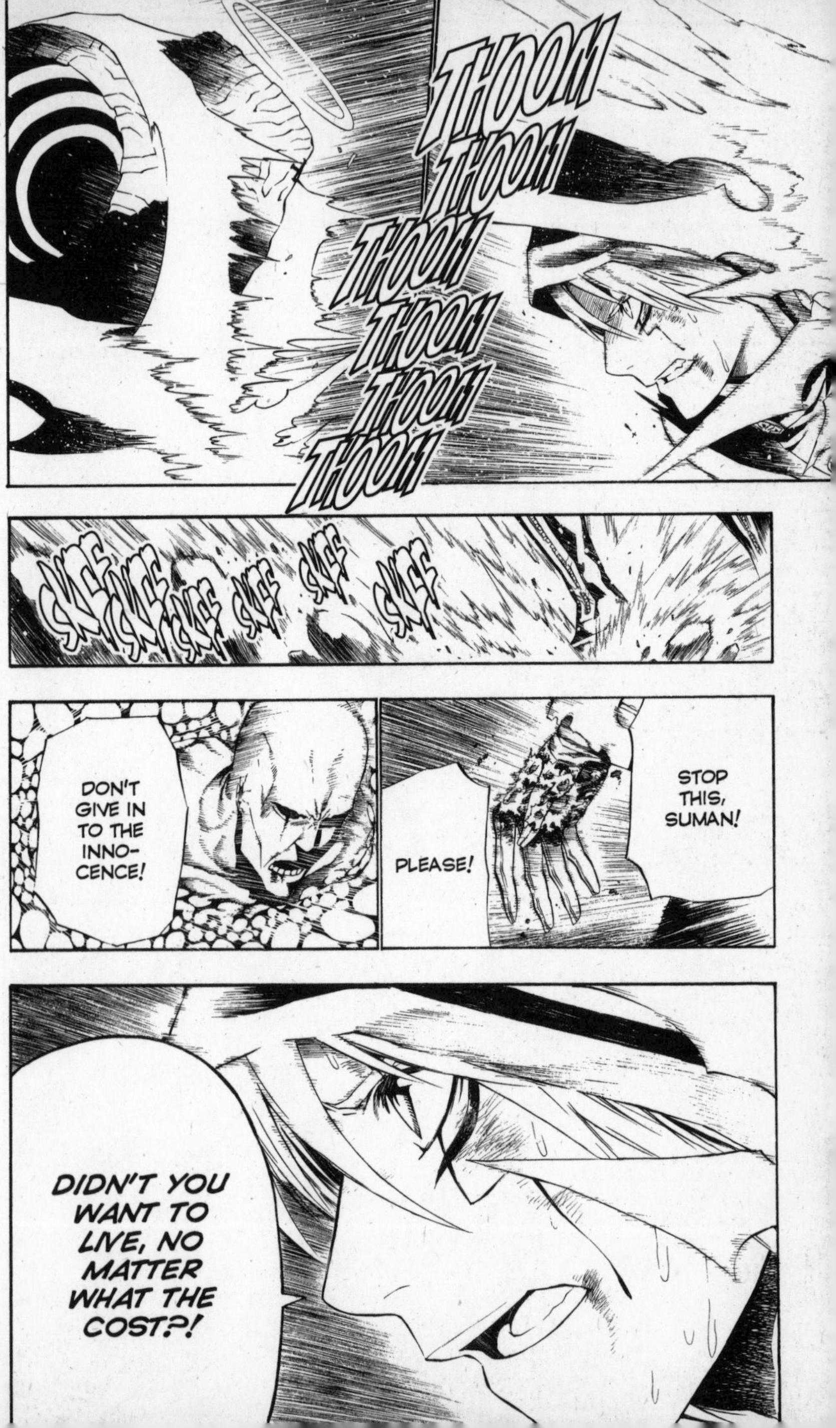
THOOM THOOM THOOM THOOM THOOM THOOM
STOP THIS, SUMAN!
PLEASE!
DON'T GIVE IN TO THE INNO-CENCE!
DIDN'T YOU WANT TO LIVE, NO MATTER WHAT THE COST?!

READ THIS WAY

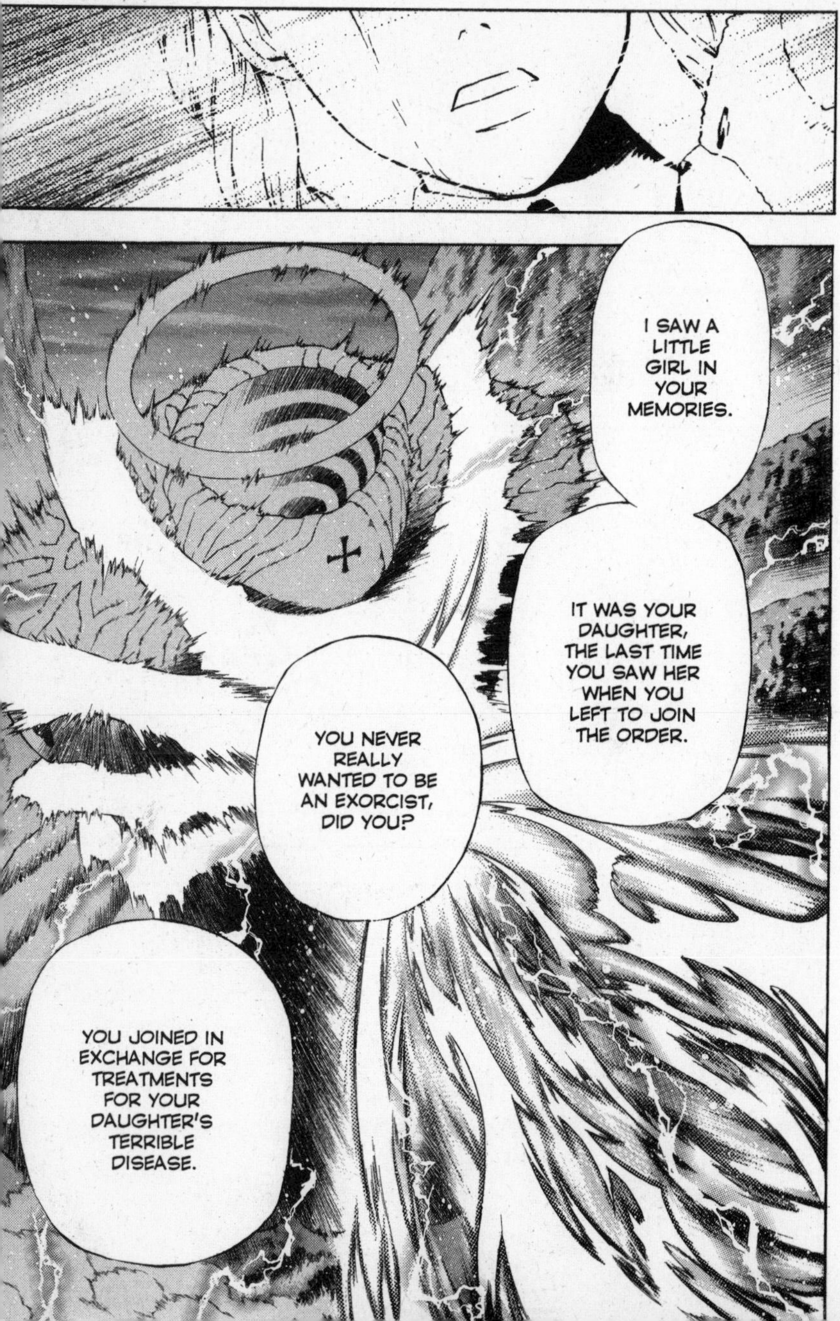
I SAW A LITTLE GIRL IN YOUR MEMORIES.
IT WAS YOUR DAUGHTER, THE LAST TIME YOU SAW HER WHEN YOU LEFT TO JOIN THE ORDER.
YOU NEVER REALLY WANTED TO BE AN EXORCIST, DID YOU?
YOU JOINED IN EXCHANGE FOR TREATMENTS FOR YOUR DAUGHTER'S TERRIBLE DISEASE.

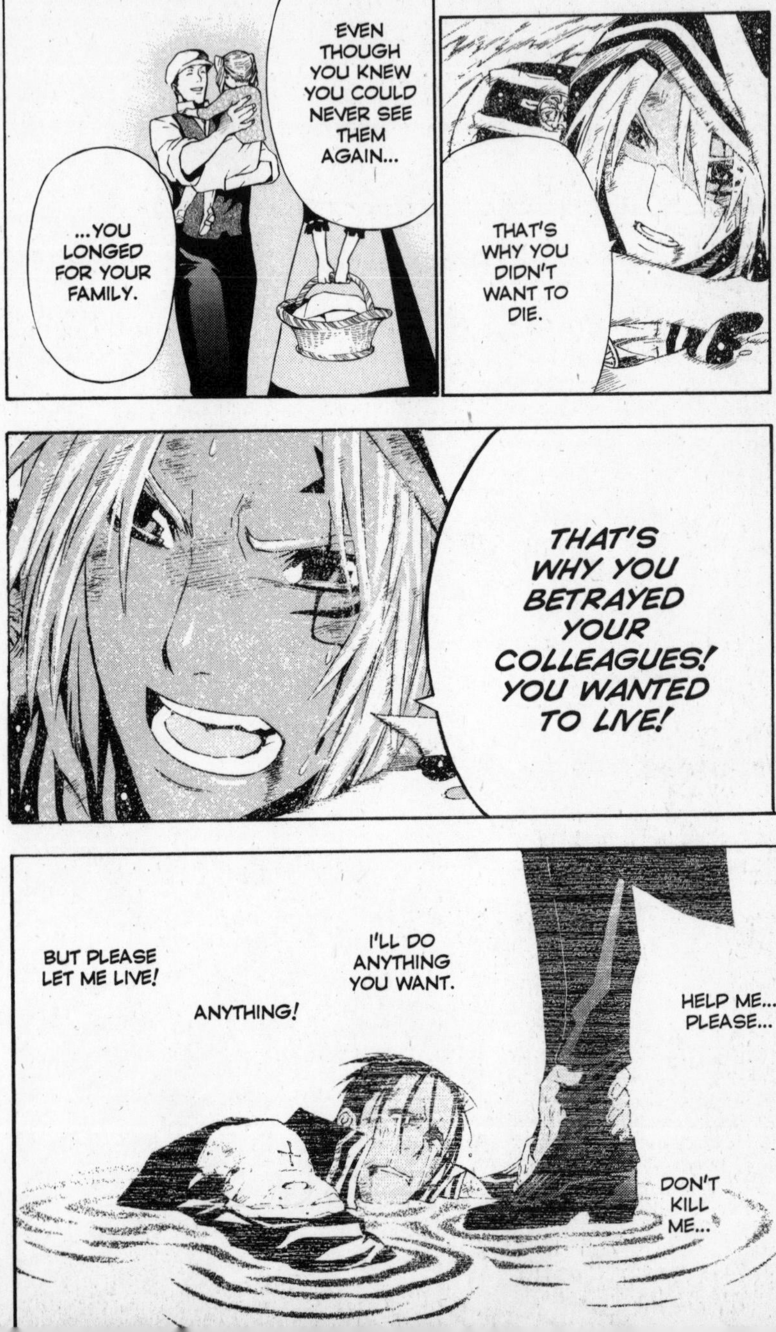
EVEN THOUGH YOU KNEW YOU COULD NEVER SEE THEM AGAIN...
...YOU LONGED FOR YOUR FAMILY.
THAT'S WHY YOU DIDN'T WANT TO DIE.
THAT'S WHY YOU BETRAYED YOUR COLLEAGUES! YOU WANTED TO LIVE!
HELP ME... PLEASE...
DON'T KILL ME...
I'LL DO ANYTHING YOU WANT.
ANYTHING!
BUT PLEASE LET ME LIVE!

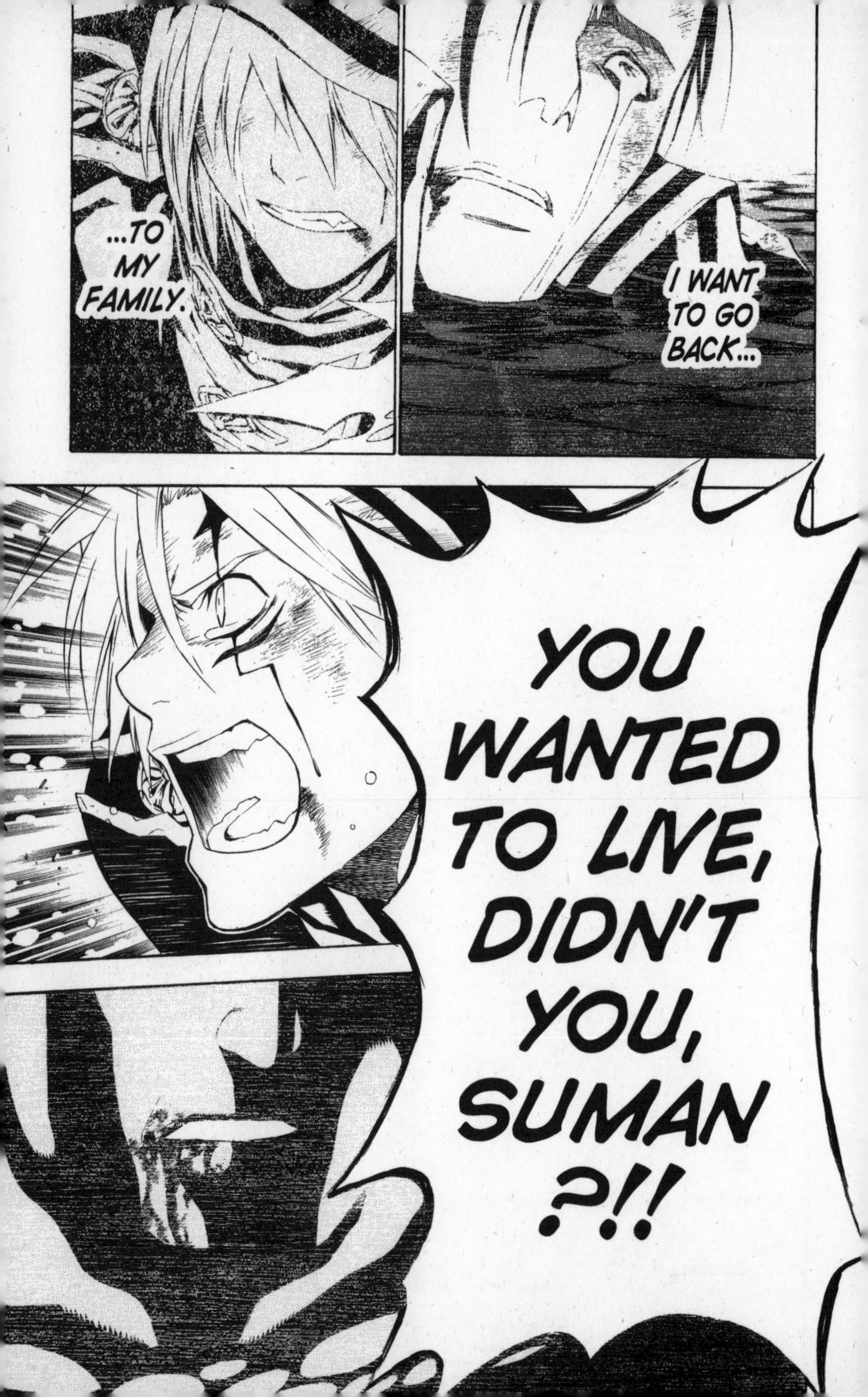
I WANT TO GO BACK...
...TO MY FAMILY.
YOU WANTED TO LIVE, DIDN'T YOU, SUMAN ?!!

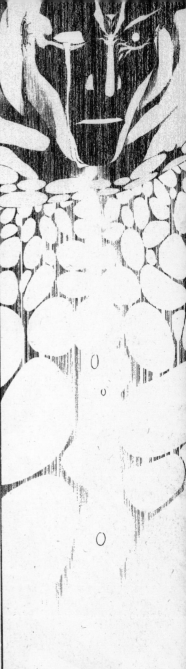

WHEN I WAS INSIDE OF SUMAN, I SAW A PARASITE-TYPE INNOCENCE IN HIS RIGHT ARM.

I'LL HAVE TO SEVER HIS ARM TO REMOVE IT.

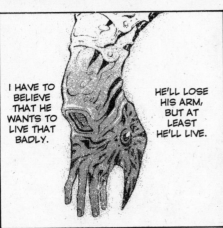

HE'LL LOSE HIS ARM, BUT AT LEAST HE'LL LIVE.

I HAVE TO BELIEVE THAT HE WANTS TO LIVE THAT BADLY.

IT'S THE ONLY WAY.

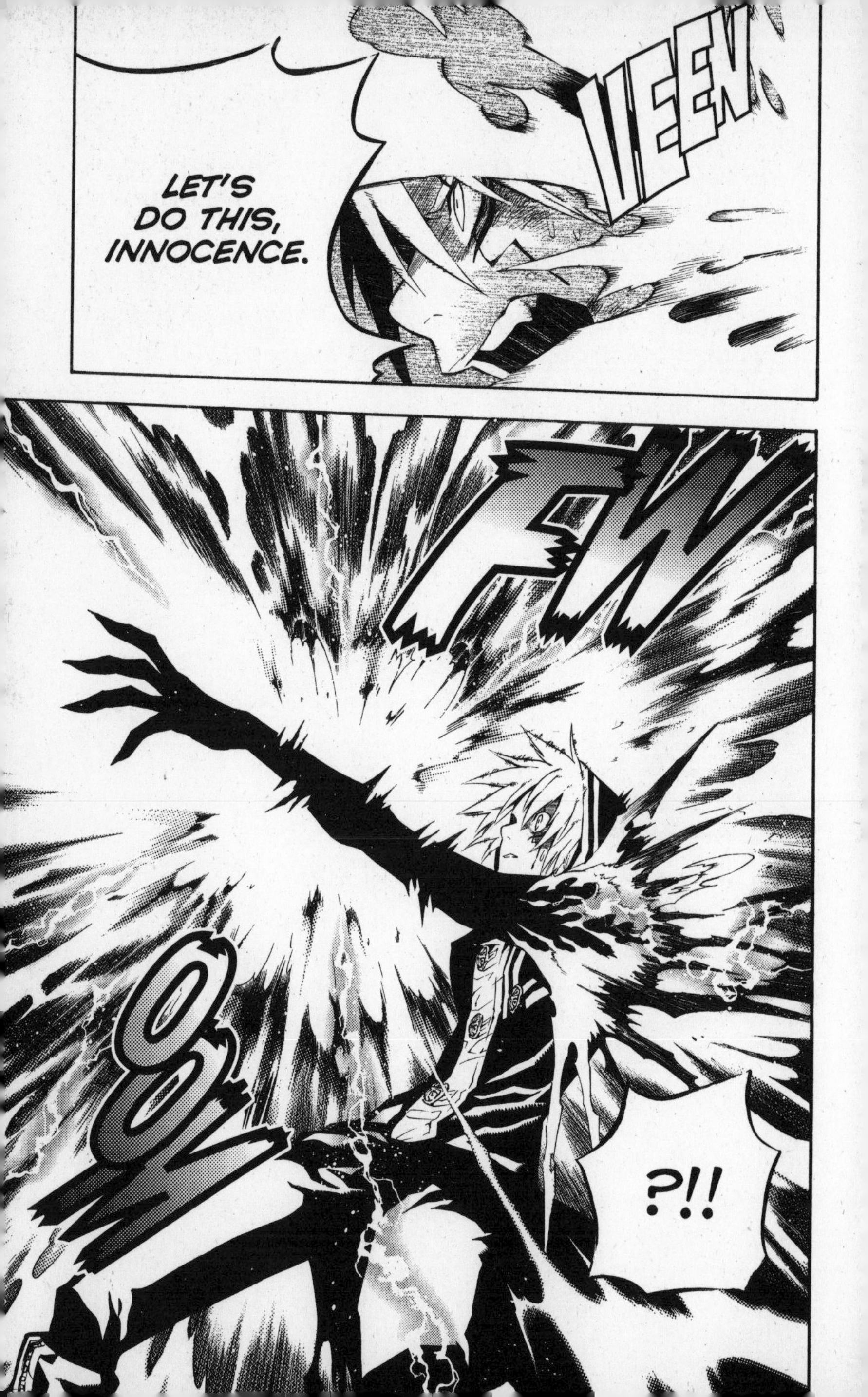
VEEN
LET'S DO THIS, INNOCENCE.
?!!

THE STORY OF THE FALLEN ONE TURNED OUT TO BE VERY TRAGIC. DRAWING IT TOOK A HEAVY TOLL ON ME EMOTIONALLY. HOWEVER, THIS ISN'T THE STORY OF A TRAITOR, BUT OF A MAN WHO LOVED HIS FAMILY MORE THAN ANYTHING, A MAN WHO WAS FORCED TO MAKE TERRIBLE CHOICES. DON'T HATE SUMAN, PITY HIM.

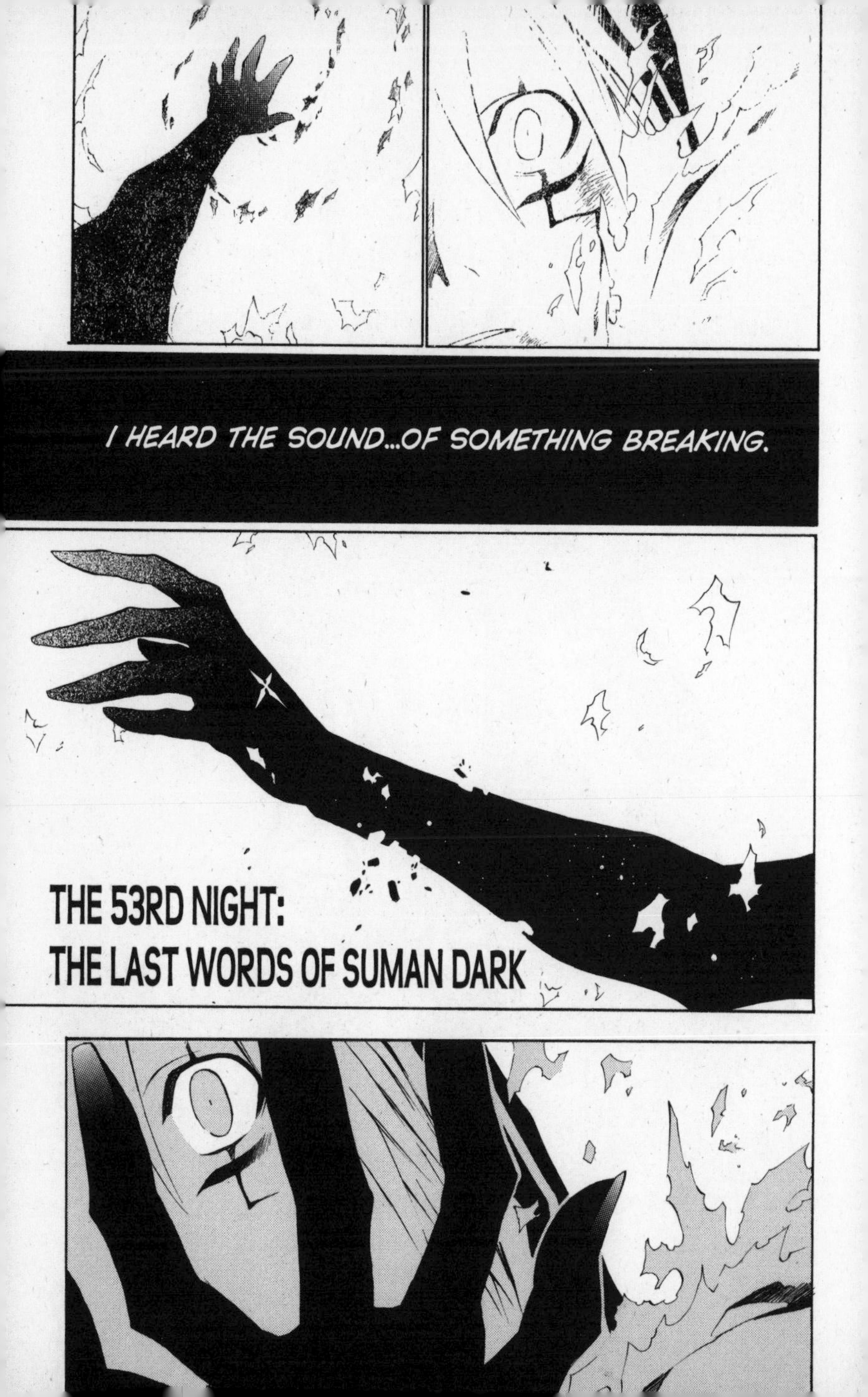
I HEARD THE SOUND...OF SOMETHING BREAKING.
THE 53RD NIGHT:
THE LAST WORDS OF SUMAN DARK

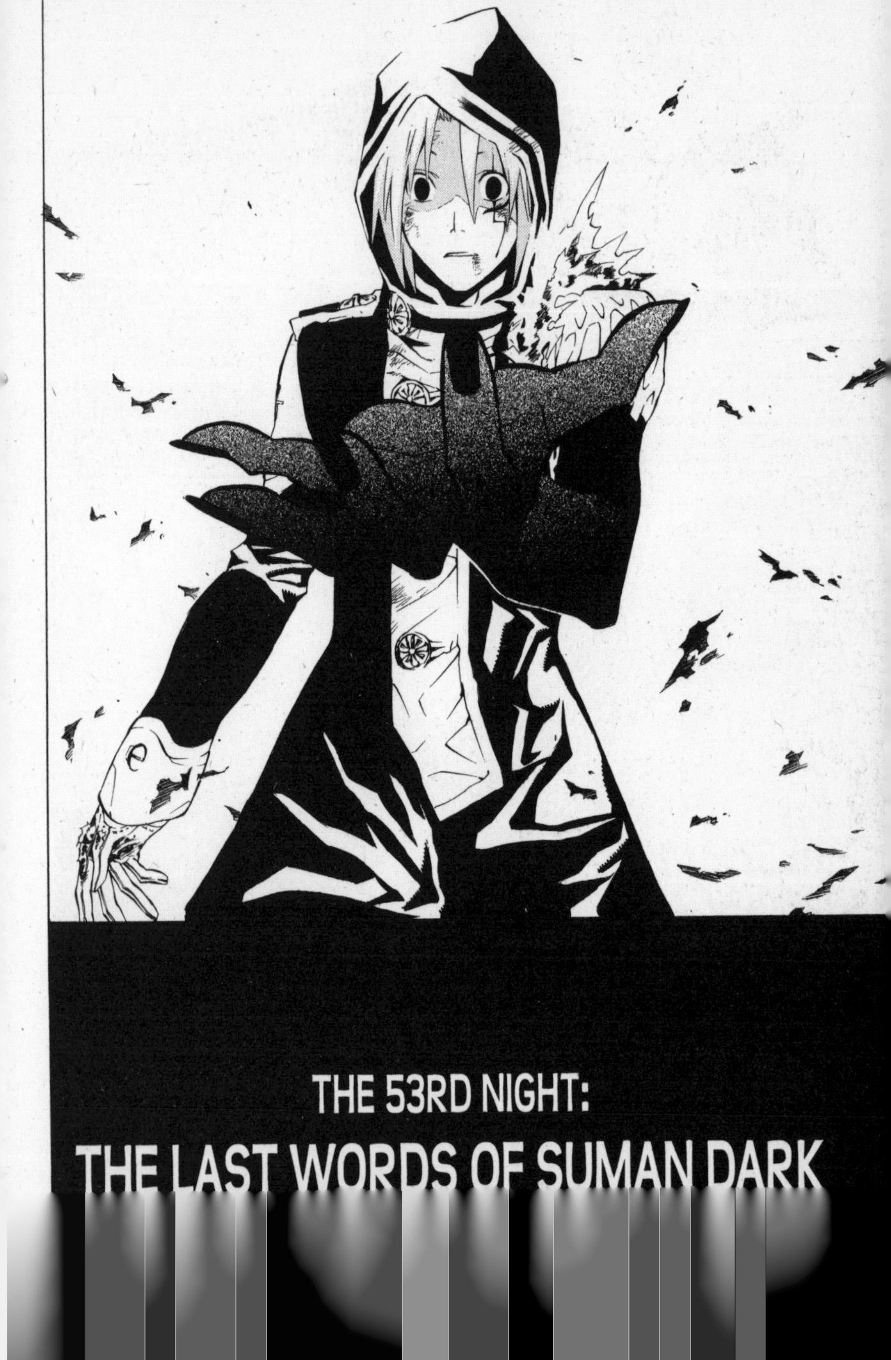

THE 53RD NIGHT:
THE LAST WORDS OF SUMAN DARK

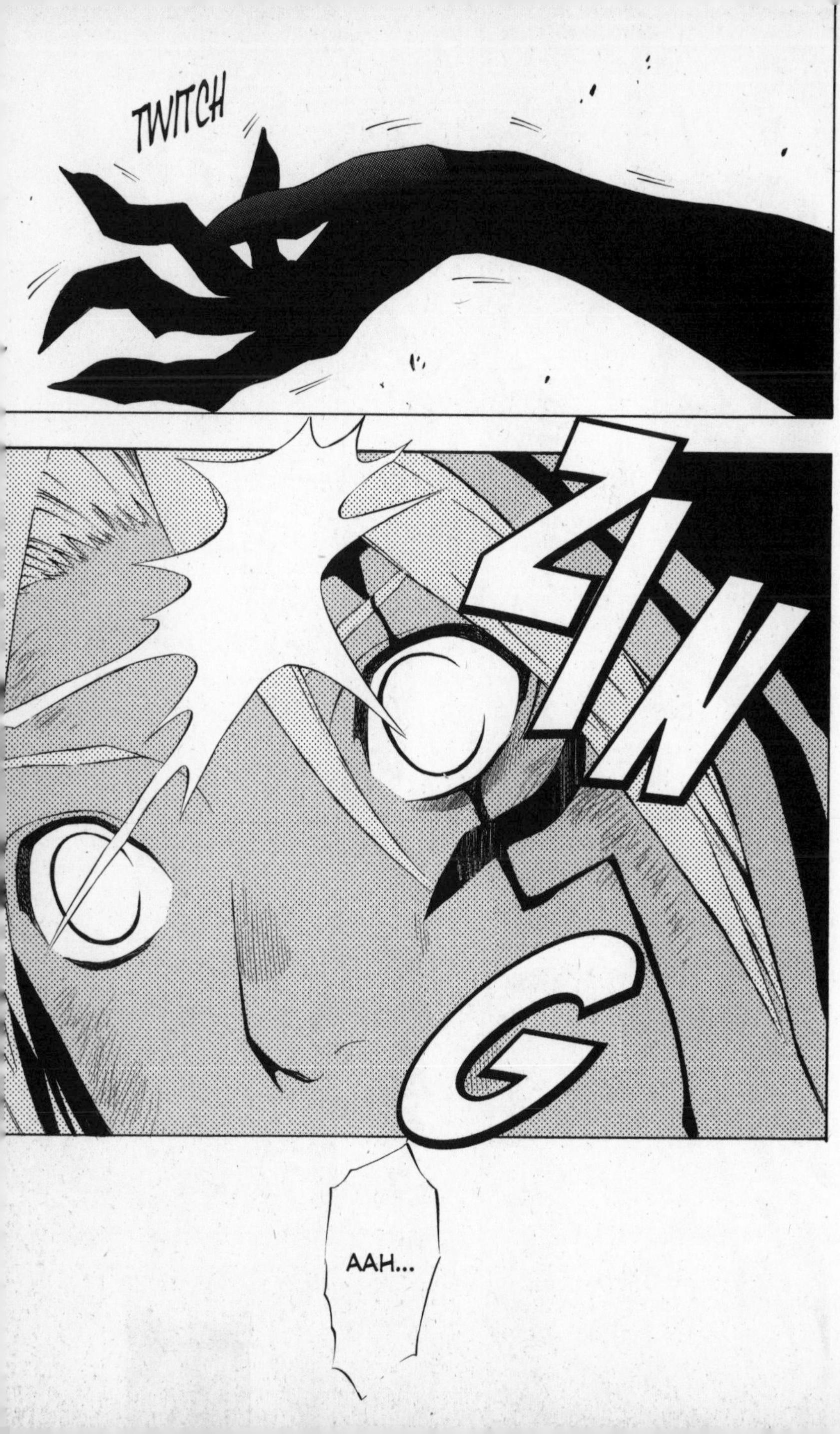
TWITCH
ZING
AAH...

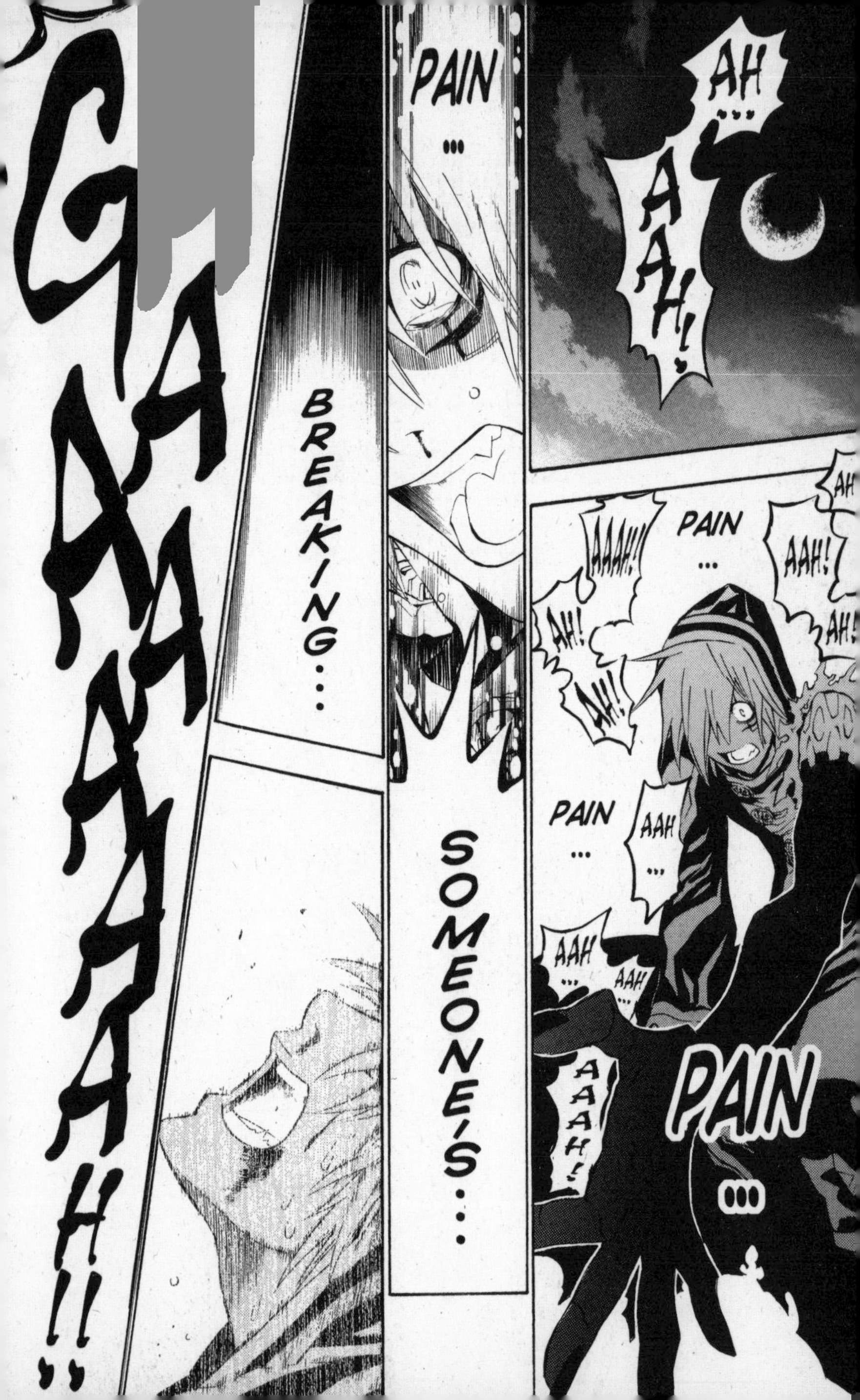
AH... AAAH!
AH
AAH!
AH!
PAIN...
AAAH!!
AH!
AH!!
AAH...
PAIN...
AAH...
AAH...
AAAAH!
PAIN...
PAIN...
SOMEONE'S...
BREAKING...
GAAAAAAH!!

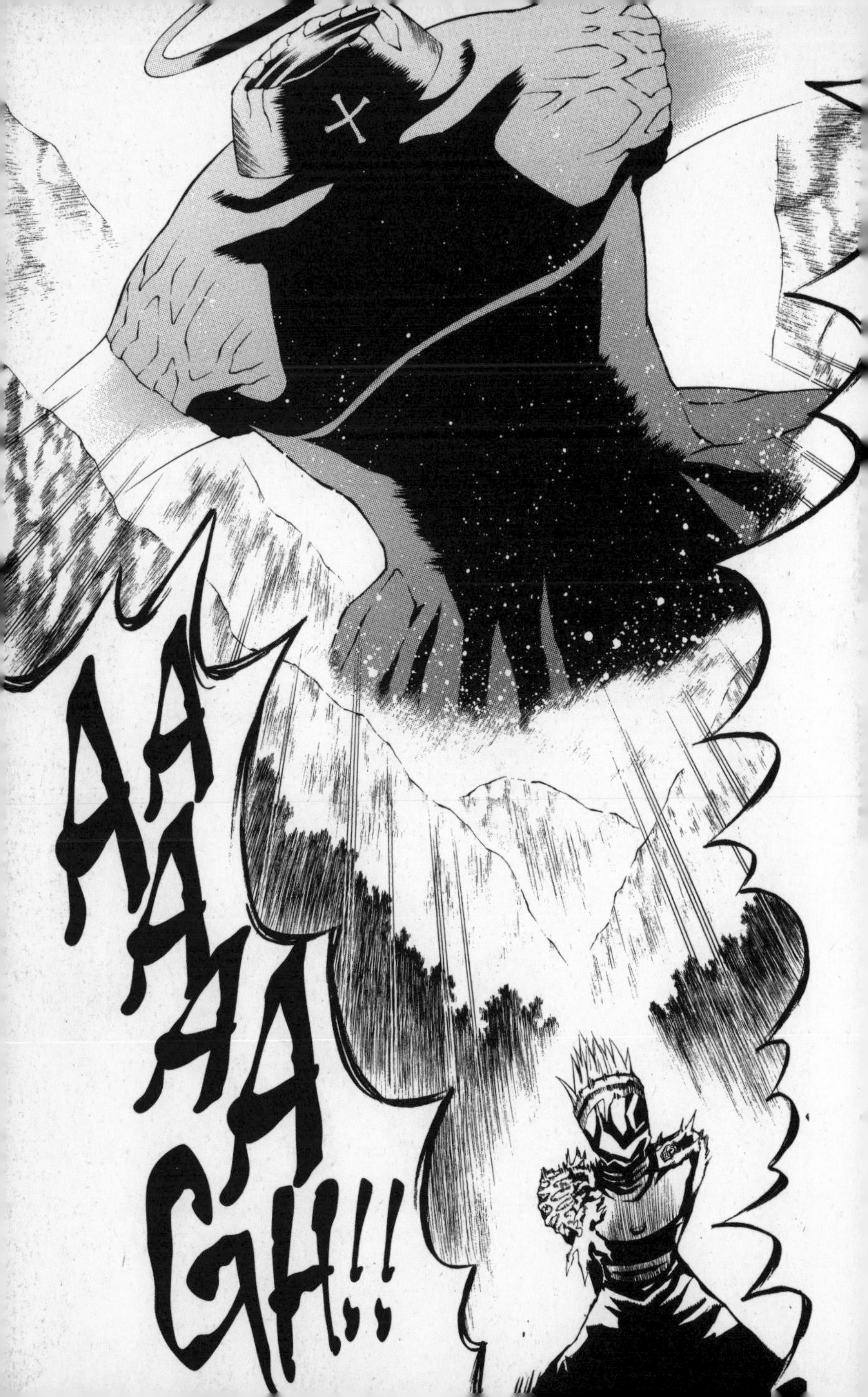
AAAAAGH!!

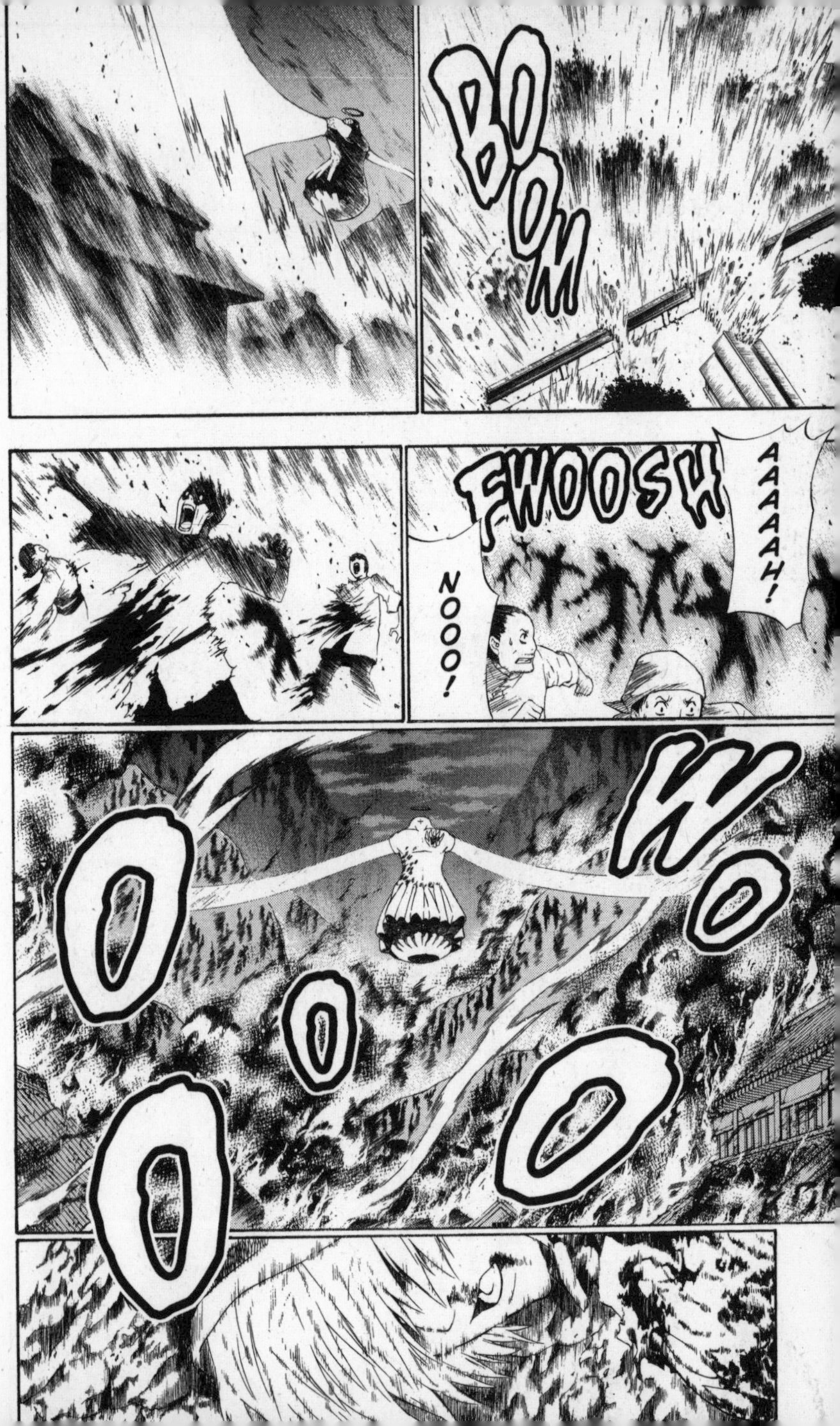
BOOOM
AAAAAH!
FWOOSH
NOOOO!
WOOOOO

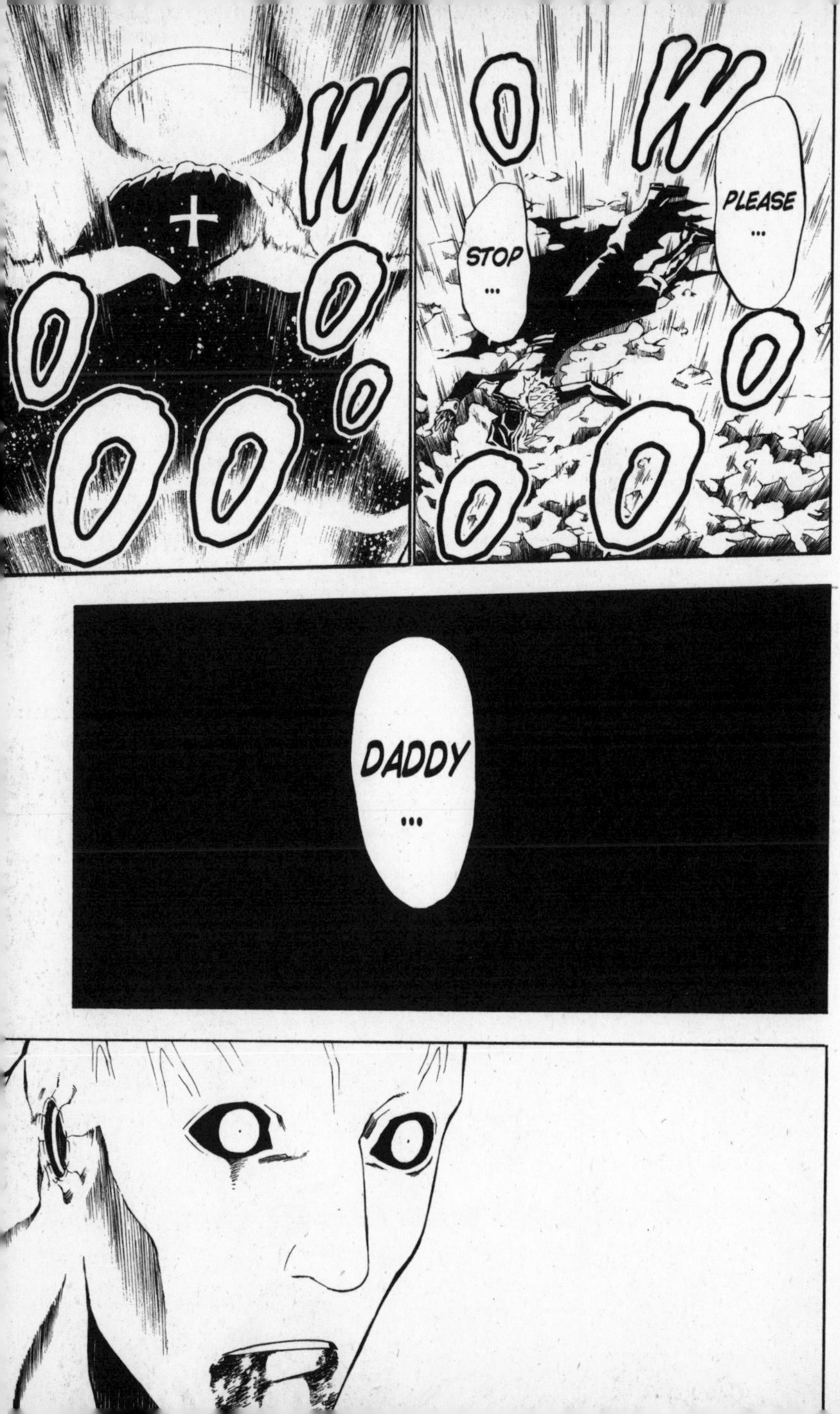
PLEASE ...
STOP ...
WOOOO
WOOOOOO
DADDY ...

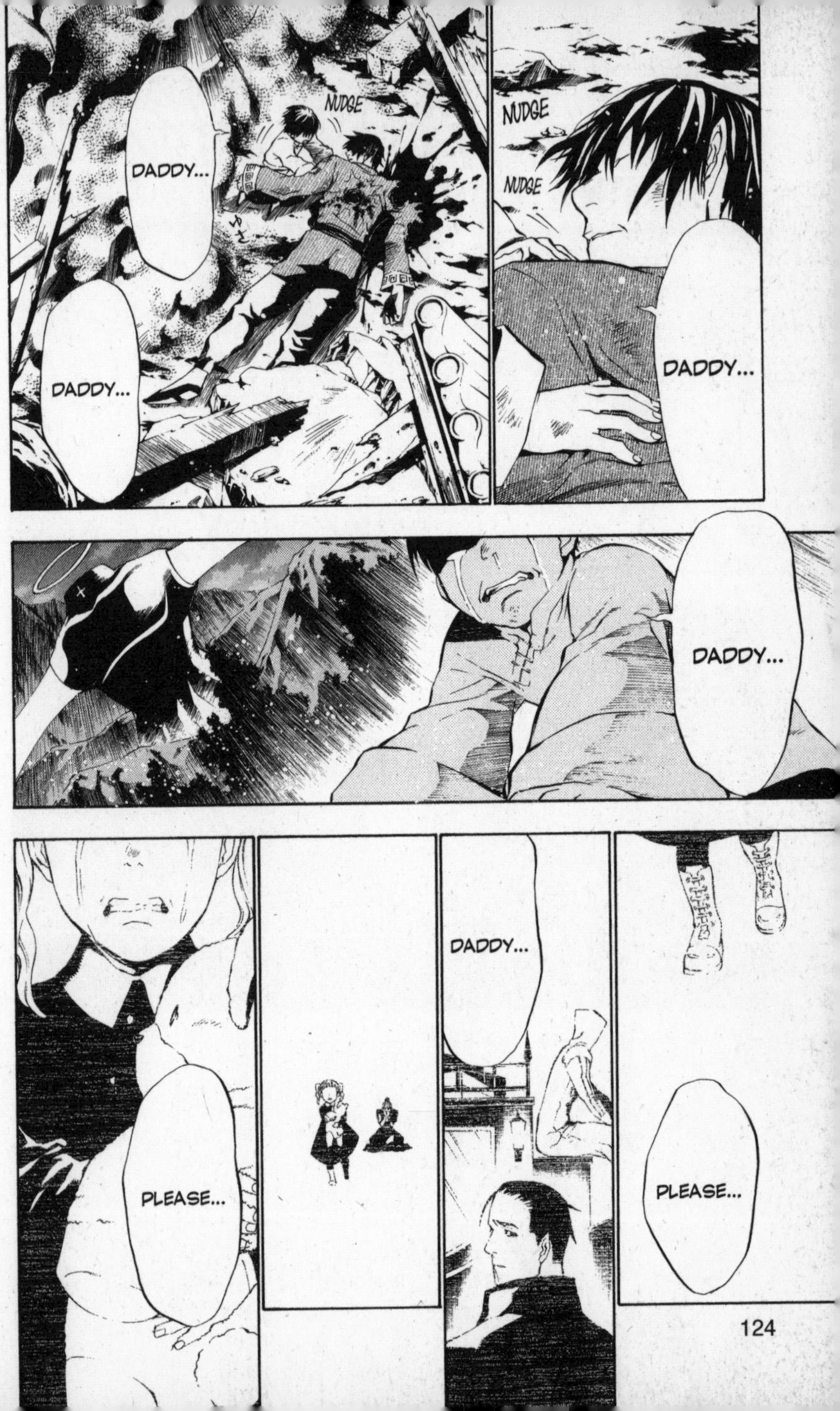
NUDGE
NUDGE
DADDY...
NUDGE
DADDY...
DADDY...
DADDY...
PLEASE...
DADDY...
PLEASE...

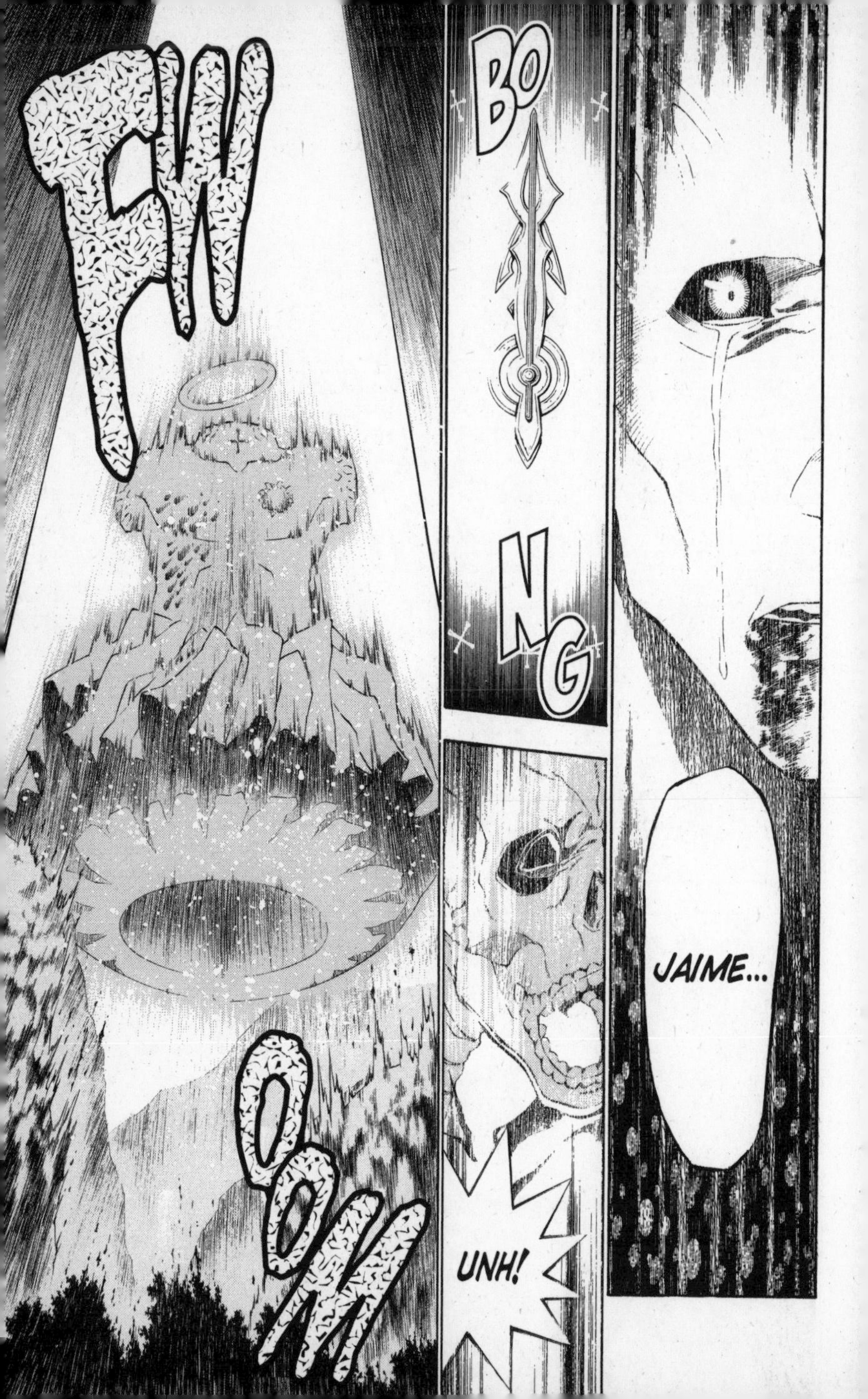
JAIME...
BONG
UNH!
FWOOM

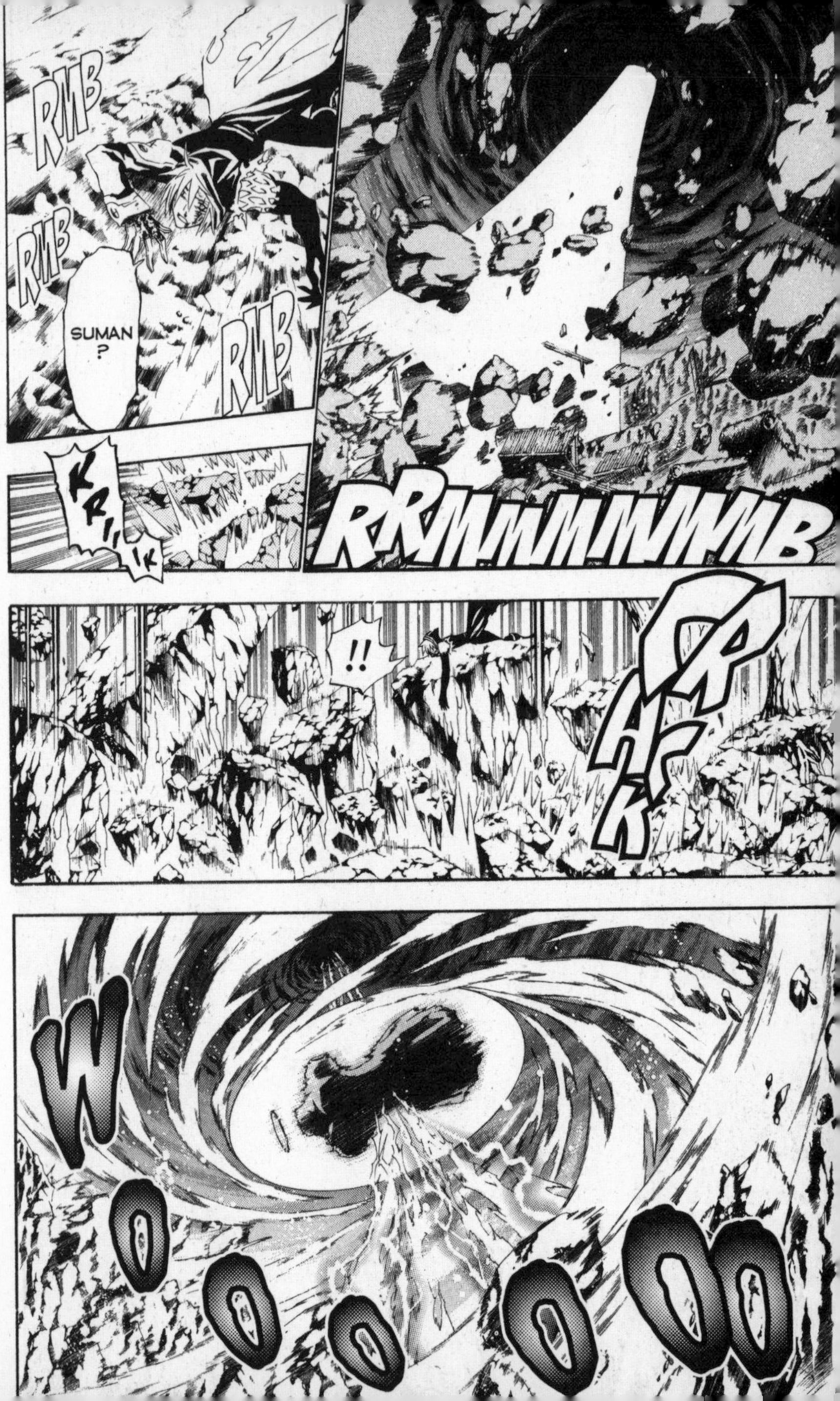
RRMMMMMMMB
RMB
RMB
SUMAN ?
RMB
KRIIIK
!!
CRACK
WOOOOOOOO

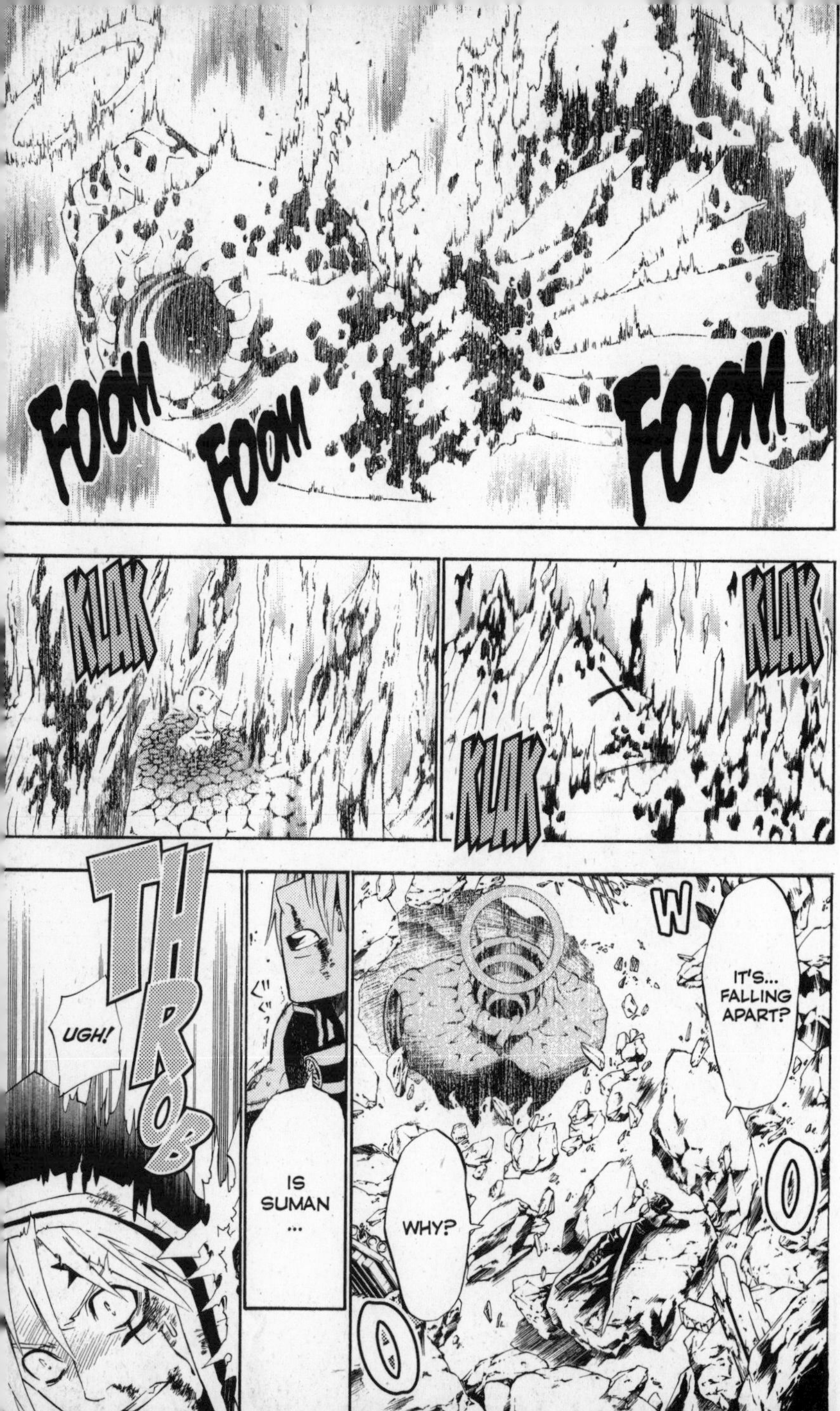
FOOM
FOOM
FOOM
KLAK
KLAK
KLAK
W
IT'S... FALLING APART?
WHY?
IS SUMAN ...
THROB
UGH!

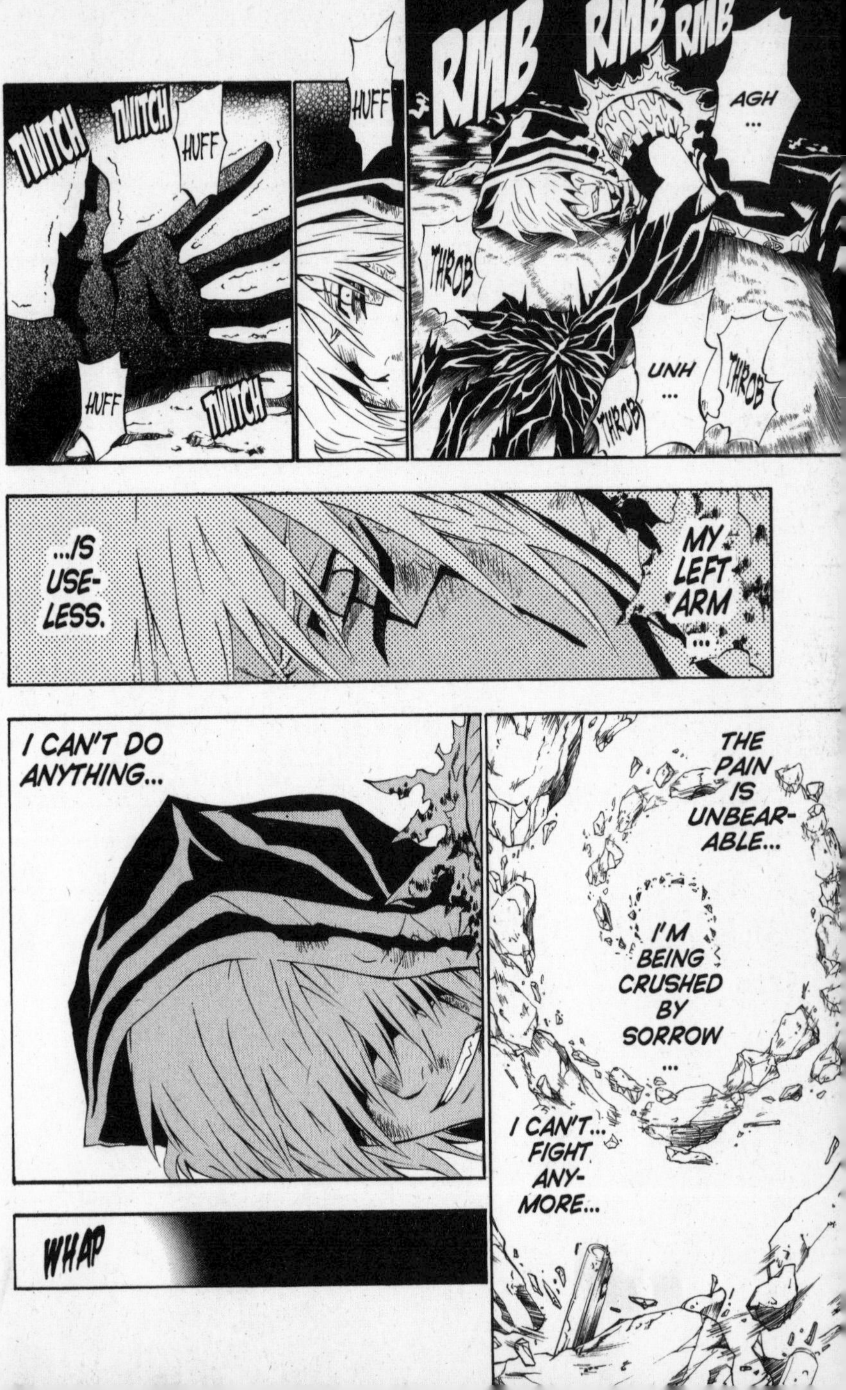
RMB RMB RMB
AGH...
THROB
UNH...
THROB
THROB
HUFF
TWITCH
TWITCH
HUFF
HUFF
TWITCH
MY LEFT ARM...
...IS USE-LESS.
THE PAIN IS UNBEAR-ABLE...
I'M BEING CRUSHED BY SORROW...
I CAN'T... FIGHT ANY-MORE...
I CAN'T DO ANYTHING...
WHAP

WHAP

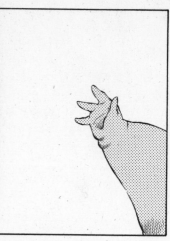

--CANPY...

TIM--

WHAT ARE YOU...

WHUP

PLURT

BLEEDING

YOWWW!!!

CHONK

WHOOM

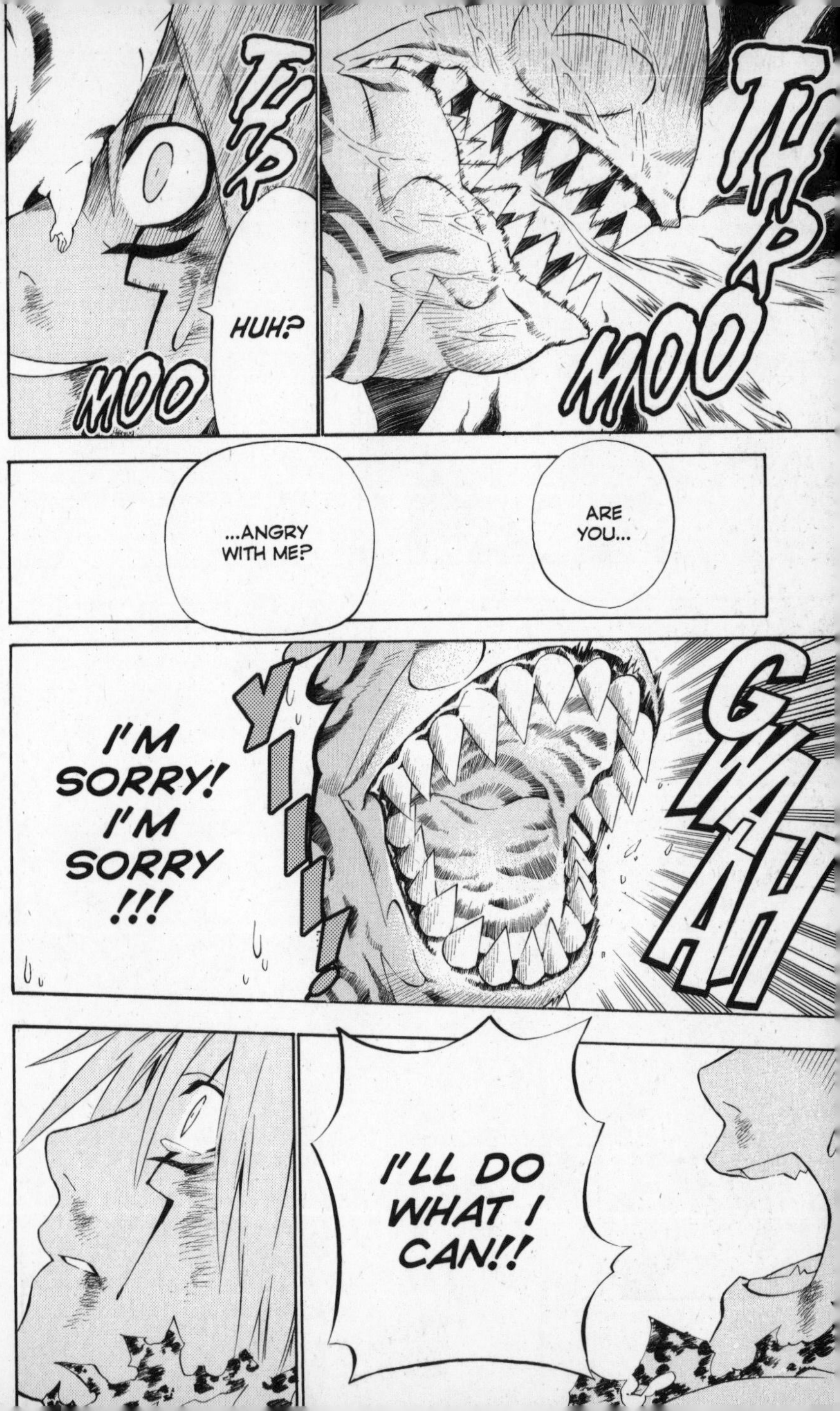
THR
MOO
THR
HUH?
MOO
ARE YOU...
...ANGRY WITH ME?
GWAAH
I'M SORRY! I'M SORRY!!!
I'LL DO WHAT I CAN!!

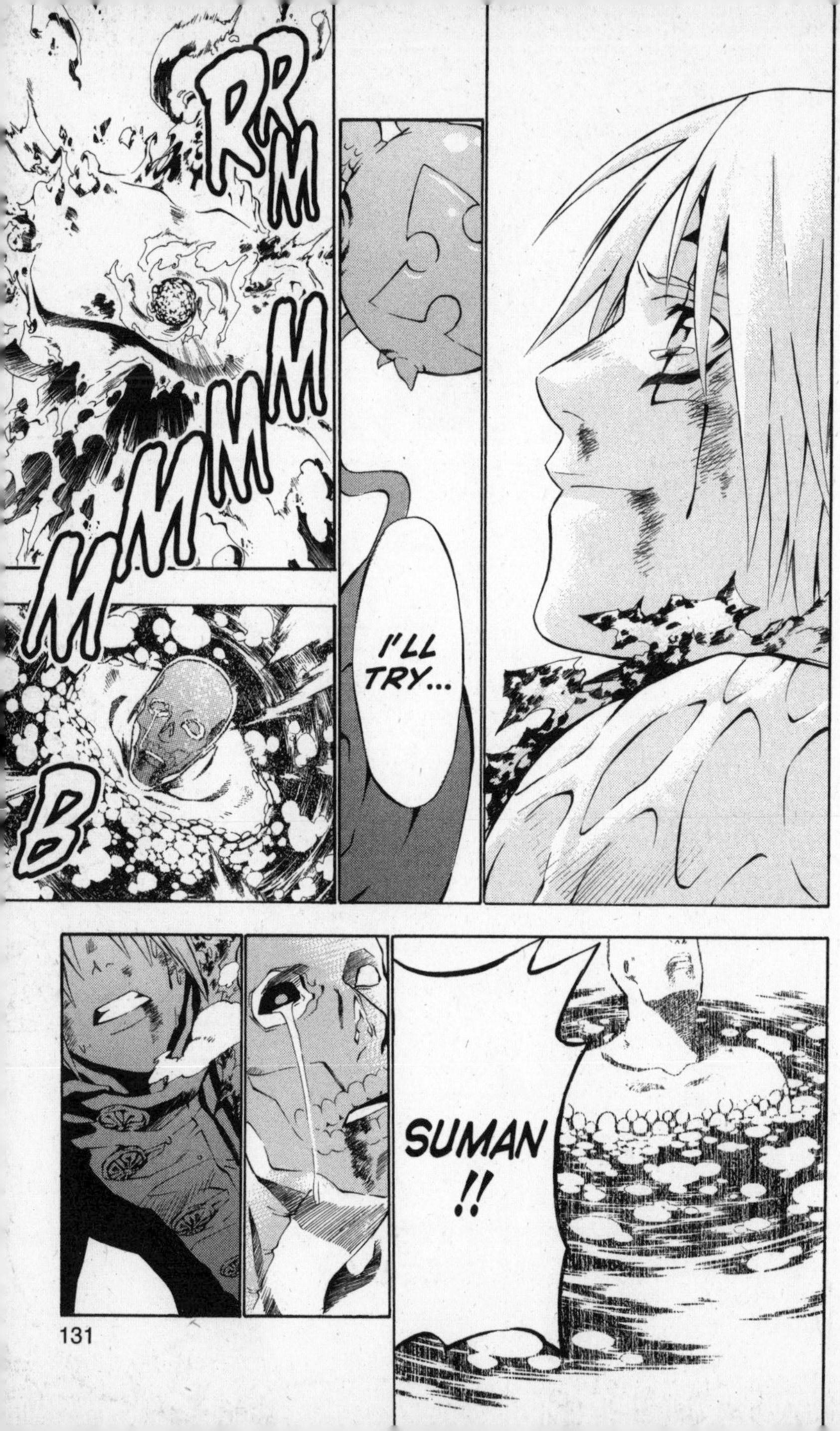
I'LL TRY...
RRMMMMMMB
SUMAN!!

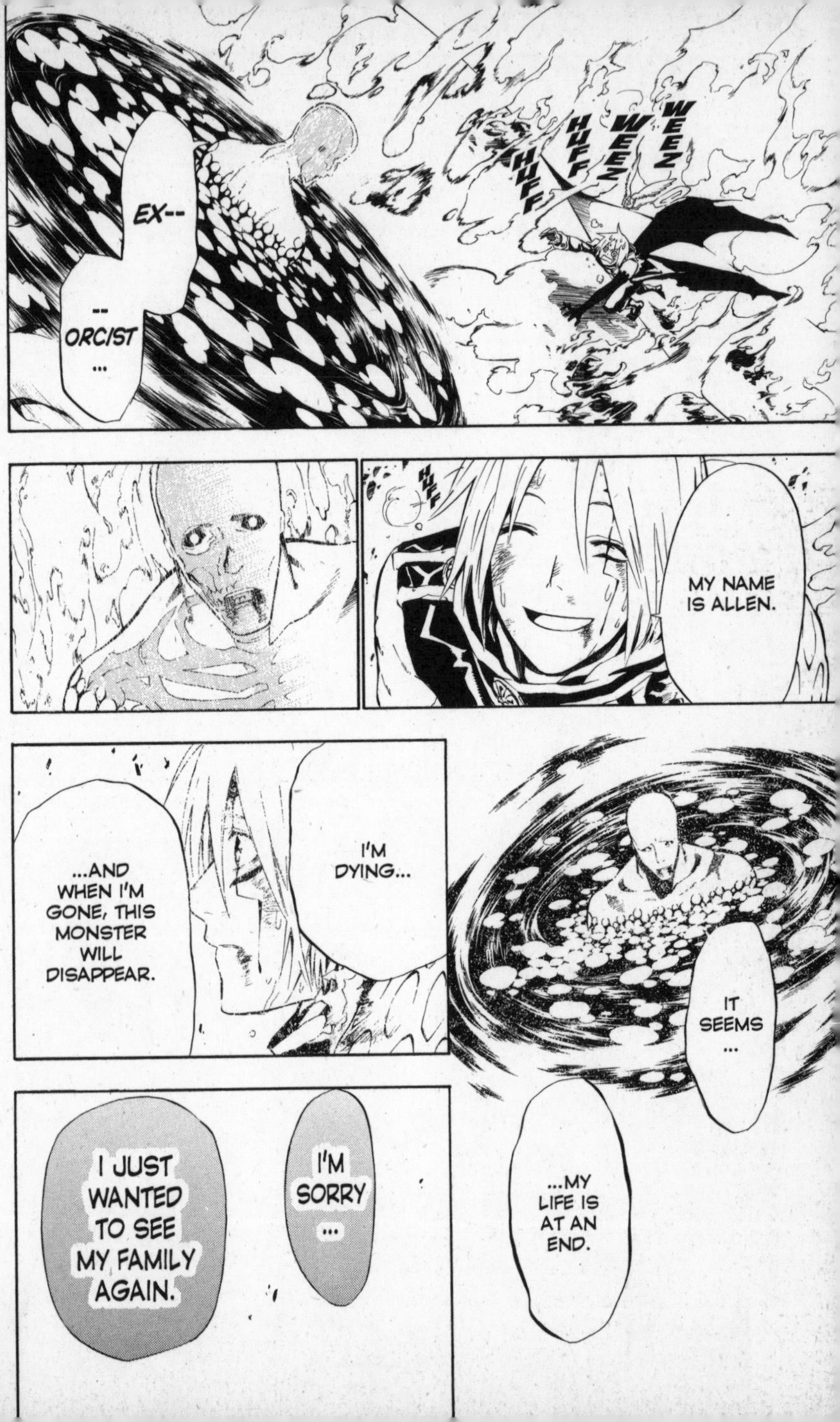
WEEZ
WEEZ
HUFF
HUFF
EX--
-- ORCIST ...
HUFF
MY NAME IS ALLEN.
IT SEEMS ...
...MY LIFE IS AT AN END.
I'M DYING...
...AND WHEN I'M GONE, THIS MONSTER WILL DISAPPEAR.
I'M SORRY ...
I JUST WANTED TO SEE MY FAMILY AGAIN.

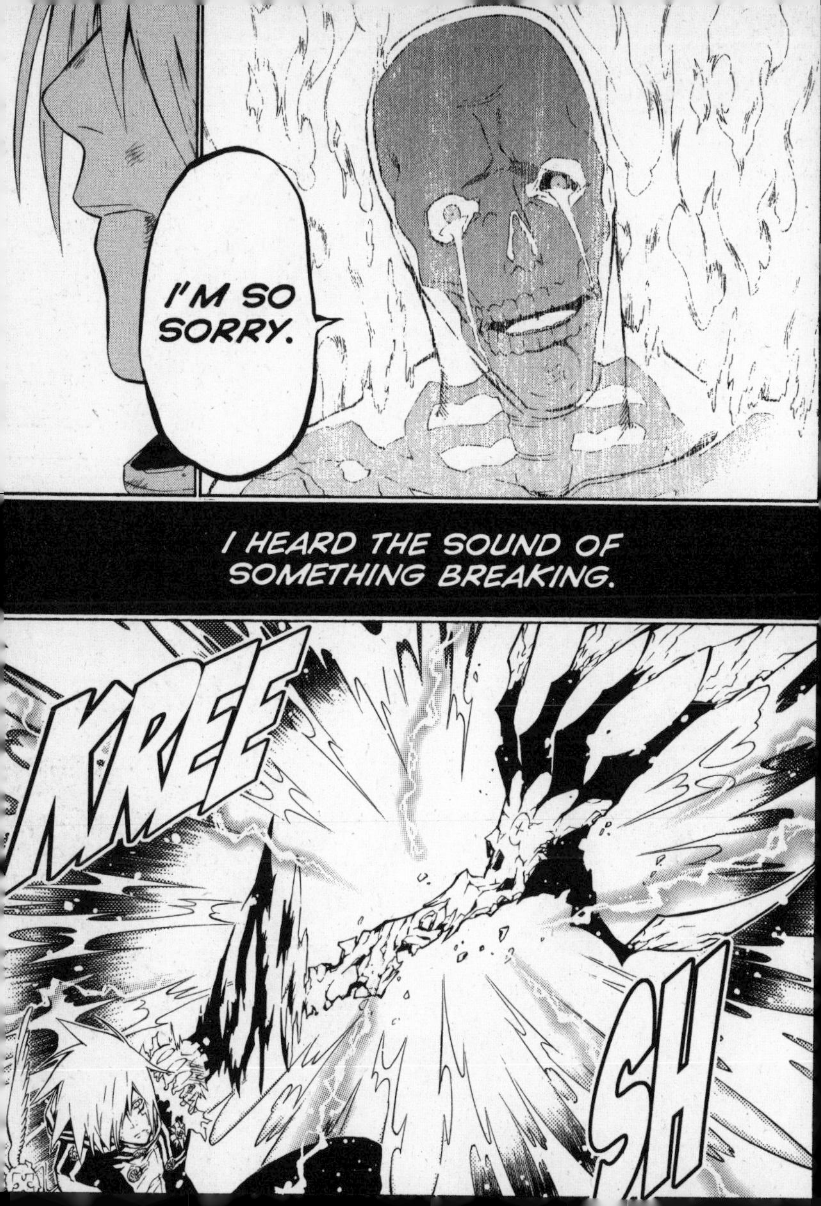
I'M SO SORRY.
I HEARD THE SOUND OF SOMETHING BREAKING.
KREE
SH

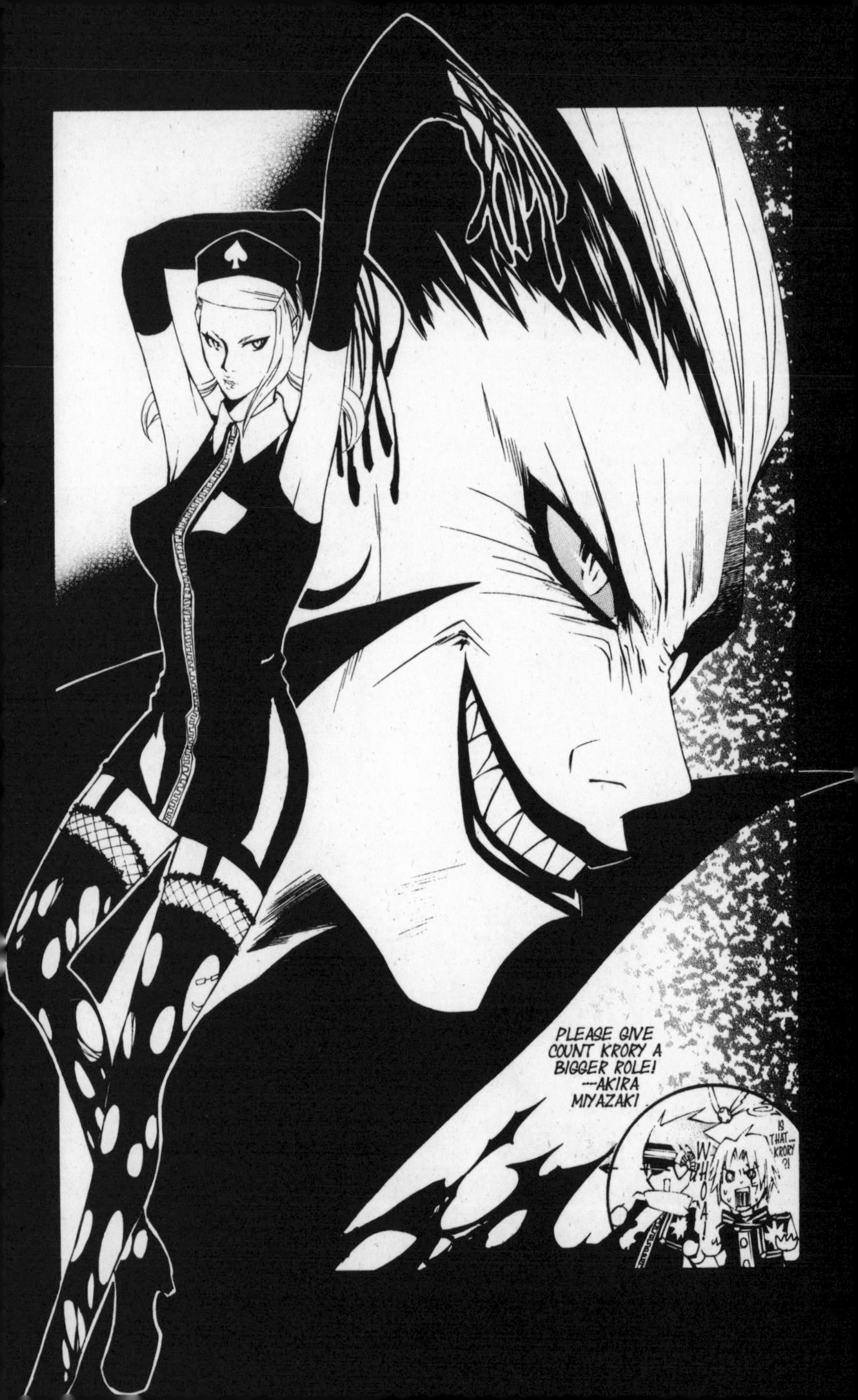
PLEASE GIVE COUNT KRORY A BIGGER ROLE! --AKIRA MIYAZAKI
IS THAT... KRORY ?!
WHOA!

THE 54TH NIGHT: REND ALLEN'S HEART

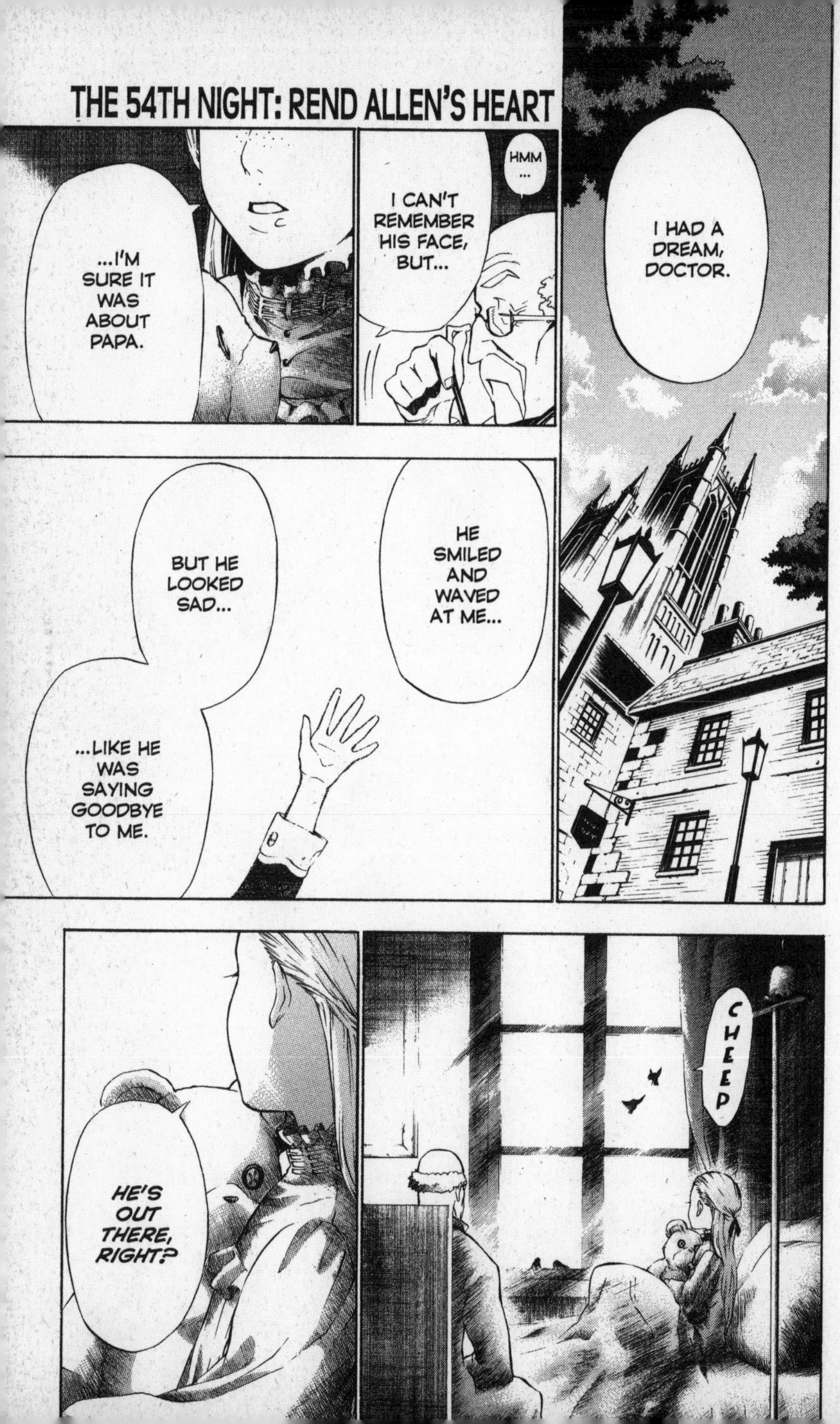
I HAD A DREAM, DOCTOR.
HMM...
I CAN'T REMEMBER HIS FACE, BUT...
...I'M SURE IT WAS ABOUT PAPA.
HE SMILED AND WAVED AT ME...
BUT HE LOOKED SAD...
...LIKE HE WAS SAYING GOODBYE TO ME.
CHEEP
HE'S OUT THERE, RIGHT?

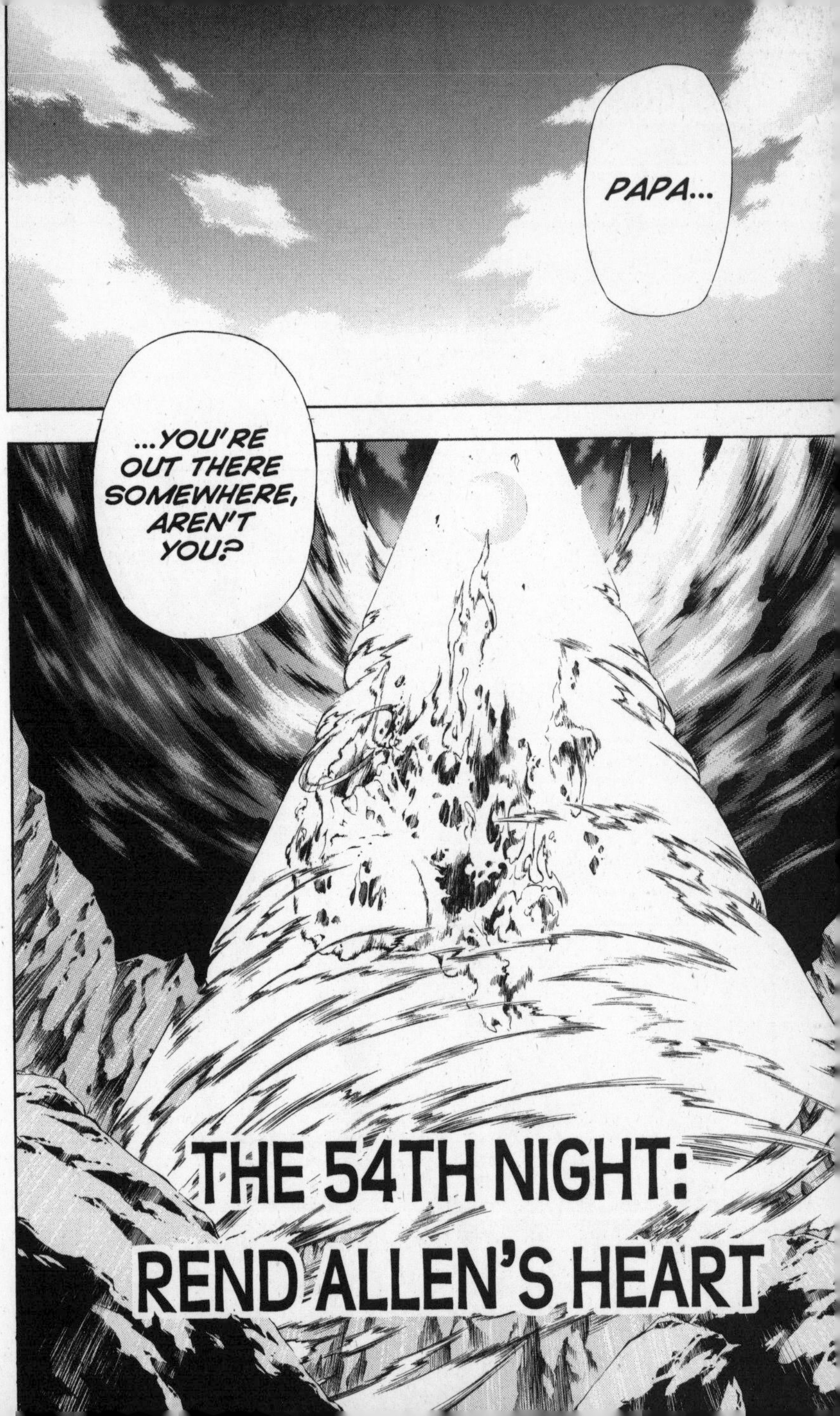
PAPA...
...YOU'RE OUT THERE SOMEWHERE, AREN'T YOU?
THE 54TH NIGHT: REND ALLEN'S HEART

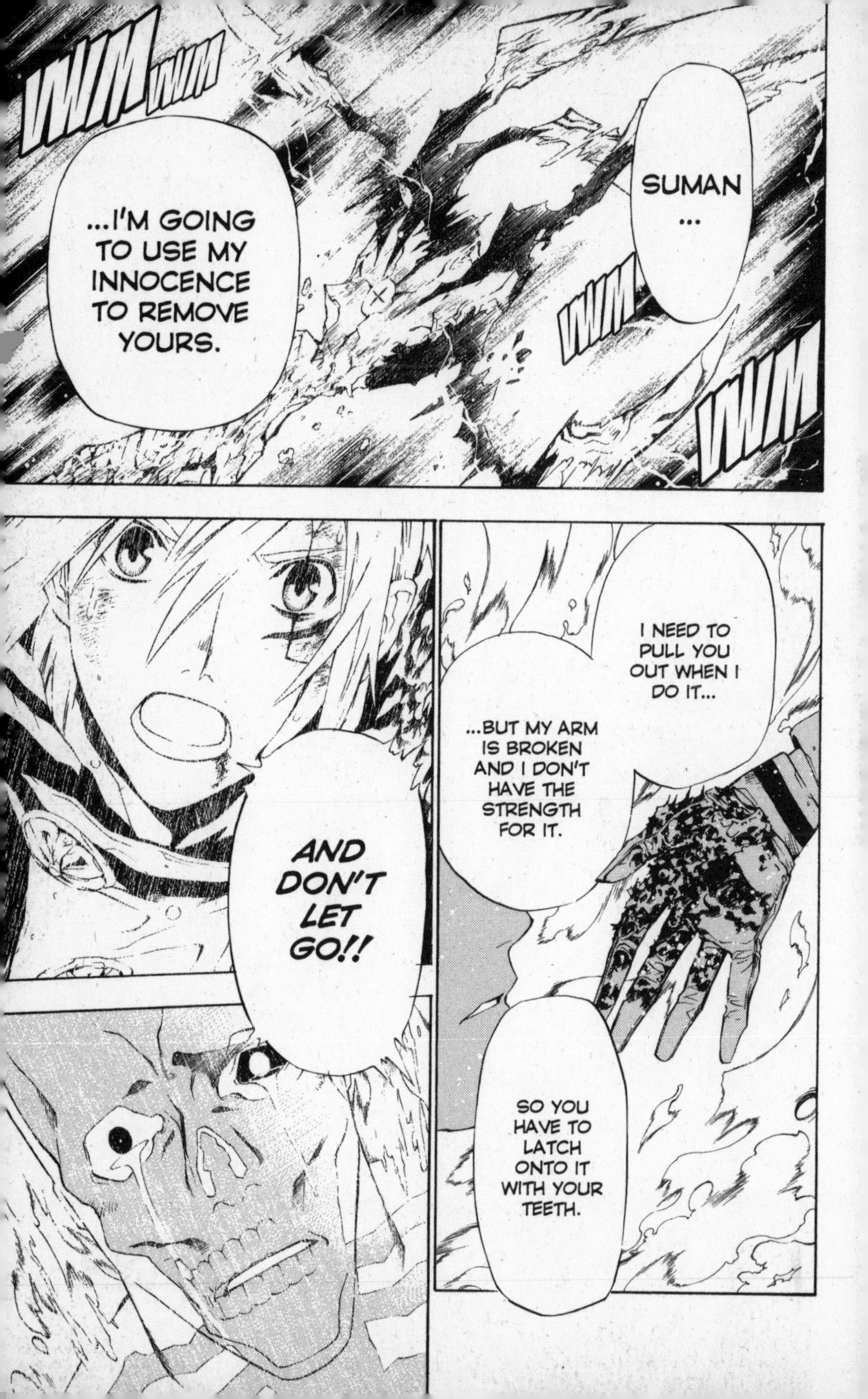
SUMAN ...
VWM
VWM
VWM VWM
...I'M GOING TO USE MY INNOCENCE TO REMOVE YOURS.
I NEED TO PULL YOU OUT WHEN I DO IT...
...BUT MY ARM IS BROKEN AND I DON'T HAVE THE STRENGTH FOR IT.
SO YOU HAVE TO LATCH ONTO IT WITH YOUR TEETH.
AND DON'T LET GO!!

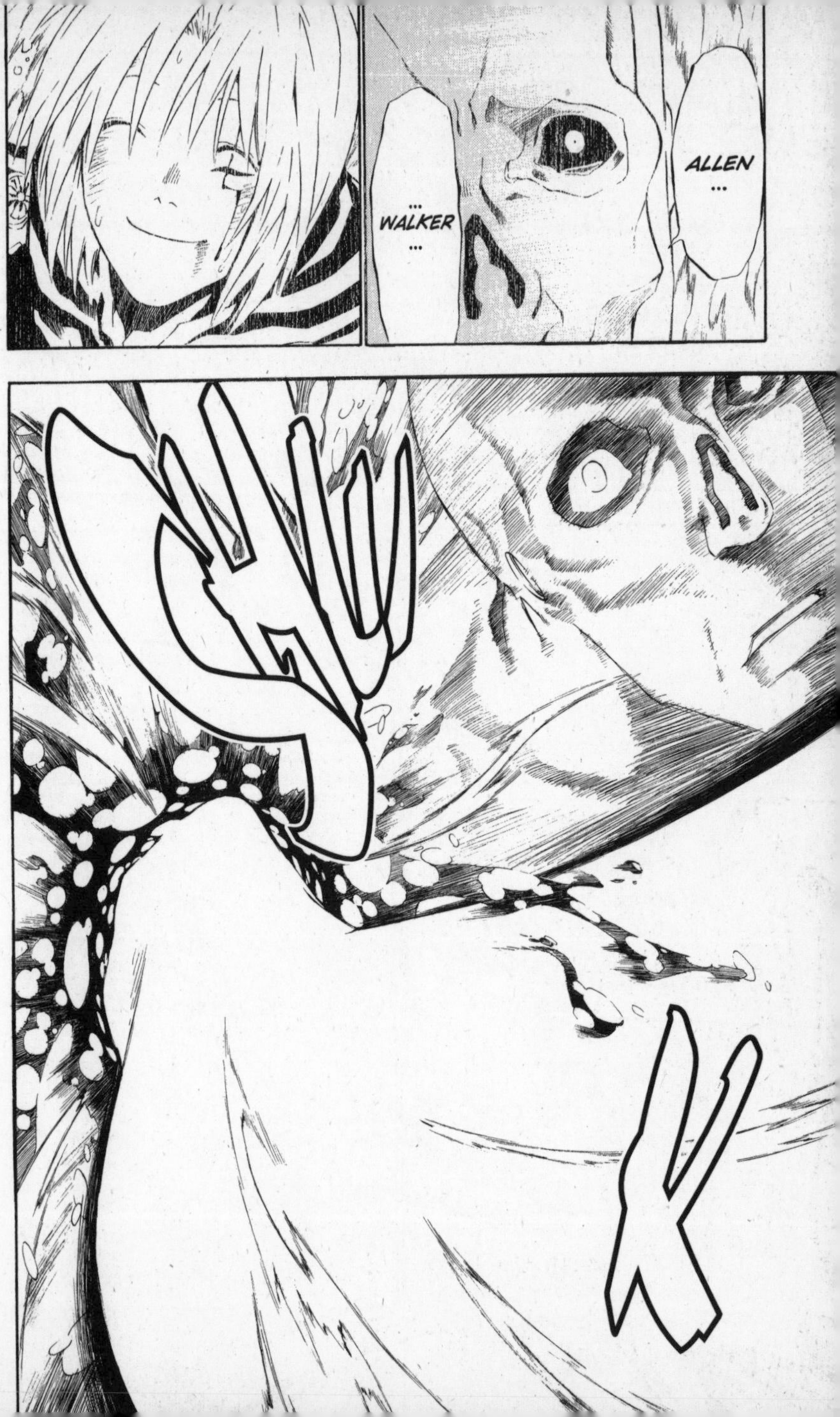
ALLEN ...
... WALKER ...

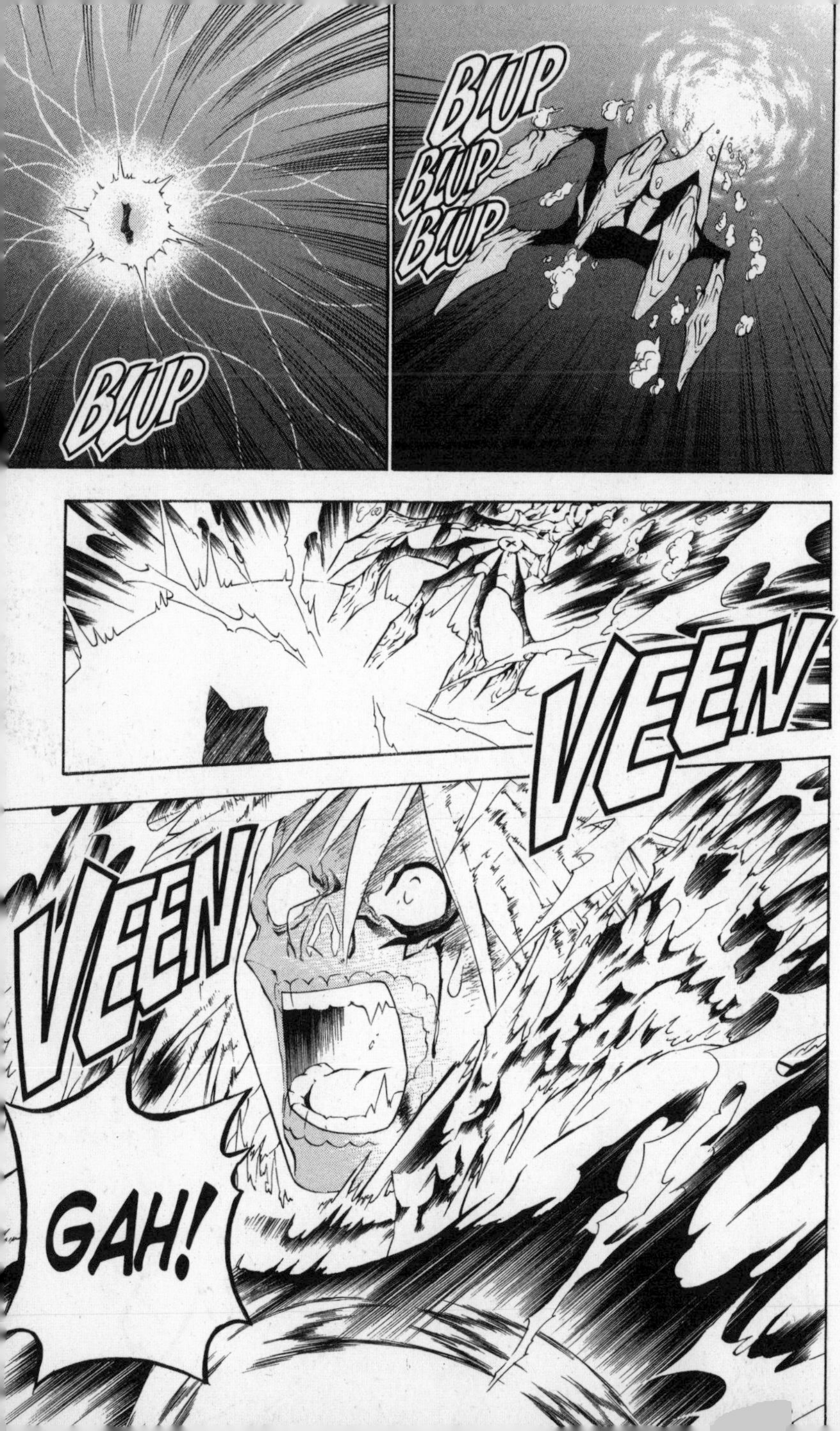
BLUP
BLUP
BLUP
BLUP
VEEN
VEEN
GAH!

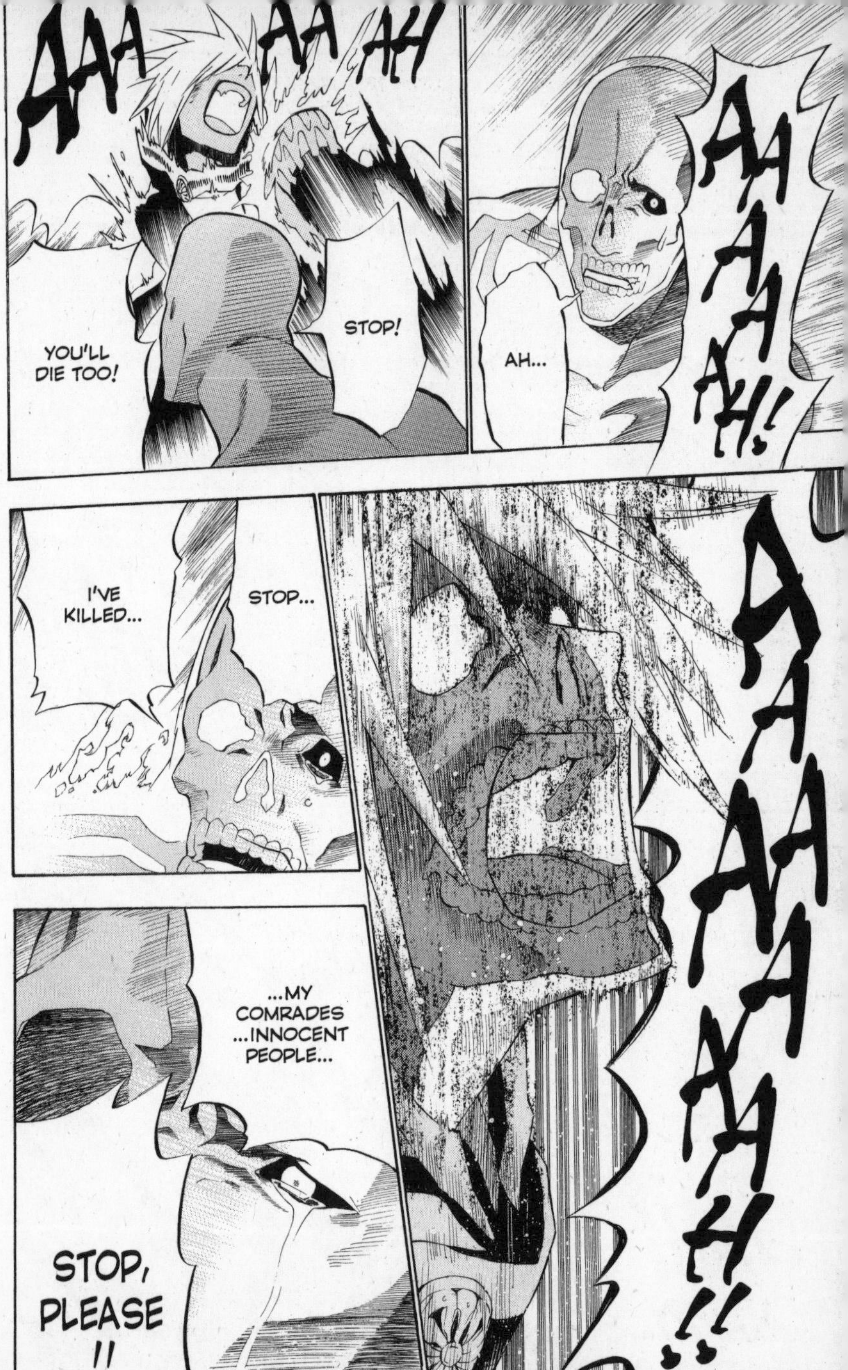
AH...
AAAAAH!
AAA AA AH
STOP!
YOU'LL DIE TOO!
AAAAAAAAH!!
STOP...
I'VE KILLED...
...MY COMRADES ...INNOCENT PEOPLE...
STOP, PLEASE!!

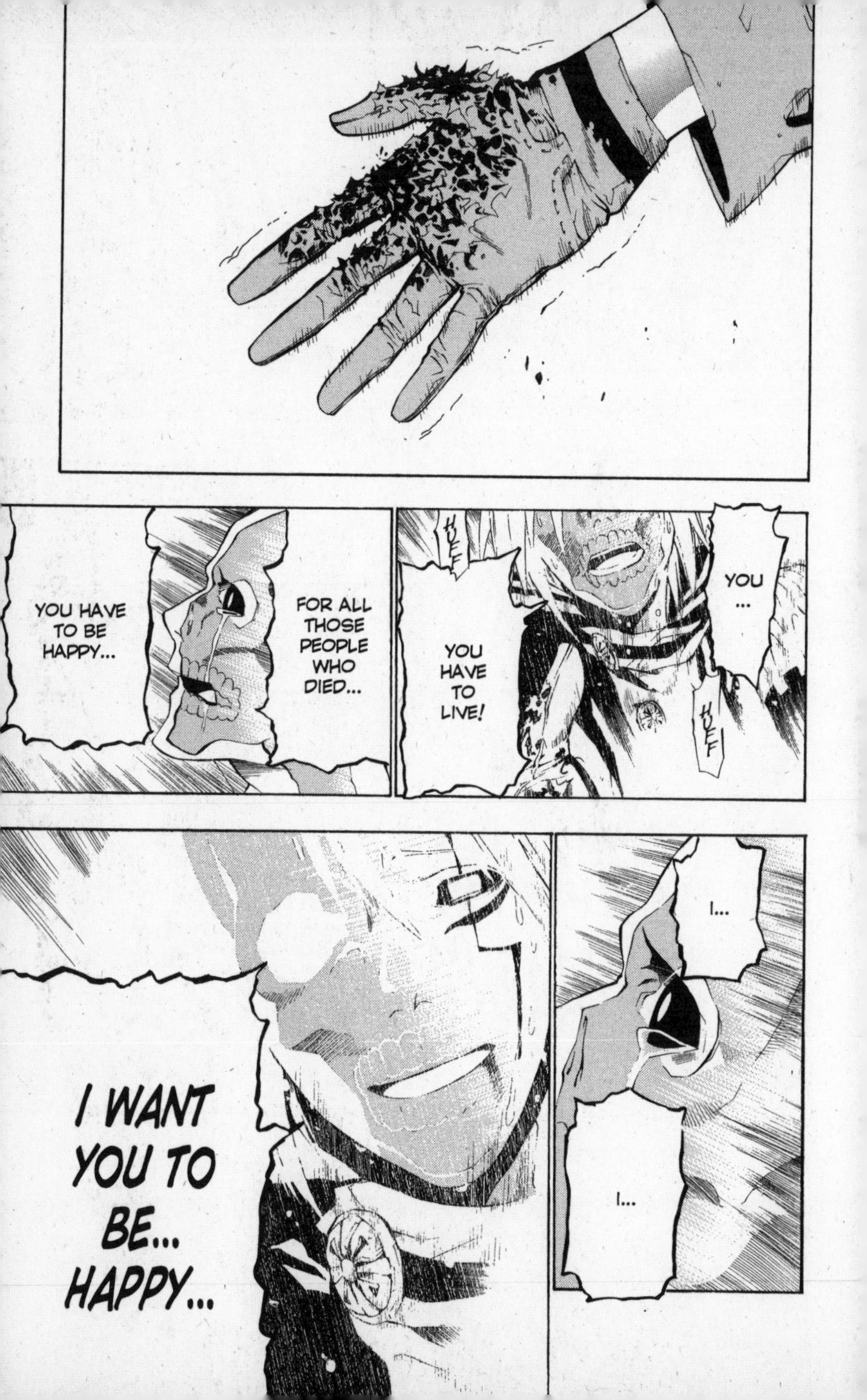
YOU ...
HUFF
YOU HAVE TO LIVE!
HUFF
FOR ALL THOSE PEOPLE WHO DIED...
YOU HAVE TO BE HAPPY...
I...
I...
I WANT YOU TO BE... HAPPY...

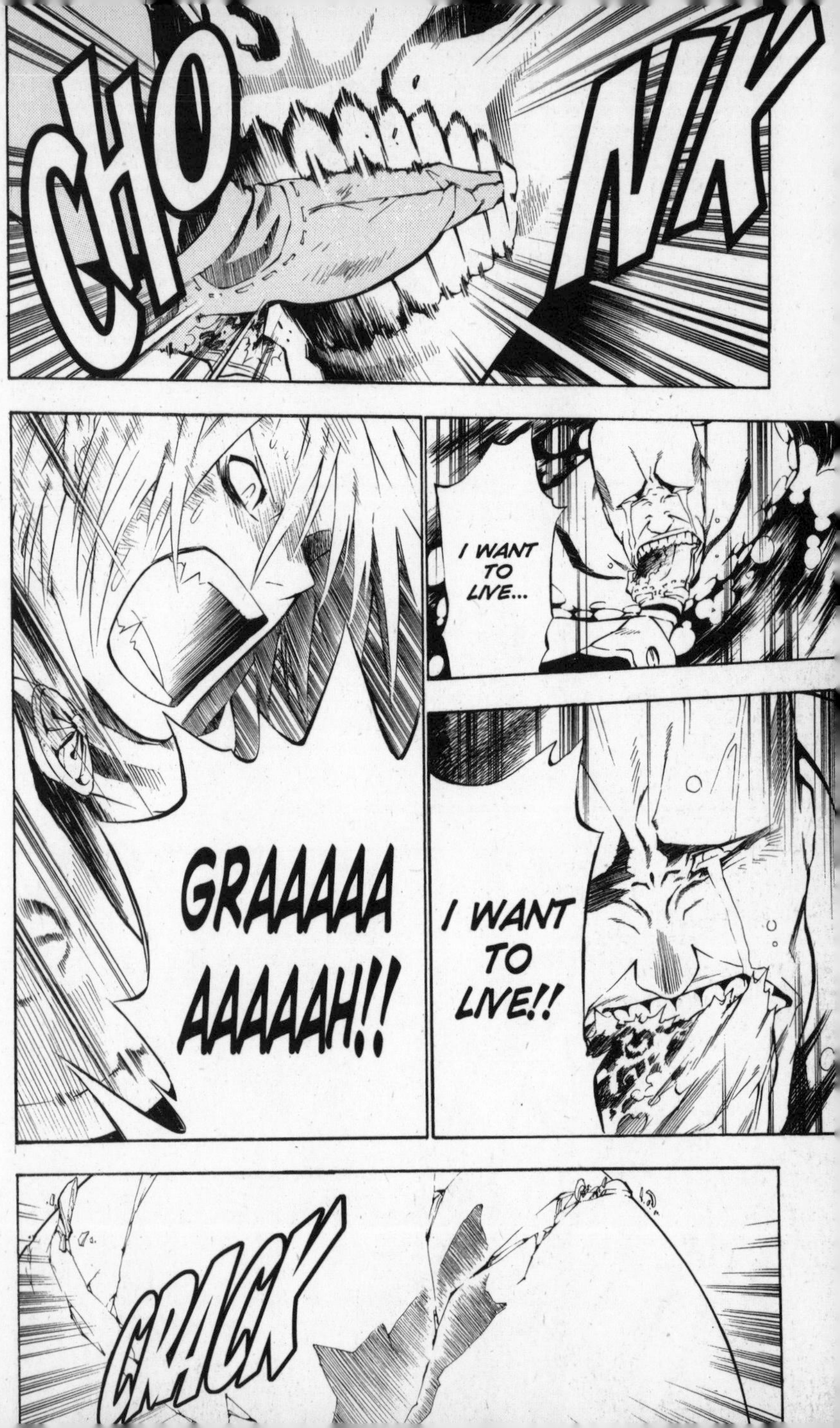
CHONK
I WANT TO LIVE...
I WANT TO LIVE!!
GRAAAAAAAAAAH!!
CRACK

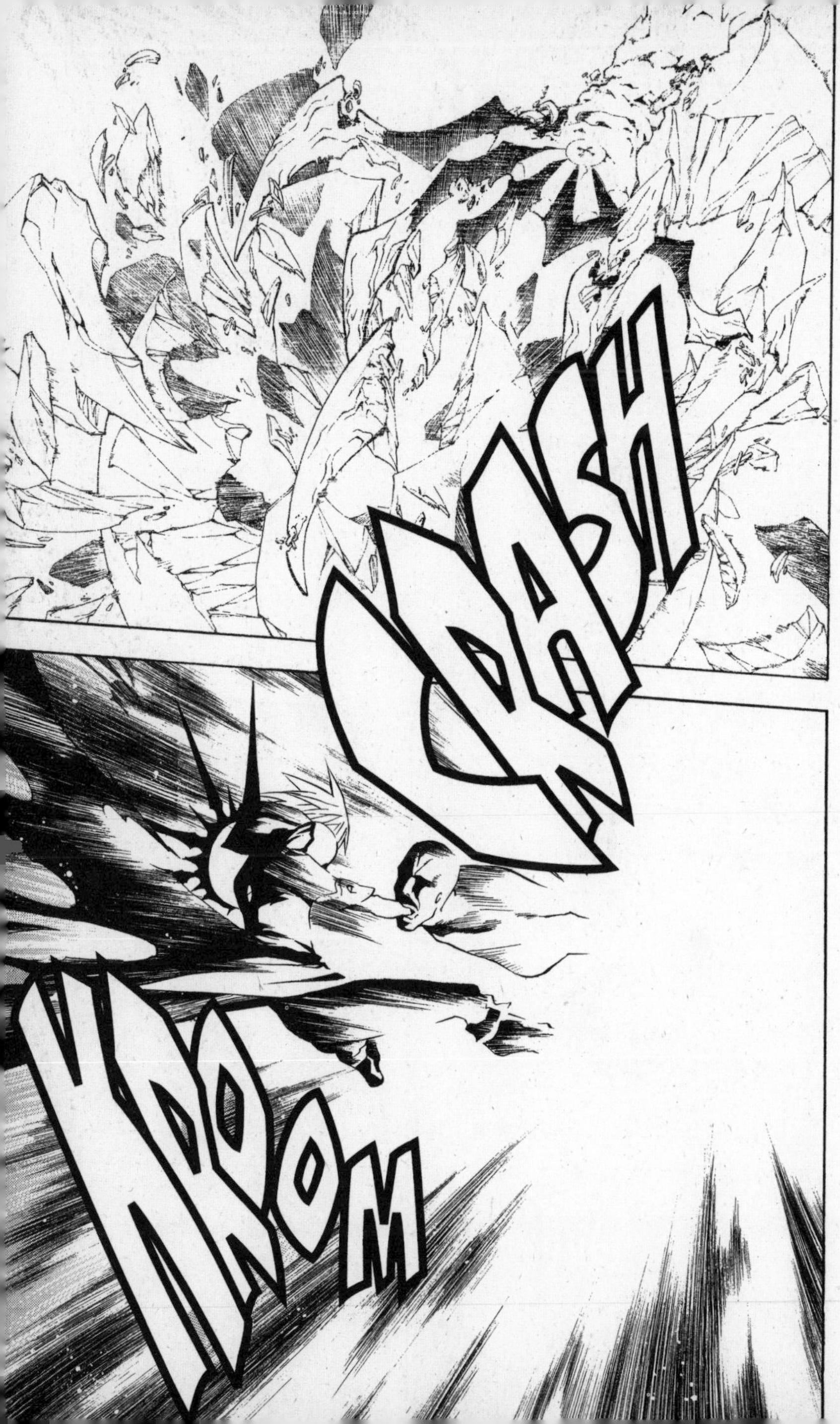
CRASH
VROOM

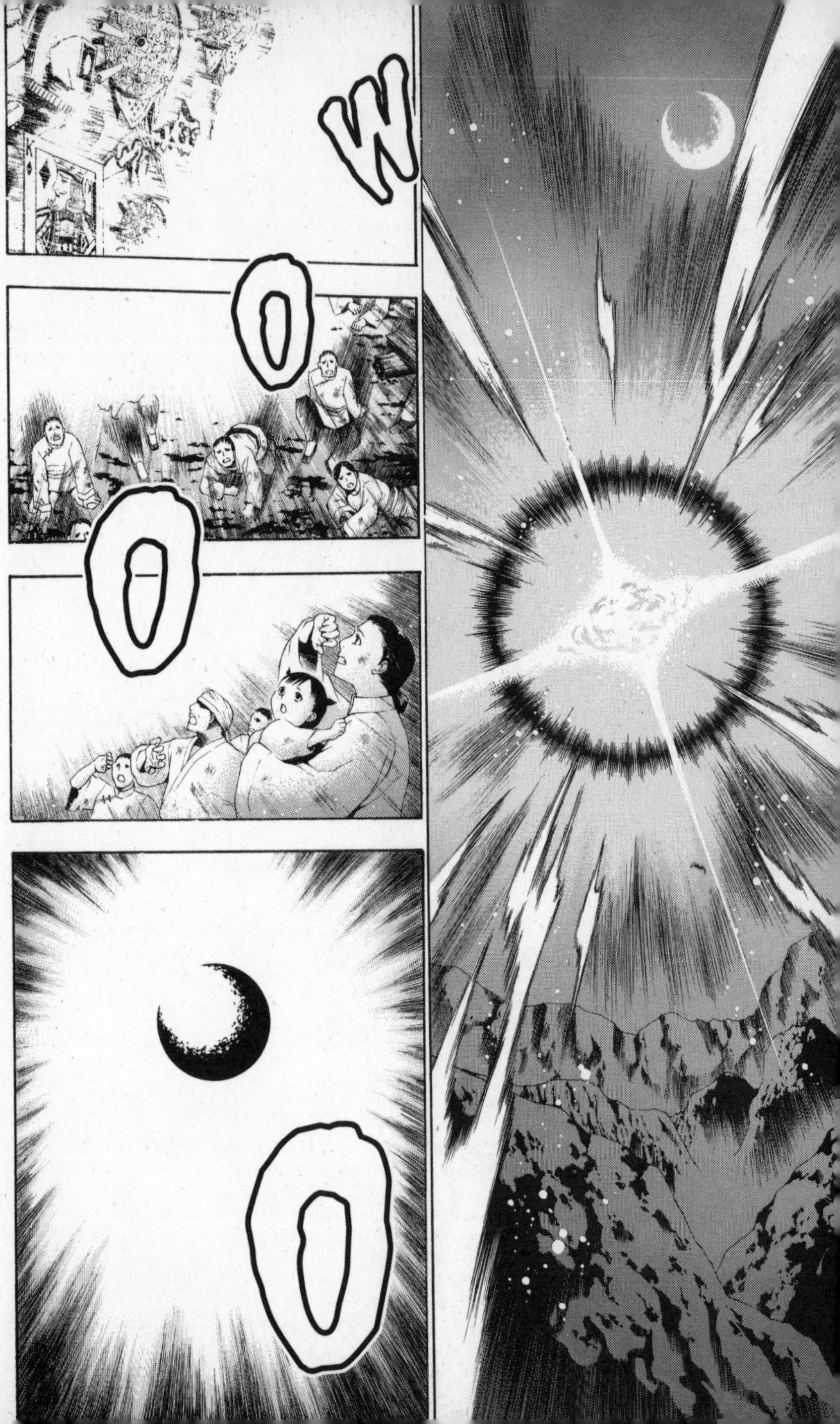
WOOO

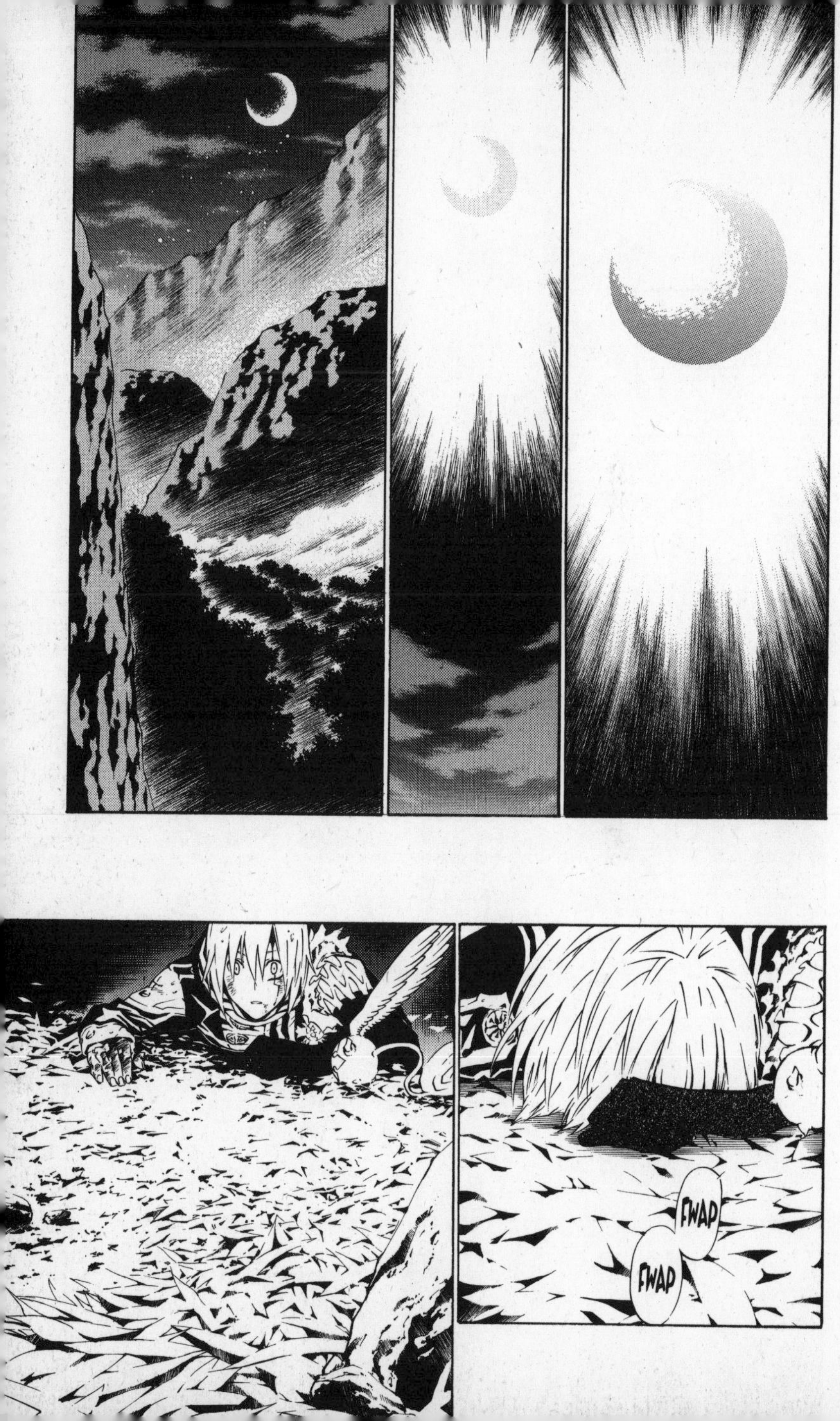
FWAP
FWAP

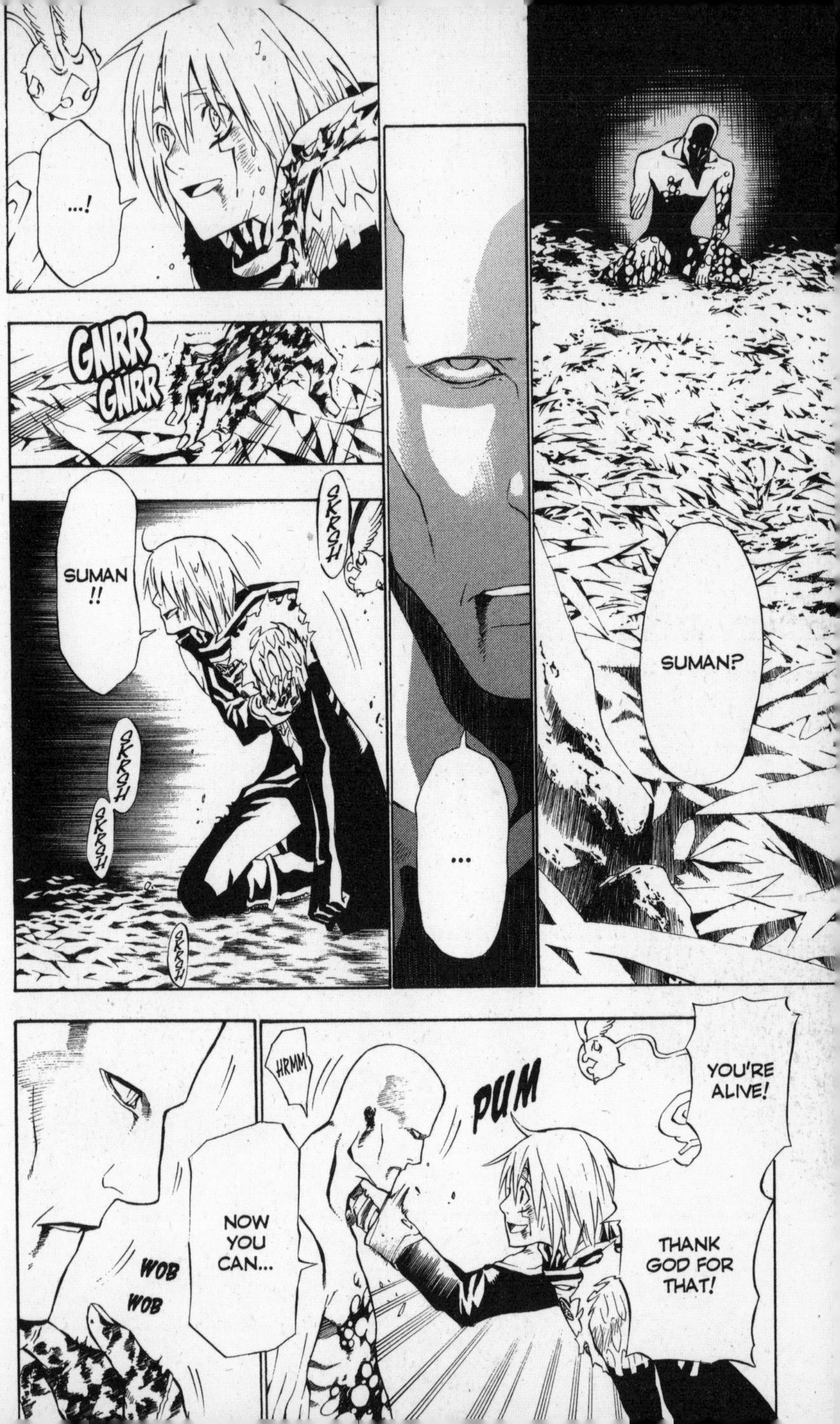
SUMAN?
...
...!
GNRR GNRR
SKRSH
SUMAN !!
SKRSH SKRSH
SKRSH
YOU'RE ALIVE!
PUM
THANK GOD FOR THAT!
HRMM
NOW YOU CAN...
WOB WOB

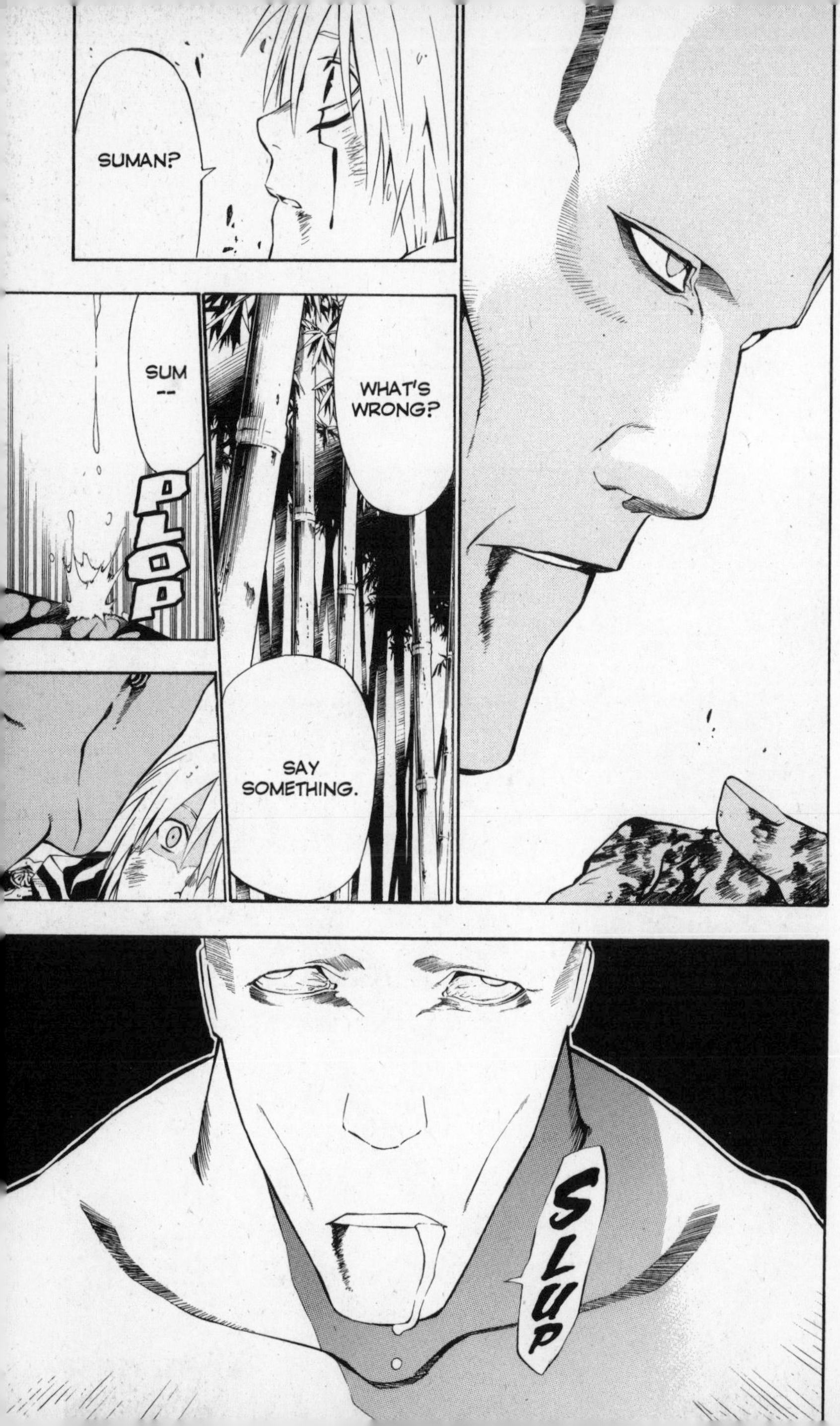

SUMAN?
WHAT'S WRONG?
SAY SOMETHING.
SUM --
PLOP
SLUP

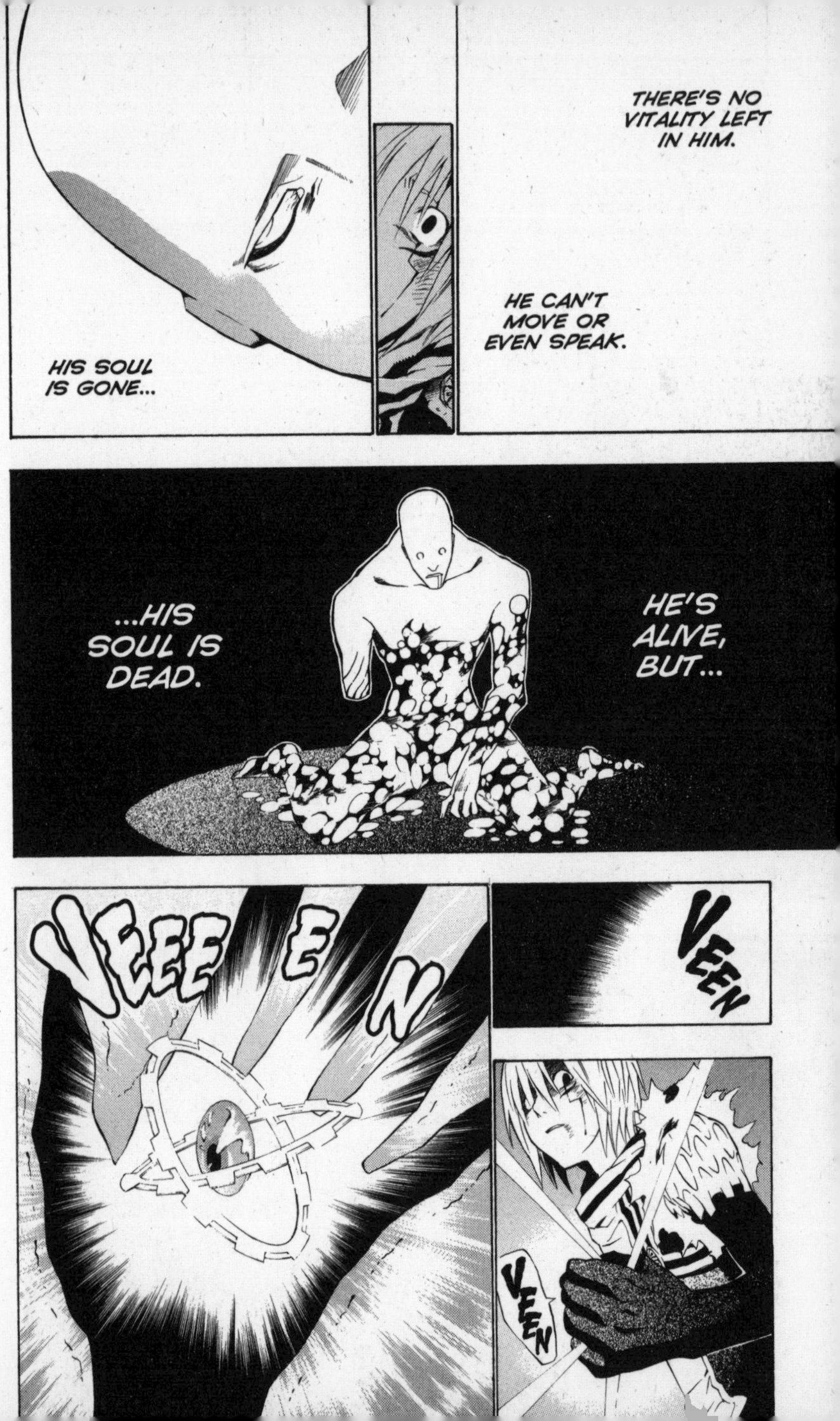
THERE'S NO VITALITY LEFT IN HIM.
HE CAN'T MOVE OR EVEN SPEAK.
HIS SOUL IS GONE...
HE'S ALIVE, BUT...
...HIS SOUL IS DEAD.
VEEN
VEEN
VEEEEN

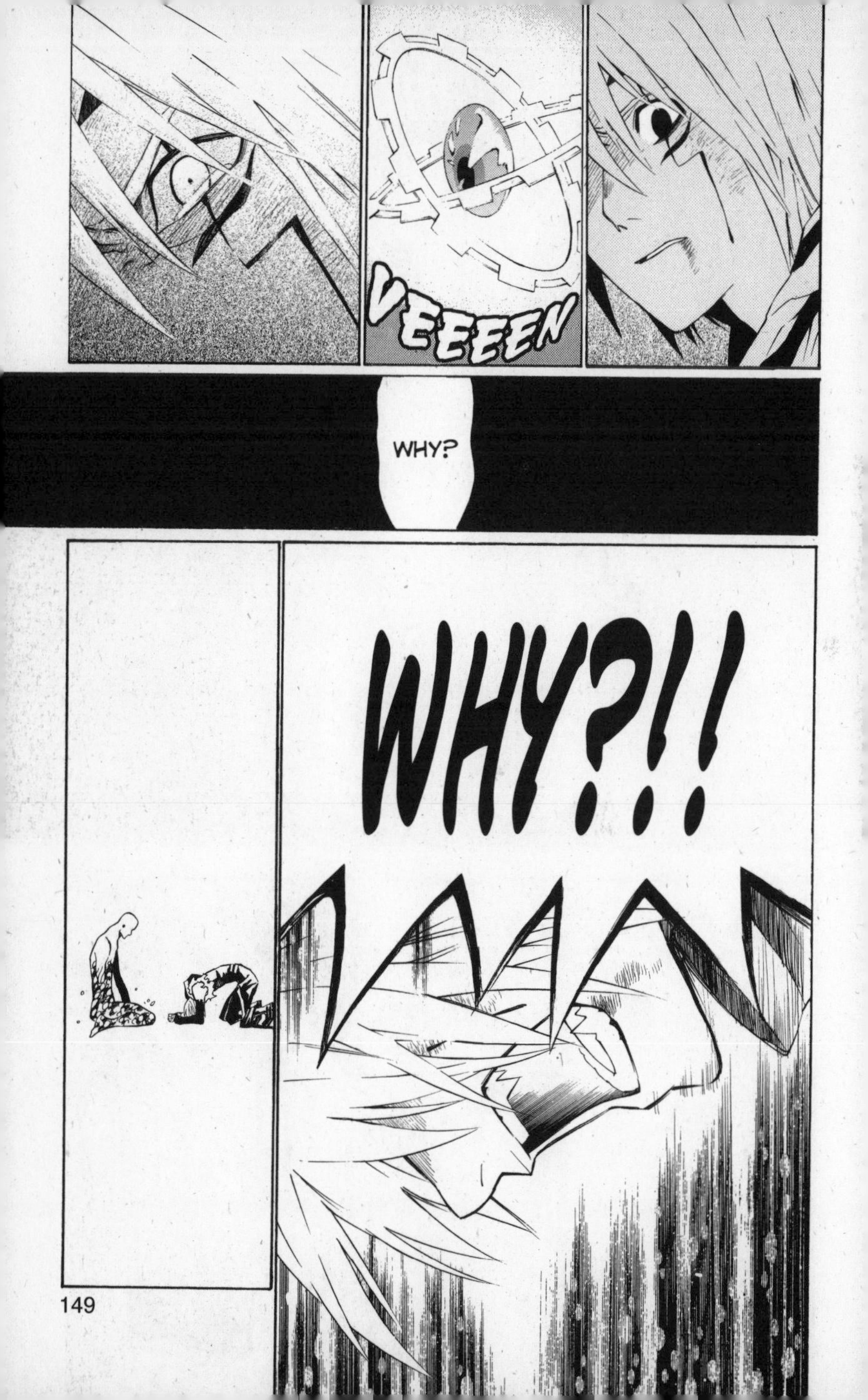
VEEEEN
WHY?
WHY?!!

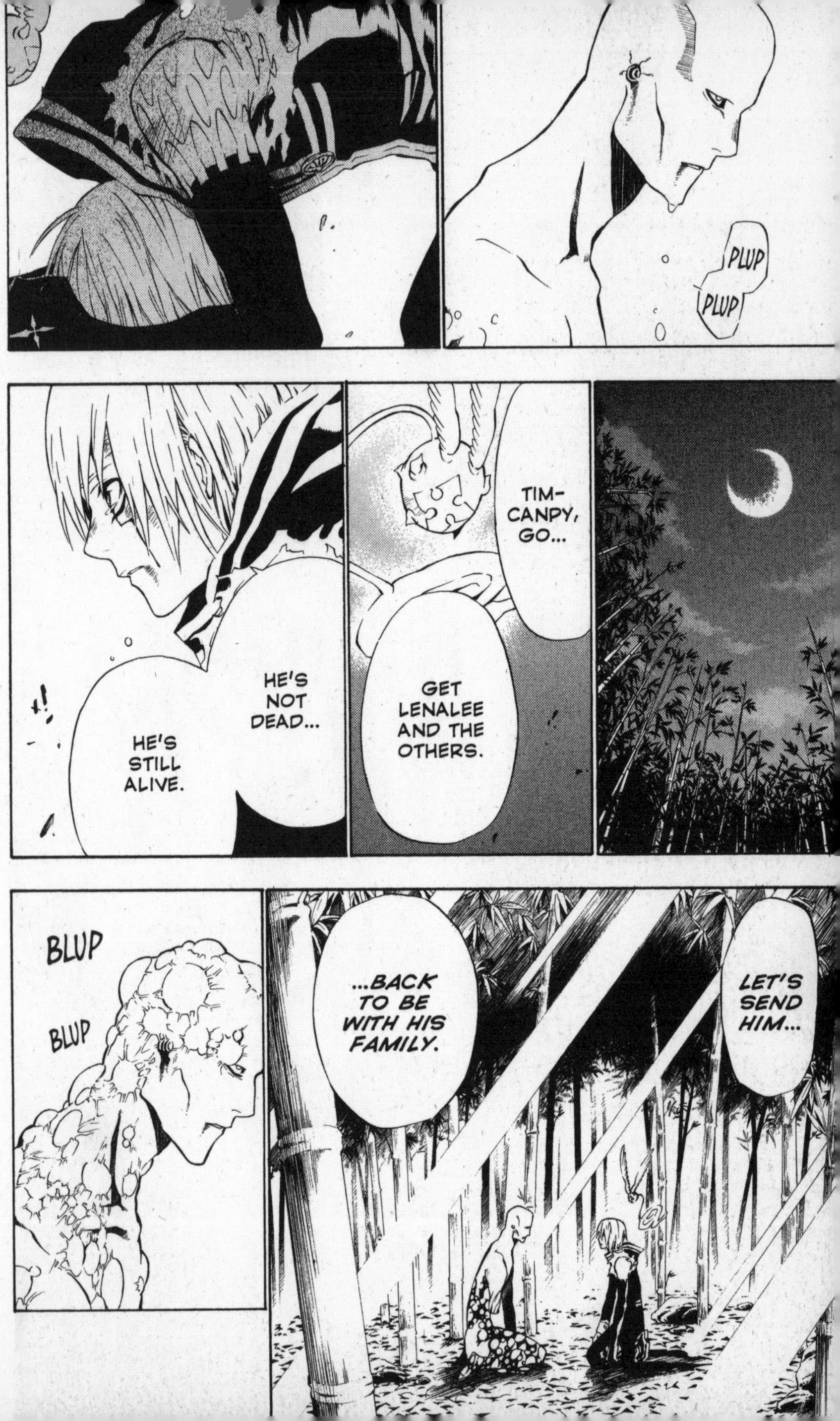
PLUP
PLUP
TIM-CANPY, GO...
GET LENALEE AND THE OTHERS.
HE'S NOT DEAD...
HE'S STILL ALIVE.
LET'S SEND HIM...
...BACK TO BE WITH HIS FAMILY.
BLUP
BLUP

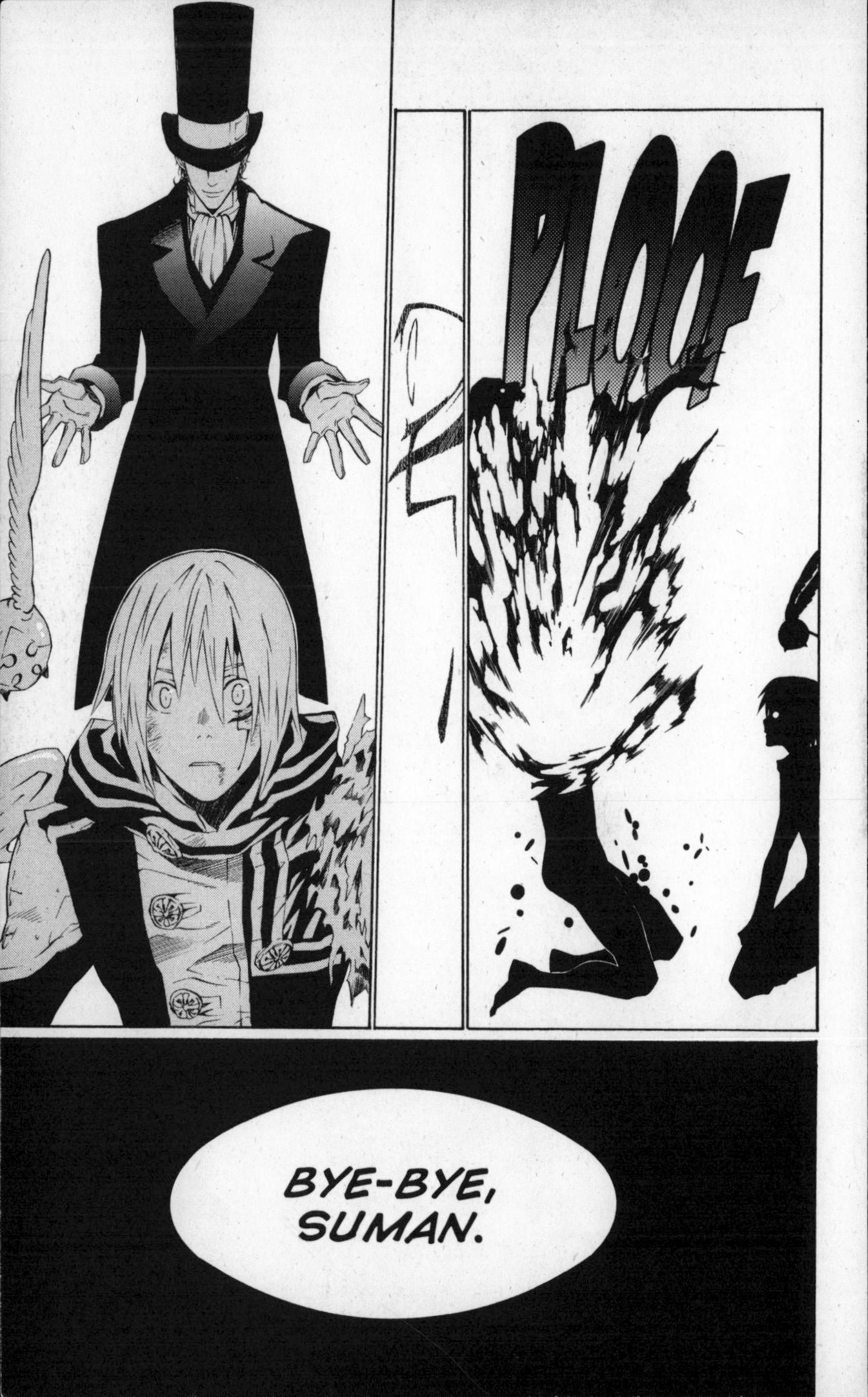
PLOOF
BYE-BYE, SUMAN.

I THINK WE CAN PLAY A GAME WITHOUT YOU CHEATING WITH THESE CARDS. ♡

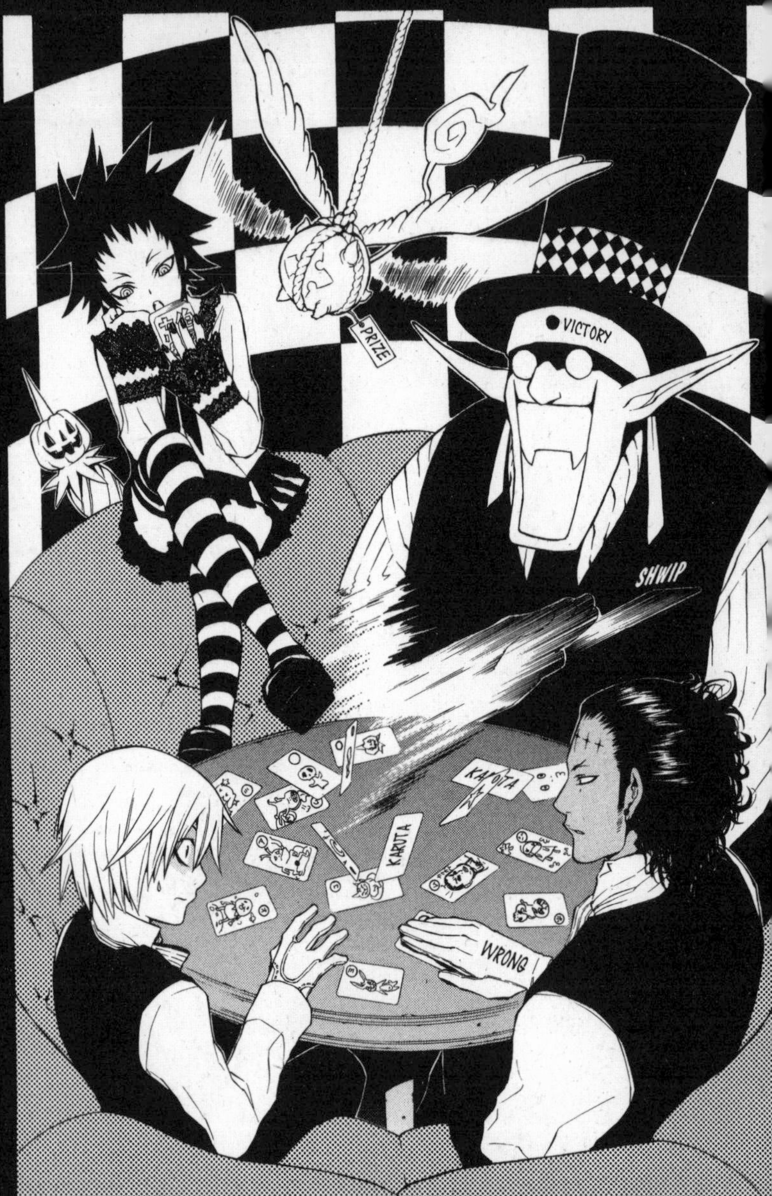
VICTORY
PRIZE
SHWIP
KARUTA
KARUTA
WRONG

THE 55TH NIGHT: DELETE

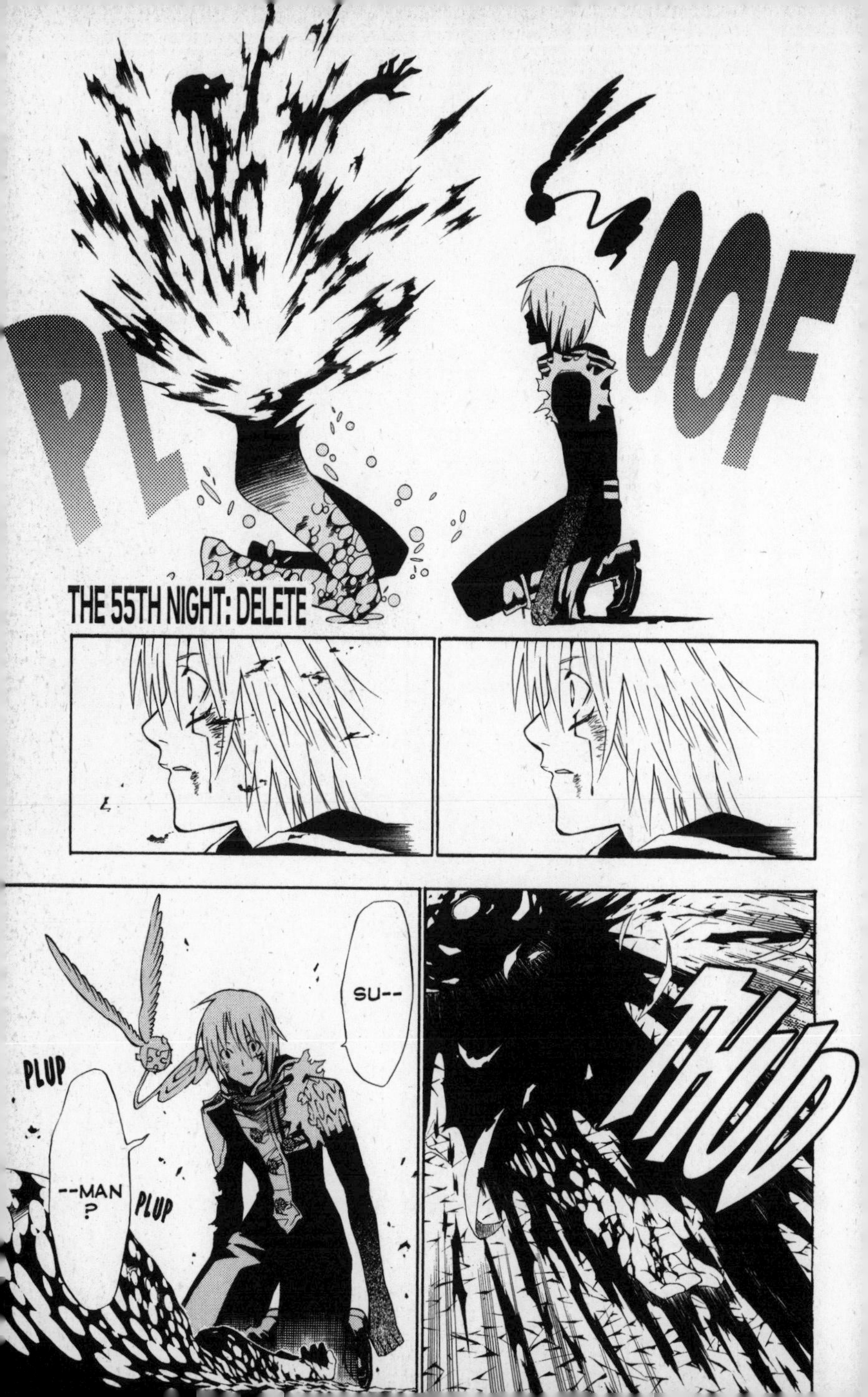
PLOOF
THUD
SU--
PLUP
--MAN ?
PLUP

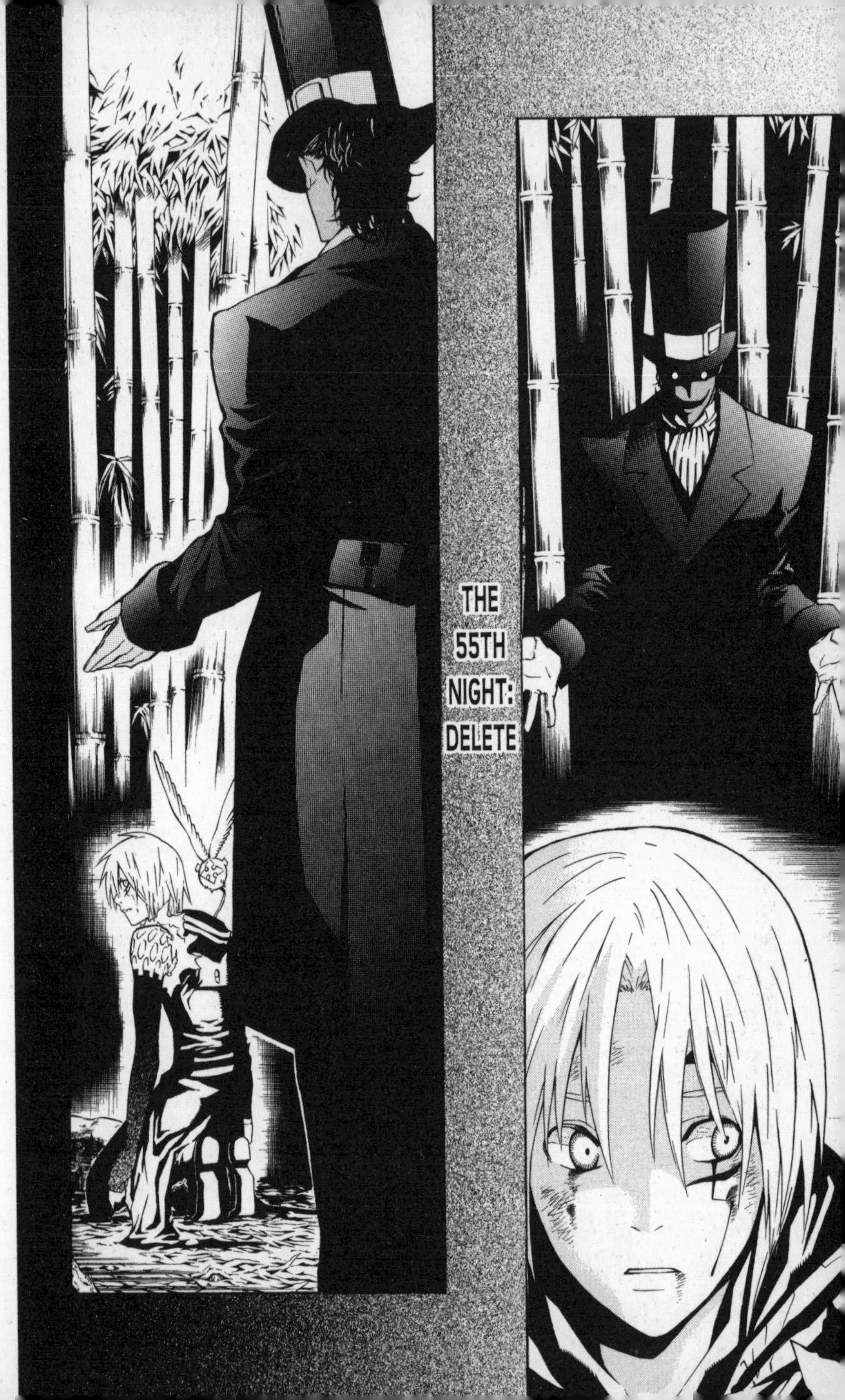
THE 55TH NIGHT: DELETE

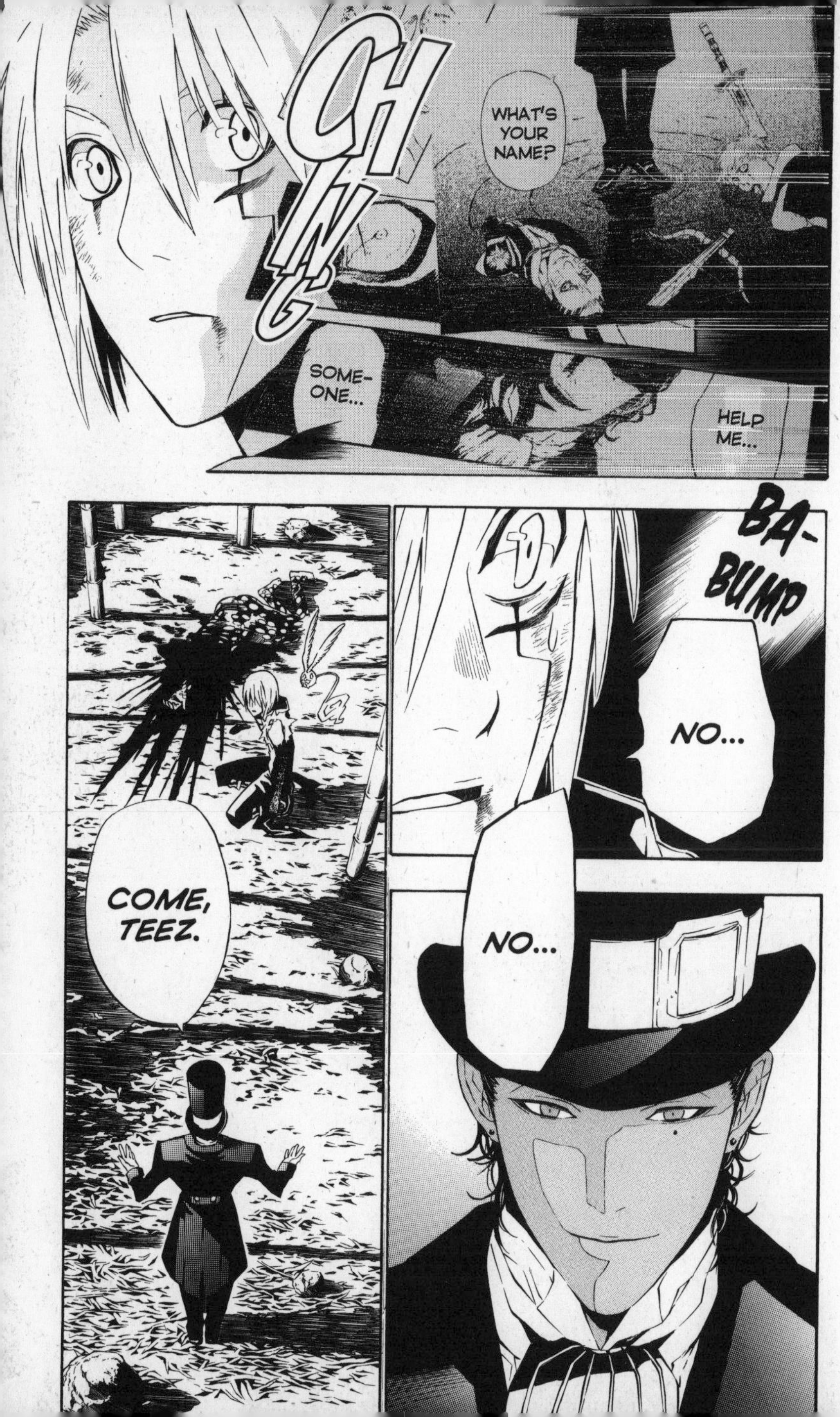
WHAT'S YOUR NAME?
CHING
SOME-ONE...
HELP ME...
BA-BUMP
NO...
NO...
COME, TEEZ.

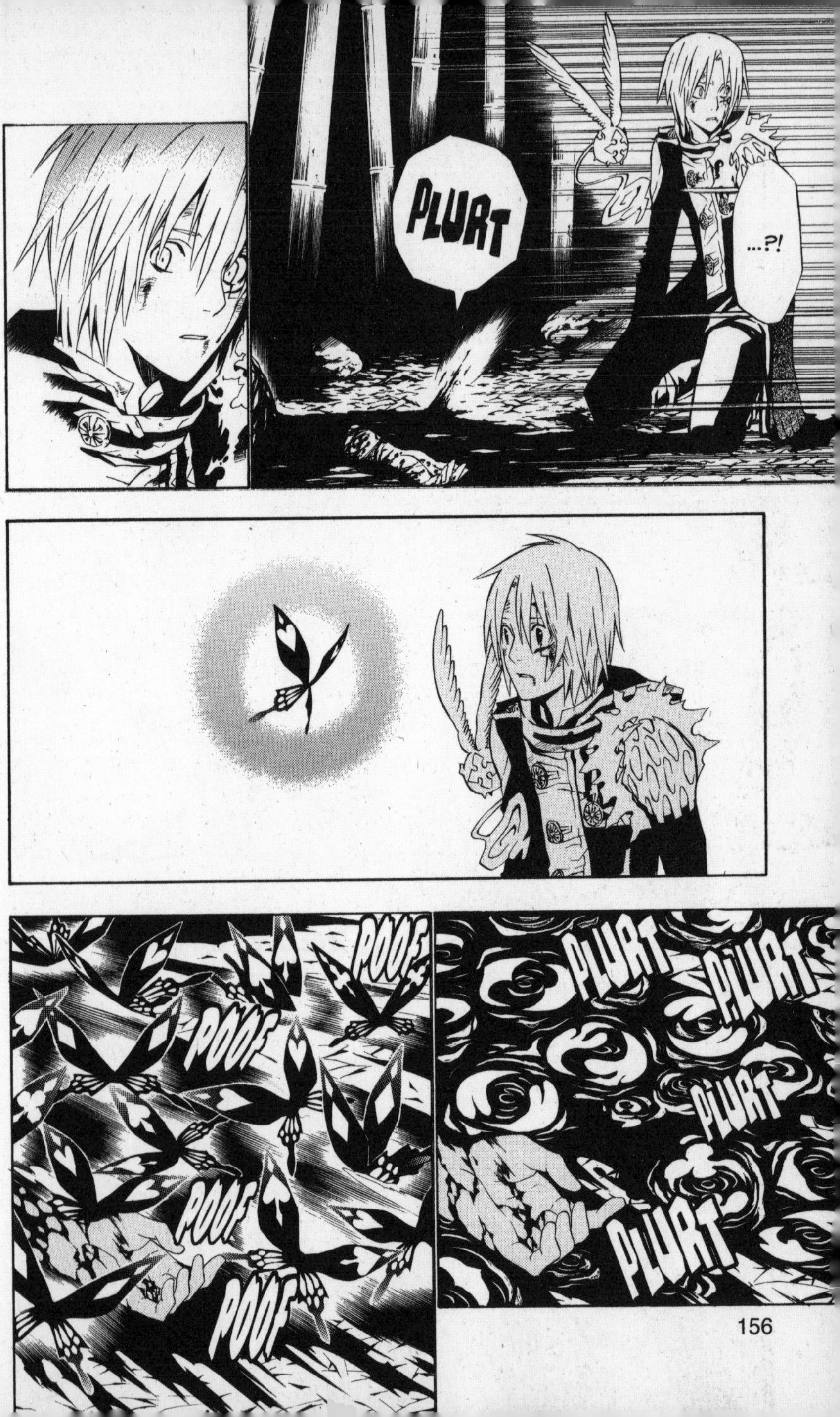
...?!
PLURT
PLURT
PLURT
PLURT
PLURT
POOF
POOF
POOF
POOF

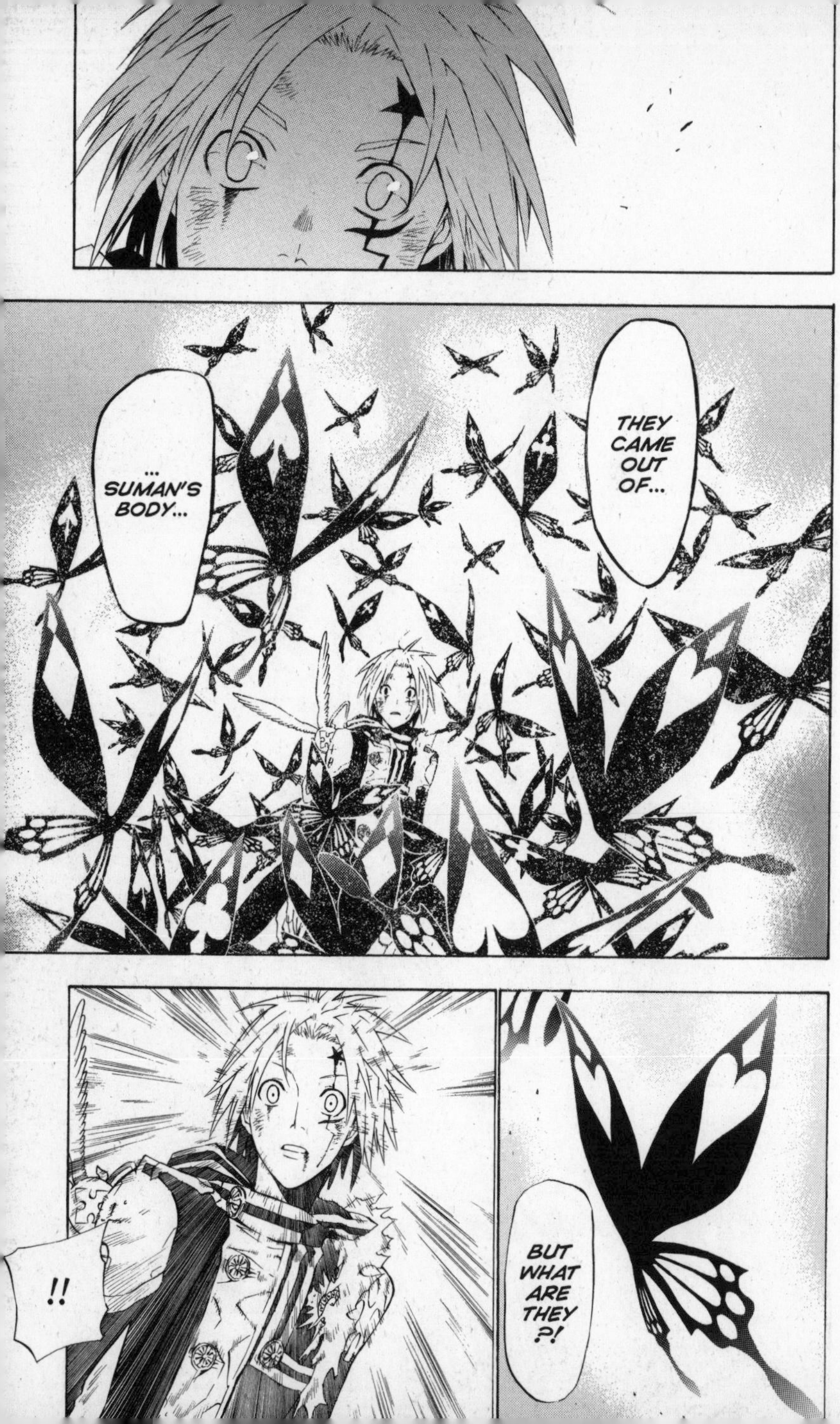
THEY CAME OUT OF...
...SUMAN'S BODY...
BUT WHAT ARE THEY ?!
!!

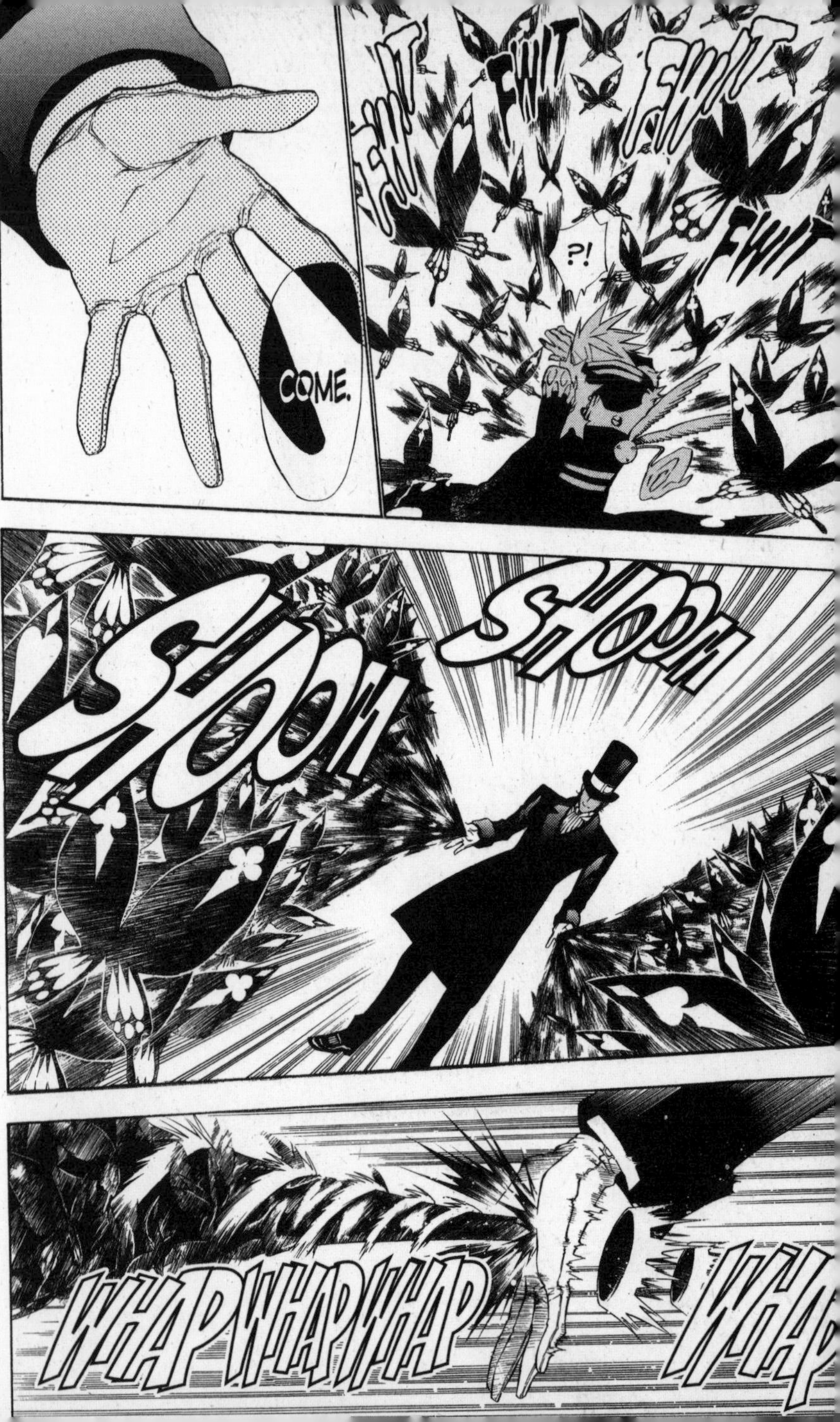
FWIT
FWIT
FWIT
FWIT
?!
COME.
SHOOM
SHOOM
WHAP
WHAPWHAPWHAP

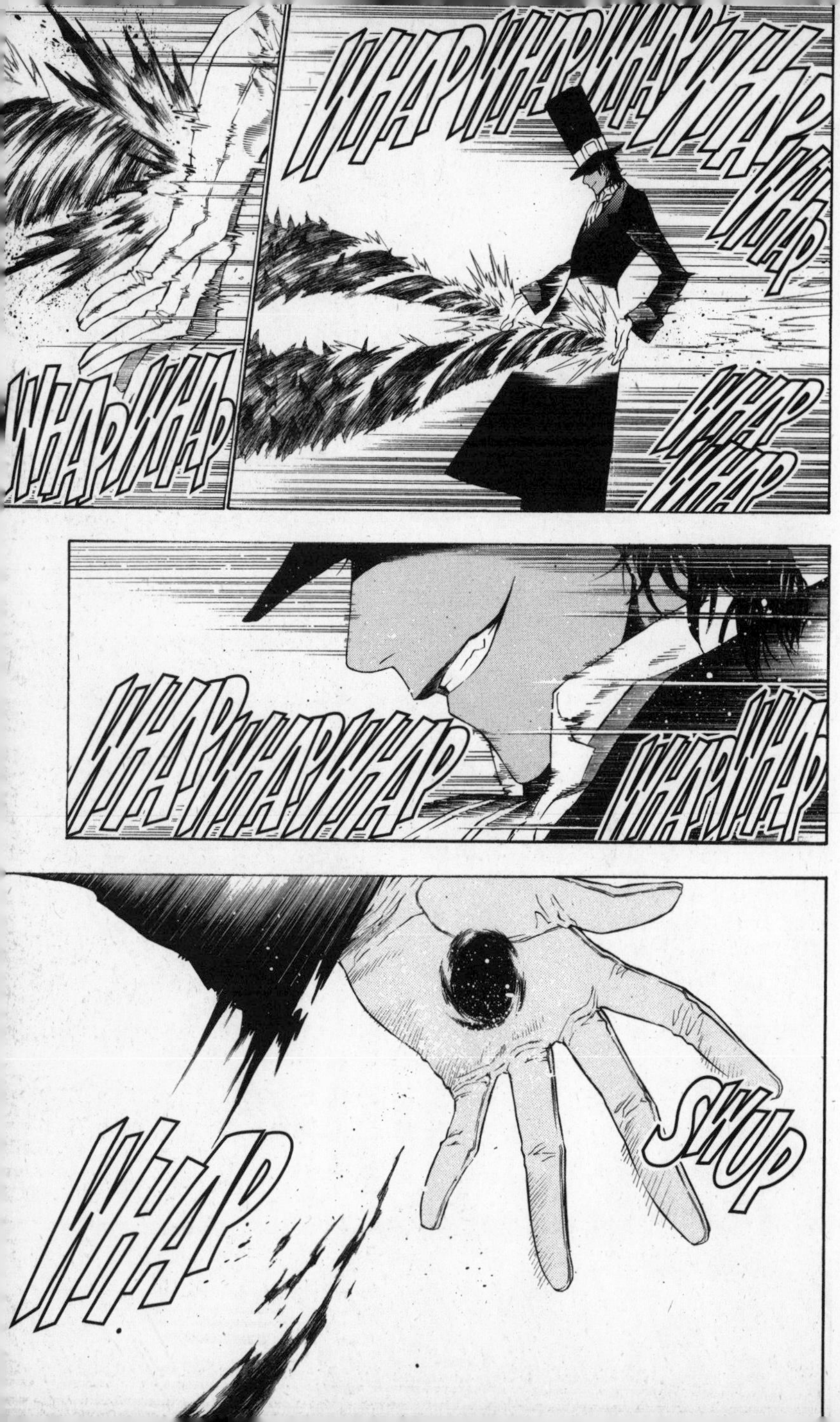
WHAPWHAPWHAPWHAP
WHAP
WHAP WHAP
WHAPWHAP
WHAPWHAP
WHAPWHAPWHAP
SHUP
WHAP

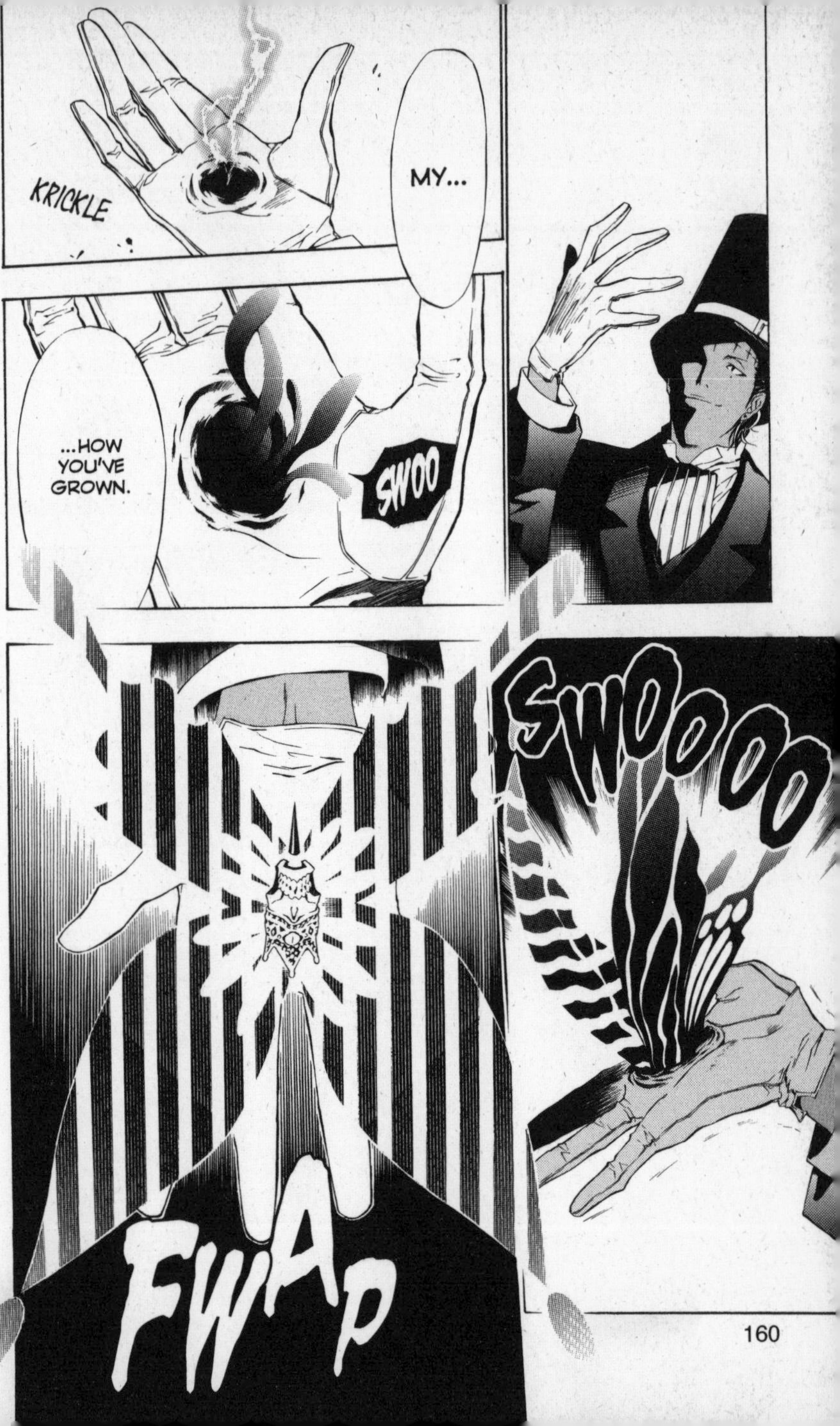
MY...
KRICKLE
...HOW YOU'VE GROWN.
SWOO
SWOOOO
FWAP

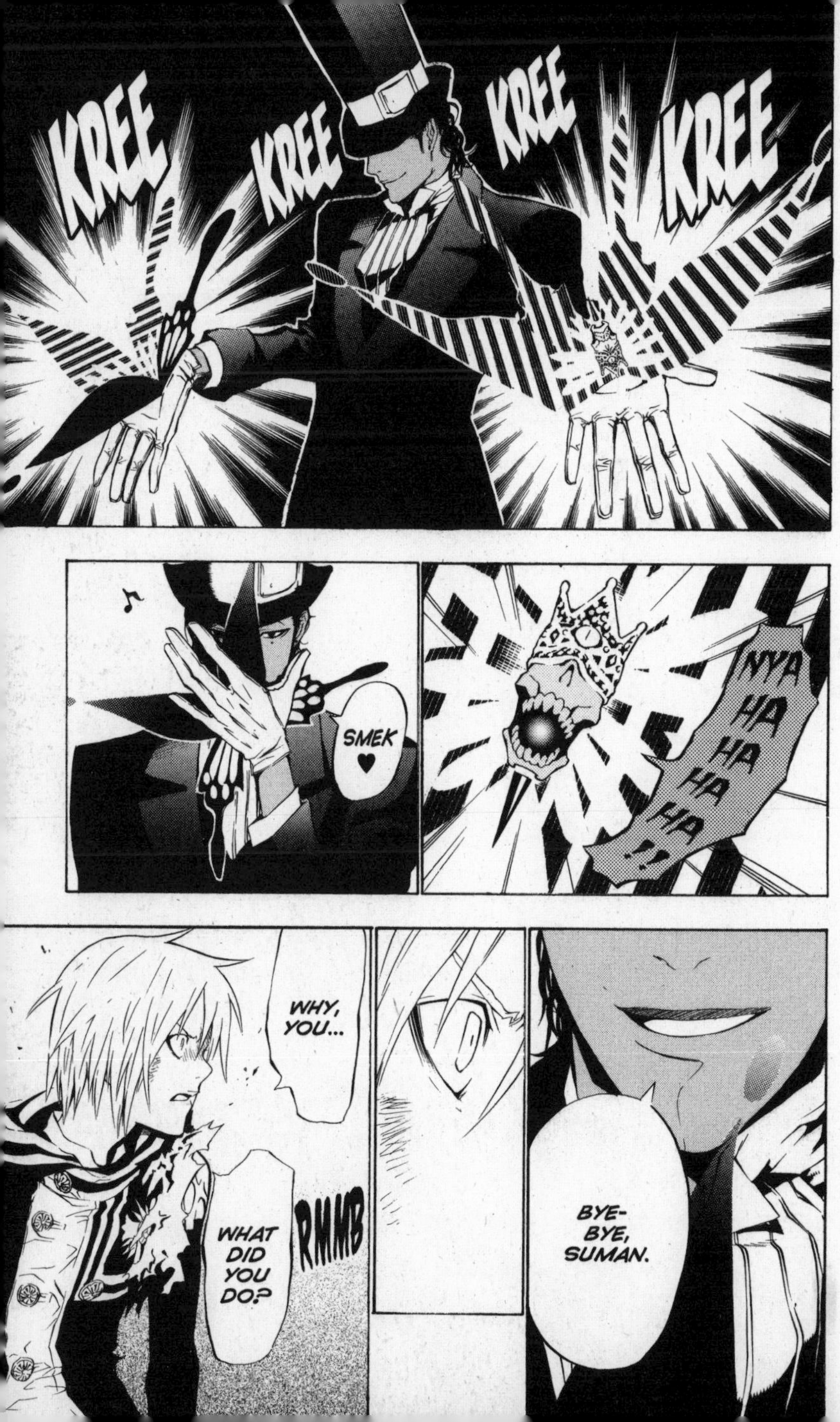
KREE
KREE
KREE
KREE
NYA HA HA HA HA!!
SMEK ♥
BYE-BYE, SUMAN.
WHY, YOU...
WHAT DID YOU DO?
RMMB

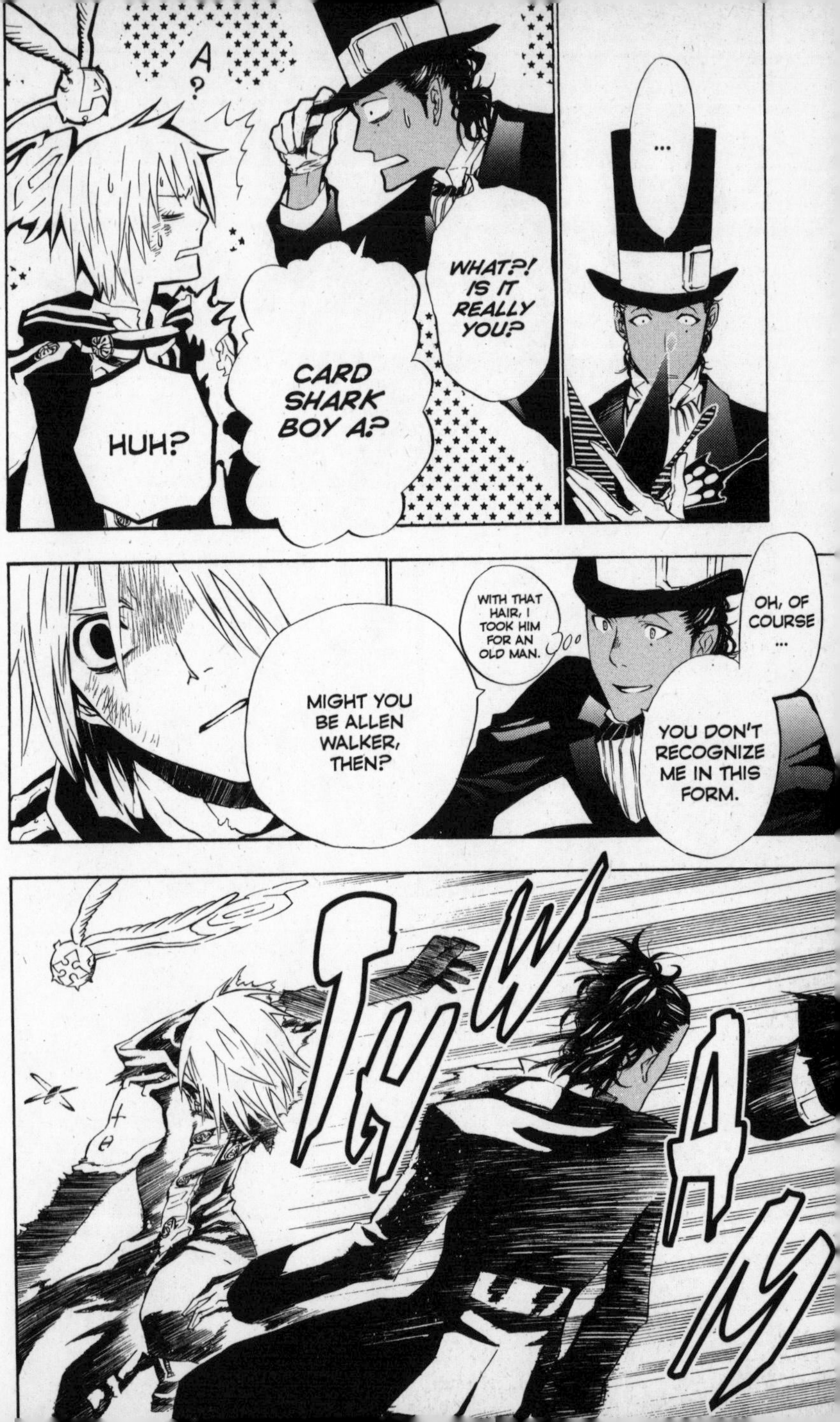
...
WHAT?! IS IT REALLY YOU?
CARD SHARK BOY A?
A?
HUH?
OH, OF COURSE...
YOU DON'T RECOGNIZE ME IN THIS FORM.
WITH THAT HAIR, I TOOK HIM FOR AN OLD MAN.
MIGHT YOU BE ALLEN WALKER, THEN?
THWAM

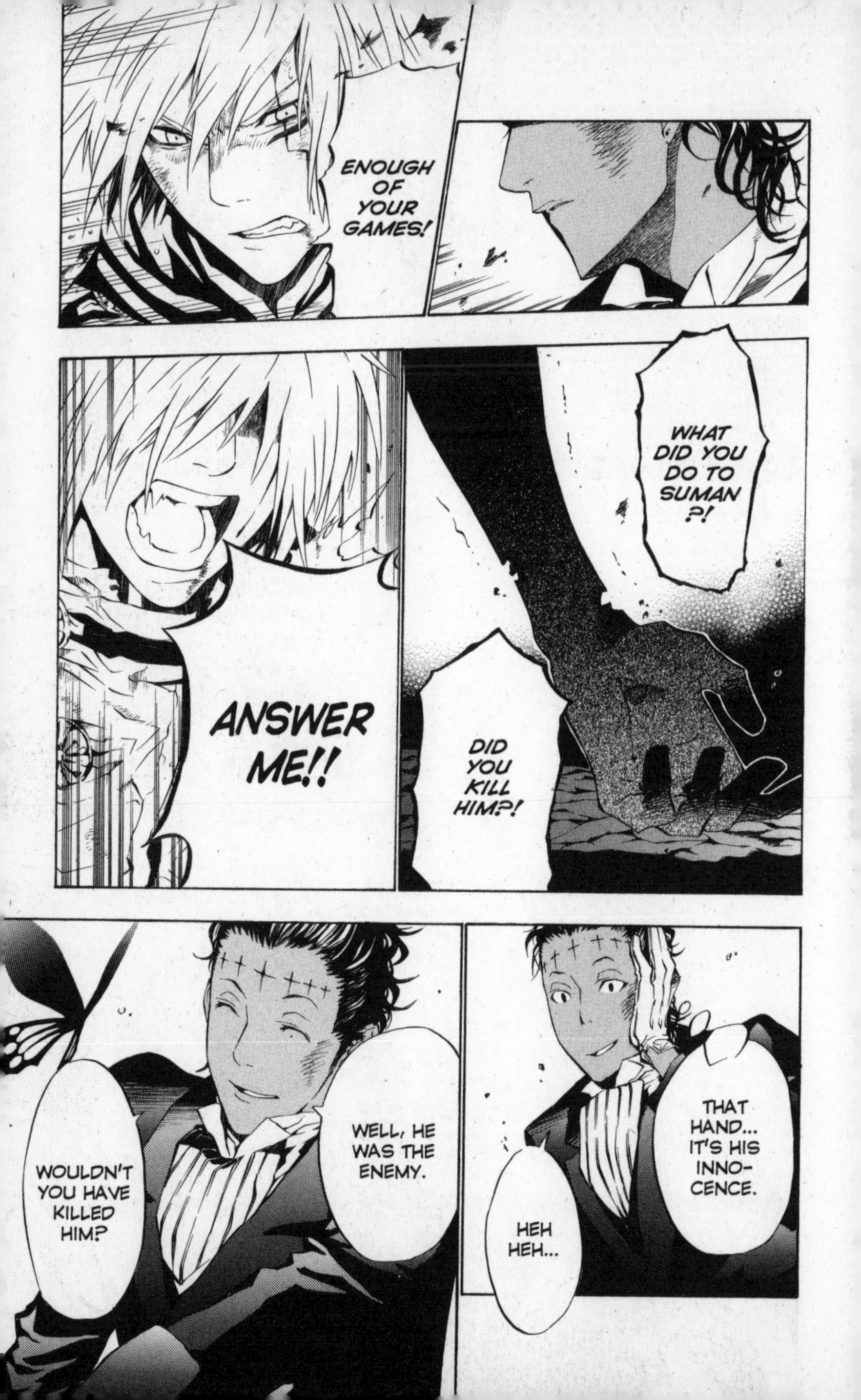
ENOUGH OF YOUR GAMES!
WHAT DID YOU DO TO SUMAN?!
DID YOU KILL HIM?!
ANSWER ME!!
THAT HAND... IT'S HIS INNOCENCE.
HEH HEH...
WELL, HE WAS THE ENEMY.
WOULDN'T YOU HAVE KILLED HIM?

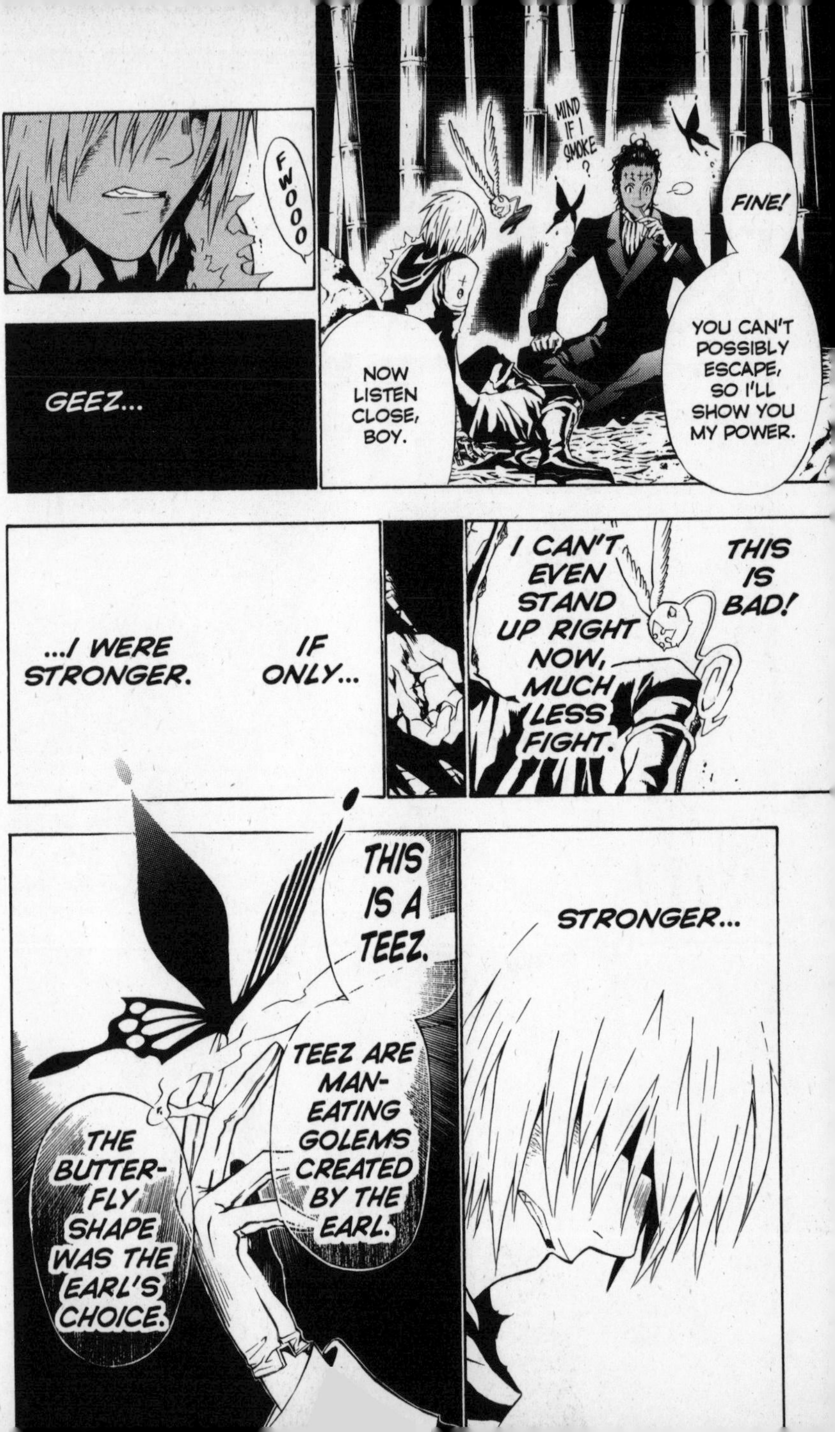
MIND IF I SMOKE?
FINE!
YOU CAN'T POSSIBLY ESCAPE, SO I'LL SHOW YOU MY POWER.
NOW LISTEN CLOSE, BOY.
FWOOO
GEEZ...
THIS IS BAD!
I CAN'T EVEN STAND UP RIGHT NOW, MUCH LESS FIGHT.
IF ONLY...
...I WERE STRONGER.
STRONGER...
THIS IS A TEEZ.
TEEZ ARE MAN-EATING GOLEMS CREATED BY THE EARL.
THE BUTTERFLY SHAPE WAS THE EARL'S CHOICE.

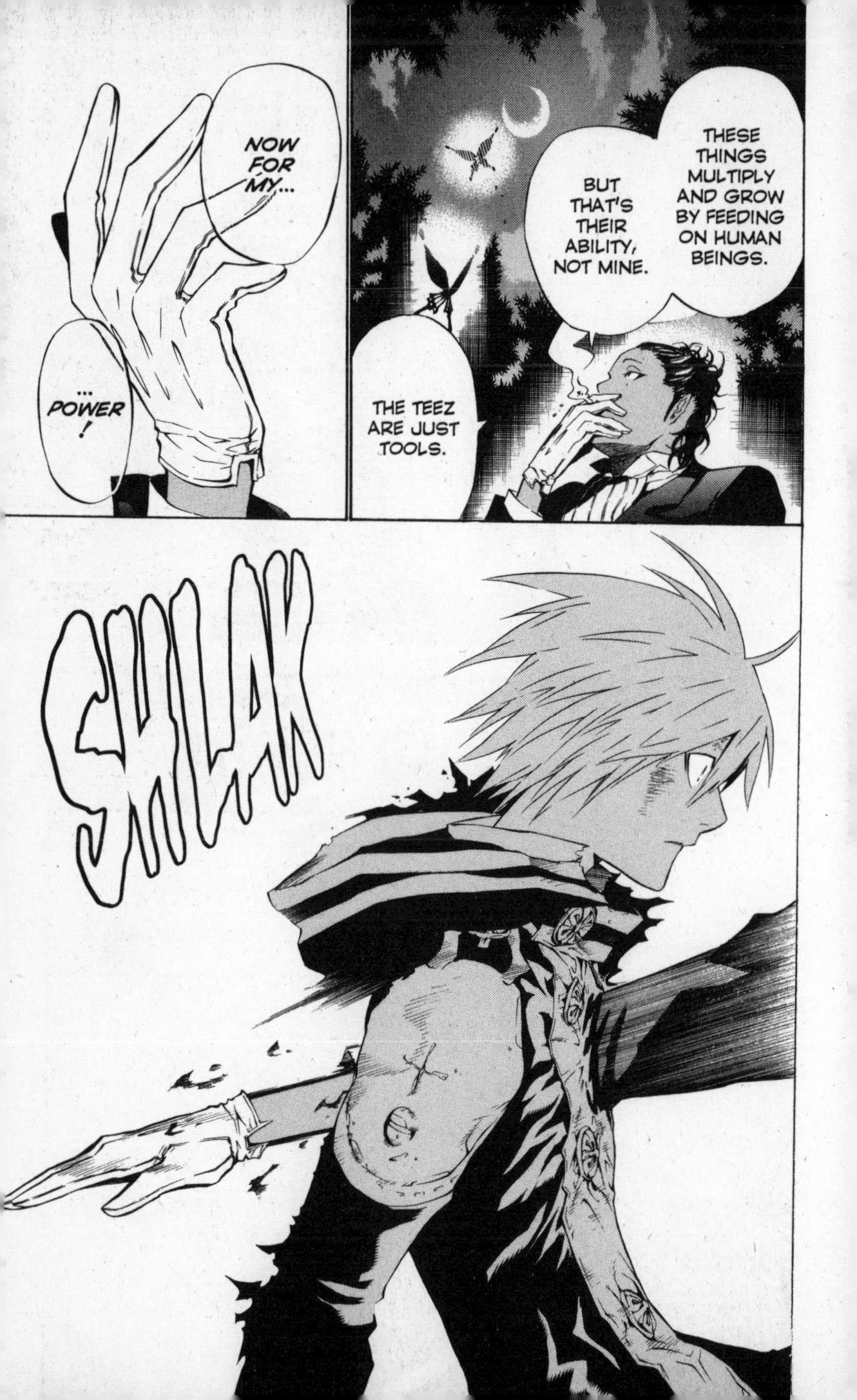
THESE THINGS MULTIPLY AND GROW BY FEEDING ON HUMAN BEINGS.
BUT THAT'S THEIR ABILITY, NOT MINE.
THE TEEZ ARE JUST TOOLS.
NOW FOR MY...
...POWER!
SHLAK

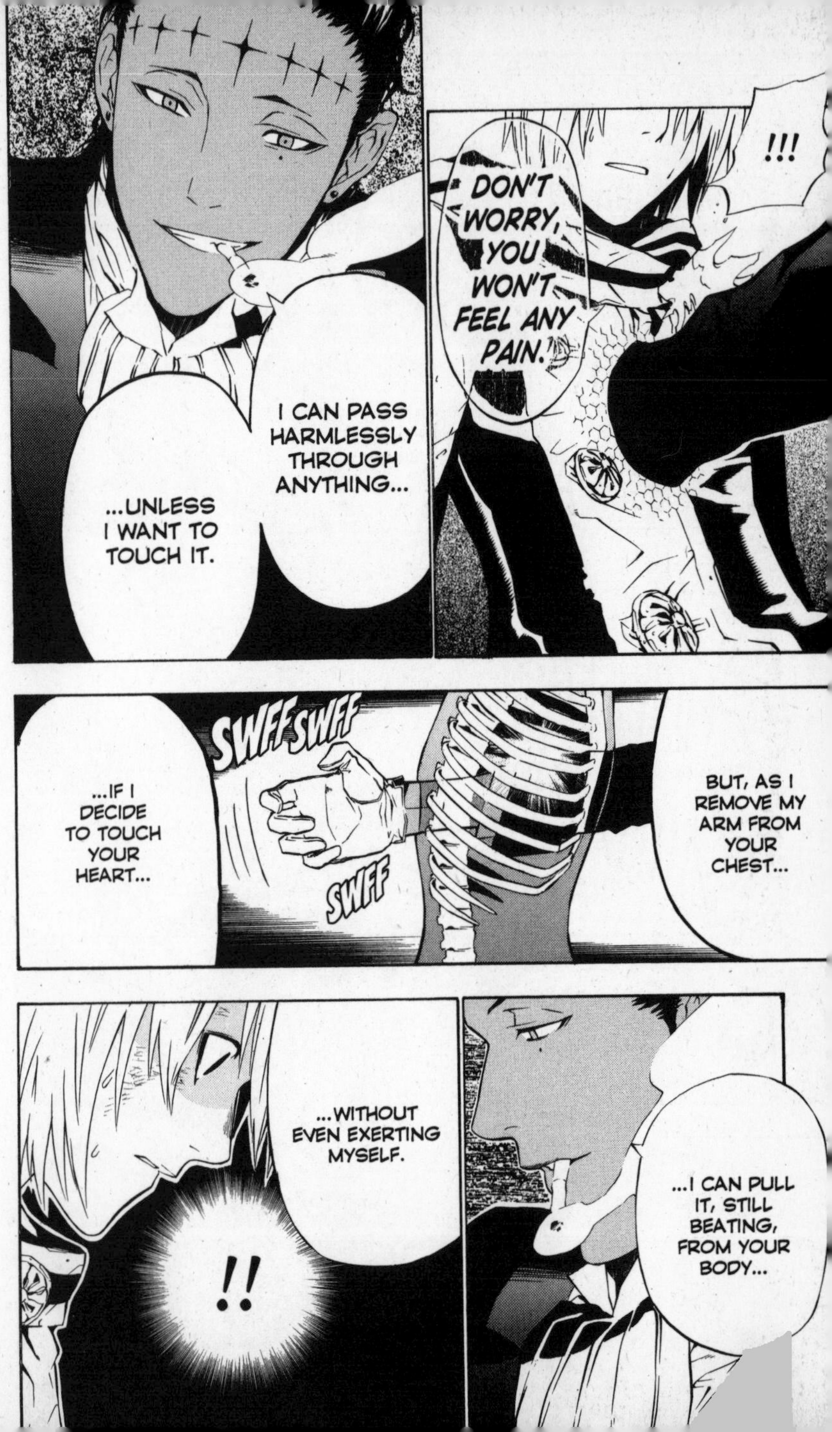
!!!
DON'T WORRY, YOU WON'T FEEL ANY PAIN.
I CAN PASS HARMLESSLY THROUGH ANYTHING...
...UNLESS I WANT TO TOUCH IT.
BUT, AS I REMOVE MY ARM FROM YOUR CHEST...
SWFF SWFF
SWFF
...IF I DECIDE TO TOUCH YOUR HEART...
...I CAN PULL IT, STILL BEATING, FROM YOUR BODY...
...WITHOUT EVEN EXERTING MYSELF.
!!

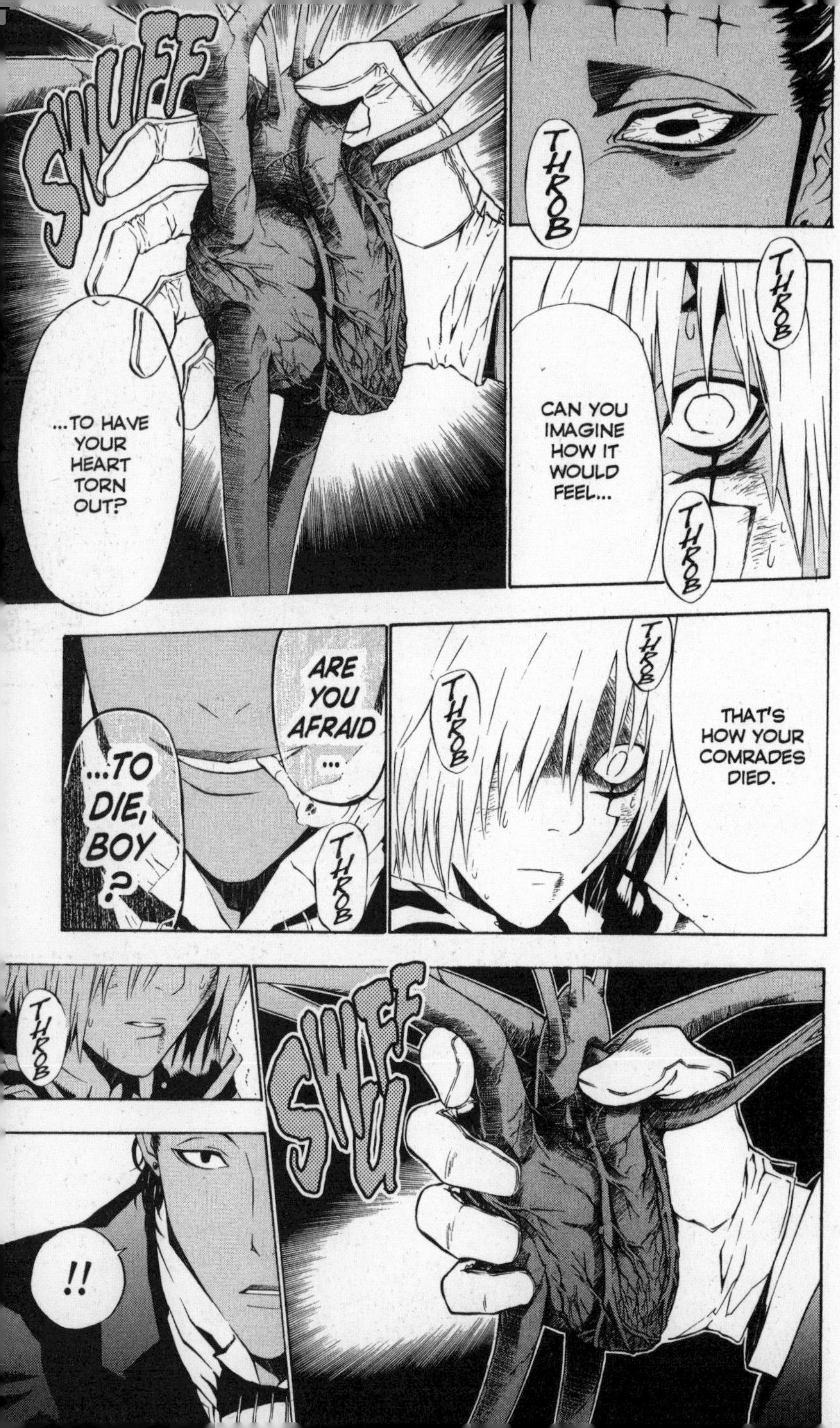
THROB
THROB
CAN YOU IMAGINE HOW IT WOULD FEEL...
THROB
SNUFF
...TO HAVE YOUR HEART TORN OUT?
THROB
THROB
THAT'S HOW YOUR COMRADES DIED.
ARE YOU AFRAID...
...TO DIE, BOY?
THROB
SNUFF
THROB
!!

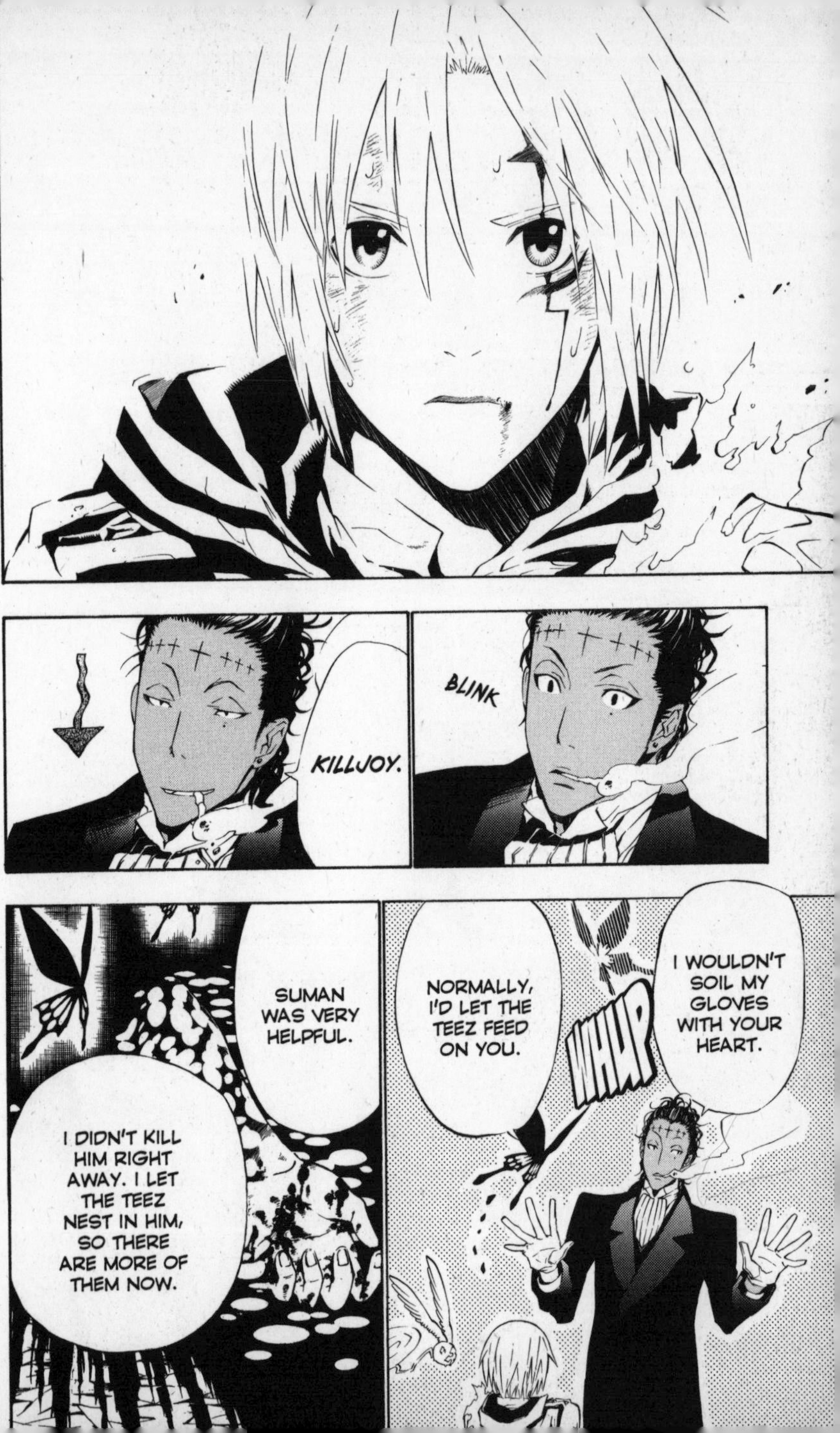
BLINK
KILLJOY.
I WOULDN'T SOIL MY GLOVES WITH YOUR HEART.
WHUP
NORMALLY, I'D LET THE TEEZ FEED ON YOU.
SUMAN WAS VERY HELPFUL.
I DIDN'T KILL HIM RIGHT AWAY. I LET THE TEEZ NEST IN HIM, SO THERE ARE MORE OF THEM NOW.

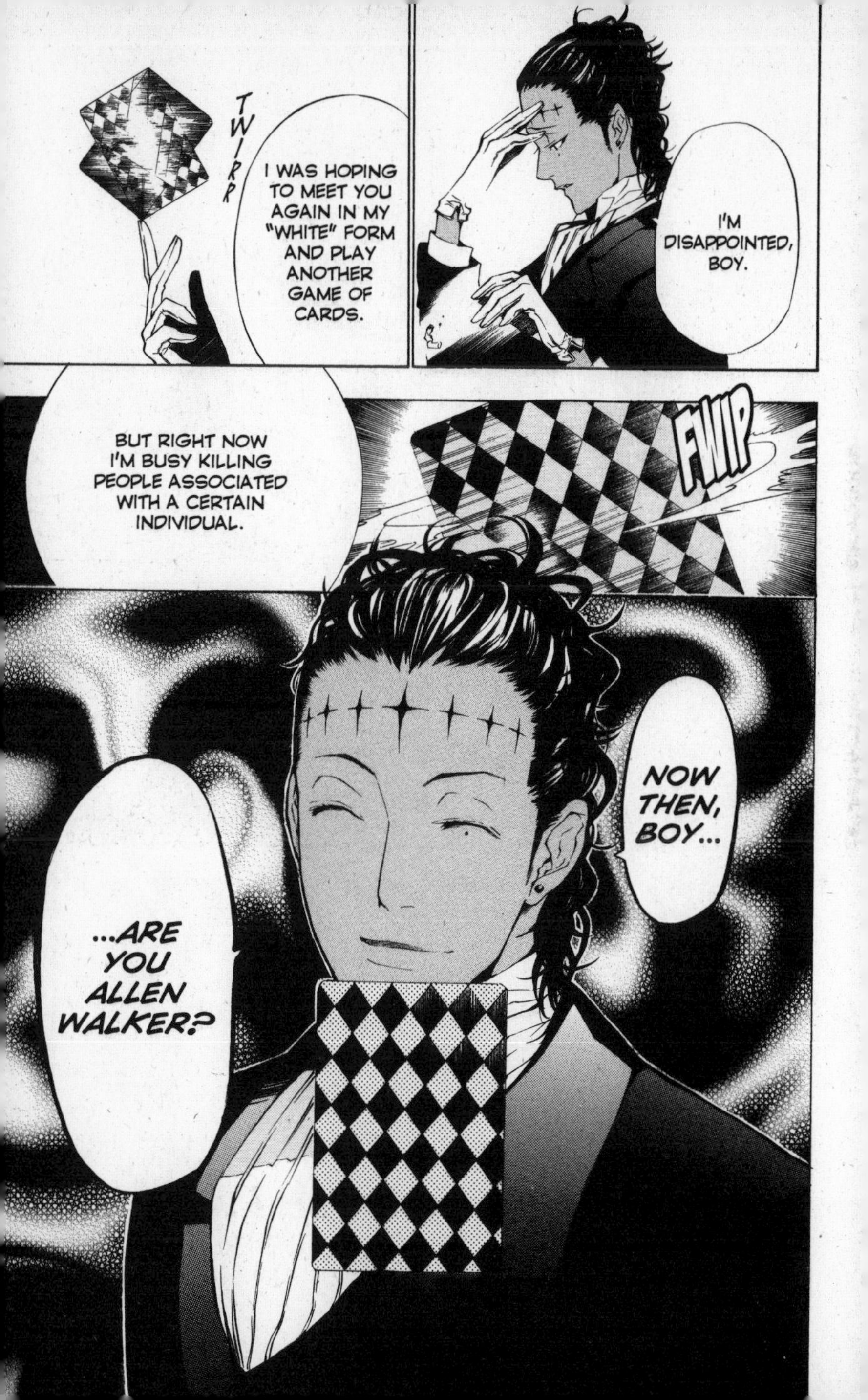
I'M DISAPPOINTED, BOY.
I WAS HOPING TO MEET YOU AGAIN IN MY "WHITE" FORM AND PLAY ANOTHER GAME OF CARDS.
TWIRR
FWIP
BUT RIGHT NOW I'M BUSY KILLING PEOPLE ASSOCIATED WITH A CERTAIN INDIVIDUAL.
NOW THEN, BOY...
...ARE YOU ALLEN WALKER?

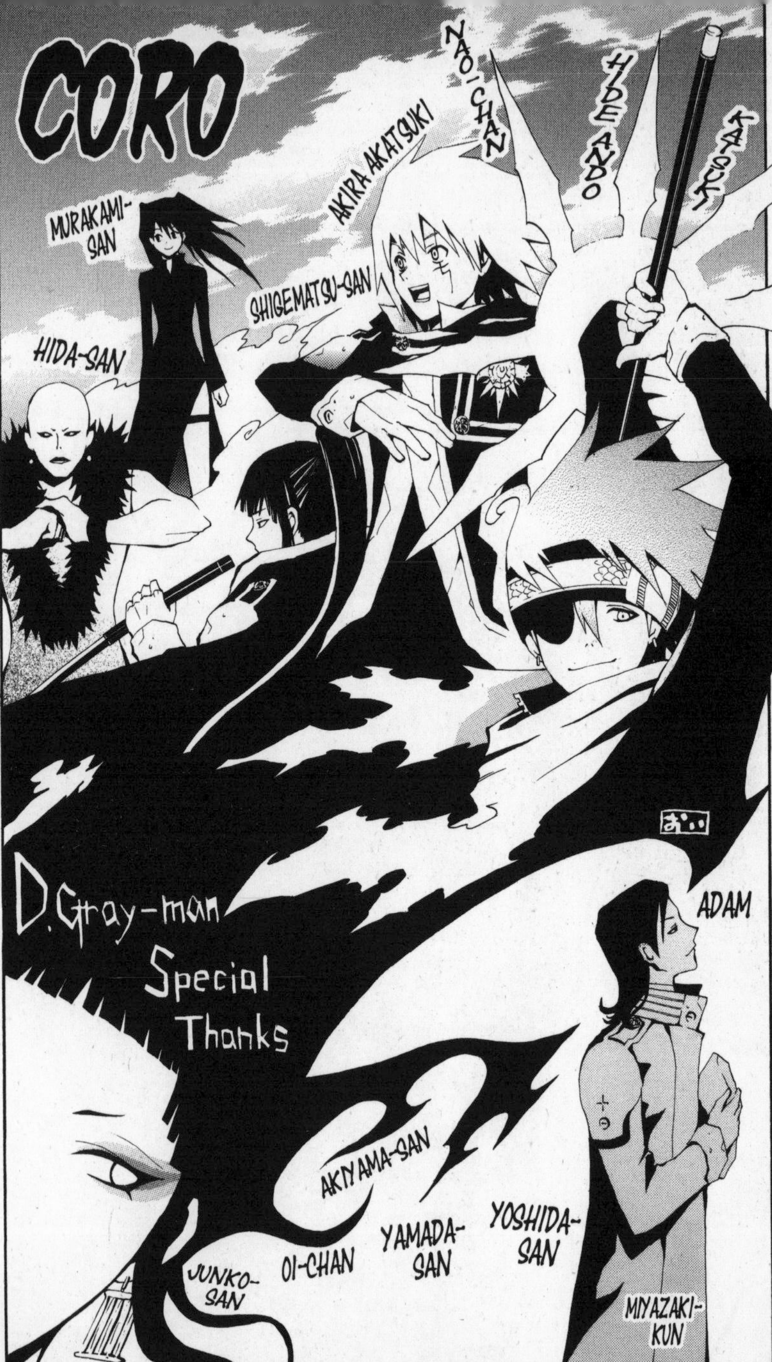
CORO
KATSUKI
HIDE ANDO
NAO-CHAN
AKIRA AKATSUKI
MURAKAMI-SAN
SHIGEMATSU-SAN
HIDA-SAN
ADAM
D.Gray-man Special Thanks
MIYAZAKI-KUN
YOSHIDA-SAN
YAMADA-SAN
AKIYAMA-SAN
OI-CHAN
JUNKO-SAN

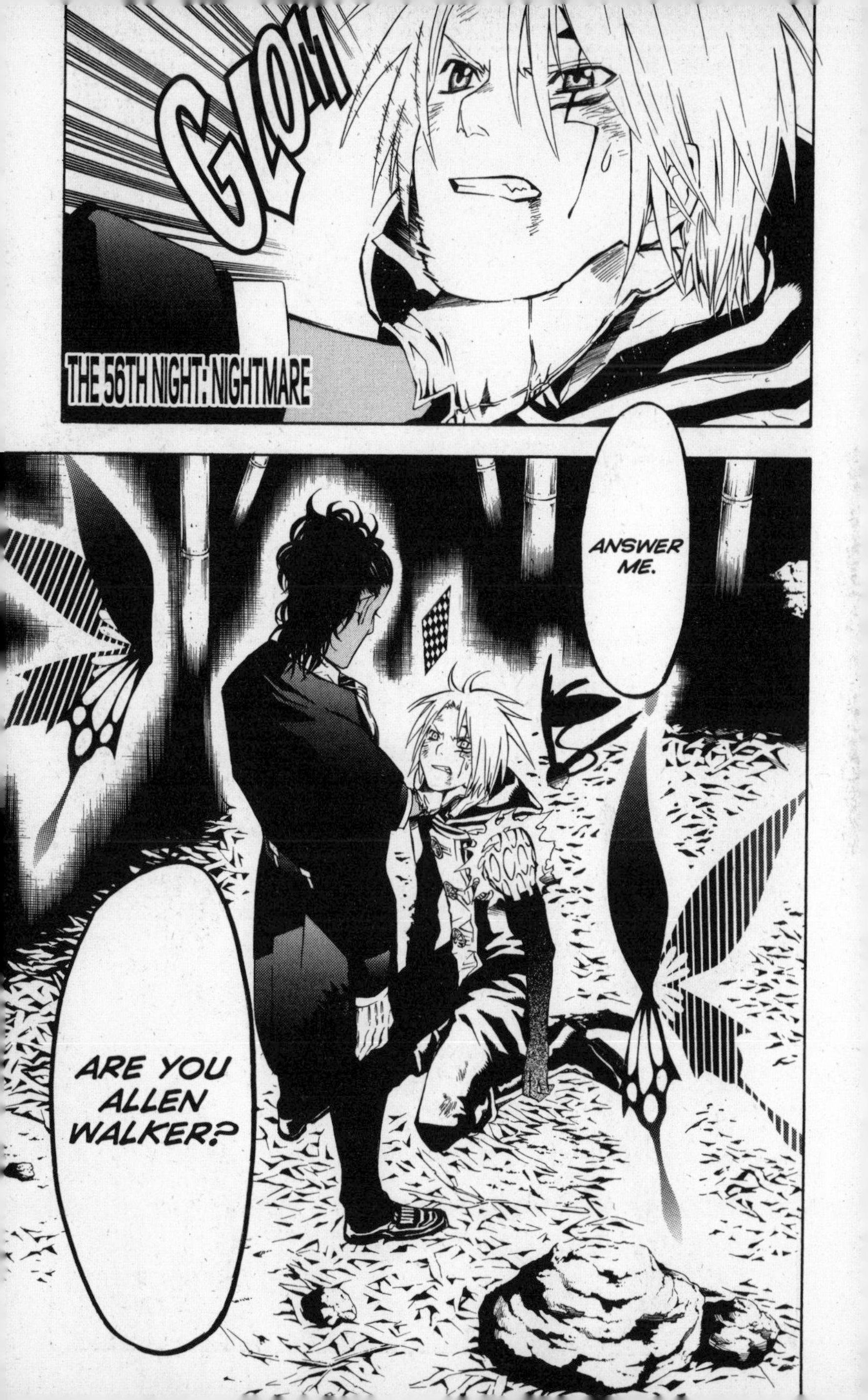
GLOM
THE 56TH NIGHT: NIGHTMARE
ANSWER ME.
ARE YOU ALLEN WALKER?

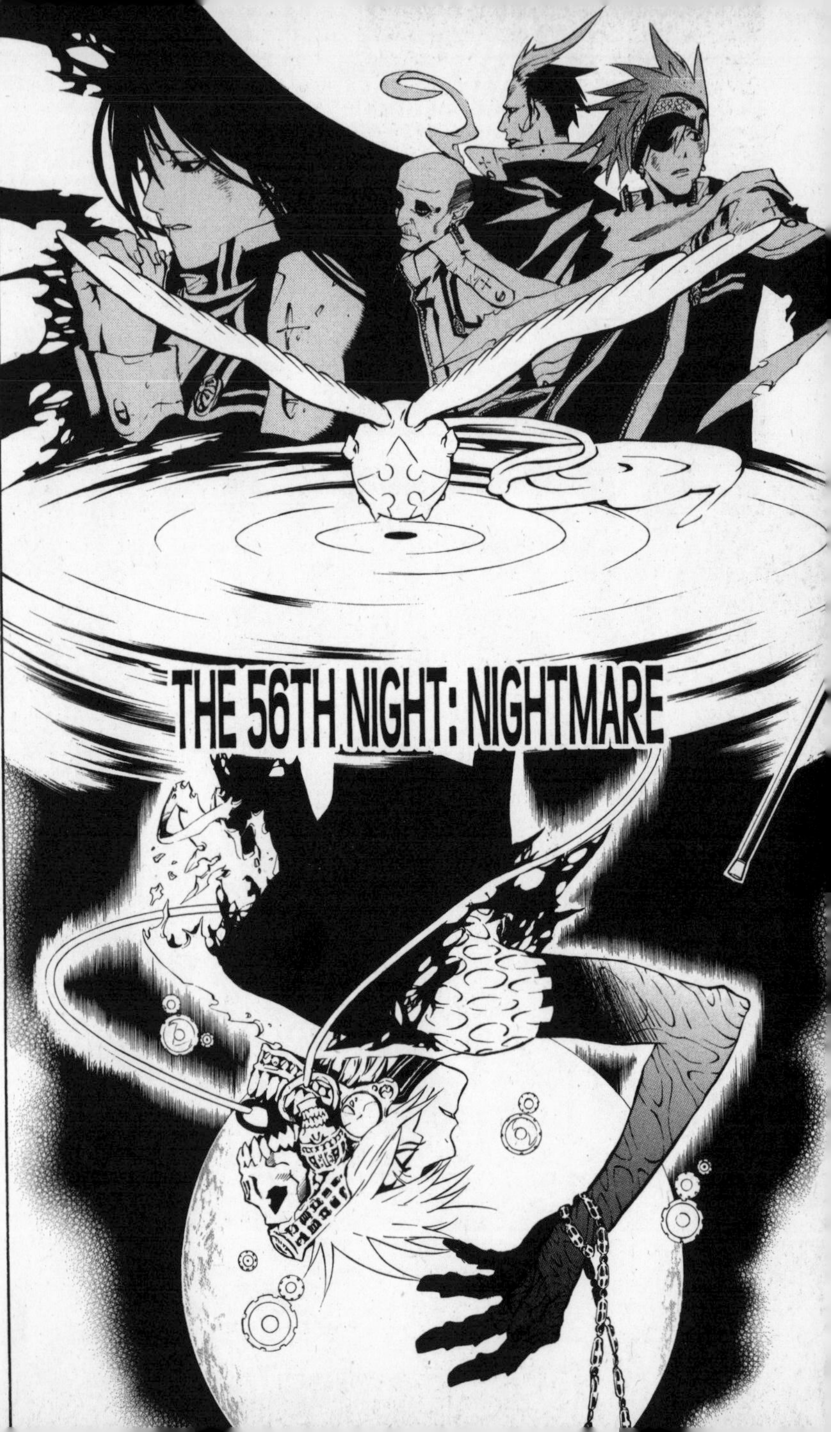
THE 56TH NIGHT: NIGHTMARE

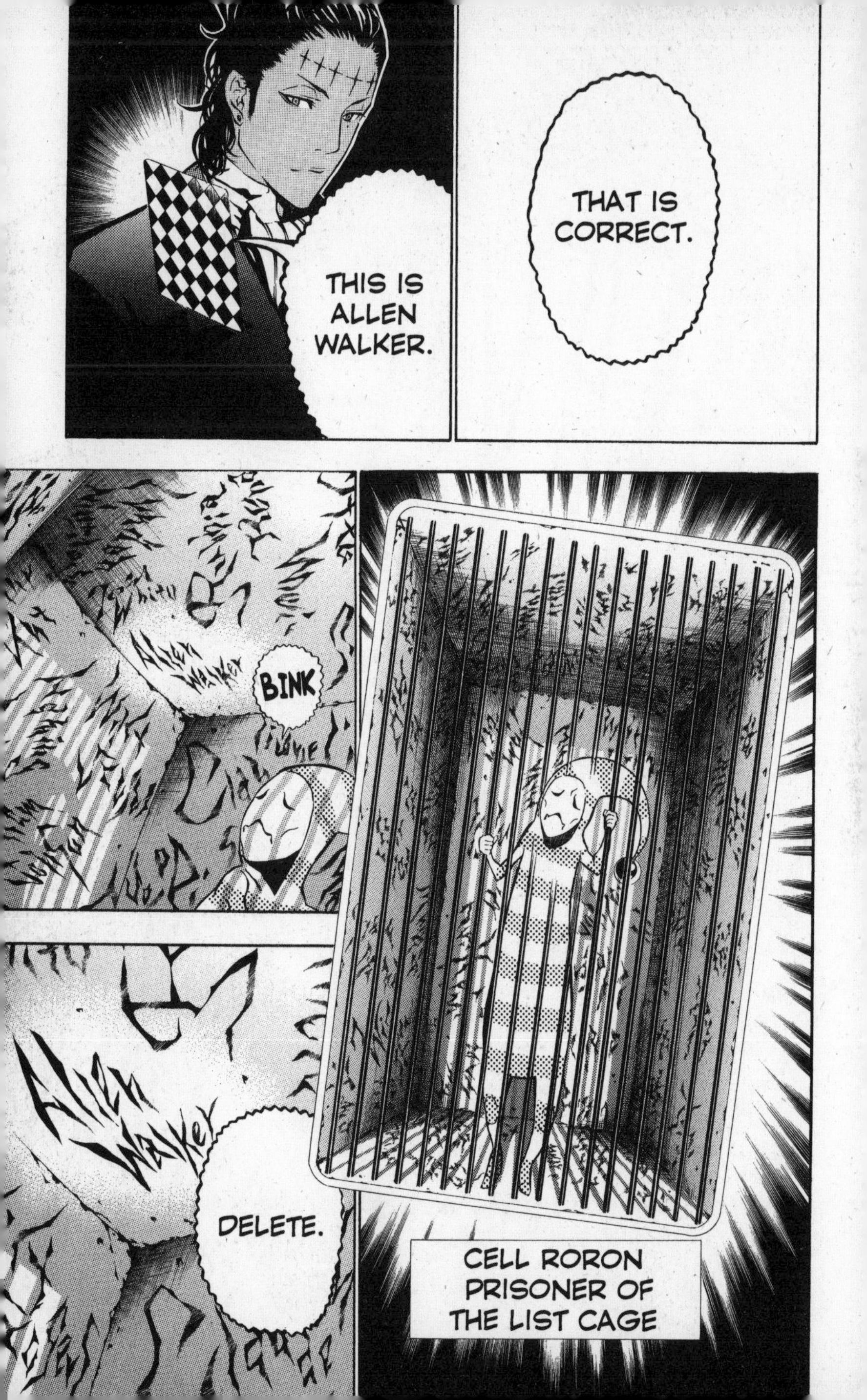
THAT IS CORRECT.
THIS IS ALLEN WALKER.
CELL RORON PRISONER OF THE LIST CAGE
Allen Walker
BINK
Allen Walker
DELETE.

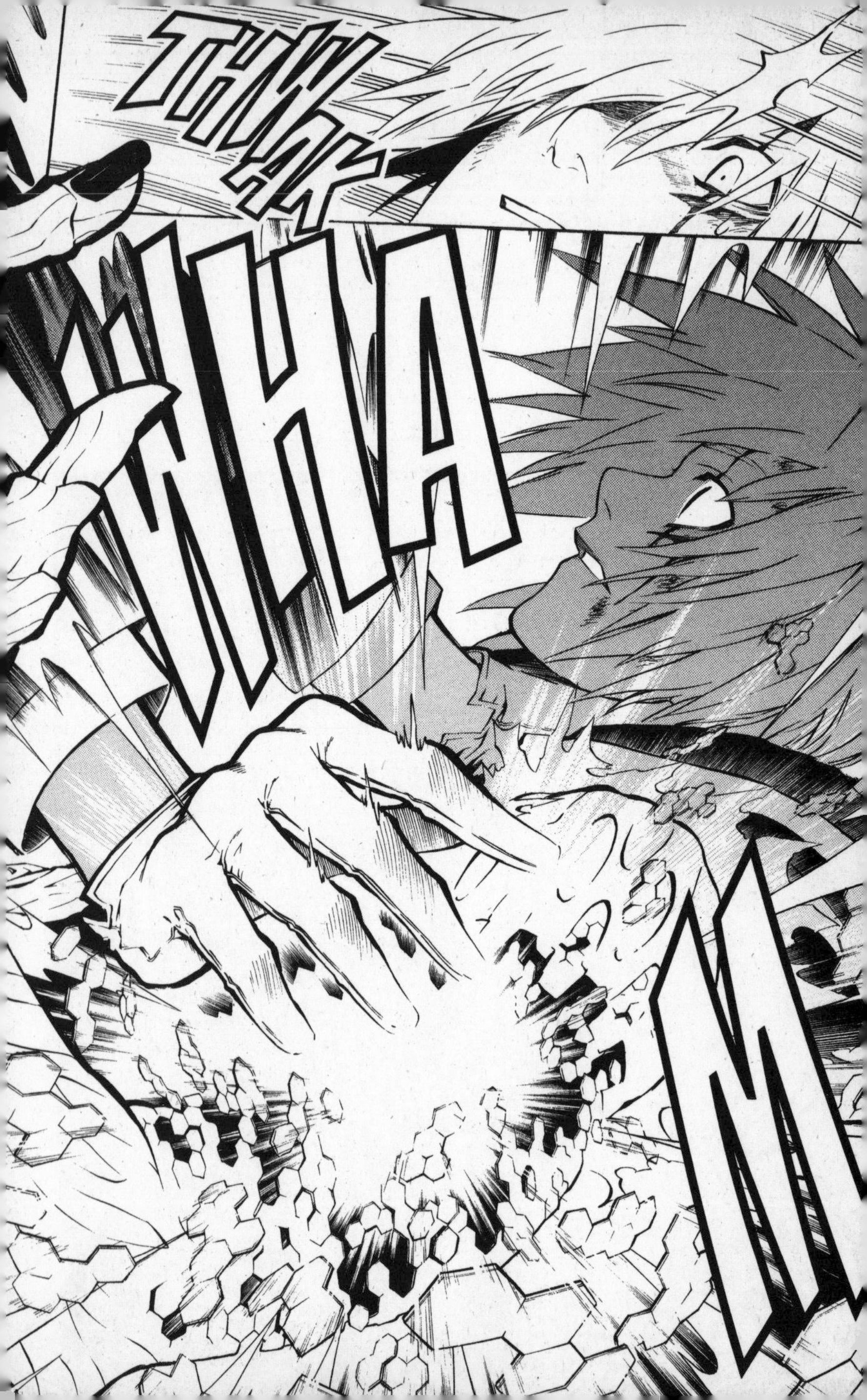
THWACK
WHAM

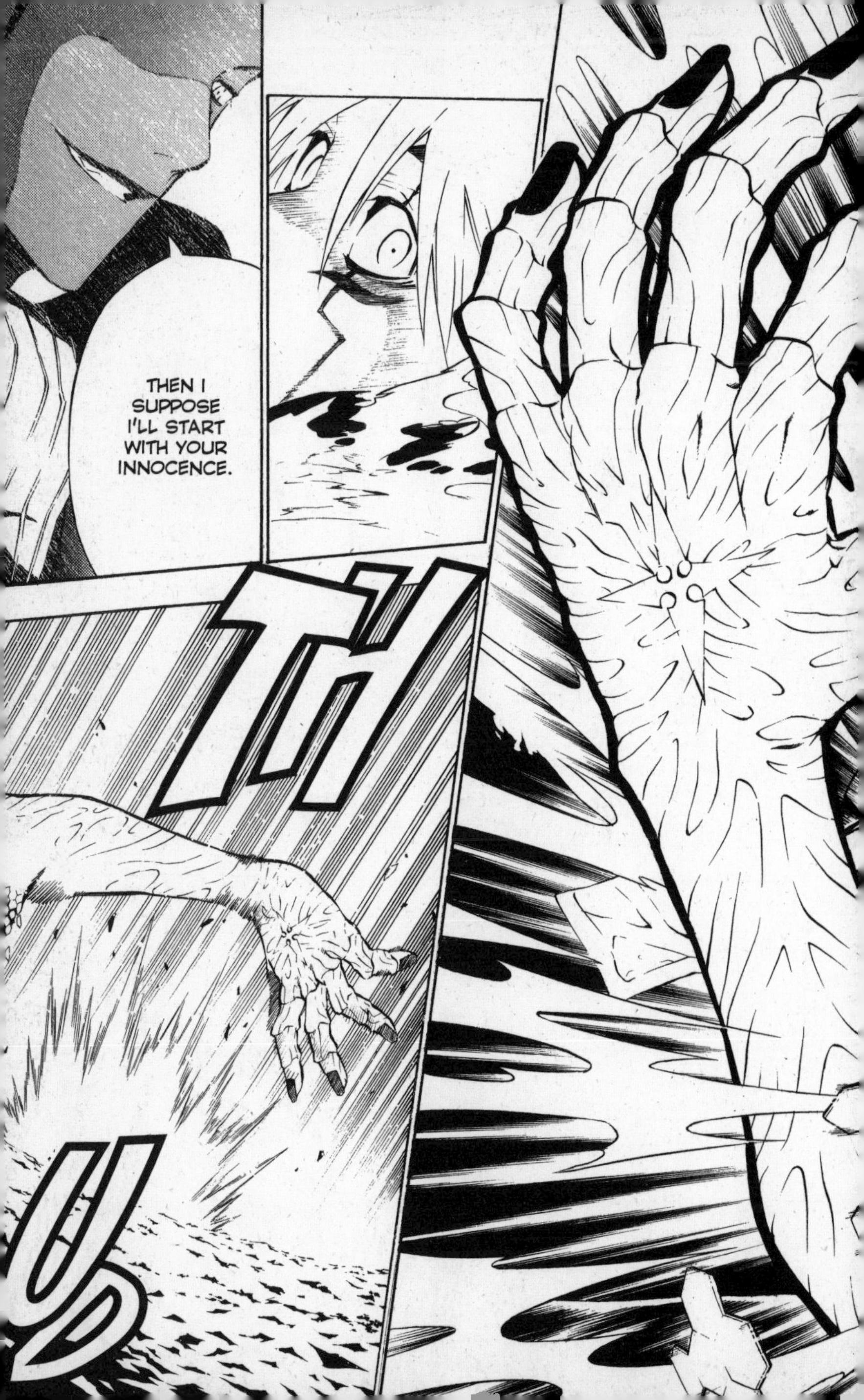
THEN I SUPPOSE I'LL START WITH YOUR INNOCENCE.

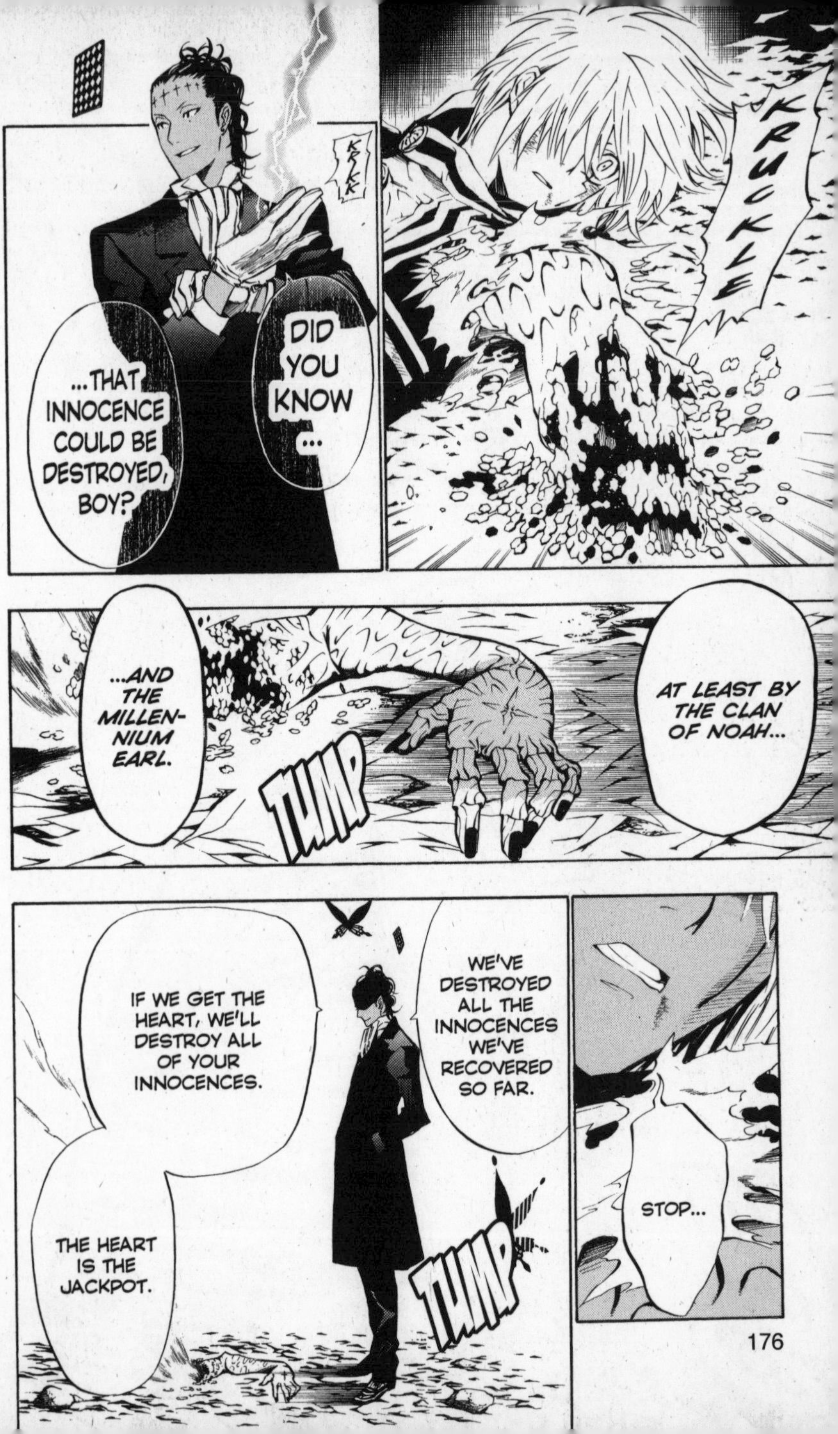
KRUCKLE
KRIKK
DID YOU KNOW ...
...THAT INNOCENCE COULD BE DESTROYED, BOY?
AT LEAST BY THE CLAN OF NOAH...
...AND THE MILLEN-NIUM EARL.
TUMP
STOP...
WE'VE DESTROYED ALL THE INNOCENCES WE'VE RECOVERED SO FAR.
IF WE GET THE HEART, WE'LL DESTROY ALL OF YOUR INNOCENCES.
THE HEART IS THE JACKPOT.
TUMP

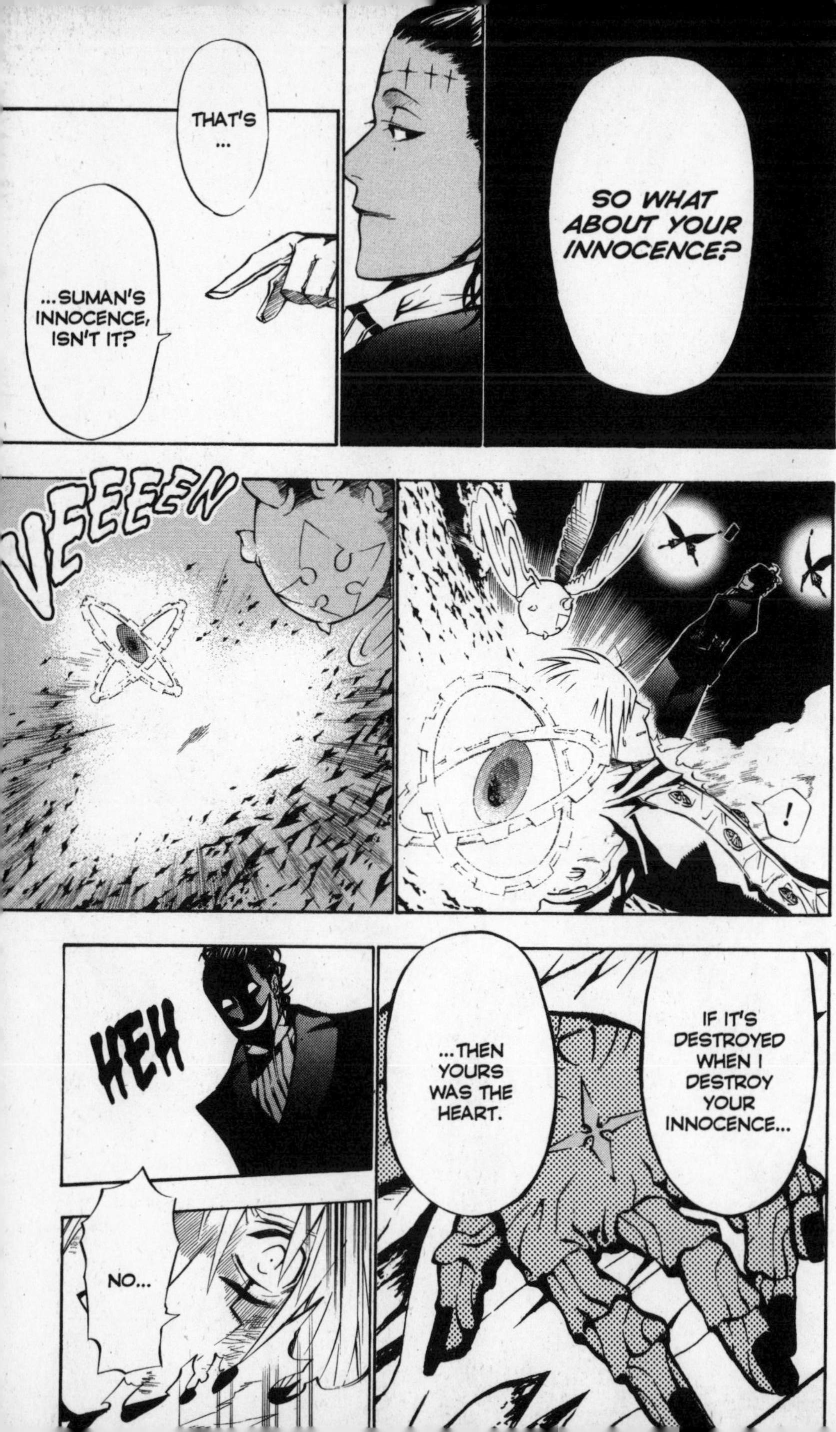
SO WHAT ABOUT YOUR INNOCENCE?
THAT'S ...
...SUMAN'S INNOCENCE, ISN'T IT?
!
VEEEEEN
IF IT'S DESTROYED WHEN I DESTROY YOUR INNOCENCE...
...THEN YOURS WAS THE HEART.
HEH
NO...

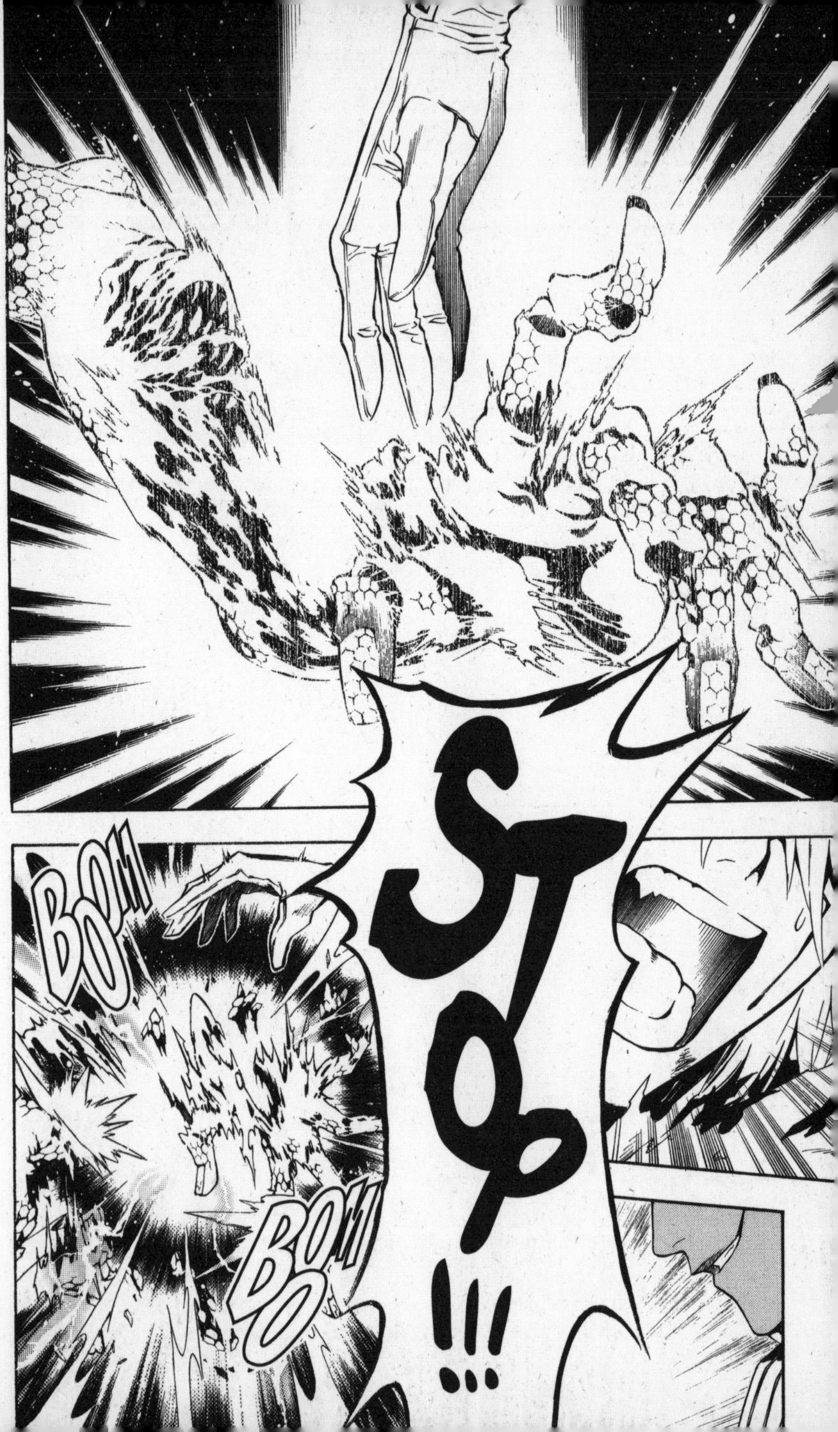
STOP!!!
BOOM
BOOM

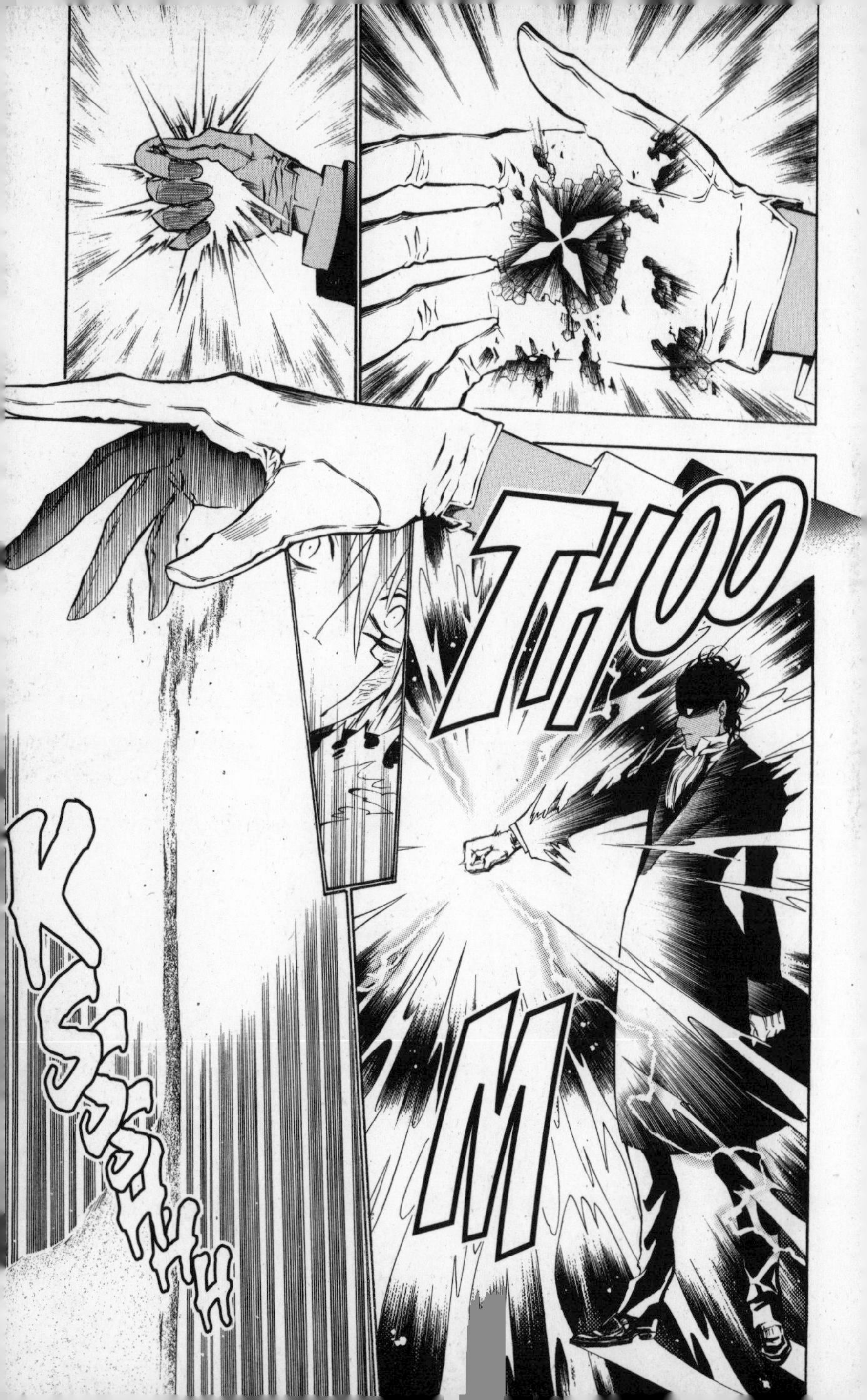
THOOM
KSSSHH

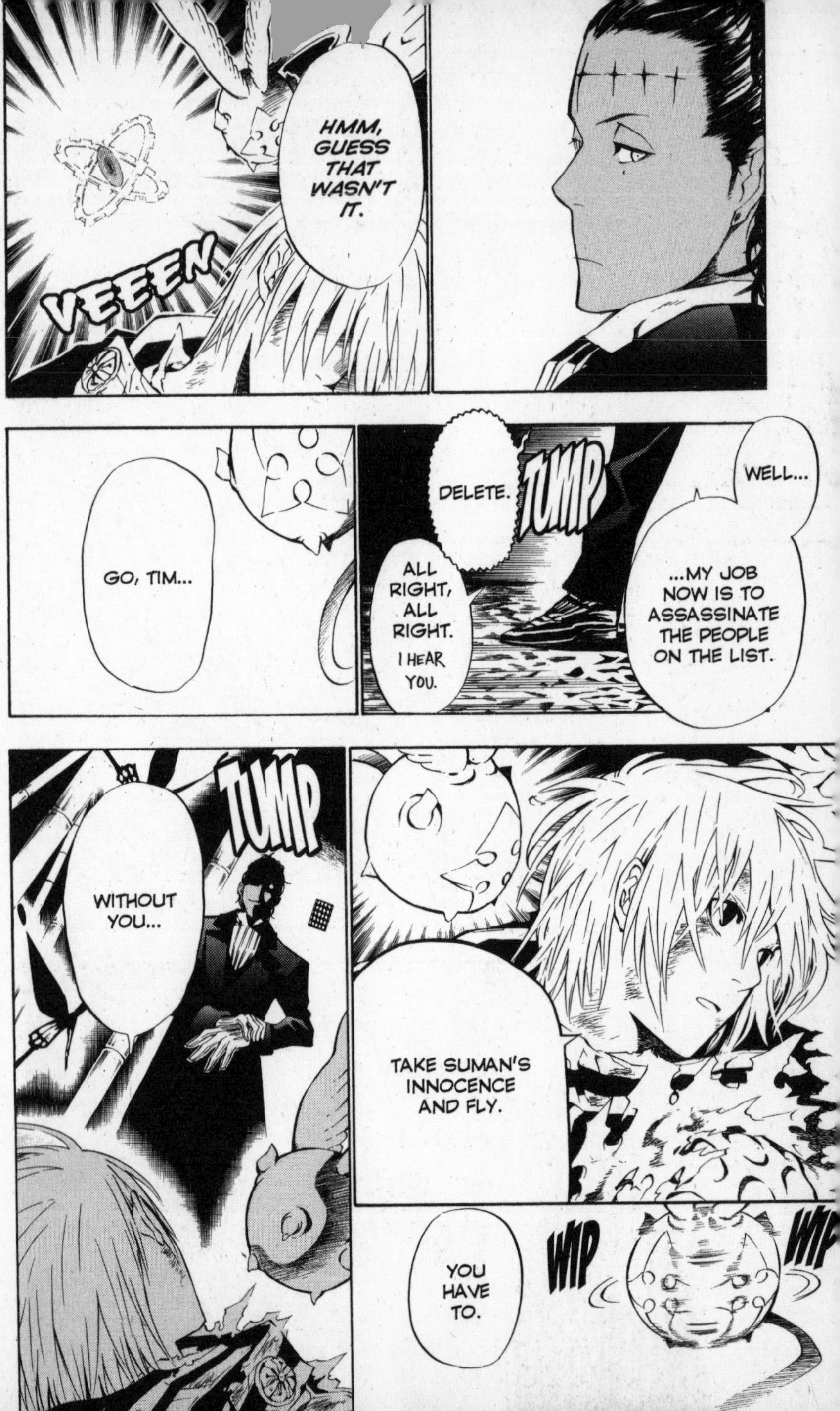
VEEEN
HMM, GUESS THAT WASN'T IT.
WELL...
...MY JOB NOW IS TO ASSASSINATE THE PEOPLE ON THE LIST.
TUMP
DELETE.
ALL RIGHT, ALL RIGHT. I HEAR YOU.
GO, TIM...
TAKE SUMAN'S INNOCENCE AND FLY.
WIP
WIP
YOU HAVE TO.
TUMP
WITHOUT YOU...

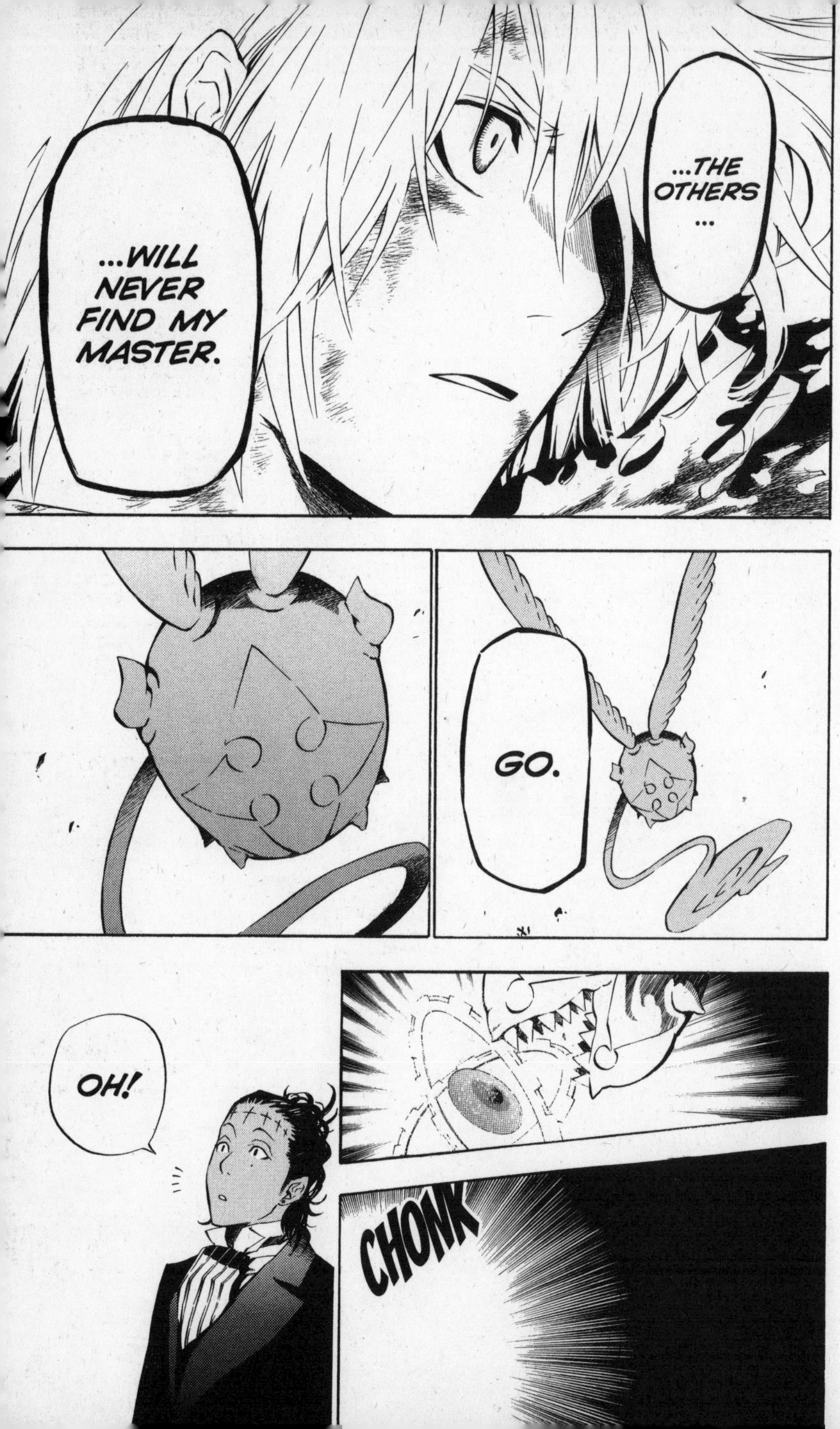
...THE OTHERS ...
...WILL NEVER FIND MY MASTER.
GO.
CHONK
OH!

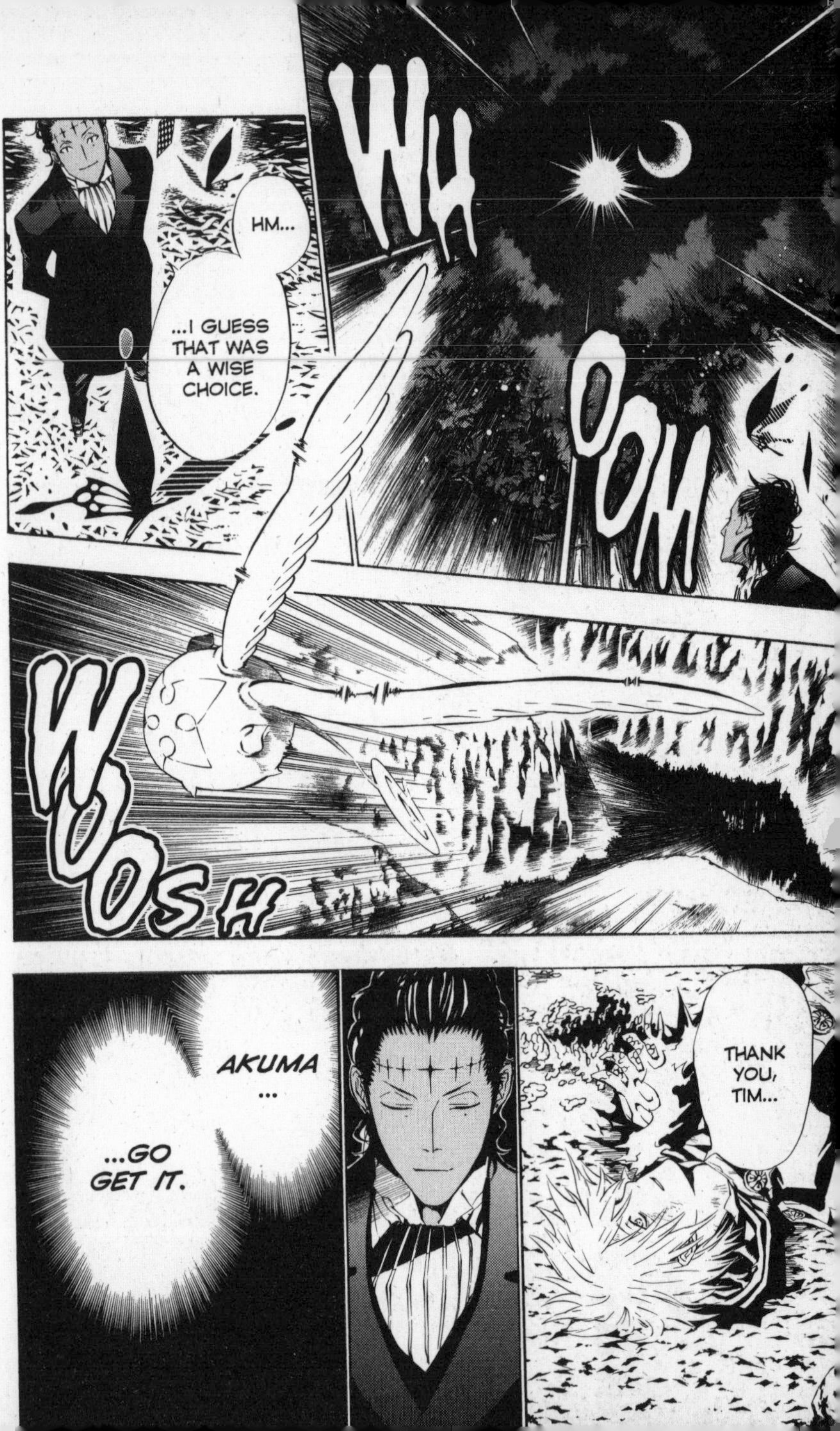
WHOOM
HM...
...I GUESS THAT WAS A WISE CHOICE.
WHOOSH
THANK YOU, TIM...
AKUMA...
...GO GET IT.

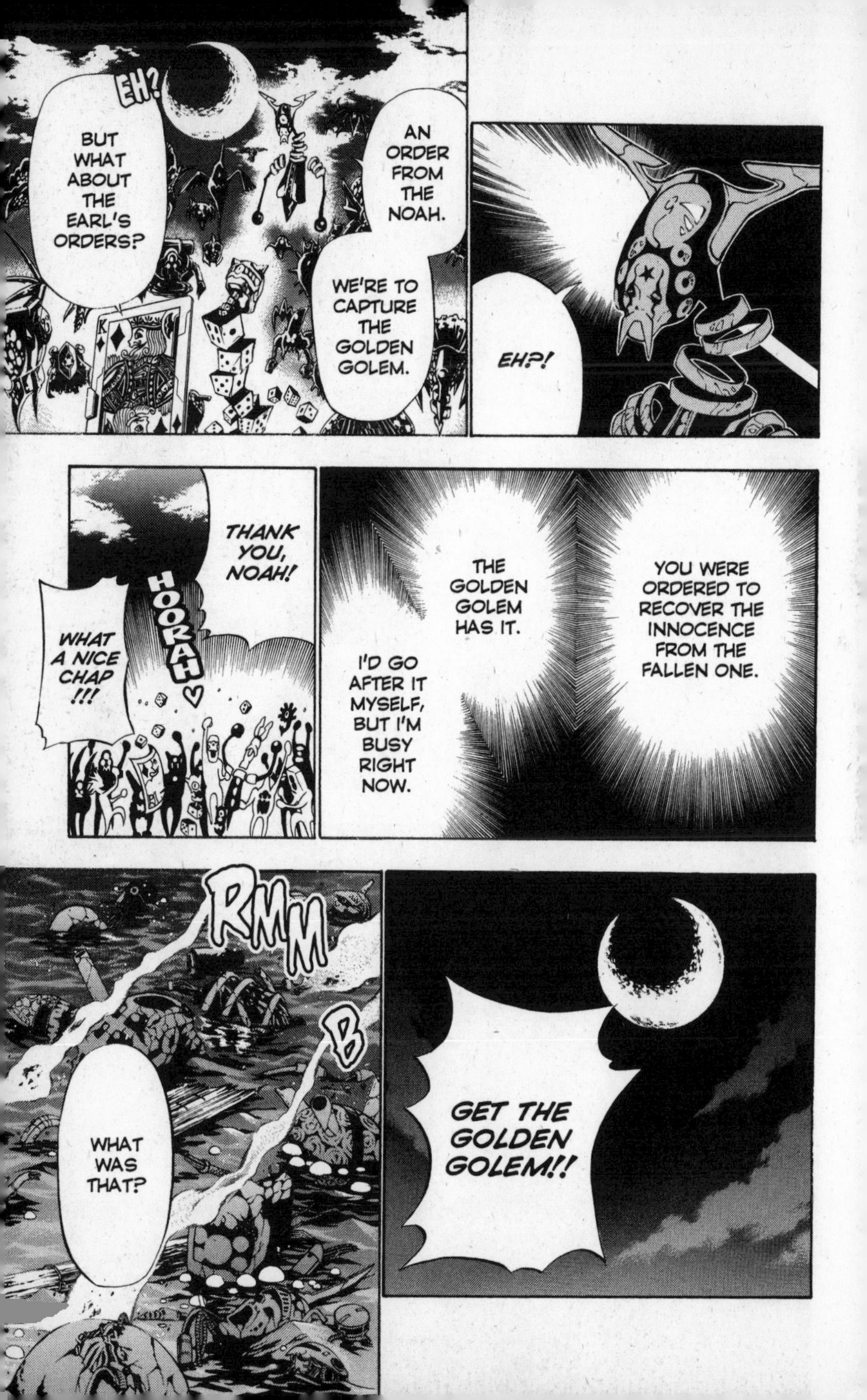
EH?!
AN ORDER FROM THE NOAH.
WE'RE TO CAPTURE THE GOLDEN GOLEM.
EH?
BUT WHAT ABOUT THE EARL'S ORDERS?
YOU WERE ORDERED TO RECOVER THE INNOCENCE FROM THE FALLEN ONE.
THE GOLDEN GOLEM HAS IT.
I'D GO AFTER IT MYSELF, BUT I'M BUSY RIGHT NOW.
THANK YOU, NOAH!
HOORAH ♥
WHAT A NICE CHAP!!!
GET THE GOLDEN GOLEM!!
RMMB
WHAT WAS THAT?

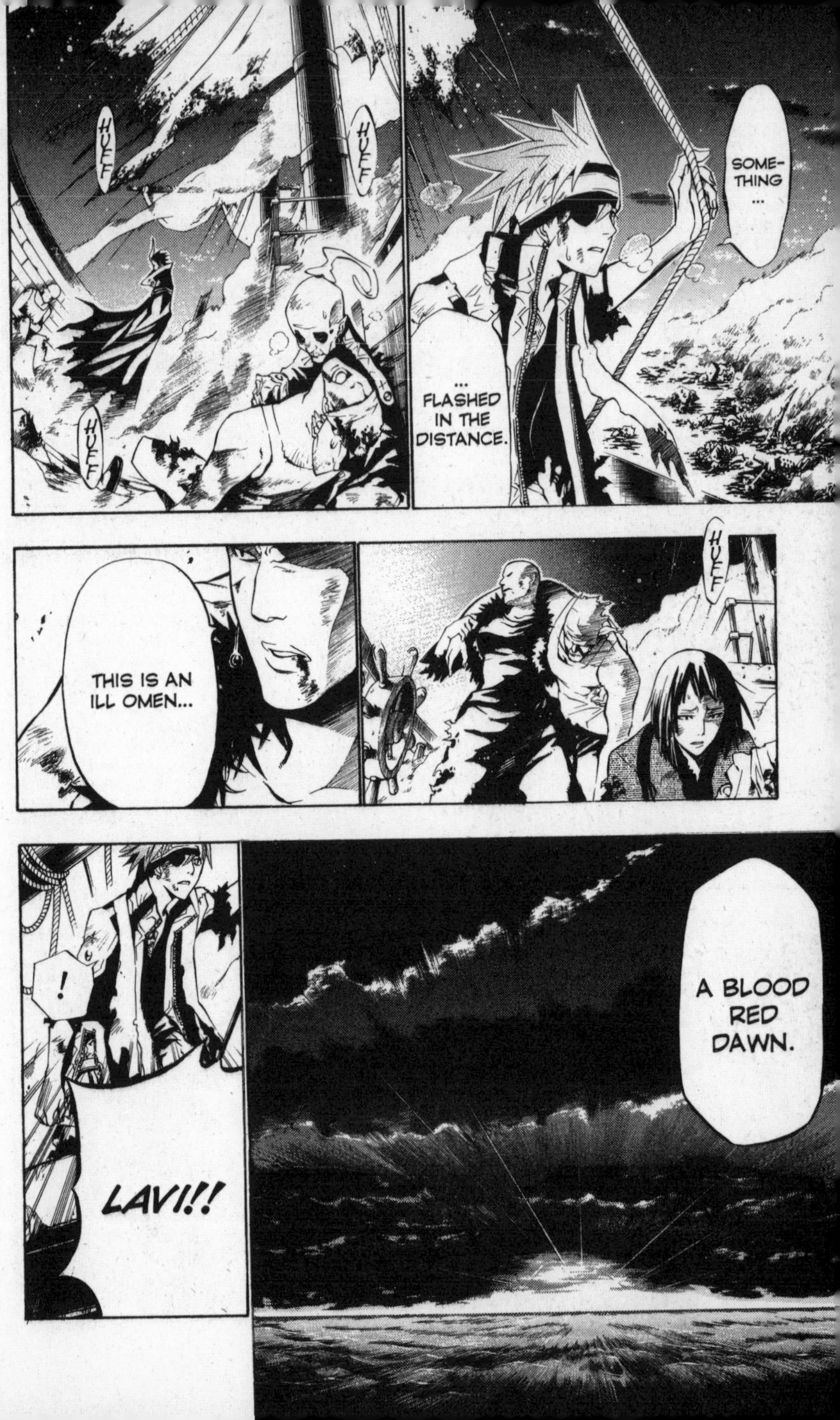
SOME-THING ...
... FLASHED IN THE DISTANCE.
HUFF
HUFF
HUFF
HUFF
THIS IS AN ILL OMEN...
A BLOOD RED DAWN.
!
LAVI!!

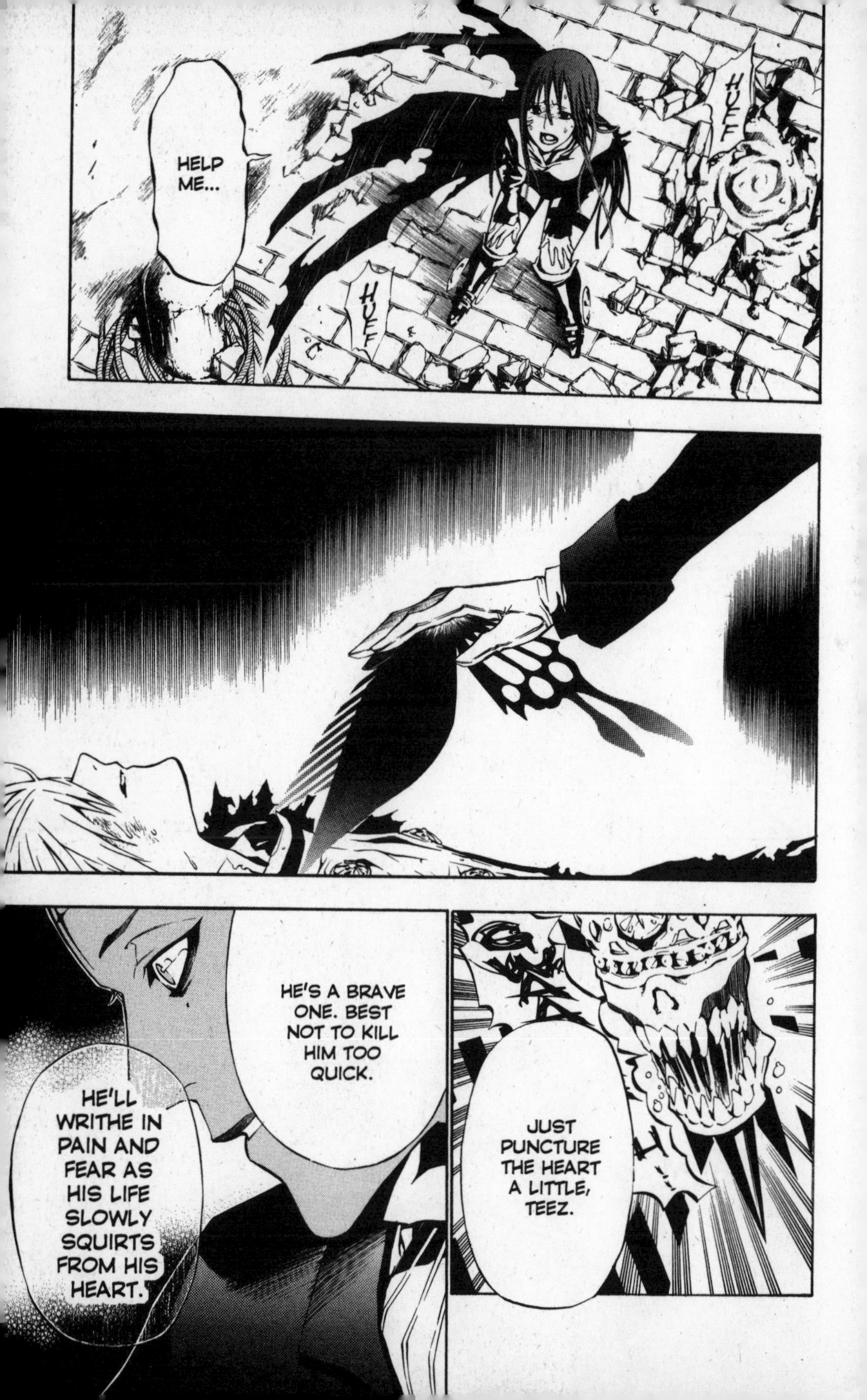
HUFF
HELP ME...
HUFF
JUST PUNCTURE THE HEART A LITTLE, TEEZ.
HE'S A BRAVE ONE. BEST NOT TO KILL HIM TOO QUICK.
HE'LL WRITHE IN PAIN AND FEAR AS HIS LIFE SLOWLY SQUIRTS FROM HIS HEART.

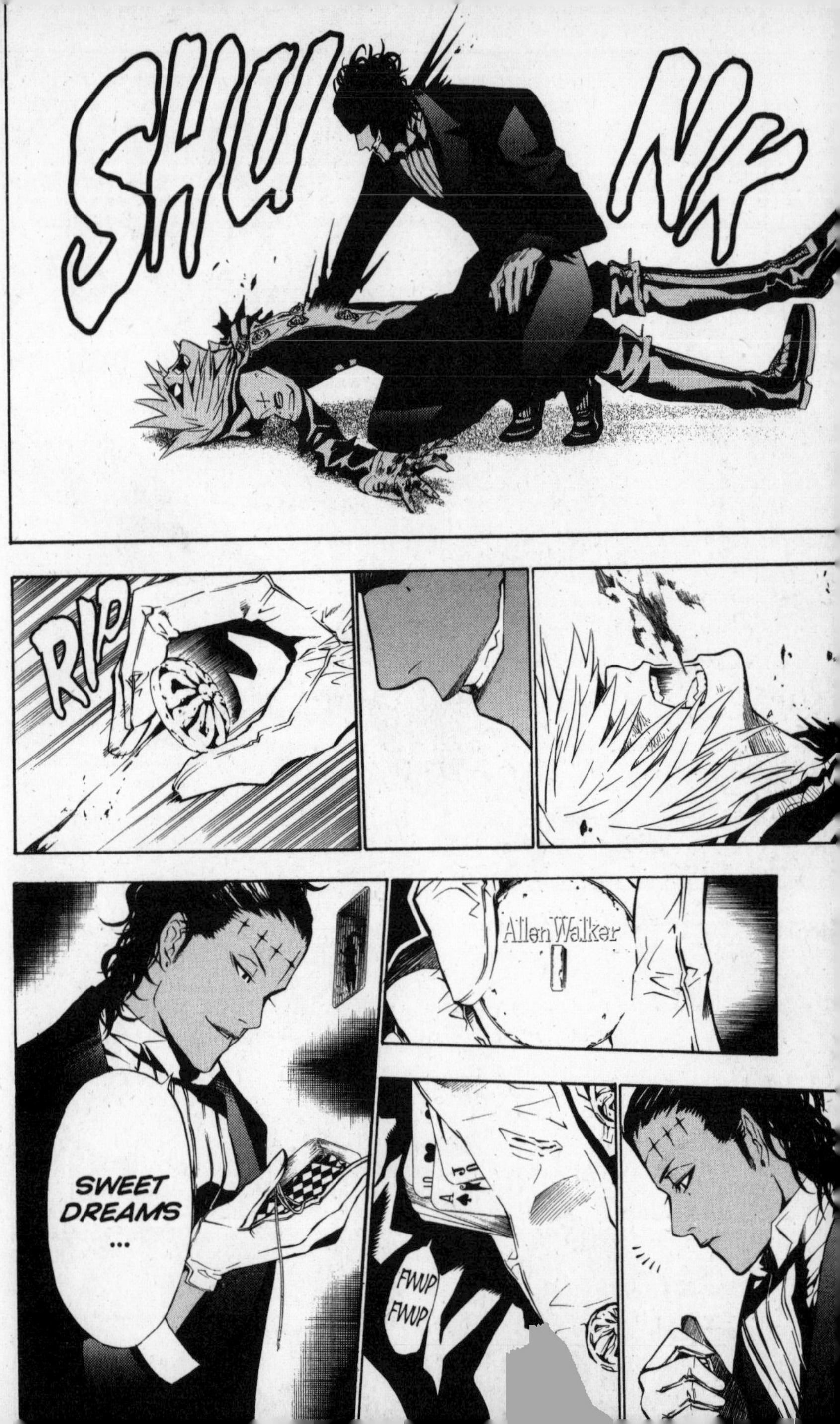
SHUNK
RIP
Allen Walker
FWUP FWUP
SWEET DREAMS ...

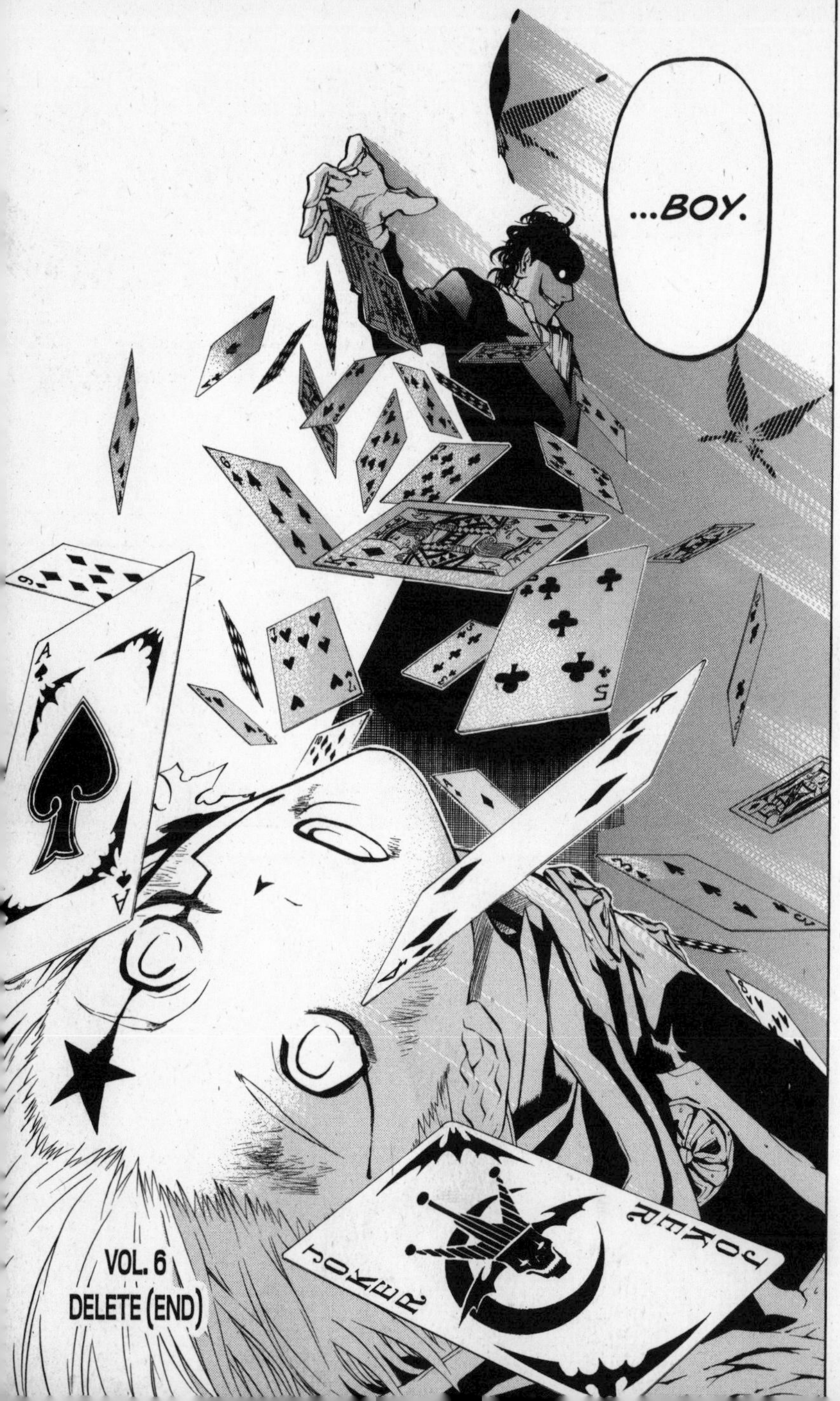
...BOY.
VOL. 6
DELETE (END)

IN THE NEXT VOLUME...

Allen has disappeared after his latest
with Tyki Mikk. Lavi and Lenalee try to
have to be satisfied with saving Timca
pursuing horde of akuma. Eventually th
their mission with Allen's replacement
Miranda Lotto. As for Allen, he has to
deal with the staggering loss of his In

Available Now!

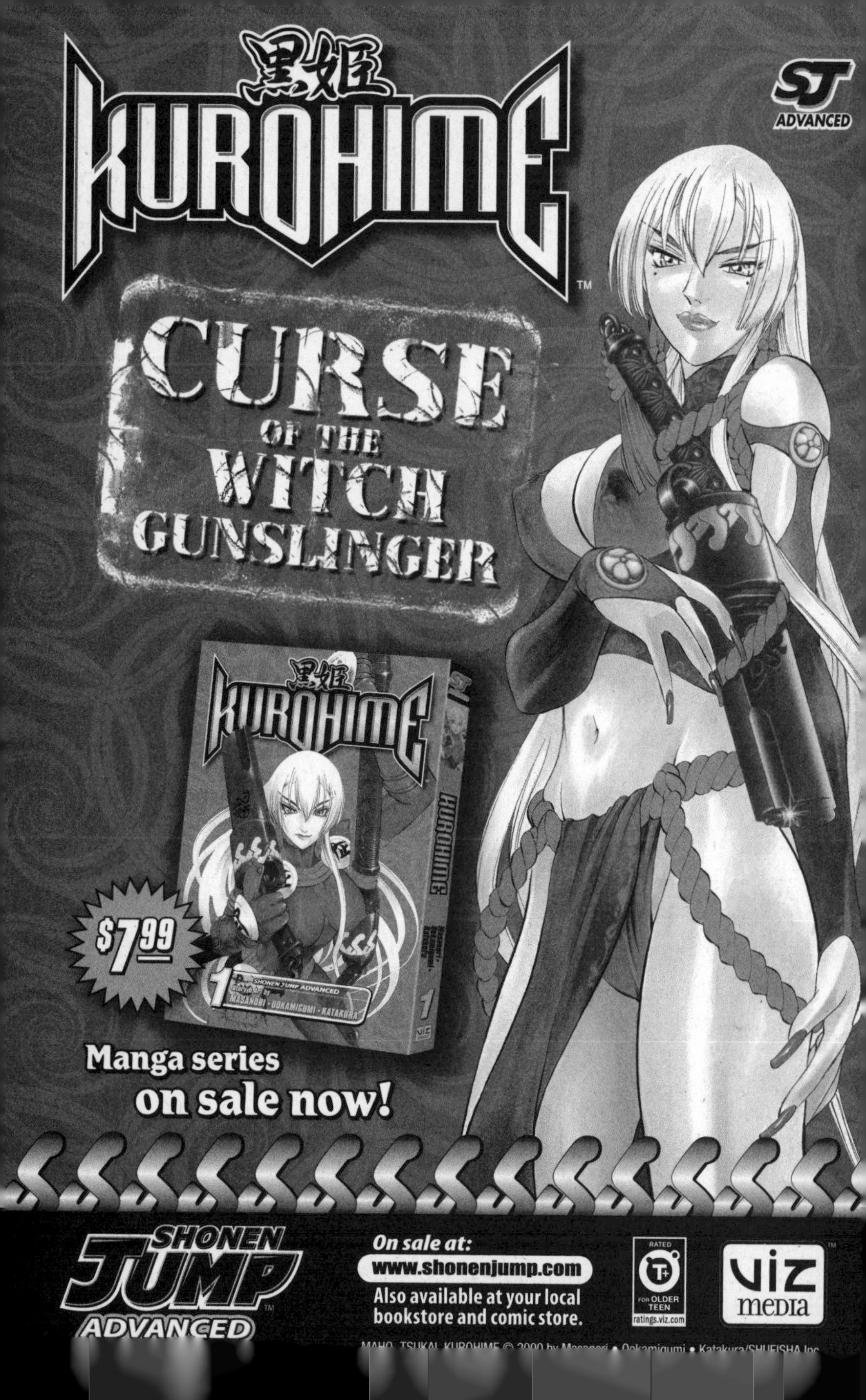
黒姫
KUROHIME
SJ ADVANCED
CURSE OF THE WITCH GUNSLINGER
$7.99
SHONEN JUMP ADVANCED
MASANORI • OOKAMIGUMI • KATAKURA
Manga series on sale now!
SHONEN JUMP ADVANCED
On sale at:
www.shonenjump.com
Also available at your local bookstore and comic store.
RATED T+ FOR OLDER TEEN
ratings.viz.com
VIZ MEDIA
MAHO TSUKAI KUROHIME © 2000 by Masanori • Ookamigumi • Katakura/SHUEISHA Inc.

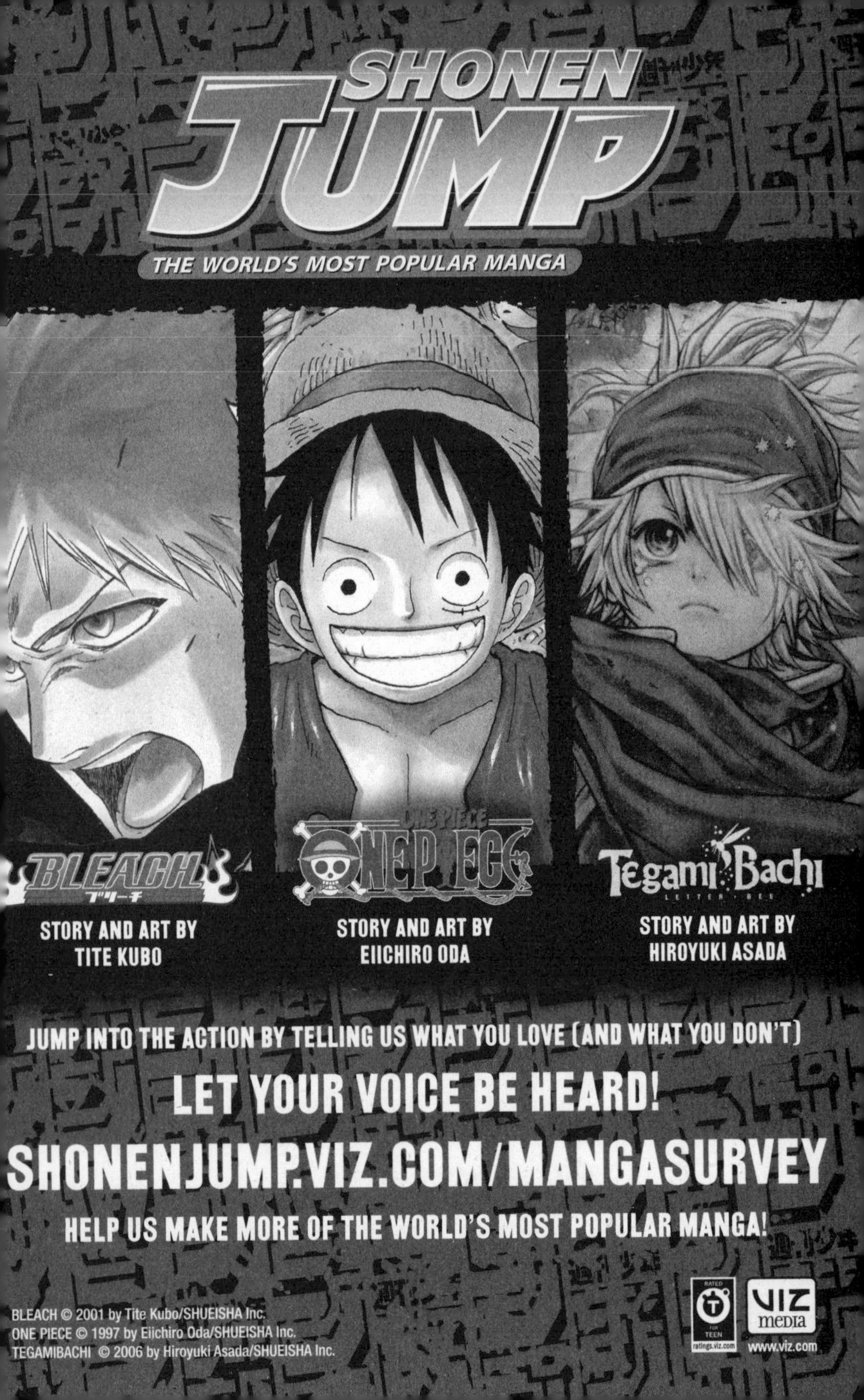
SHONEN JUMP
THE WORLD'S MOST POPULAR MANGA
BLEACH
ブリーチ
STORY AND ART BY
TITE KUBO
ONE PIECE
STORY AND ART BY
EIICHIRO ODA
Tegami Bachi
LETTER BEE
STORY AND ART BY
HIROYUKI ASADA
JUMP INTO THE ACTION BY TELLING US WHAT YOU LOVE (AND WHAT YOU DON'T)
LET YOUR VOICE BE HEARD!
SHONENJUMP.VIZ.COM/MANGASURVEY
HELP US MAKE MORE OF THE WORLD'S MOST POPULAR MANGA!
BLEACH © 2001 by Tite Kubo/SHUEISHA Inc.
ONE PIECE © 1997 by Eiichiro Oda/SHUEISHA Inc.
TEGAMIBACHI © 2006 by Hiroyuki Asada/SHUEISHA Inc.
RATED T FOR TEEN
ratings.viz.com
VIZ media
www.viz.com